Digital Image Processing

DIGITAL IMAGE PROCESSING

By

ABHISHEK YADAV
B.E. and M.E. in Electronics and Communication

POONAM YADAV
B.Tech. and MBA

UNIVERSITY SCIENCE PRESS

(An Imprint of Laxmi Publications Pvt. Ltd.)

An ISO 9001:2008 Company

BENGALURU • CHENNAI • COCHIN • GUWAHATI • HYDERABAD
JALANDHAR • KOLKATA • LUCKNOW • MUMBAI • RANCHI • NEW DELHI
BOSTON (USA) • ACCRA (GHANA) • NAIROBI (KENYA)

DIGITAL IMAGE PROCESSING

Printed and bound in India
Typeset at : Shubham Composer, Delhi.
First Edition : 2009, *Reprint* : 2014,2016
ISBN : 978-81-318-0524-4

Branches

Bengaluru	080-26 75 69 30
Chennai	044-24 34 47 26
Cochin	0484-237 70 04, 405 13 03
Guwahati	0361-254 36 69, 251 38 81
Hyderabad	040-27 55 53 83, 27 55 53 93
Jalandhar	0181-222 12 72
Kolkata	033-22 27 43 84
Lucknow	0522-220 99 16
Mumbai	022-24 91 54 15, 24 92 78 69
Ranchi	0651-220 44 64

PUBLISHED IN INDIA BY
UNIVERSITY SCIENCE PRESS
(An Imprint of Laxmi Publications Pvt. Ltd.)
An ISO 9001:2008 Company
113, GOLDEN HOUSE, DARYAGANJ, NEW DELHI-110002, INDIA
Telephone : 91-11-4353 2500, 4353 2501
Fax : 91-11-2325 2572, 4353 2528
www.laxmipublications.com info@laxmipublications.com

C—10762/015/09
Printed at : Ajit Printing Press, Delhi.

Dedicated to
Dr. S.S. Pattnaik
Professor and Head
ECE & Television and Media
Department, NITTTR Chandigarh

CONTENTS

PREFACE

"Digital Image Processing" is now-a-days a demanding and interesting field. It is a core subject for Electronics and Communication and Computer Engineering. On the other hand it is the interdisciplinary subject that is a part of different branches of engineering. This shows the importance of the subject.

But the deficiency of this area is that there are very few books available in the market for a general Indian student. I have tried here to represent all the fundamentals of Digital Image Processing in an easy way.

Here we start the discussion with the chapter 1 that deals with *Fundamentals of Image Processing*. Here we will discuss some familiar examples of Image Processing, Components of Image Processing System and Generation of Digital Image. Chapters 2 and 3 deal with *Image Enhancement Techniques* in *Spatial Domain* and *Frequency Domain* respectively. Image Enhancement is the most demanding field and mostly applicable area of Image Processing.

In the next chapter, we discuss *Image Restoration*. The image is degraded due to noise that is to be restored at the receiver side by using different filtering methods. Till this chapter, we have discussed the gray level image. In chapter 5, these concepts of *Gray Images* are explained for Color Image.

Next chapter deals with *Morphological Image Processing*. From this chapter onwards, we consider the features and attributes of an Image. Chapter Registration deals with transformation of image at different planes for different purposes. In next chapter, we discuss the *Image Segmentation* that is very important and fundamental step of image processing. By the chapter *Data Compression*, we become familiar with the data compression techniques that will help us to save the bandwidth and space.

Now we got the features and attributes of an image, but these are not ready for the use. Chapter *Feature Extraction and Description* deals with the way to represent and describe these features and attributes of an image for the use in computer and other applications. In the last chapter Object Recognition, I conclude with final representation, description and comparing of image features and attributes for different applications.

I definitely must not say that I have explained any extraordinary and new area of Image Processing in this book. But I have tried to explain all the best and recent ideas of this field at a place. I explained all those areas in which the students feel uneasy. I feel grateful if this book helps to all the respected faculty members and my dear students to study this subject with interest. I have put my best efforts in bringing this book to you. Any suggestion regarding the improvement of this book will be appreciated. I will feel happy to get the suggestions and queries of all and try to solve them as early as possible.

—Author

ACKNOWLEDGEMENT

I pay my all regards to **Dr. S.S. Pattnaik,** Professor & Head, Electronics & Communication Department, NITTTR Chandigarh through this book who always inspired me to do hard and honest work. I am also thankful to **Dr. L.N. Paliwal** (Presently Director of ITS Engineering College, Greater Noida) for his great support and encouragement.

I am grateful to **Mrs. Swapna Devi,** Assistant Professor, Electronics & Communication Department, NITTTR Chandigarh who firstly introduced me to the deep fundamentals of Digital Image Processing with great interest.

I am thankful to **Mr. Rabi Narayan Panda,** Assistant Professor, KIET, Ghaziabad who always suggested me during the preparation of the book. I should be grateful to **Mr. Subash Chandra Arya,** Lecturer, GIIT Greater Noida for his suggestion and great support.

I am thankful to my dear son **Mr. Krishnabhishek** and daughter **Kr. Divyankasksha** who always fill my life with great happiness. I am really humble respect to my wife for her great patience during the preparation of this book.

I am thankful to my parents and almighty God as they gave me opportunity to serve the field of technical education.

—Author

CHAPTER 1

INTRODUCTION & FUNDAMENTALS

The basic aim of study of digital image processing is to process the image (in digital form) for—

1. improvement of image for human interpretation and
2. processing of image data for storage, presentation and transmission of image by machine.

1.1 DEFINITION OF IMAGE AND DIGITAL IMAGE PROCESSING

Before studying digital image processing, first of all we should be cleared about image.

"An image may be defined as a two dimensional function $f(x, y)$, where x and y are spatial (plane) co-ordinates. The amplitude of 'f' at any pair of co-ordinate (x, y) is called the intensity '*or*' gray level of the image at that point".

When (x, y) and amplitude values of 'f' are all finite, discrete quantities, we call the image a digital image.

Now we should define digital image processing. Digital image processing may be defined as a

1. *"Discipline in which both input and output of a process are image"*.

   and
2. *"Process of extracting attributes from images (up to the level till we are able to recognize the individual object)"*.

1.2 EXAMPLES OF DIGITAL IMAGE PROCESSING

For human being, the meaning of an image is to see an image by eyes. But unlike humans, who are limited to the visual band of electromagnetic (EM) spectrum, imaging covers almost the entire EM spectrum ranging from gamma to radio waves. Examples are ultrasound, X-Rays, electron microscopy, computer generated images etc. Thus we conclude that digital image processing has a wide area of study. That's why here we will study some practical examples of digital image processing.

So to study systematically, first of all we should know about electromagnetic spectrum of radiations.

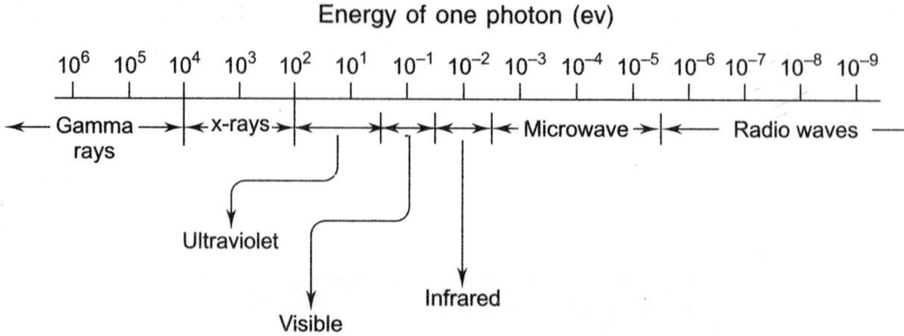

Fig. 1.1 *Electromagnetic spectrum.*

Now we can study the practical examples of each part of EM spectrum.

1. **Gamma Rays :** Gamma rays are basically used in nuclear medicine and astronomical observations. In nuclear medicine, patient is injected with a radioactive isotope that emits gamma rays as it decays. Now these emissions are collected by gamma ray detector thus an image is produced.
2. **X-ray Imaging :** The uses of X-rays are very well-known in medical diagnostics. But they are also used in industries and astronomy.
   Basic method of taking X-rays images can be explained as follows :
   (*a*) In a vacuum tube, we have a cathode and anode. Cathode is heated that causes the emission of electrons. Now these electrons hit the anode and causes the emission of X-rays.
   (*b*) Number of X-rays can be controlled by current applied to cathode and energy of X-rays can be controlled by positive voltage applied to anode. According to energy of X-rays, rays will penetrate in the body of patient.
   (*c*) When X-rays passes through the body of patient, intensity of X-rays is varied and the resulting energy falling on the film develops image by same method as photographic film.
3. **Ultraviolet Rays :** The area of application of ultraviolet rays includes lithography, microscopy, lasers, biological imaging, astronomical observation etc.
   Ultraviolet rays is not visible, but when a photon of ultraviolet radiations collides with an electron in an atom of fluorescent material, it elevates the electron to a higher energy level and when electron returns back to real energy level, it emits visible light (radiations).
4. **Visible and Infrared Rays :** The infrared band is used along with visible band. The area of application of this combination includes light microscopy, remote sensing, industry etc.
   Here in the given table, we will get some interesting use of visible band.

Table 1.1 ***Bands and Application***

Band No.	*Name*	*Wavelength (μm)*	*Characteristics and Uses*
1.	Visible Blue	0.45 – 0.52	Maximum water penetration
2.	Visible Green	0.52 – 0.60	Good for measuring plant vigor
3.	Visible Red	0.63 – 0.69	Vegetation discrimination
4.	Near Infrared	0.76 – 0.90	Biomass and shoreline mapping
5.	Middle Infrared	1.55 – 1.75	Moisture content of soil and vegetation
6.	Thermal Infrared	10.4 – 12.5	Soil moisture and thermal mapping

5. **Microwave Rays :** The well-known area of application of microwave rays is 'Radar'. By radar imaging, we can collect data over any region at any time regardless of weather 'or' ambient lighting conditions.
6. **Radio Waves :** As at the one end we use gamma for medicine and astronomy, radio waves are also used marjorly in medical and astronomy. The most well-known application of radio waves in medical field is Magnetic resonance imaging (MRI).

   In this technique (MRI), we place a patient in a powerful magnet and passes radio waves through body of patient in the form of short pulses. Each pulse causes a responding pulses of radio waves to be emitted by the patient's tissues. The location from which these signals originated and their strength are determined by a computer.

   Thus we have concluded all the major applications of image processing.

1.3 FUNDAMENTAL STEPS IN DIGITAL IMAGE PROCESSING

Till now, it should be clear that the area of digital image processing is very broad. To study the digital image processing, the whole process has been divided into some fundamental steps as shown in Figure 1.2.

{Output of these processes are generally images}

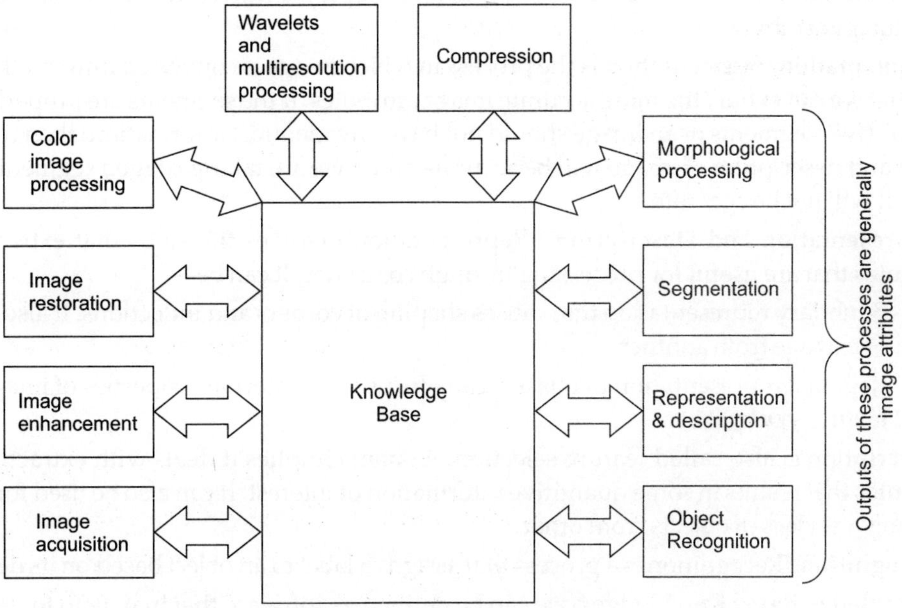

Fig. 1.2 *Fundamental steps in digital image processing.*

Now let us define the each step one by one.

1. **Image Acquisition :** This is the first step of digital image processing. Definitely first step of digital image processing should be sensing of an image. So in an image acquisition, image is sensed by *'illumination'* from source and *'reflection'* or *'observation'* from sensors. It will also involves preprocessing, such as scaling. Example of image acquisition is to take an image by a camera.
2. **Image Enhancement :** After taking an image, it is some time required to highlight certain features of image. So image enhancement is simply to highlight certain features of image.

Example of image enhancement is simply to increase the contrast of image so that it looks better.

3. **Image Restoration :** Restoration means to restore an image that is not looking good due to some distortion (Noise). Thus, we can say that restoration also involves the process so that image looks better just like image enhancement. But image enhancement is a subjective process that is based on human perception only. Here we see that image appearance is increasing but we don't bother about '*why*' and '*how*'?

   On the other hand, image restoration is a objective process. It is based on mathematical and probabilistic models of image degradation. Here we analysis '*why*' and after getting the reason of image degradation, we remove that by developing some methods (after using some mathematical analysis).

4. **Color Image Processing :** Color image processing deals with modeling and pocessing of color images.
5. **Wavelets and Multiresolution Processing :** Wavelets are the foundation for representing images in various degree of resolution.
6. **Compression :** Compression is a technique that is used for reducing the storage space for saving an image and reducing the bandwidth required for transmission of image.
7. **Morphological Processing :** It basically deals with tools for extracting image components that are useful for representation and description of shape. Definitely the outputs of this process are image attributes.
8. **Segmentation :** Segmentation is the process in which image is converted into small segments so that we can extract the more accurate image attributes. If the segments are properly autonomous (two segments of an image should not have any identical information) then representation and description of image will be accurate and if we are taking rugged segmentation, the result will not be accurate.
9. **Representation and Description :** Representation involves the steps that extracts the attributes that are useful for processing through computer. It can be—
   (*a*) Boundary representation that causes shaping of corners and inflections. It also separates one image from another.
   (*b*) Regional representation that is basically focused on internal properties of image such as texture, contrast etc.

   Description is also called feature selection. As name implies it deals with extracting the attributes that results in some quantitive information of interest. It can also be used for differentiating one class of objects from other.

10. **Recognition :** Recognition is a process that assigns a label to an object based on its descriptors.
11. **Knowledge Base :** Knowledge base can be defined as software that may help to user proper image enhancement, restoration 'or' compression technique. It may help user in segmentation of an image.

It is only the base that helps to synchronize all the processes to each other.

1.4 COMPONENTS OF AN IMAGE PROCESSING SYSTEM

Although the components of an image processing system differs according to different types of images, for example; satellite images and X-ray images cannot be processed by same type of image processing system. But to have a knowledge about the minimum requirement of an image processing system, we can study the block diagram given below of a general purpose image processing system.

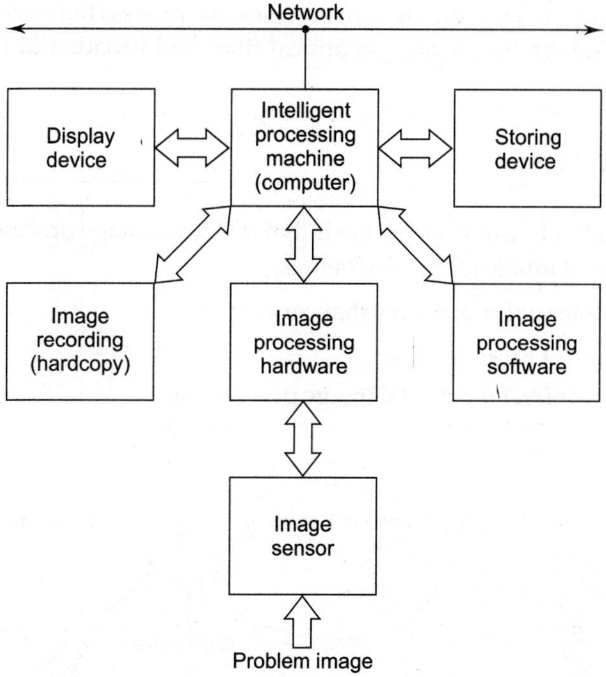

Fig. 1.3 *Components of digital image processing system.*

Now we study each part one by one :

1. **Image Sensor :** First basic requirement is image sensor. It has basically two parts :
   (*a*) A physical device that will sense the energy radiated by the object we wish to image.
   (*b*) A second device that is called digitizer that will convert the output of physical device into digital form.
2. **Image Processing Hardware :** Image processing hardware is here used just before the intelligent device (generally a super computer) because it will perform the specialized process on image but with high speed. For example, it may take average of different samples of an image for reduction of noise.
3. **Intelligent Processing Machine (Computer) :** It basically may be a general purpose PC *'or'* a supercomputer according to task to be performed. The basic use of this device is that it will perform all digital image processing task off line. Off line means once, we have taken image, we can apply different enhancement techniques (and other processes also).
4. **Image Processing Software :** Image processing softwares are specially designed programming modules that perform specific tasks. Some software also provides the facility that a user can also write programming codes for some purposes.

   Storing Device : Storing devices are used for storing of an image for different purposes. On the basis of tasks, the storing.device can be of three types :
   (*a*) Short-term storage for use during process.
   (*b*) On-line storage for relatively fast recall.
   (*c*) Storage for frequent use.

6. **Display Device :** Display device is generally a color monitor.
7. **Image Recording (Hard Copy) :** It may be only one of leser printers, inkjet units, CD-ROMs etc.
8. **Networking :** By networking, one system user can also process the system at another place. For image, we require high bandwidth so optical fiber and broadband technologies are better options.

1.5 VISUAL PERCEPTION

The basic purpose of study of visual perception is that in digital image processing, we concern about the better representation of image for human beings.

So now we will study about human eyes that covers :

1. Physical limitations of human vision.
2. The factors that will effect the digital image processing.

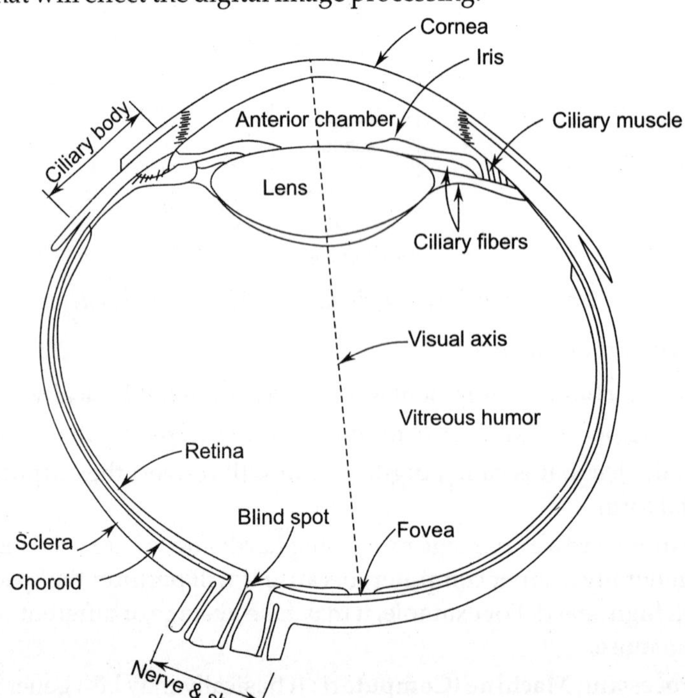

Fig. 1.4 *Human eyes (cross section view).*

So let us start with Fig. 1.4 that shows the horizontal cross section of human eye. The eye is nearly a sphere with an average diameter of approximately 20 mm. Three membranes encloses the eyes.

(*a*) Cornea and Sclera that are the outer covers of eyes.

(*b*) Choroid that has further two parts called ciliary body and iris diaphragm.

(*c*) Retina that has two classes of receptors called cones and rods.

Besides, these three types of membranes eyes also have one lens. Now we will study them in detail.

First membrane that is also the outer cover of eyes includes cornea and sclera. The cornea is a tough, transparent tissue that covers the whole surface of eyes. At optic globe (lens), the sclera provides the safety to the eye.

Second membrane is just below than cornea and sclera. The basic purpose of this membrane is to provide nutrition to the eye. It contains a network of blood vessels. It also provides the protection to the eye by reducing the amount of extreme light to the eyes and back scatter with in lens. As we know that choroid is divided into two parts called ciliary body and the iris diaphragm, here the work of iris is very interesting. As we may see in figure. 1.4 the central opening of iris varies in diameter from 2 to 8 mm approximately. This variation is according to the amount of light entering the eyes. The front end of iris contains visible pigment of eyes and back of iris contains the black pigment of eyes.

Third and innermost membrane is called retina, when eyes is properly focused, light from an object outside the eyes is imaged on retina. For image formation these are light receptors on the surface of retina. As discussed, there are two types of receptors called cones and rodes. The cones in each eye number between 6 and 7 million. They are located at the central portion of eyes (also called fovea). Cones are very much sensitive to color. Cones can resolve fine details because each cone is connected to its own nerve. Cone vision is called photopic 'or' bright-light vision. The number of rods is much larger approximately 75 to 150 millions are distributed over the retina surface. But the rods are unable to solve the fine details because all rods are connected to a single nerve. Rods generally provide a general overall view of image. It should be cleared that rods are not sensitive for color vision and are very much sensitive to low illumination.

Figure 1.5 shows the density of rods and cones v/s degrees for visual axis (center of fovea) see the cross section of eyes, we have a blind spot, where we don't have cones 'or' rods. By the figure 1.5 it should be cleared that cones are most dense in the center of retina and rods increase in density from center out to approximately 20° off axis and then decrease in density out of extreme periphery of retina.

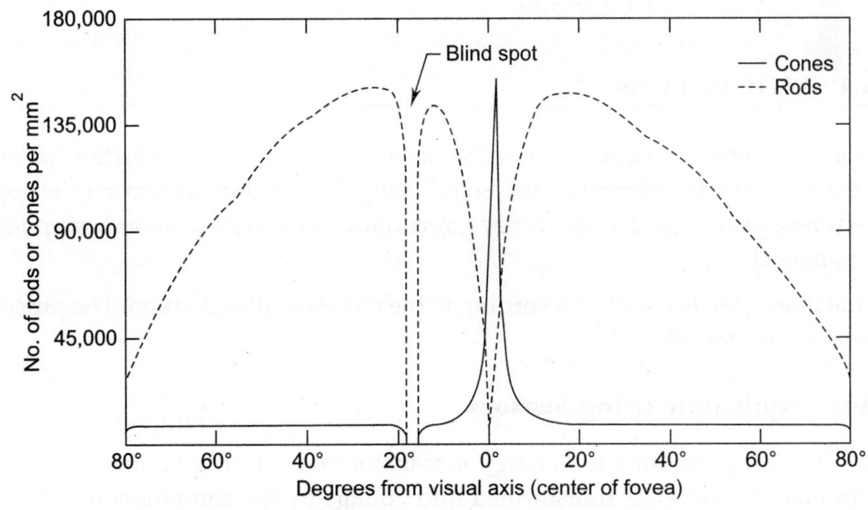

Fig. 1.5 *Density of cones and rods.*

Now we come to the final part of interest that is lens. The lens is made up of concentric layers of fibrous cells. It contains 60 to 70% water, about 6% fat and more protein than any other tissue in eyes.

The lens is colored by a slightly yellow pigmentation that increases with age. The lens absorbs approximately 8% of visible light. Note that both infrared and ultraviolet lights are absorbed significantly by eyes. If it is in excessive amount, it can damage the eyes.

1.5.1 Image Formation in Eyes

The principle difference between the lens of eye and ordinary lens is that eyes lens is flexible. The shape of the lens is controlled by ciliary body. To focus on distant objects, ciliary body muscles allow the lens to be relatively flattened. Similarly if object is very near, then these muscles allow the lens to be thicker.

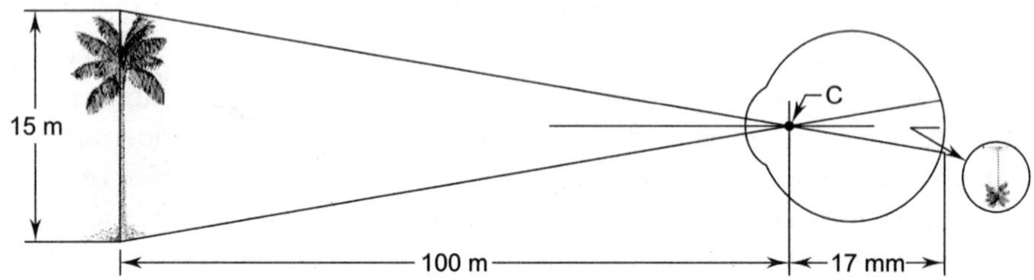

Fig. 1.6 *Image formation in eyes.*

The distance between the center of lens and the retina is called focal length. This length varies from 17 mm to 14 mm according to refractive power of lens. When object is away them about 3 mm, then lens has its lower refractive power. If the object is nearer then 3 mm, lens has its higher refractive index. By very small mathematical calculation, we can easily calculate the retinal height of image of object as for example :

$$\frac{15}{100} = \frac{h}{17}$$

Then $h = 2.55$ mm.

1.6 IMAGE ACQUISITION

The images are generated by combination of an *"illumination"* source and the reflection 'or' absorption of energy from that source by the elements of the *"scene"* being imaged. Illumination may be originated by a radar, infrared energy source and X-ray energy source, ultrasound energy source, computer generated illumination pattern etc.

To sense the image, we use sensor according to the nature of illumination. The process of image sense is called image acquisition.

1.6.1 Image Acquisition Using Sensors

By the sensor, basically illumination energy is transformed into digital image. The idea is that incoming illumination energy is transformed into voltage by the combination of input electrical energy and sensor material that is responsive to the particular type of energy being detected. The output waveform is the response of sensor and this response is digitalized to obtain digital image.

These sensors may be of different type such as:

1. Single image sensor

2. Sensor strips that may be linear or circular.
3. Array sensors.

1.6.1.1 Image Acquisition using Single Image Sensor

The basic idea of image acquisition using single image sensor has been shown in Fig. 1.7.

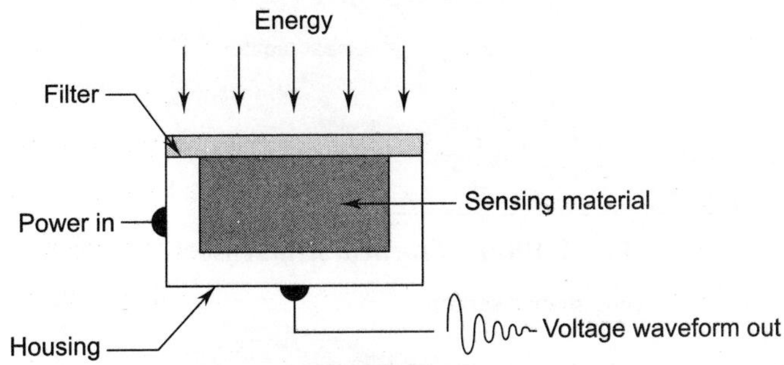

Fig. 1.7 *Single image sensor.*

The photodiode is also single sensor that generate output wave form according to illumination coming on the photodiode.

To generate a 2-D image, the sensor must have relative displacement in both X- and Y- direction between the sensor and the area to be imaged. Fig. 1.8 shows the basic arrangement for generation of 2-D image. Here a negative film is mounted on drum. The mechanical moment of drum provides the displacement in one direction. The single sensor is mounted on the lead screw that provides motion in perpendicular direction (motion in other direction). This method of image acquisition is slow but with high precision.

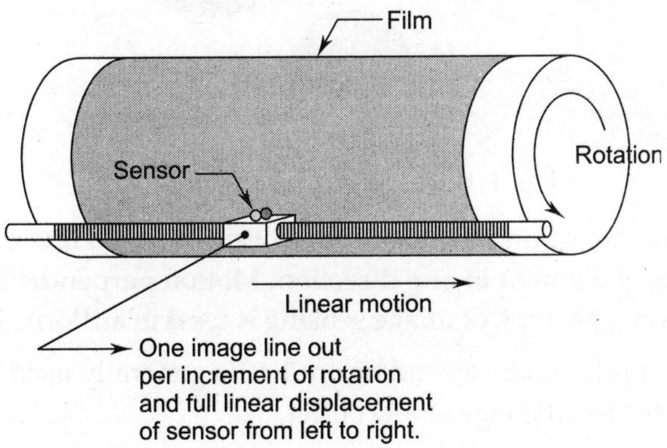

Fig. 1.8 *Single image sensor for 2-D image.*

1.6.1.2 Image Acquisition using Sensor Strip

The two frequently used strip sensors have been shown in Figs. 1.9 and 1.10 given below :

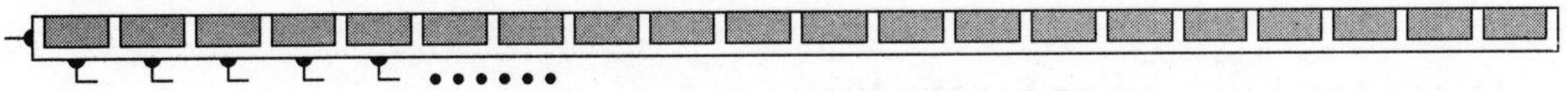

Fig. 1.9 *Strip image sensor.*

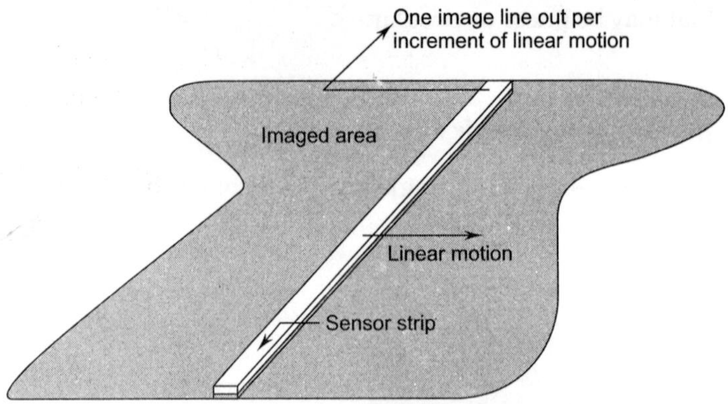

Fig. 1.10(a) *Practical strip sensors.*

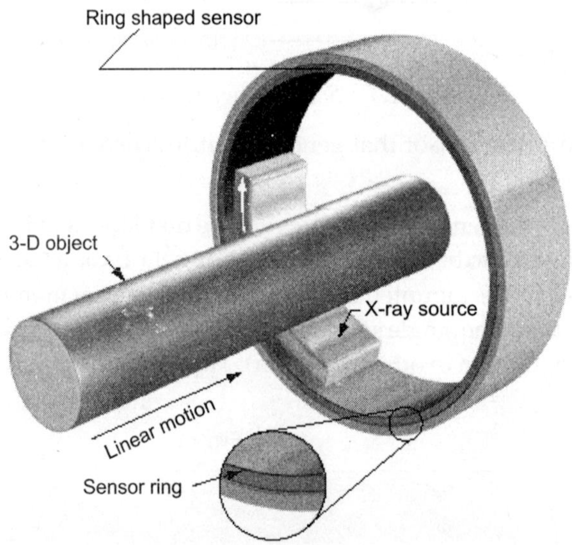

Fig. 1.10(b) *Practical strip sensors.*

In first figure 1.9, a number of single sensors have been arranged linearly to form a sensor strip. The strip provides imaging element in one direction. Motion perpendicular to the strip provides imaging in other direction. This type of image sensing is used in airborne imaging applications.

The sensor arrangement shown in second figure 1.10 is generally used in medical and industry imaging to obtain cross-sectional image of 3-D object.

Here sensor strips is mounted in a ring configuration. A rotating X-ray source provides illumination and the portion of the sensors opposite to the source collect the X-ray energy that passes through the object. Examples of this type of imaging are :

Computerized axial tomography (CAT), Magnetic resonance imaging (MRF), Positron emission tomography (PET) etc.

1.6.1.3 Image Acquisition using Sensor Arrays

This type of image acquisition is used in digital camera. A typical sensor for these cameras is an CCD array. In this type of sensor we use 4000 × 4000 elements as shown in Fig. 1.11.

Fig. 1.11 *Array sensor.*

The response of each sensor is proportional to the integral of the light projected on the surface of sensor. This type of arrangement is used in astronomical and other applications.

1.7 A SIMPLE IMAGE MODEL

Now we will proceed for mathematical representation of image. As we have already discussed, image can be presented by two-dimensional function $f(x, y)$ where (x, y) are the co-ordinates and amplitude of 'f' is called gray level '*or*' intensity level of image. Practically an image $f(x, y)$ must be non-zero and finite quantity ; that is

$$0 < f(x, y) < \infty$$

It is also discussed that for an image $f(x, y)$, we have two factors :

(*a*) The amount of source illumination incident on the scene being imaged. Let us represent it by $i(x, y)$.

(*b*) The amount of illumination reflected 'or' absorbed by objects in the scene. Let us represent it by $r(x, y)$.

Then $f(x, y)$ can be represented by

$$f(x, y) = i(x, y) \, . \, r(x, y)$$

Where $$0 < i(x, y) < \infty$$

it means illumination will be a non-zero and finite quantity and its quantity will depend upon illumination source

and $$0 < r(x, y) < 1$$

that indicate '*0*' means no reflection and total absorption and '*1*' means, no absorption and total reflection. The quantity of absorption '*or*' reflection depends upon characteristics of the imaged object.

1.7.1 Image Sampling and Quantization

We have acquired image by different sensor methods. But the response of all sensors is a continuous. Now to create a digital image, continuous sensed data should be converted into digital form. This involves two processes called sampling and quantization.

As we know the image is represented by $f(x, y)$, that is to be converted into digital form. An image $f(x, y)$ may be continuous with respect to x and y co-ordinates and also in amplitude. So,

1. *"Digitizing the coordinates values is called sampling"* ; and
2. *"Digitizing the amplitude values is called quantization"*.

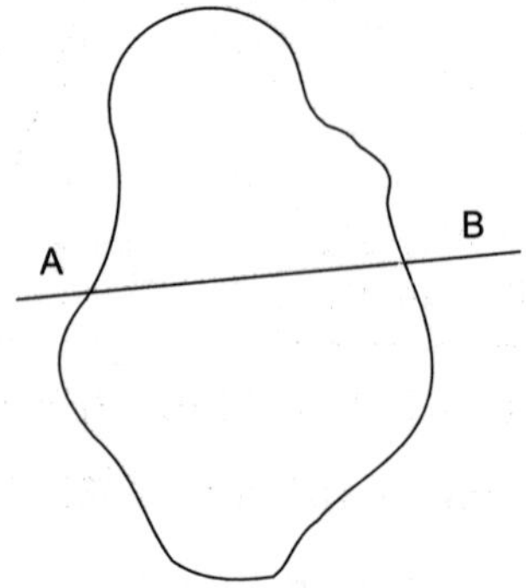

Fig. 1.12(a) *Test Image.*

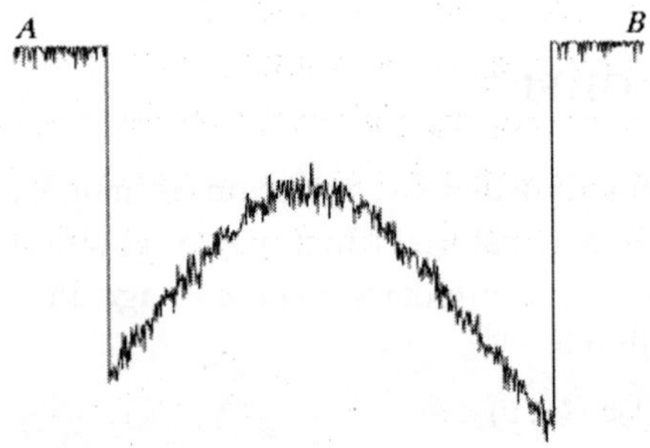

Fig. 1.12(b) *One-dimensional function of AB.*

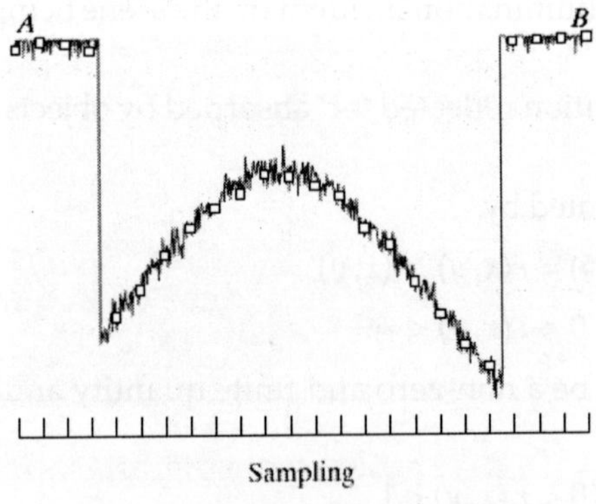

Fig. 1.12(c) *Sampled output.*

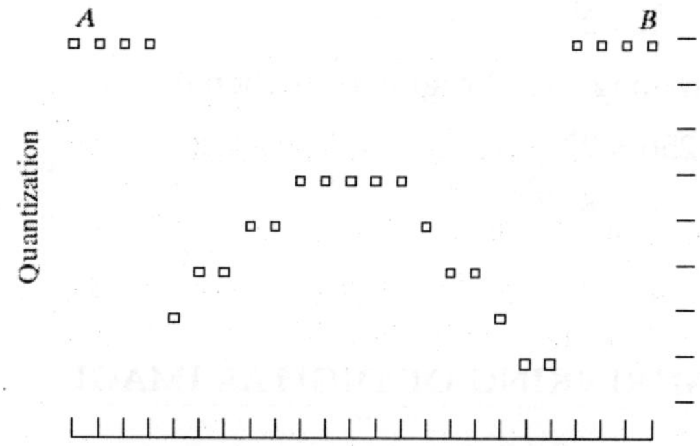

Fig. 1.12(d) *Quantized output.*

Here in Fig. 1.12 (*b*), we have drawn one dimensional function of line AB of an image shown in Fig. 1.12 (*a*). The random variations are due to noise. Now by sampling, we get the white squared output as shown in Fig. 1.12 (*c*). But still image is continuous on the gray scale. Finally after quantization we get complete digital output as shown in Fig. 1.12 (*d*).

If image is generated by single sensor ; the process of sampling and quantization will be same as shown in figure and discussed so far.

When image is generated by sensor strip ; the sampling is limited in one direction. But if image is taken by sensor array ; sampling is limited by both direction. Quantization process remains the same for all the methods.

1.7.2 Representation of Digital Image

The result of sampling and quantization is a matrix of real numbers.

Assuming that an image $f(x, y)$ is sampled so that resulting digital image has M rows and N columns. Now

(*a*) The co-ordinate at origin are

$$(x, y) = (0, 0)$$

(*b*) The co-ordinate at first row will be

$$(0, 0), (0, 1), (0, 2), \ldots\ldots (0, N-1)$$

and so on.

Here (0, 1) shows the second sample at first row. So we have matrix in the form given below :

$$f(x, y) = \begin{bmatrix} f(0,0) & f(0,1) & \ldots\ldots & f(0, N-1) \\ f(1,0) & f(1,1) & \ldots\ldots & f(1, N-1) \\ \vdots & \vdots & & \vdots \\ f(M-1, 0) & f(M-1, 1) & \ldots\ldots & f(M-1, N-1) \end{bmatrix}$$

Values of M and N are totally positive and cannot be negative.

Thus amplitude of '*f*' called gray level has also been digitized in the range [0, L–1] means in total L levels. This range is called dynamic range of an image.

Here if we talk about the storage of an image in computer then we have to calculate the gray level in terms of bits. If number of bits are K, then gray levels will be

$$L = 2^K$$

It means if we say that an image has 256 gray level then it is an

$$256 = 2^K$$

or $$K = 8$$

8 bit image.

1.8 ZOOMING AND SHRINKING OF DIGITAL IMAGE

Zooming may be viewed as oversampling, while shrinking may be viewed as undersampling. Definitely both can be applied to the digital image only. In the zooming, we simply create new pixel location and assign gray levels for these new location.

If zooming is done by non-integer times (say 1.5 times to original image) ; then for assigning new gray level we follow nearest neighbour interpolation. It means for example we have 500 × 500 pixel image that is zoomed by 1.5 times. Due to this zooming we get new image of 750 × 750 pixel. Now new pixels are assigned gray level according to nearest gray level.

If zooming is done by integer times (say 2 times) ; then we may use pixel replication method. It means we duplicate each column if we are zooming image in horizontal direction and we duplicate each row, if we are zooming image in vertical direction.

For shrinking, we apply same process but in reverse direction (in place of duplication of pixel values, we delete rows and columns).

Summary

1. The aim of digital image processing is the improvement in the quality of image and make it suitable for different processes such as storage, transmission 'or' presentation.
2. Image is defined by two-dimensional function $f(x, y)$, where x, y are spatial (plane) co-ordinates and amplitude of $f(x, y)$ is called intensity level.
3. There may be following fundamental steps of image processing—Image Acquisition, Image Enhancement, Image Restoration, Color Image Processing, Wavelet and Multiresolution Processing, Image Compression, Morphological Processing, Image Segmentation, Representation and Description and Object Recognition.
4. The components of an image processing system may consist of the following parts :
   Image Sensor, Image Processing Hardware, Intelligent Processing Machine, Display device, Storing Device, Image Recording System and Image Processing Software etc.
5. Image acquisition means—*'illumination'* from energy source and *'reflection'* *'or'* absorption by object to be imaged.
6. Acquisition is done with the help of image sensor. Sensor may be a single image sensor, strip type sensor *'or'* array type sensor.
7. After taking image by a sensor ; image is digitalized with the help of digitalizer.
8. Digitalizing of co-ordinate values is called *'Sampling'*.
9. Digitalizing of amplitude values is called *'Quantization'*.
10. Zooming may be viewed as *'Oversampling'* and shrinking may be viewed as *'undersampling'*.

Review Questions

1. Define the image and image processing system.
2. Draw the electromagnetic spectrum of light. Find the applications of Gamma rays, X-rays, microwave and radio waves.
3. What are the fundamental steps of digital image processing ?
4. What are the major components of an image processing system ?
5. Draw the cross section view of human eyes ? Define the effects of rods and cones in eyes.
6. What do you understand by image sampling and quantization.
7. Define the process of oversampling and undersampling of an image.

CHAPTER 2

IMAGE ENHANCEMENT IN SPATIAL DOMAIN

2.1 INTRODUCTION

"The objective of enhancement is to process an image so that the result is more suitable for human being in comparison to original image".

Image enhancement's approaches falls two categories :

(*a*) **Spatial Domain :** Spatial means the plane of image itself. So spatial domain is based on direct manipulation of pixels of an image. Term spatial domain refers to the aggregate of pixels composing an image.

(*b*) **Frequency Domain :** Frequency domain processing techniques are based on manipulation in Fourier transform of image.

Enhancement is a subjective matter. The image can be *'good'* for one human being and can be *'bad'* for other person. Thus, for applying any enhancement technique, first of all we apply trial and error method.

2.2 MATHEMATICAL ANALYSIS OF ENHANCEMENT IN SPATIAL DOMAIN

1. Spatial domain analysis is applied directly to the pixels of image so it can be shown by

$$\boxed{g(x, y) = T[f(x, y)]} \qquad \text{... (2.1)}$$

$f(x, y)$ = Input image

$g(x, y)$ = Output image.

T = Operator of $f(x, y)$ whose value depends the neighbourhoods of (x, y).

2. **Gray-level transformation (Intensity Mapping) :** It is the simplest form of spatial domain, if we take the value of *'T'* when the neighbourhoods is size of 1×1 (single pixel). In this case, $g(x, y)$ depends upon $f(x, y)$ only. In this case, this is called gray-level transformation *'or'* mapping. It is represented by:

$$S = T(r) \quad \text{... (2.2)}$$
$$S = g(x, y)$$
$$r = f(x, y)$$

3. **Contrast Stretching :** The spatial domain equation (2.2) shows basically the image we get after equation (2.2) would be of high contrast.

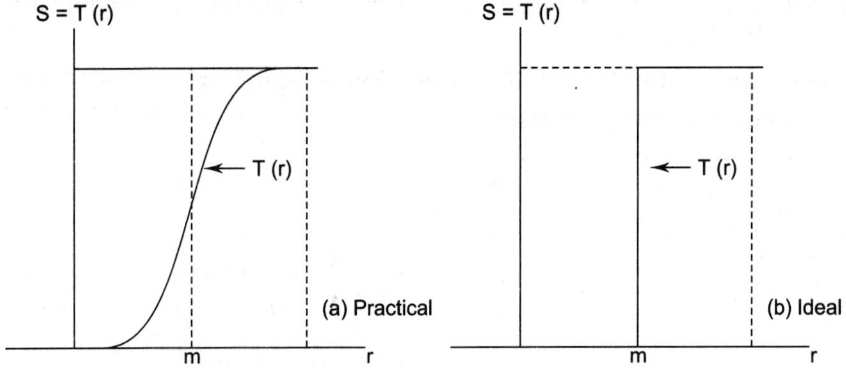

Fig. 2.1 *Contrast stretching and thresholding.*

4. **Thresholding :** The result of equation 2.2 is also thresholding of image. If pixel has value less then *'m'*, we get dark pixel and if pixel has value high then *'m'*, we get light pixel.

Because enhancement at any point in an image depends only on the gray level at that point, so this technique is also referred as point processing.

This is always done with the help of mask, that will be discussed later.

2.3 BASIC GRAY LEVEL TRANSFORMATION

Basically we have different types of gray level transformations

1. Point transformation.
2. Linear (negative and identity) transformation.
3. Logarithmic (log and inverse log) transformation.
4. Power-low transformation.
5. Piece-wise linear transformation.

2.3.1 Point Transformation

By equation,

$$S = T(r) \quad \text{(By equation 2.2)}$$

where T = transform operator, this can be done by using 1×1 window that means only a single pixel; that type of transformation is called point transformation.

Basically use of point transformation is masking of a particular pixel.

2.3.2 Linear Transformation

Positive *'or'* identity transformation does not play an important role in image processing, because transformed image is image itself.

Negative transformation plays a vital role in image processing. Suppose we have total number of gray level = L

Then the range of gray levels = [0, L – 1] so the negative imaging can be presented by equation,

$$\boxed{S = (L - 1) - r} \quad \text{... (2.3)}$$

The application of negative imaging is to create a negative of image. If black area is dominant area in image that can be converted into white area and very small but important white in real picture is now converted into black spot. So now,

Black area with small spot white = White area with small spot black

Underlined image can be analysed easily.

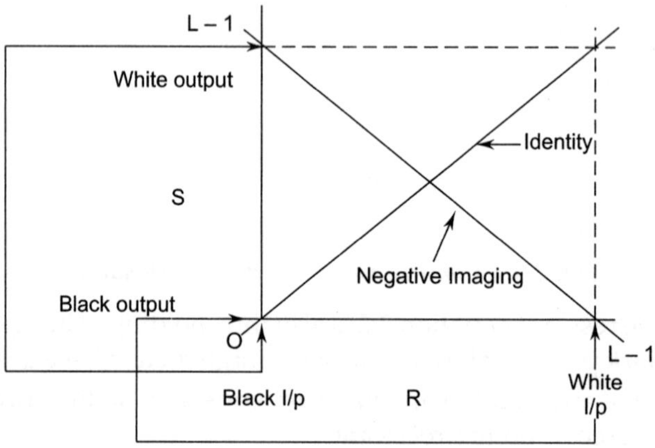

Fig. 2.2 *Line or transformation.*

2.3.3 Log Transformation

A general equation for log transformation is given by

$$\boxed{S = c \log (1 + r)} \quad \text{... (2.4)}$$

where c = constant and

$r \geq 0$.

The transfer characteristics has been drawn below :

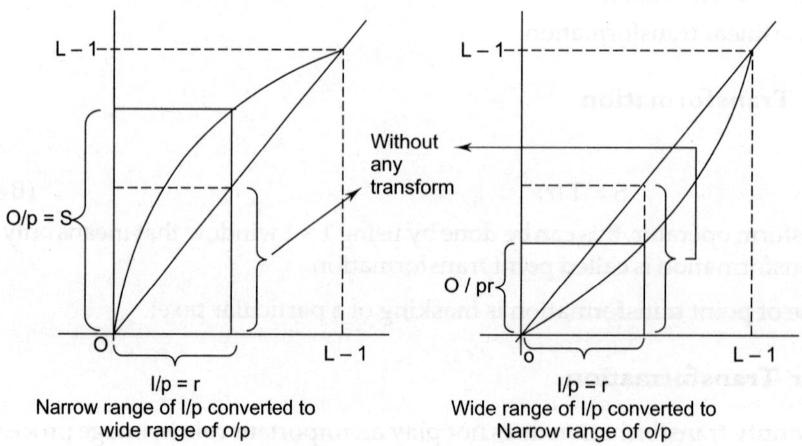

Fig. 2.3 *Log transformation.*

That shows that by log transformation, we get spreading / compressing of gray levels (that can also be done by power low transformation). But the actual advantage of log-transformation is compression and expansion of an image.

2.3.4 Power Low Transformation (n^{th} power and n^{th} root transformation).

The basic equation for power low transformation is

$$S = cr^{\gamma} \qquad \text{... (2.5)}$$

transfer function can be drawn as given below :

(*i*) for $\gamma > 1$ It is n^{th} power

(*ii*) for $\gamma < 1$ It is n^{th} root of pixel.

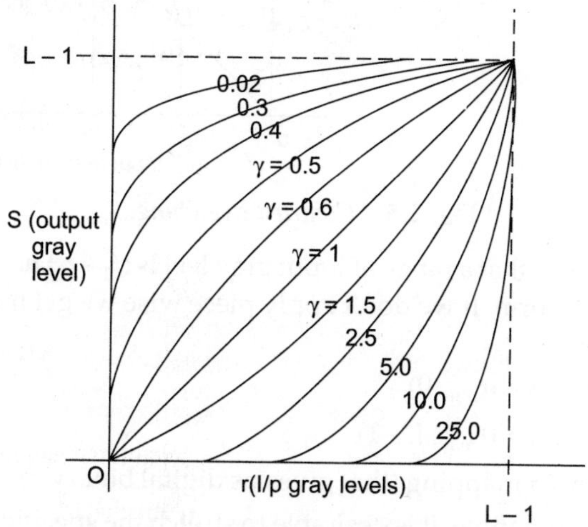

Fig. 2.4 *Power low transformation.*

(also called gamma correction due to the use of gamma as constant). Basically γ correction plays same role as log-transformation ; but now with small variation in the value of γ causes a long range (dynamic range) coverage. The most popular advantage of gamma level-correction is in CRT.

As at internet, a single picture in a website is visited by different peoples having different CRT. So many CRT has automatic gamma correction and some have manual that carries to see the image according to our choice and our monitor.

2.3.5 Piece-wise Linear Transformation

In the transformations discussed till now has one disadvantage that "*transformation is applied to whole image. On the other hand, if we require to enhance a particular part of image, we generally prefer a piece-wise linear transformation*".

Now we will discuss different types of piece-wise transformation functions and their applications.

(*a*) **Contrast Stretching :** Basically due to different reasons such as :

(*i*) Poor illumination.

(*ii*) Lack of dynamic range in imaging sensor.

(*iii*) Wrong setting of lens aperture during image acquisition.

We get poor contrast, so to get good contrast, we apply contrast stretching. The transfer function has been drawn below :

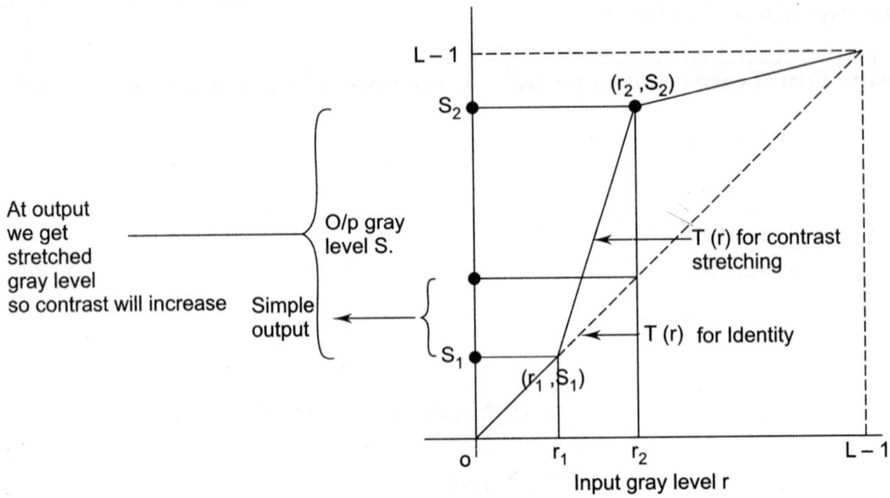

Fig. 2.5 *Contrast stretching.*

This figure clearly shows that a range of input gray levels $(r_1 - r_2)$ has been stretched $(s_1 - s_2)$ by piece-wise linear transform. If we don't apply piece wise we get normal unstretched output image.

If $\quad (r_1, s_1) = (r_{min}, 0)$

and $\quad (r_2, s_2) = (r_{max}, L-1) \quad \text{... (2.6)}$

it is also called threshold mapping (that gives us digital binary image).

(*b*) **Gray Level Slicing :** Sometime, it is desirable to stretch the specific range of image should be enhanced not the whole image.

So gray level slicing provide this facility, by two possible ways.:

(*i*) One approach is that we boast up the desired range of gray levels and other gray levels are suppressed.

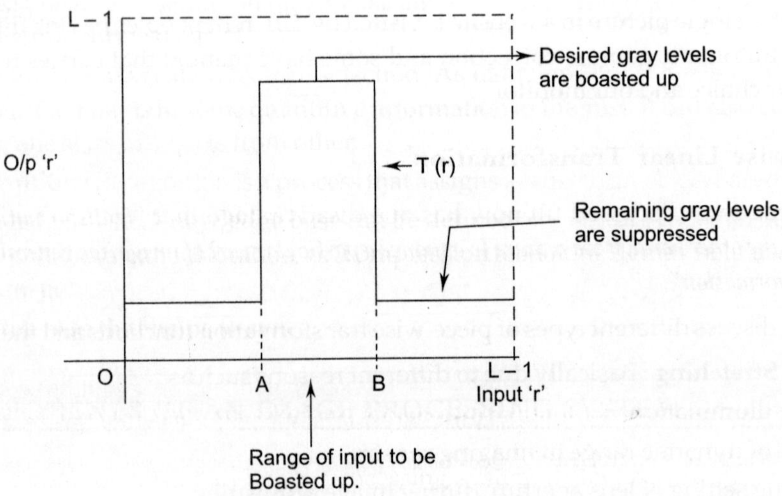

Fig. 2.6(a) *Gray level slicing.*

(*ii*) Another approach is that, we boast up the desired range of input, but also preserve the quantity of remaining part of input.

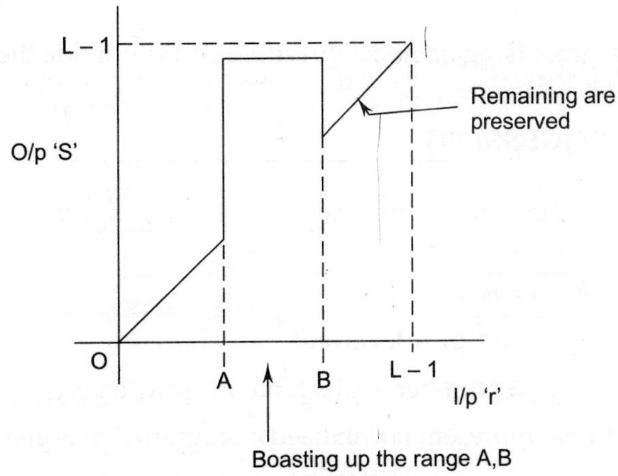

Fig. 2.6(b) *Gray level slicing.*

(*c*) **Bit-Plane Slicing :** Sometime it is also desired to know the contribution of each bit in an image. Suppose that we have 8 bits in each pixel.

Pixel having 8 Bits

$$\begin{bmatrix} a_{11} & a_{12} & \cdots\cdots & a_{1N} \\ a_{21} & a_{22} & \cdots\cdots & a_{2N} \\ \vdots & \vdots & & \vdots \\ a_{M1} & a_{2M} & \cdots\cdots & a_{MN} \end{bmatrix}_{M \times N} \qquad \ldots (2.7)$$

So it can be divided into 8-plane. Plane 0 will have all LSBs and plane '7' will have all MSB.

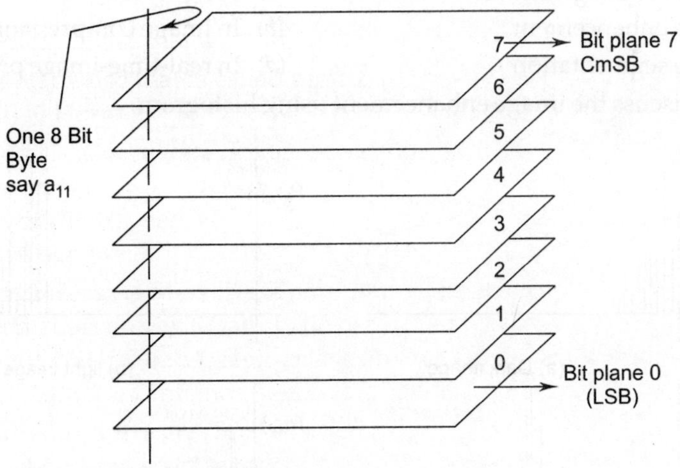

Fig. 2.7 *Bit plane slicing.*

It should be cleared that all LSB means plane '0' will play very less significant role and plane '7' will play very much significant role in image.

We may follow the following steps for bit slicing:

1. We have total $2^8 = 256$ levels. So by a appropriate threshold divide the levels 0 – 127 and 129–255.
2. Thus, we get two segments, again make threshold and subdivide the levels.

2.4 HISTOGRAM PROCESSING

1. The histogram of a digital image with gray levels in the range [0, L – 1] is a discrete function and given by

$$\boxed{h(r_k) = n_k} \quad \text{... (2.8)}$$

where $r_k = k^{\text{th}}$ gray level and

n_k = Number of pixels having gray level r_k.

2. Practically generally we represent normalized histogram that is given by

$$\text{Normalized Value} = \frac{\text{That value}}{\text{Total number of values}}$$

Thus, we have

$$\boxed{P(r_k) = \frac{n_k}{n}} \quad \text{... (2.9)}$$

Loosely speaking,

$P(r_k)$ = Probability of occurring k_{th} level.

Simply,

Addition of all terms to normalised histogram is always = 1.

3. Applications of histogram are:
   (*a*) In image enhancement
   (*b*) In image compression
   (*c*) In image segmentation
   (*d*) In real-time-image processing.
4. Now let us discuss the image enhancement using histogram.

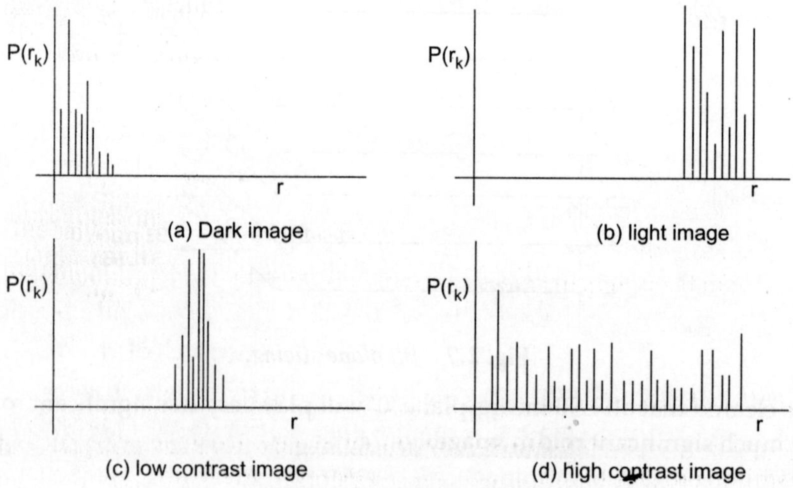

Fig. 2.8 *Histogram.*

As seen in diagram,

(*a*) A dark image will have histogram very near to origin.
(*b*) A light image will have histogram very far from origin near the maximum levels at r scale.
(*c*) A low contrast image will have very narrow and at middle histogram.
(*d*) A high contrast image will contain a wide dynamic range of pixels thats why its histogram will be uniformly distributed through scaler.

So, in general case, we have to apply a software that will convert each image histogram in form of image '*d*' automatically.

2.5 HISTOGRAM EQUALIZATION

"In histogram equalization, we get the image that has equalized gray levels".

By the equation,

$$S = T(r) \quad 0 \leq r \leq 1 \text{ for} \qquad \text{(by equations 2.2)}$$

binary scheme for histogram equalization transformation function must satisfy the following conditions.

(*a*) T (r) should be single valued that sures that the inverse transform will exist, and T (r) should be monotonically increasing that assure us that image is moving from black to white.
(*b*) And $0 \leq T(r) \leq 1$ that for $0 \leq r \leq 1$ so that input and output image have same size.

Now our basic aim is to get the

1. Input signal histogram.
2. A transfer function that will generate a equalized histogram of input signal.
3. To verify whether the output histogram generated is equalized '*or*' not.

Input signal histogram can be generated using probability density function (PDF) because the gray levels in a image are random distributed and PDF is only the tool by which we can calculate the histogram. It can be shown that if

$P_r(r)$ = PDF of input image gray levels.

and $T(r)$ = The transfer function for equalization are known, we have output $P_s(s)$ by relation,

$$P_s(s) = P_r(r)\left|\frac{dr}{ds}\right| \qquad \text{... (2.10)}$$

As we are using PDF for generating the histogram of input signal, the transform function should be in form of CDF (commulative distribution function).

So we have a new relation

$$S = T(r) = \int_0^r P_r(w)\, dw \qquad \text{... (2.11)}$$

w = dummy variable for integration

Now to verify that this T (r) will generate a output image that has equalized histogram ; let us calculate

$$\frac{ds}{dr} = \frac{d}{dr}\left[\int_0^r P_r(w) . dw\right]$$

$$\frac{ds}{dr} = P_r(r)$$

or
$$\left|\frac{dr}{ds}\right| = \frac{1}{P_r(r)} \qquad \text{... (2.12)}$$

Substituting equation (2.12) in equation (2.11), we have

$$P_s(s) = P_r(r) \times \frac{1}{P_r(r)}$$

$$P_s(s) = 1 \qquad \text{... (2.13)}$$

That means output is totally independent upon input. It will generate a equalized histogram of an image.

Thus, if we apply any image to equation (2.11) we will get equalized histogram of image.

2.6 HISTOGRAM MATCHING

In histogram equalization, we get the output image that has equalized gray levels. But sometime, it is required that we want a specific shape of histogram of image.

So "*to generate a image that has the histogram of our desire is known as histogram matching 'or' histogram specifications*".

Mathematical Analysis

Suppose that we have image 's' and PDF of it is $P_s(s)$. Now we want to generate a image 'z' with PDF $P_z(z)$ of specific value. So, we know that

$$S = T(r) = \int_0^r P_r(w)\, dw \qquad \text{... (2.14)}$$

Again for specific

$$S = G(z) = \int_0^z P_z(k)\, dk \qquad \text{... (2.15)}$$

'S' is finally the basic image for both.

So,
$$Z = G^{-1}(s) = G^{-1}[T(r)] \qquad \text{... (2.16)}$$

is the required image. For this we should follow the steps:

1. Calculate T (*r*) for original image.
2. Calculate G (z) for desired image.
3. Now apply equation (2.16) to get that desired values of 'z'. Now for each value of z calculate s by equation (2.15). Graphically, the method is shown on next page :

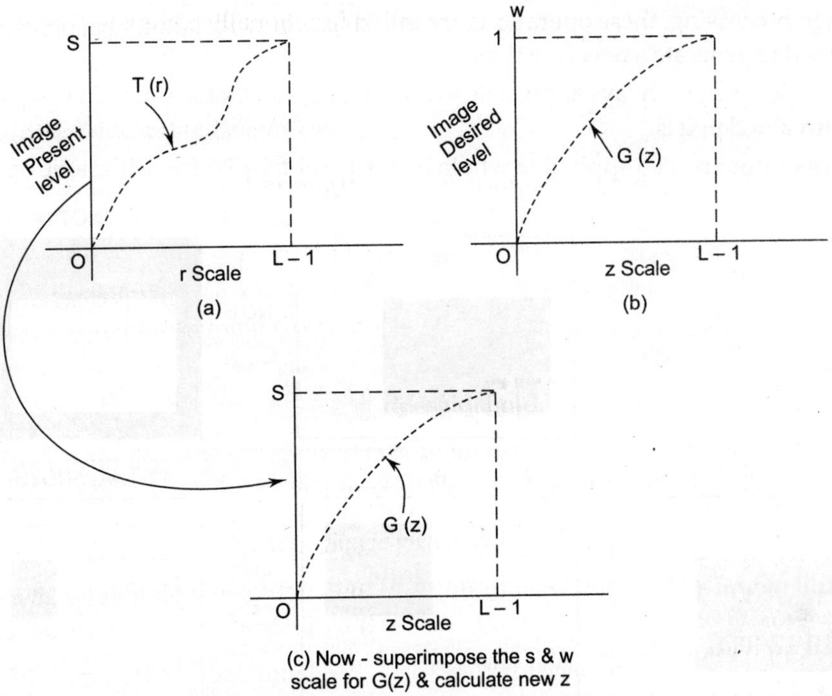

Fig. 2.9 *Process of histogram matching.*

2.7 IMAGE ENHANCEMENT USING ARITHMETIC AND LOGICAL OPERATION

1. The arithmatic operation between p and q are denoted as follows :

$$\begin{aligned} \text{Addition} &= p + q \\ \text{Subtraction} &= p - q \\ \text{Multiplication} &= p * q \ (pq \text{ 'or' } p \times q) \\ \text{Division} &= \frac{p}{q}. \end{aligned} \qquad ...(2.17)$$

2. It is performed on whole image by pixel to pixel (just like logical operation).
3. → Basic use of addition is for image averaging to reduce error.
   → Basic use of subtraction is medical imaging, where we have to remove the static background information.
   → Basic use of image multiplication is gray-level modification.

For Logic Operation :

1. The principle logic operators used in DIP are

$$\begin{aligned} \text{AND} &= p \,.\, q \\ \text{OR} &= p + q \\ \text{Complement} &= \bar{q} \ (\text{'or'}) \ \bar{p} \end{aligned} \qquad ...(2.18)$$

2. In image processing, these operations are called functionally completed. Because they can be combined to generate a new function.
3. Logical operation is always applicable to binary images whereas arithmetic operations, apply to multivalued pixels.
4. Logic operator are also applied to whole image pixel-by-pixel as arithmetic operation.

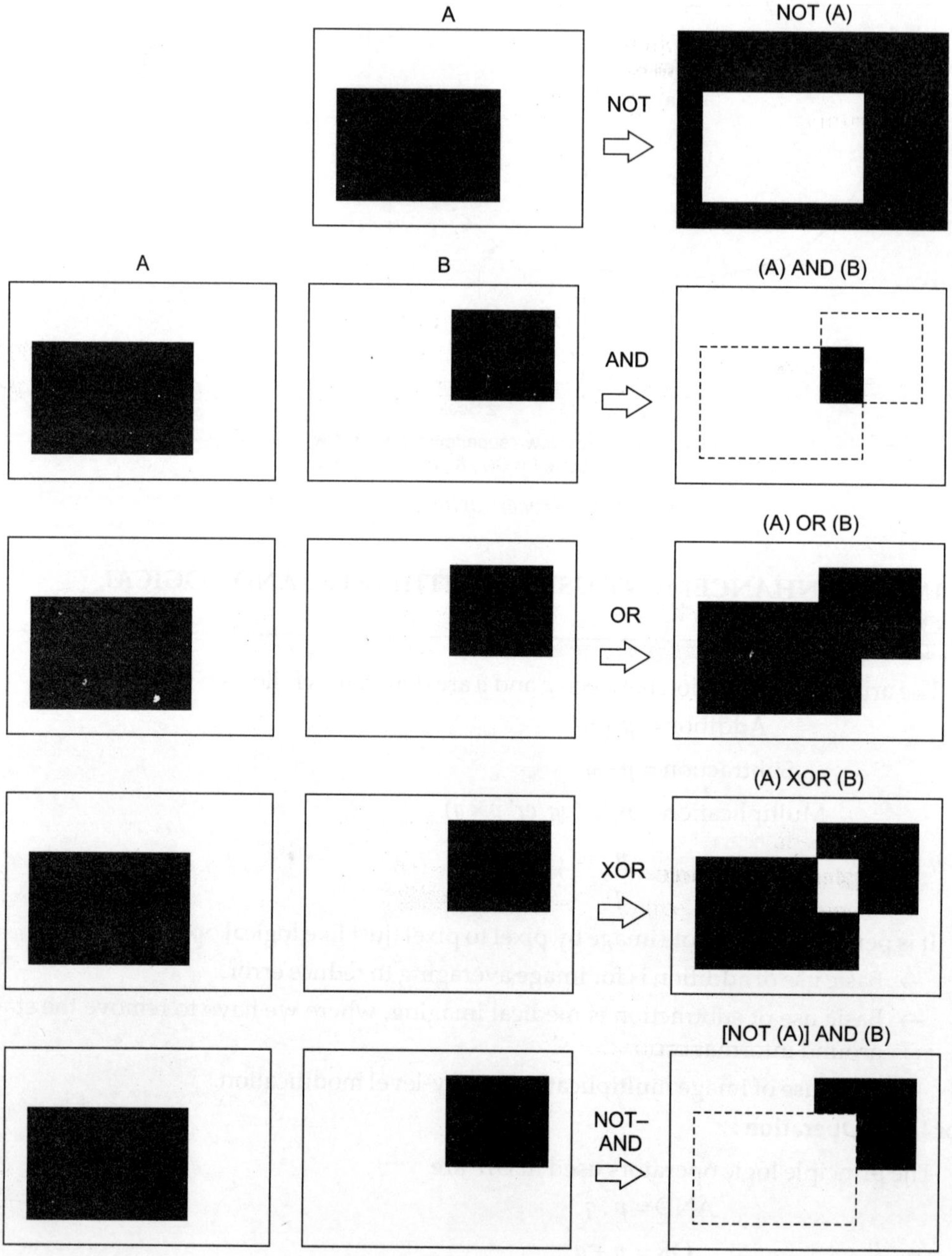

Fig. 2.10 *Logical operations.*

2.8 BASIC TRANSFORMATIONS

(*a*) **Translation :** Suppose that, we make translation of a point (X, Y, Z) to a new location by using displacement (X_0, Y_0, Z_0). Then translation can be done by using

$$X^* = X + X_0$$
$$Y^* = Y + Y_0 \quad \text{... (2.19)}$$
$$Z^* = Z + Z_0$$

where $\left(X^*, Y^*, Z^*\right)$ = New co-ordinate after translation.

In the form of matrix

$$\begin{bmatrix} X^* \\ Y^* \\ Z^* \\ 1 \end{bmatrix} = \begin{bmatrix} 1 & 0 & 0 & X_0 \\ 0 & 1 & 0 & Y_0 \\ 0 & 0 & 1 & Z_0 \\ 0 & 0 & 0 & 1 \end{bmatrix} \begin{bmatrix} X \\ Y \\ Z \\ 1 \end{bmatrix} \quad \text{... (2.20)}$$

So, the matrix used for translation of a point is

$$T = \begin{bmatrix} 1 & 0 & 0 & X_0 \\ 0 & 1 & 0 & Y_0 \\ 0 & 0 & 1 & Z_0 \\ 0 & 0 & 0 & 1 \end{bmatrix} \quad \text{... (2.21)}$$

(*b*) **Scaling :** Scaling by factor S_X, S_Y, S_Z along the points X, Y and Z ; then transformation matrix :

$$S = \begin{bmatrix} S_X & 0 & 0 & 0 \\ 0 & S_Y & 0 & 0 \\ 0 & 0 & S_Z & 0 \\ 0 & 0 & 0 & 1 \end{bmatrix} \quad \text{... (2.22)}$$

(*c*) **Rotation :** To rotate any point ; just do the following steps :

(*a*) Shift that point at origin.

(*b*) Now apply the rotation.

(*c*) Again reshift that point to original condition.

Rotation about Z-axis by angle 'θ' then transformation matrix is given by

$$R_\theta = \begin{bmatrix} \cos\theta & \sin\theta & 0 & 0 \\ -\sin\theta & \cos\theta & 0 & 0 \\ 0 & 0 & 1 & 0 \\ 0 & 0 & 0 & 1 \end{bmatrix} \quad \text{... (2.23)}$$

Rotation about 'X' axis by angle 'α' then transformation matrix is given by

$$R_\alpha = \begin{bmatrix} 1 & 0 & 0 & 0 \\ 0 & \cos\alpha & \sin\alpha & 0 \\ 0 & -\sin\alpha & \cos\alpha & 0 \\ 0 & 0 & 0 & 1 \end{bmatrix} \quad \text{... (2.24)}$$

Rotation about Y-axis by angle 'β' then transformation matrix is given by

$$R_\beta = \begin{bmatrix} \cos\beta & 0 & -\sin\beta & 0 \\ 0 & 1 & 0 & 0 \\ \sin\beta & 0 & \cos\beta & 0 \\ 0 & 0 & 0 & 1 \end{bmatrix} \quad \text{... (2.25)}$$

(*d*) **Perspective Transformations :**

(*i*) A perspective transformation projects 3:D point on to a plane.

(*ii*) This is totally non-linear transformation because it is divided by some co-ordinate value.

Perspective transformation matrix is given by

$$P = \begin{bmatrix} 1 & 0 & 0 & 0 \\ 0 & 1 & 0 & 0 \\ 0 & 0 & 1 & 0 \\ 0 & 0 & -\frac{1}{\lambda} & 1 \end{bmatrix} \quad \text{... (2.26)}$$

2.9 BASICS OF SPATIAL FILTERING

The basic of spatial filtering has been shown in Fig. 2.11. The process is simple that we move the filter mask from point to point of an image.

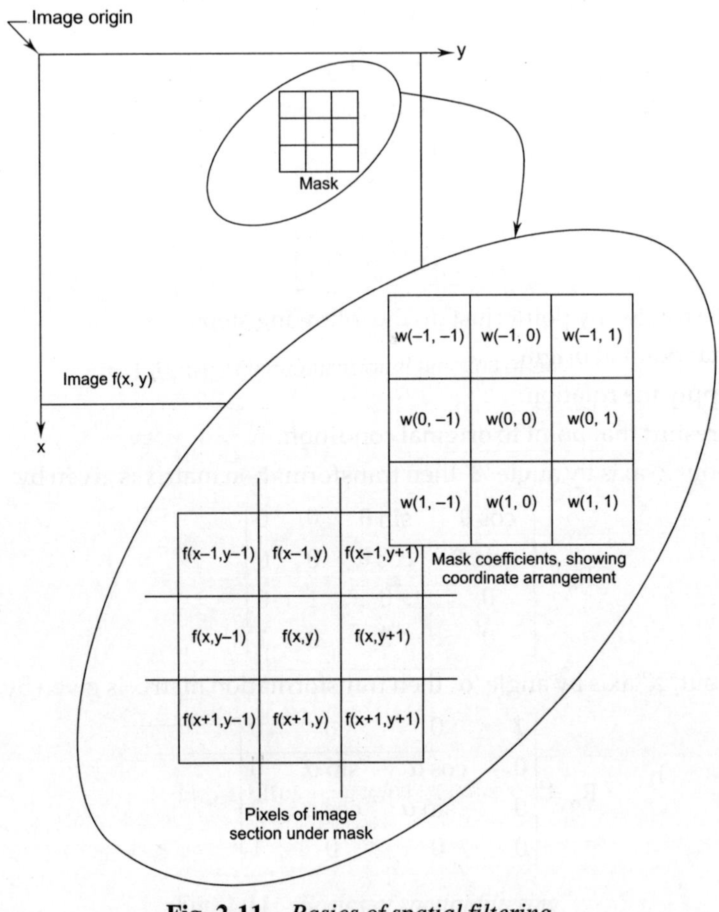

Fig. 2.11 *Basics of spatial filtering.*

At each point of image, the response of filter is calculated using a predefined relationship. For *"linear filtering, the response is given by sum of products of filter coefficients and the corresponding image pixels in the area directly under the mask"*.

For 3×3 filter mask, the response '*R*' of linear filtering at any point (x, y) is given by

$$R = w(-1,-1) f(x-1, y-1) + w(-1,0) \cdot f(x-1, y) + \ldots\ldots w(0,0) \cdot f(x, y) + \ldots\ldots + w(1,0) \cdot f(x+1, y+1) + w(1,1) \cdot f(x+1, y+1) \quad \ldots (2.27)$$

It is very easy, we can see that we have multiplied mask coefficient with respective image coefficient and after that added all, simple to say that 3×3 mask will have total '9' product terms.

In general, linear filtering of an image *f* of size M × N with a filter mask of size $m \times n$ is given by

$$R = g(x, y) = \sum_{s=-a}^{a} \sum_{t=-b}^{b} w(s, t) f(x+s, y+t) \quad \ldots (2.28)$$

where *a* and *b* are integer values. It is better to opt always a odd size filter because they have clear center point so easy to be located at image.

2.9.1 Smoothing Spatial Filtering

"The basic use of smoothing filter method is for blurring and for noise reduction".

"Blurring is a process to fill up the small gaps in lines 'or' curves. It is also used as a preprocessing for removal of small object before extracting large object information from image. In practical meaning, blurring means to reduce the sharpness".

2.9.1.1 Mean Smoothing Spatial Filtering

There may be a number of smoothing filtering methods (which will be discussed as per requirement). But at this stage, we will discuss about mean smoothing spatial filters.

"In mean filtering, we replace the value of every pixel in an image by the average / arithmetic mean of the gray levels in the neighbourhood defined by the filter mask".

The basic advantage of mean filtering is that by this type of filtering, the very small irrelevant areas of images are removed (as small areas have very small values and if we take further averaging of these areas definitely the result will be smaller so negligible). But only the disadvantage is that by mean filtering, we may loose the edges (sharp information) of an image.

Figure given below shows the basic 3×3 filter used for averaging.

$$\frac{1}{9} \times \begin{array}{|c|c|c|} \hline 1 & 1 & 1 \\ \hline 1 & 1 & 1 \\ \hline 1 & 1 & 1 \\ \hline \end{array}$$

Fig. 2.12 *3 × 3 filter for averaging.*

If we apply simply masking formula, we get response

$$R = \frac{1}{9} \sum_{i=1}^{9} Z_i \quad \ldots (2.29)$$

as we see that all filter co-efficients are equal so it is also called box filter.

"Sometime it is necessary to protect some information of our choice during averaging, for that purpose, we use weighted averaging". In this type of averaging/mean, we multiply the pixels of an image with different co-efficient. The pixels having high importance are multiplied by co-efficients of high values in comparison to others. Sometime, it is a practical approach that we use high valued co-efficients at center and decreasing the values of co-efficients as we go away from center. For example, take the 3×3 mask given below :

$$\frac{1}{16} \times \begin{array}{|c|c|c|} \hline 1 & 2 & 1 \\ \hline 2 & 4 & 2 \\ \hline 1 & 2 & 1 \\ \hline \end{array}$$

Fig. 2.13 *Another mask for averaging.*

Here the sum of all co-efficients of mask is *'16'*. So for averaging, we divide the total values by 16. So for averaging, we may conclude with general expression for filtering.

$$g(x, y) = \frac{\sum_{s=-a}^{a} \sum_{t=-b}^{b} \omega(s,t) f(x+s, y+t)}{\sum_{s=-a}^{a} \sum_{t=-b}^{b} \omega(s,t)} \qquad \text{... (2.30)}$$

2.9.1.2 *Non-Linear Smoothing Spatial Filtering*

The method discussed above is linear smoothing spatial filtering. But in some cases, we require response of filtering based on ordering 'or' ranking of pixels. They have really advantages in case of presence of impulse noise. Here at a glance, we will discuss some non-linear smoothing filters.

(*a*) **Median Filer :** Let $S_{x,y}$ represent the set of co-ordinates in a rectangular mask of size $m \times n$ centered at point (x, y). The given image is g (x, y). Then median is given by

$$R = \underset{(s,t) \in S_{xy}}{\text{Median}} \{g(s,t)\} \qquad \text{... (2.31)}$$

Thus, now each pixel value of $g(x, y)$ is replaced by median of its neighbourhood pixel under mask.

(*b*) **Maximum and Minimum Filtering :** Median filter represents the 50th percentile of ranked set of pixels. For some purposes, we may use 100th percentile *'or'* 0th percentile filter. The filter that is using 100th percentile of ranked set of pixel is called max filter and given by

$$R = \max_{(s,t) \in S_{xy}} \{g(s,t)\} \qquad \text{... (2.32)}$$

The filter that is using 0th percentile of ranked set of pixel is called min filter and given by

$$R = \min_{(s,t) \in S_{xy}} \{g(s,t)\} \qquad \text{... (2.33)}$$

Max filter is useful for finding brightest point of an image and minimum filter is useful for finding darkest point of image.

(*c*) **Mid-point Filtering :** Mid-point filter simply computes the mid-point between the maximum and minimum values in the area covered by the filter/mask.

$$\text{So, } R = \frac{1}{2} [\max \{g(s,t)\} + \min \{g(s,t)\}] \qquad \text{... (2.34)}$$

$(s, t) \in S_{xy}$ $(s, t) \in S_{xy}]$

This filter is combination of statistics and averaging.

It is very useful for enhancement if image is corrupted with gaussian *'or'* uniform noise.

2.9.2 Sharpening Spatial Filter

As sometime it is required to suppress some irrelevant information by blurring, it is sometime essential for image enhancement, to sharp some small but relevant information. So process opposite to blurring is sharpening.

"Sharpening is a process to highlight fine detail in an image 'or' enhance detail that has been blurred, either in error 'or' as a natural effect of particular method of image acquisition".

One main difference between blurring and sharpening is also that in blurring, we take averaging of neighbouring pixel averaging of pixels is equivalent to integration of pixel.

So Blurring = Average of neighbouring pixels = Integration of pixels.

So definitely logically sharpening should be equal to derivative of pixels.

So sharpening = Derivative of pixels.

As we know that mathematically, derivative can be of

1. First derivative that can be represented by

$$\frac{\partial f}{\partial x} = f(x+1) - f(x)$$

or

$$\frac{\partial f}{\partial y} = f(y+1) - f(y) \qquad \text{... (2.35)}$$

For an image $f(x, y)$; so at a time, we take partial derivative along one axis.

2. Second derivative that can be represented by

$$\frac{\partial^2 f}{\partial x^2} = f(x+1) + f(x-1) - 2f(x)$$

$$\frac{\partial^2 f}{\partial y^2} = f(y+1) + f(y-1) - 2f(y) \qquad \text{... (2.36)}$$

So now, we will discuss first derivative and second derivative in detail for image enhancement.

2.9.2.1 *Use of First Derivative for Enhancement (The Gradient)*

The basic properties that should be followed by first derivative are :

1. First determine should be zero at the area of constant gray levels (also called flat segments of image).
2. Must be non-zero at gray-level step *'or'* ramp.

Both properties are easily understandable mathematically. Practically, first derivative in image processing are implemented using magnitude of the gradient. For a function $f(x, y)$, the gradient of at co-ordinates (x, y) is defined as the two-dimensional column vector.

$$\nabla f = \begin{bmatrix} G_x \\ G_y \end{bmatrix} = \begin{bmatrix} \frac{\partial f}{\partial x} \\ \frac{\partial f}{\partial y} \end{bmatrix} \qquad \text{... (2.37)}$$

The magnitude of this vector is given by $meg\,(\nabla f)$

$$= \left[G_x^2 + G_y^2\right]^{\frac{1}{2}}$$

$$= \left[\left(\frac{\partial f}{\partial x}\right)^2 + \left(\frac{\partial f}{\partial y}\right)^2\right]^{\frac{1}{2}} \quad \text{... (2.38)}$$

It should be cleared :

1. Gradient vector itself is a linear operator. But its magnitude is a squaring a square root means non linear operator.
2. Magnitude of gradient vector is referred as gradient.

Here for easy calculation, we approximate gradient by

$$\nabla f \simeq |G_x| + |G_y| \quad \text{... (2.39)}$$

that serves our purpose sufficiently.

Now let us discuss the calculation of G_x and G_y by the use of different filters. Here we have drawn the filter in terms of $z_1, ..., z_9$ in stead of $f(-1,-1), ...f(1,1)$ only for simplicity. Both have same meaning.

One of the simplest ways to implement a first order derivative is to use Robert-Cross gradient operators.

$$G_x = (z_9 - z_5)$$

and

$$G_y = (z_8 - z_6) \quad \text{... (2.40)}$$

But it is not practical to use 2×2 mask, as it does not have any center.

An approach using masks of size 3×3 is given by

$$G_x = (z_7 + z_8 + z_9) - (z_1 + z_2 + z_3)$$

and

$$G_y = (z_3 + z_6 + z_9) - (z_1 + z_4 + z_7) \quad \text{... (2.41)}$$

In this formulation, the difference between first and third row of the 3×3 image region calculate the derivative in x-direction. The difference between the third and first columns calculate the derivative in y-direction.

This mask is called prewitt operators. A slight variation of these two equations uses a weight of 2 in the center co-efficient.

$$G_x = (z_7 + 2z_8 + z_9) - (z_1 + 2z_2 + z_3)$$

and

$$G_y = (z_3 + 2z_6 + z_9) - (z_1 + 2z_4 + z_7).$$

A weight value of '2' is used to achieve some smoothing by giving more importance to the center point. To implement these derivative, we use sobel operators as shown in figure 2.14.

One thing should be cleared to the students that the addition of all co-efficients should be zero.

z_1	z_2	z_3
z_4	z_5	z_6
z_7	z_8	z_9

−1	0
0	1

0	−1
1	0

Roberts

−1	−1	−1
0	0	0
1	1	1

−1	0	1
−1	0	1
−1	0	1

Prewitt

-1	-2	-1
0	0	0
1	2	1

-1	0	1
-2	0	2
-1	0	1

Sobel

Fig. 2.14. *Mask used for Gradient.*

2.9.2.2 *Use of Second Derivative for Enhancement (the Laplacian)*

Second derivative must follow the properties given below :

1. Second derivative must be at constant gray-level areas (called flat segment of image).
2. Must be non-zero at gray-level ramp.
3. Must be zero at gray-level ramp of constant slope.

The Laplacian of a 2D function f (x, y) is a second-order derivative defined as

$$\nabla^2 f = \frac{\partial^2 f}{\partial x^2} + \frac{\partial^2 f}{\partial y^2} \quad \text{... (2.42)}$$

For a 3×3 region, one of the two forms encountered most frequently in practice is

$$\nabla^2 f = 4z_5 - (z_2 + z_4 + z_6 + z_8). \quad \text{... (2.43)}$$

Another digital approximation including the diagonal neighbours is given by

$$\nabla^2 f = 8z_5 - (z_1 + z_2 + z_3 + z_4 + z_6 + z_7 + z_8 + z_9) \quad \text{... (2.44)}$$

Both equations are isotropic for rotation increments of 90° and 45° respectively.

Because, the Laplacian is a derivative operator, its use high lights gray-level discontinuities in an image and de-emphasizes regions with slowly varying gray levels.

So by Laplacian, we get response with very highlighted edges and totally suppressed low gray-level area. So if we add original image with Laplacian of Image ; Resultant image will have highlighted edges along with all other information. Thus, we use Laplacian for image enhancement by the following expression :

$$g(x, y) = \begin{cases} \{f(x, y) - \nabla^2 f(x, y) \text{ ; if the center co-efficient of the Laplacian mask is negative} \\ f(x, y) + \nabla^2 f(x, y) \text{ if the center co-efficient of the Laplacian mask is positive} \end{cases} \quad \text{... (2.45)}$$

0	1	0
1	-4	1
0	1	1

1	1	1
1	-8	1
1	1	1

0	-1	0
-1	4	-1
0	-1	0

-1	-1	-1
-1	8	-1
-1	-1	-1

Fig. 2.15. *Mask used to implement ine digital laplacian.*

(Remember a the gradient and Laplacian will be discussed under the topic *'edge detection'*. Reader need not be confused. By sharpending, we mean that we are highlighting some fine details of image that are also called edges of an image. So sharpening and edge detection both are same).

Summary

1. Objective of the image enhancement is to process an image so that result is more suitable for human being.
2. Image enhancement is categorized in two categories : spatial domain and frequency domain.
3. Spatial domain is based on direct manipulation of pixels of an image. It is also called aggregate of pixels.
4. Spatial domain enhancement is a subjective analysis.
5. For enhancement purpose, we use different gray level transformation functions such as point, linear, log a power low and piece-wise linear transformation.
6. For image enhancement, image segmentation, image compression, it is better to represent an image by its histogram.
7. In histogram, we draw a plot between different possible values of gray levels and the number of pixels having these values.
8. In histogram equalization, we get an image that has equalized gray levels.
9. By histogram matching, we get an image of our desired histogram.
10. By different arithmetic and logical operations, enhancement of an image may be achieved.
11. Basic purpose of spatial filtering in smoothing and sharpening of an image. Spatial filtering is done with the help of masks.
12. Smoothing is a process that removes the noise and blurr the image. Smoothing is done with the help of mean-filters.
13. Sharpening is process that removes blurring of an image and sharps the edges of an image. Sharpending is done with the help of Robert cross gradient, prewitt and sobel operators that provides the first derivative of an image. For second derivative, we use Laplacian.

Review Questions

1. What do you mean by image enhancement ? What are different methods of image enhancement?
2. What are the basic gray level transformation ?
3. What do you mean by histogram processing ?
4. What do you understand by:
   (*a*) Histogram equalization
   (*b*) Histogram matching
   How do these process enhance the image?
5. Write short notes on
   (*a*) Smoothing spatial filtering
   (*b*) Sharpening spatial filtering.

Test Figure 2.1 *Image with low contrast*

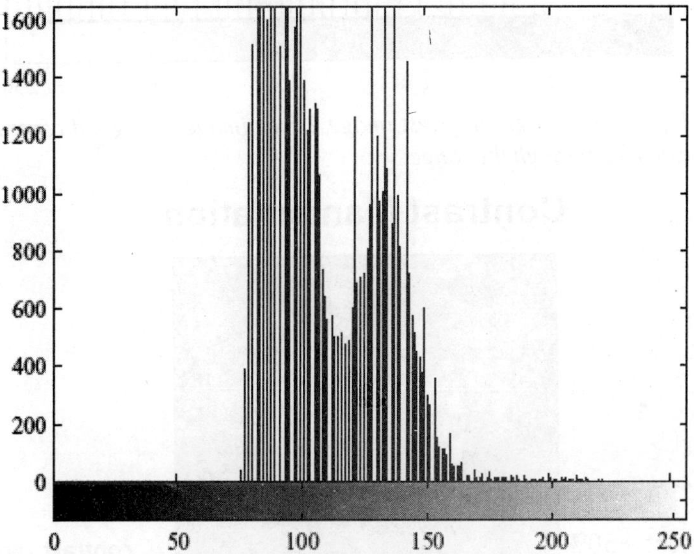

Test Figure 2.2 *Histogram of Image shown in Test figure 2.1*

Test Image 2.3 *Image of test image 2.1 after contrast stretching*

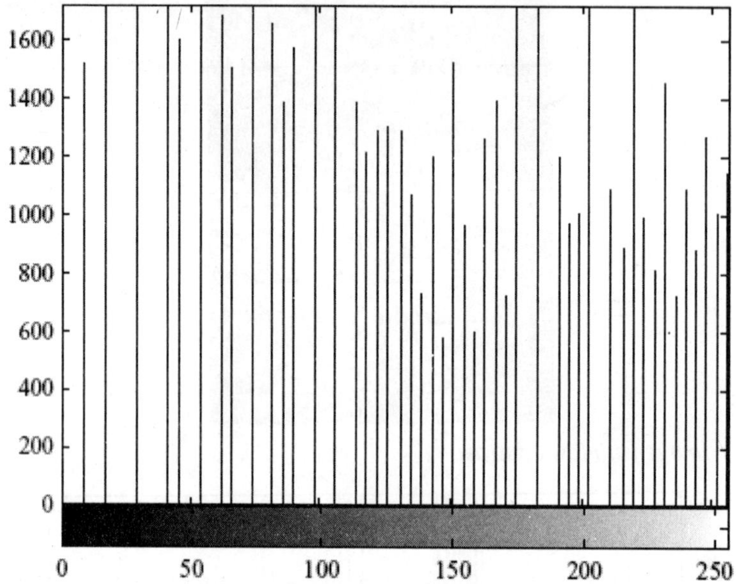

Test Image 2.4 *Equalized histogram of test image 2.3 as image is of good contrast; histogram is extended through the range*

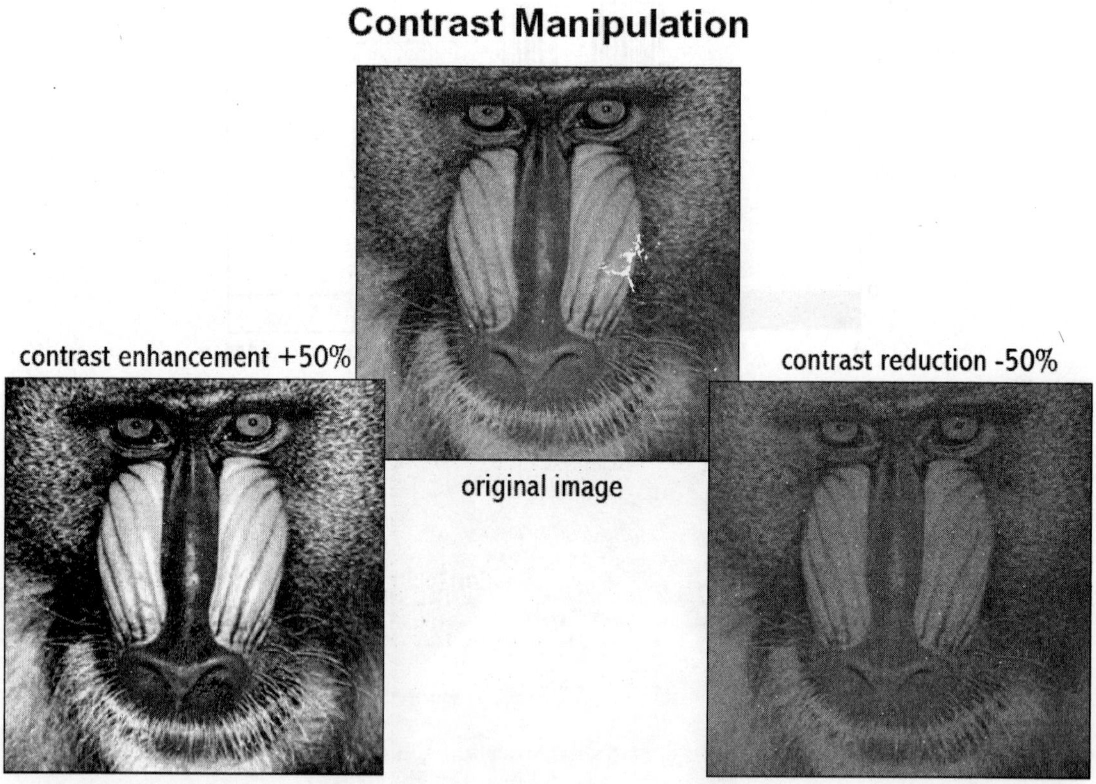

Test Image 2.5 *Effect of varying contrast of an image.*

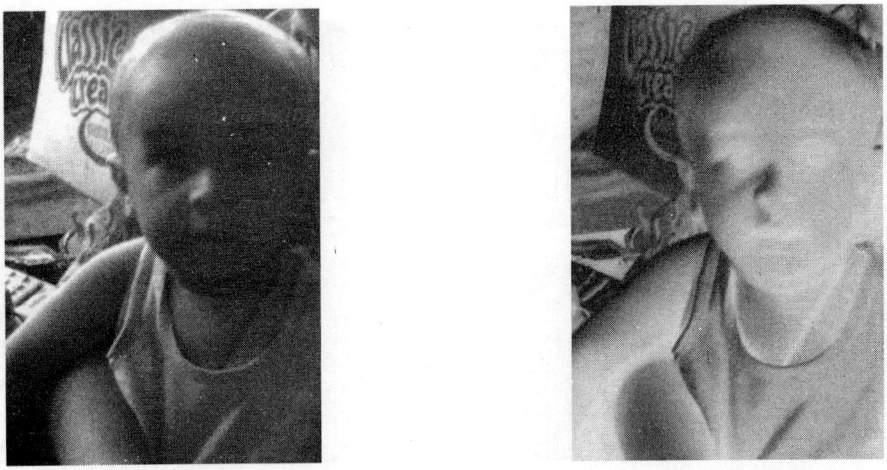

Original Image **After transform**

Test Image 2.6 *Result of negative transformation on an image*

Original Image **After equalization**

Test Image 2.7 *Result of Equalization on a image*

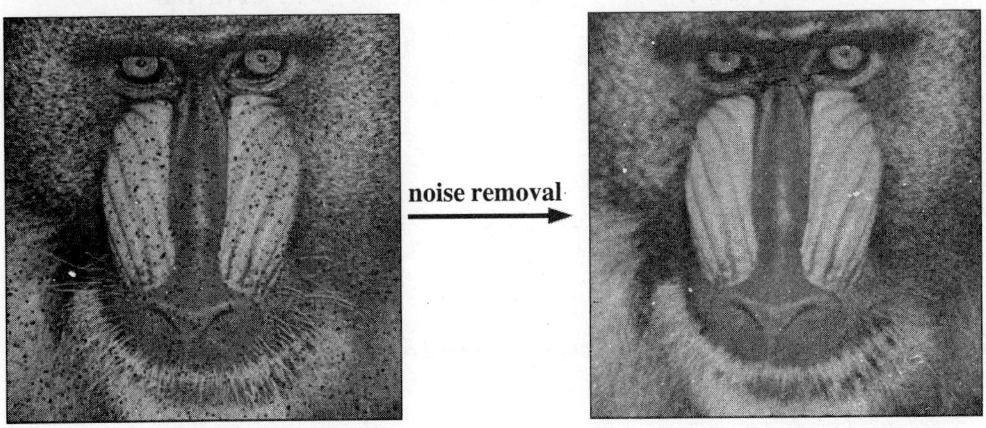

Test Image 2.8 *Effect of Smoothing of an image (it also reduces the noise and sharpness of an image)*

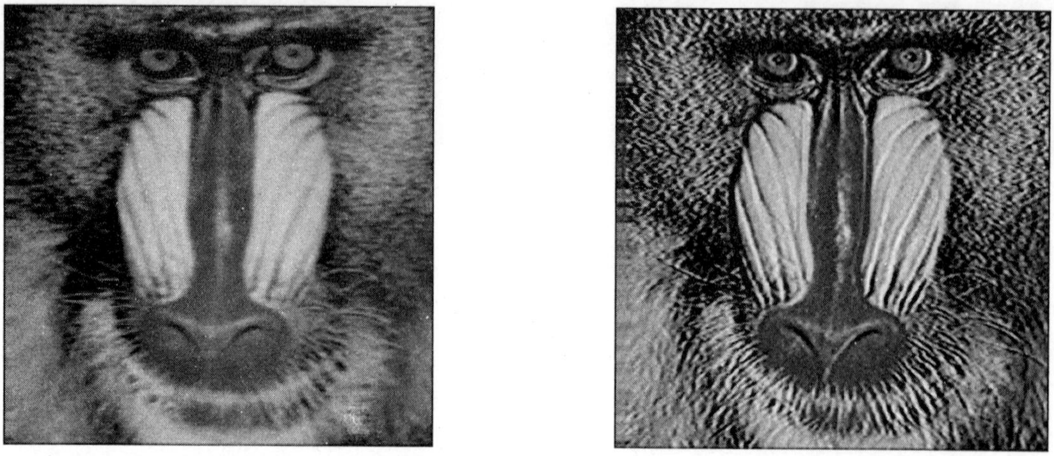

Test Image 2.9 *Effect of Sharpening of an image*

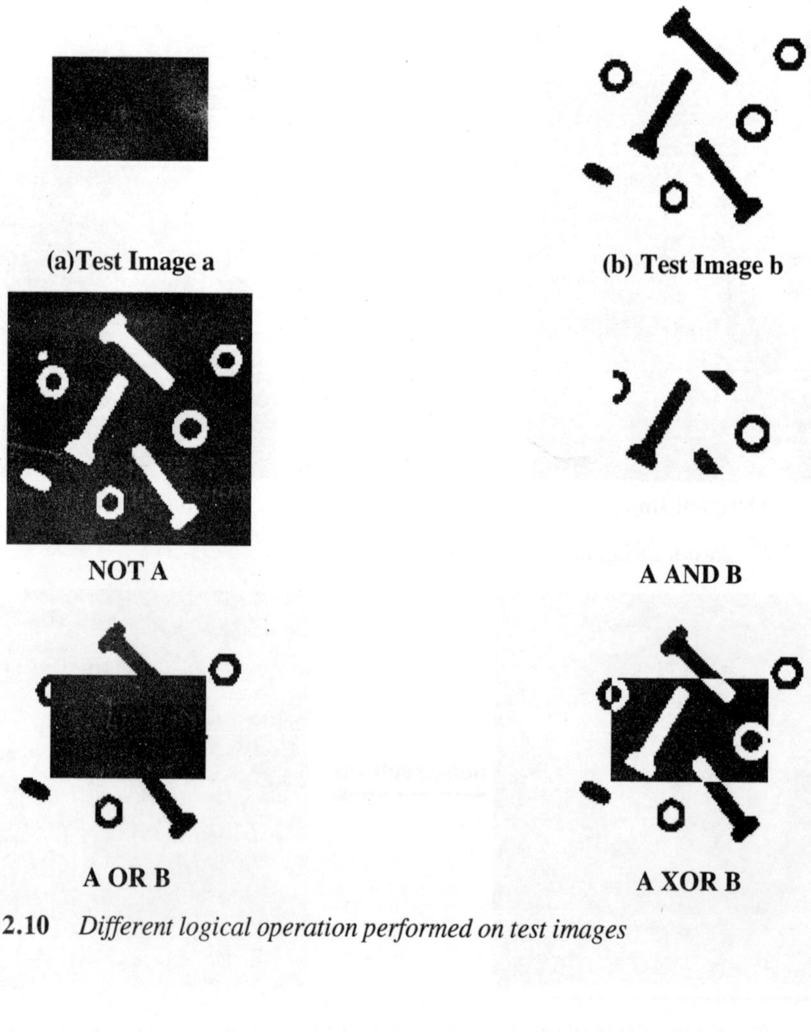

Test Image 2.10 *Different logical operation performed on test images*

3 CHAPTER

IMAGE ENHANCEMENT IN FREQUENCY DOMAIN

One method of image enhancement has been discussed in previous chapter. Now we will discuss another method called frequency domain image enhancement. As discussed previously, *"In this method, Enhancement is applied on the fourier transform of whole image"*.

So before going in detail for image enhancement using frequency domain, we just revise the fourier transform of a function because we will use fourier transform for converting an image from time domain to frequency domain.

3.1 ONE DIMENSIONAL FOURIER TRANSFORM AND ITS INVERSE

The fourier transform of a single variable, continuous function, $f(x)$ is defined by equation

$$F(u) = \int_{-\infty}^{\infty} f(x) . e^{-j2\pi ux} \, dx \qquad \text{... (3.1)}$$

Inverse fourier transform for a given $F(u)$ is given by

$$f(x) = \int_{-\infty}^{\infty} F(u) . e^{j2\pi ux} \, du \qquad \text{... (3.2)}$$

If given function $f(x)$ is a discrete function of one variable $x = 0, 1, \ldots\ldots, M - 1$; then fourier transform is called discrete fourier transform (DFT) and given by

$$F(u) = \frac{1}{M} \sum_{x=0}^{M-1} f(x) . e^{-j2\pi ux/M} \qquad \text{... (3.3)}$$

for $u = 0, 1, 2, \ldots\ldots, M - 1$

Simply the inverse discrete fourier transform is given by

$$f(x) = \sum_{u=0}^{M-1} F(u) . e^{j2\pi ux/M} \qquad \text{... (3.4)}$$

for $x = 0, 1, 2, \ldots\ldots, M - 1.$

3.2 TWO DIMENSIONAL FOURIER TRANSFORM AND ITS INVERSE

If we have two variable u and v ; then fourier transform is given by

$$F(u,v) = \int_{-\infty}^{\infty}\int_{-\infty}^{\infty} f(x,y) \,.\, e^{-j2\pi(ux+vy)} \,.\, dx \,.\, dy \qquad \text{... (3.5)}$$

and similarly its inverse fourier transform is given by

$$f(x,y) = \int_{-\infty}^{\infty}\int_{-\infty}^{\infty} F(u,v) \,.\, e^{-j2\pi(ux+vy)} \,.\, du \,.\, dv \qquad \text{... (3.6)}$$

The discrete fourier transform (DFT) of $f(x,y)$ of size $M \times N$ (two dimensional) is given by equation

$$F(u,v) = \frac{1}{N}\sum_{x=0}^{M-1}\sum_{y=0}^{N-1} f(x,y)\, e^{-j2\pi\left(\frac{ux}{M}+\frac{vx}{N}\right)} \qquad \text{... (3.7)}$$

where $u = 0, 1, 2, \ldots\ldots, (M-1)$

and $v = 0, 1, 2, \ldots\ldots, (N-1)$.

Similarly the inverse fourier transform is given by

$$f(x,y) = \sum_{u=0}^{M-1}\sum_{v=0}^{N-1} F(u,v)\, e^{j2\pi\left(\frac{ux}{M}+\frac{vx}{N}\right)} \qquad \text{... (3.8)}$$

again $x = 0, 1, \ldots\ldots, (M-1)$

and $y = 0, 1, \ldots\ldots, (N-1)$.

3.3 BASICS OF FILTERING IN FREQUENCY DOMAIN

Filtering in frequency domain is easy and straight forward. It consists of the following steps :

1. Multiply the input image by $(-1)^{x+y}$ to center the transform (to take the image at its original place after transformation). It should cleared to the students that by equation :

$$F(u,v) = \frac{1}{MN}\sum_{x=0}^{M-1}\sum_{y=0}^{N-1} f(x,y) \,.\, e^{-j2\pi(ux+vy)} \qquad \text{... (3.9)}$$

   $f(x, y)$ has been multiplied by exponential function that will cause to shift the function by shifting property of fourier transform. (It is called preprocessing on image).

2. Now compute $F(u, v)$, the DFT of image from step '1'.
3. Now for enhancement of image, we multiply any filter (according to our choice and requirement) $H(u, v)$ to the image so.

$$G(u,v) = H(u,v) \,.\, F(u,v) \qquad \text{... (3.10)}$$

   Definitely $G(u, v)$ is called enhanced image.

   Practically we prefer real function $H(u, v)$ that's why it will not provide any phase shift to the image (if any function has imaginary value and it is multiplied to another function, the result will be phase shift in the second function). So it is called zero-phase shift filter.

4. Now calculate the IDFT (Inverse DFT) of image of step (3).

   So filtered image $= F^{-1}[G(u,v)] = g(x,y)$.

5. Now to compensate step (1) again multiply the image by $(-1)^{x+y}$ that is called post processing of image.

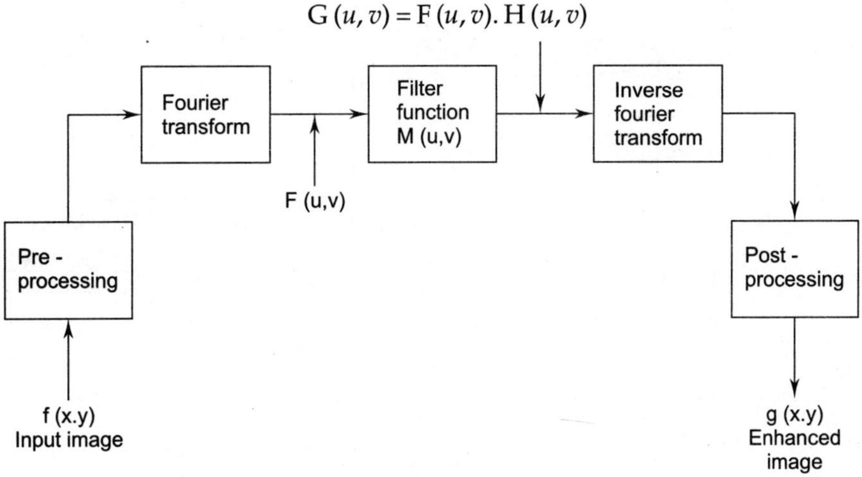

Fig. 3.1 *Basic steps for enhancement—Enhanced Image.*

3.4 BASIC FREQUENCY DOMAIN FILTERS

Now we will study the basic filters used for enhancement. Just like spatial filtering, frequency domain filtering also has two types :

(*a*) Smoothing frequency domain filtering and

(*b*) Sharpening frequency domain filtering.

Now we will study them in detail.

3.4.1 Smoothing Frequency Domain Filtering

As discussed in spatial domain also, smoothing is a process that will blur the sharp edges *'or'* transition of images. In term of frequency domain, smoothing simply reflect the same process. Sharp edges *'or'* transition, after taking fourier transform produces high frequency components. So *"in frequency domain smoothing means suppressing high frequency component from image"*. As we know that low pass-filters are used for removing high frequency components.

(*a*) **Low Pass Filtering :** A 2-D ideal low-pass filter is one whose transfer function satisfies the relation

$$H(u, v) = \begin{cases} 1 & \text{if} \quad D(u, v) \leq D_0 \\ 0 & \text{if} \quad D(u, v) > D_0 \end{cases} \qquad \text{... (3.11)}$$

where D_0 is a specified non-negative quantity, and $D(u, v)$ is the distance from point (u, v) to the origin of the frequency plane ; that is

$$D(u, v) = \left[u^2 + v^2\right]^{\frac{1}{2}} \qquad \text{... (3.12)}$$

Figure 3.2 shows the plot of H (u, v) of an ideal low pass filter.

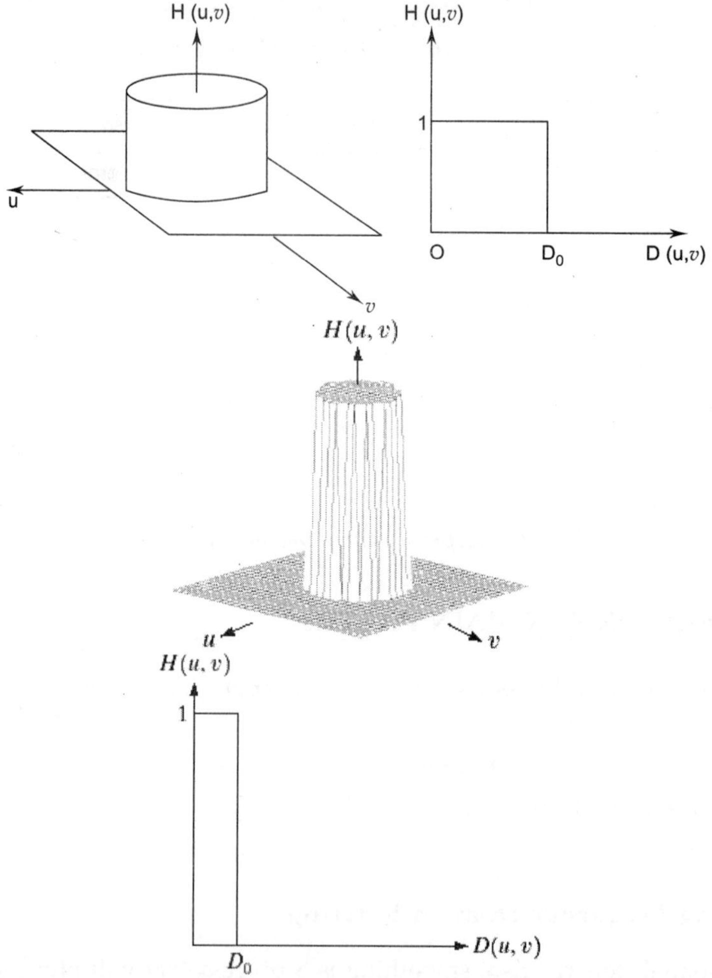

Fig. 3.2 *Ideal low-pass filter.*

Thus, this low-pass filter will pass all frequency components inside D_0 and all frequency components outside the circles are suppressed. D_0 is called the cut-off frequency of filter. Practically this much sharp cut-off is not possible. Due to sharp cut-off frequencies ; ideal low pass filter has ringing problem. The solution of this problem is Butterworth filter.

(*b*) **Butterworth low-pass filter :** The transfer function of the butterworth low-pass filter (BLPF) of order '*n*' and with cut-off frequency locus at a distance D_0 from the origin is defined by the relation

$$\mathrm{H}(u, v) = \frac{1}{1 + \left[\dfrac{\mathrm{D}(u, v)}{\mathrm{D}_0}\right]^{2n}} \quad \text{... (3.13)}$$

Where, $\mathrm{D}(u, v) = \left[u^2 + v^2\right]^{\frac{1}{2}}$ (From equation 3.12)

The plots for BLPF has been shown in Fig. 3.3. BLPF of order '1' has no ringing problem. But higher order BLPF has the ringing problem.

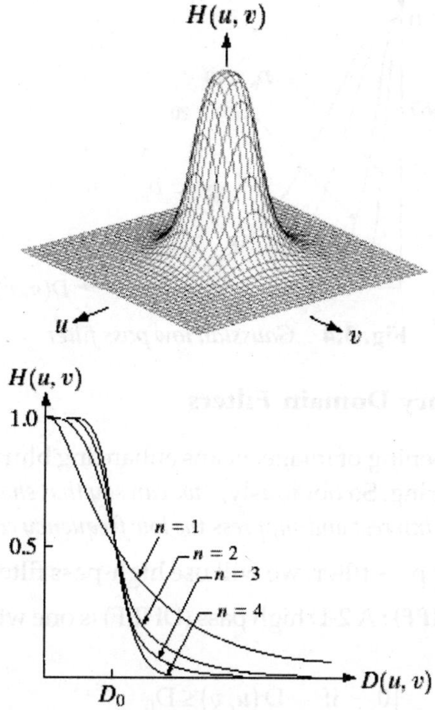

Fig. 3.3 *Butterworth low pass filter.*

(*c*) **Gaussian low-pass filter :** The transfer function of GLPF is given by

$$H(u, v) = e^{-D^2(u,v)/2\sigma^2} \quad \text{... (3.14)}$$

where, $D(u, v) = \left[u^2 + v^2\right]^{\frac{1}{2}}$ (From equation 3.12)

and σ = is the measure of spread of Gaussian curve.

If $\sigma = D_0$, then

$$H(u, v) = e^{-D^2(u,v)/2D_0^2} \quad \text{... (3.15)}$$

The basic property of GLPF is that it will not have ringing problem. The plots for GLPF has been drawn in Fig. 3.4.

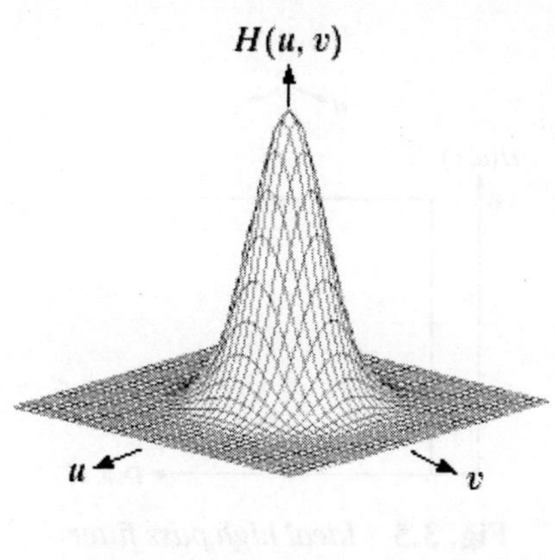

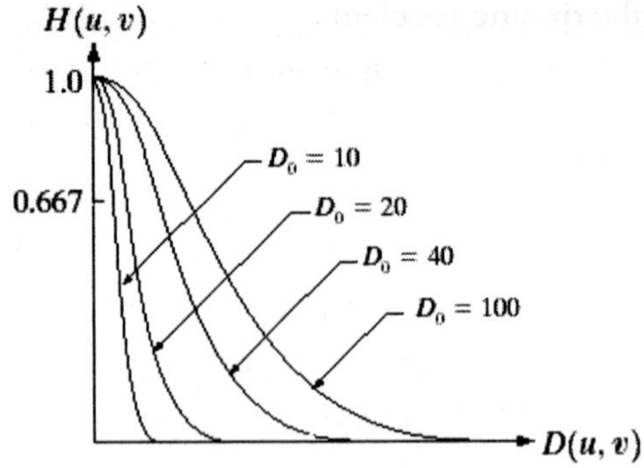

Fig. 3.4 *Gaussian low pass filter*

3.4.2 Sharpening Frequency Domain Filters

As discussed previously, sharpening of image means enhancing blurred information of image. It is opposite to the smoothing filtering. So obviously, *"we can say that sharpening means, we allow to pass high frequency components of our interest and suppress the low frequency components"*.

So now instead of using low pass filter, we will use high-pass filter for sharpening.

(*a*) **Ideal high pass filter (IHPF) :** A 2-D high pass (DHPF) is one whose transfer function satisfies the relation.

$$H(u, v) = \begin{cases} 0 & \text{if} \quad D(u, v) \le D_0 \\ 1 & \text{if} \quad D(u, v) > D_0 \end{cases} \qquad \text{... (3.16)}$$

where $D(u, v) = \left[u^2 + v^2\right]^{\frac{1}{2}}$ (From equation 3.12)

and D_0 = Cutoff distance measured from the origin of the frequency plane.

Thus, IHPF attenuate all the frequency components inside D_0 and allows all the frequency components to be passed outside D_0. As in case of ILPF, IHPF is also practically not realizable. The plots has been drawn in Fig. 3.5.

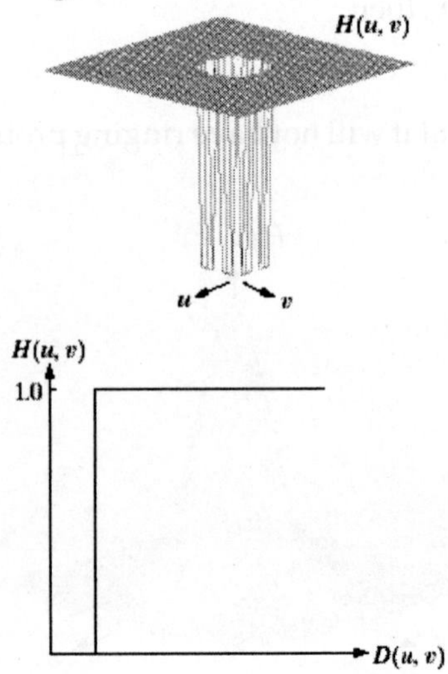

Fig. 3.5 *Ideal high pass filter*

(*b*) **Butterworth high pass-filter (BHPF) :** The transfer function of BHPF of order '*n*' and with cut-off frequency locus D_0 from the origin is defined by the relation.

$$H(u,v) = \frac{1}{\left[1 + \frac{D_0}{D(u,v)}\right]^{2n}} \qquad \text{... (3.17)}$$

The plots have been drawn in Fig. 3.6.

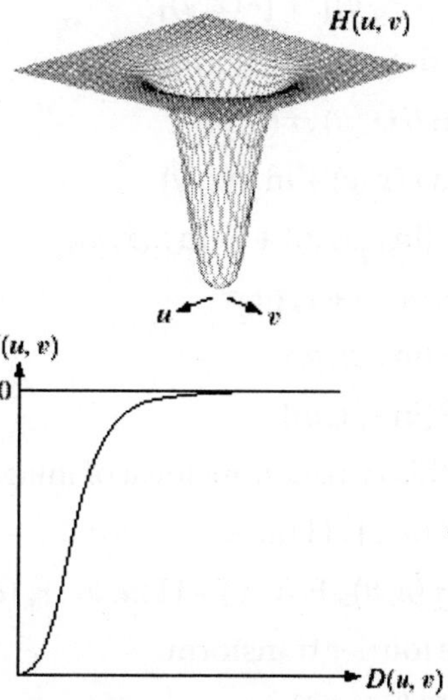

Fig. 3.6 *Butterworth high pass filter*

(*c*) **Gaussian High Pass Filtering :** The transfer function of the GHPF with cut-off frequency locus at a distance D_0 from the origin is given by

$$H(u,v) = 1 - e^{-D^2(u,v)/2D_0^2} \qquad \text{... (3.18)}$$

The plot has been given in figure 3.7.

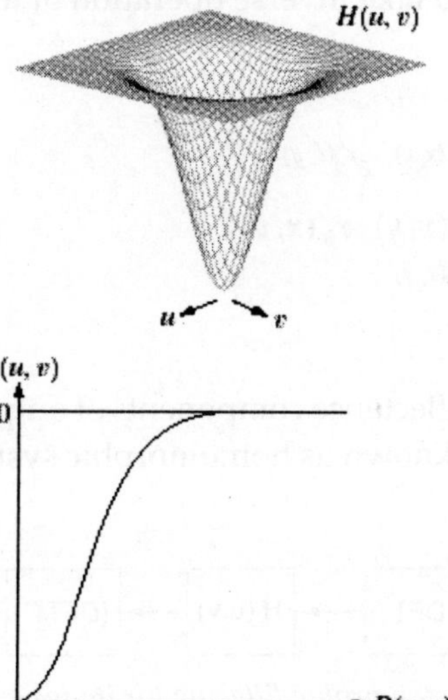

Fig. 3.7 *Gaussian High pass filter*

3.5 HOMOMORPHIC FILTERING

Now we will discuss *"a special method of enhancement in which we deal with illumination and reflectance component specially"*. Let us start with basic definition of image, according to that

$$f(x, y) = i(x, y) \,.\, r(x, y) \quad \text{... (3.19)}$$

Taking fourier transform of this function directly is not possible in other words :

$$\mathrm{F}\{f(x, y)\} \neq \mathrm{F}[i(x, y)] \,.\, \mathrm{F}[r(x, y)] \quad \text{... (3.20)}$$

So a better mathematical way is defining $Z(x, y) = \ln f(x, y)$ ... (3.21)

$$= \ln\{i(x, y) \,.\, r(x, y)\}$$

$$Z(x, y) = \ln i(x, y) + \ln r(x, y) \quad \text{... (3.22)}$$

Now $\mathrm{F}\{Z(x, y)\} = \mathrm{F}\{\ln i(x, y)\} + \mathrm{F}\{\ln r(x, y)\}$

$$Z(u, v) = F_i(u, v) + F_r(u, v) \quad \text{... (3.23)}$$

where $F_i(u, v) = \mathrm{F}\{\ln i(x, y)\}$

and $F_r(u, v) = \mathrm{F}\{\ln r(x, y)\}$

Now second step is to multiply this fourier transform of image by a filter function $H(u, v)$.

So $S(u, v) = Z(u, v) \,.\, H(u, v)$

$$S(u, v) = H(u, v) \,.\, F_i(u, v) + H(u, v) \,.\, F_r(u, v)$$

Now third step is to take inverse fourier transform.

$$S(x, y) = F^{-1}\{S(u, v)\}$$

$$= F^{-1}\{H(u, v)\, F_i(u, v)\} + F^{-1}\{H(u, v) \,.\, F_r(u, v)\}$$

$$S(x, y) = i'(x, y) + r'(x, y) \quad \text{... (3.24)}$$

where $i'(x, y) = F^{-1}\{H(u, v)\, F_i(u, v)\}$

$$r'(x, y) = F^{-1}\{H(u, v)\, F_r(u, v)\}$$

Now final step is that we have to take inverse operation of logarithm applied at beginning. So enhanced image

$$g(x, y) = e^{s(x, y)}$$

$$= e^{i'(x, y)} \,.\, e^{r'(x, y)}$$

$$g(x, y) = i_0(x, y) \,.\, r_0(x, y) \quad \text{... (3.25)}$$

where $i_0(x, y) = e^{i'(x, y)}$

$$r_0(x, y) = e^{r'(x, y)}$$

These are the illumination and reflectance components of output image. This method is based on a special case of a class of systems known as homomorphic system. The all steps has been drawn below in block diagram.

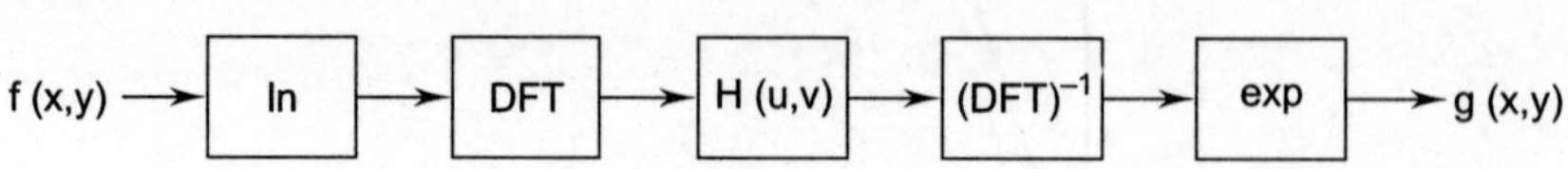

Fig. 3.8 *Homomorphic filtering for image enhancement.*

Summary

1. Second method of image enhancement is frequency domain enhancement. In frequency domain enhancement, we apply enhancement an fourier transform of image.
2. Steps for image enhancement using frequency domain can be defined as pre-processing, fourier transform of that image, apply desired enhancement function on image, now take the inverse fourier transform of resultant. If required apply post-processing on the output of process.
3. Same as spatial domain filtering, frequency domain filtering also is of two types—smoothing filtering and sharpening filtering.
4. As in case of spatial filtering ; in frequency domain also, smoothing filter blurs the image. By blurring here we mean removing high frequency components of an image so smoothing in frequency domain is achieved by low-pass-filters.
5. Here also, by sharpening we again means to enhance the blurred image. In frequency domain, it means allowing high frequency components, so we use high pass filter in frequency domain.
6. Homomorphic filtering is a special method of enhancement in frequency domain. In homomorphic filtering, we deal with illumination and reflectance components of an image.

Review Questions

1. What are the fundamental steps of frequency domain enhancement ?
2. Differentiate between spatial domain enhancement and frequency domain enhancement.
3. What are basic smoothing frequency domain filtering ? Co-relate frequency domain filtering to spatial domain filtering.
4. What do you understand by blurring ? How can it be removed ?
5. What is homomorphic filtering ?

4

CHAPTER

IMAGE RESTORATION

4.1 INTRODUCTION

Image restoration by definition is also to process the image so that it looks better. But the basic difference between image restoration and image enhancement can be listed as given below :

1. Image enhancement is a subjective analysis on the other hand image restoration is an objective process.
2. Image restoration involves modelling of degradation in image and apply some mechanism to get image back. On the other hand, Image enhancement involves the process to manipulate the image in order to take the psychophysical advantage of human being.

For example, contrast stretching is a image enhancement technique but removing of blurring from an image by applying deburring filter is a image restoration process.

4.2 MODEL OF THE IMAGE DEGRADATION / RESTORATION PROCESS

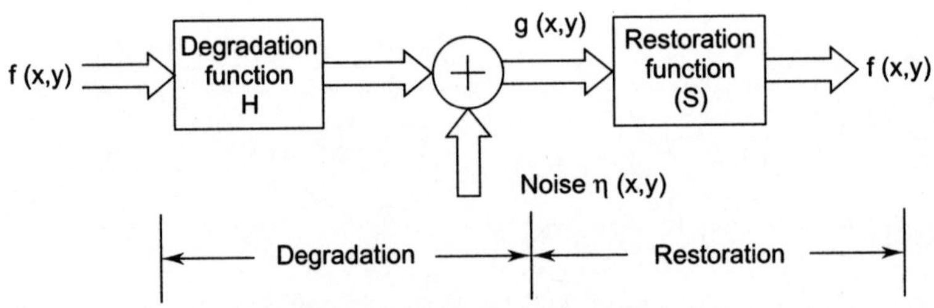

Fig. 4.1 *Degradation Model.*

Here we have input image $f(x, y)$. This image is degraded by a degradation function $H(x, y)$. Now during the channel transmission, we have noise $\eta(x, y)$. Thus, we have

$$g(x, y) = h(x, y) * f(x, y) + \eta(x, y) \quad \text{... (4.1)}$$

If we take frequency domain

$$G(u, v) = H(u, v) F(u, v) + N(u, v) \quad \text{... (4.2)}$$

Thus if we have some knowledge about H (u, v) and noise ($\eta\,(x, y)$ '*or*') N (u, v) then we get an image $\hat{f}\,(x, y)$ that is very close to real image $f\,(x, y)$.

4.3 NOISE MODELS

Different noises and their PDF are given below

(*a*) **Gaussian Noise :** PDF of gaussian (white noise)is given by

$$\text{P}(z) = \frac{1}{\sqrt{2\pi\sigma^2}} e^{-(z-\mu)^2/2\sigma^2} \qquad \text{... (4.3)}$$

Where, z = gray levels

μ = mean value of z

σ = standard deviation

σ^2 = variance of z.

Gaussian Noise is generated due to

- Electronic circuit noise
- Sensor noise due to poor illumination
- Sensor noise due to high temperature.

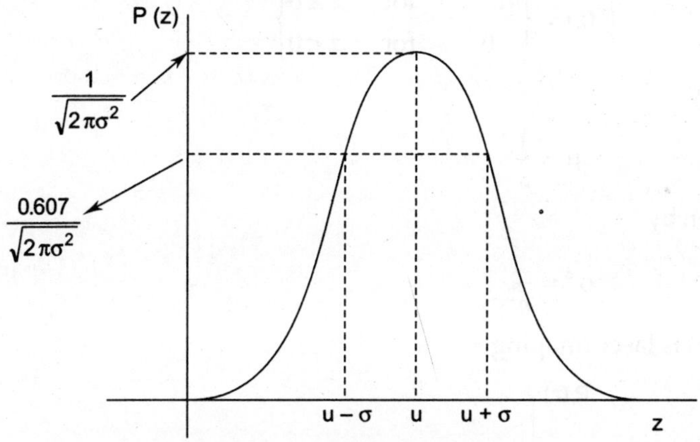

Fig. 4.2 *Gaussian Noise.*

(*b*) **Rayleigh Noise :** The PDF of Rayleigh noise is given by

$$\text{P}(z) = \begin{cases} \frac{2}{b}(z-a)\,e^{-(z-a)^2/b} & \text{for} \quad z \geq a \\ 0 & \text{for} \quad z < a \end{cases} \qquad \text{... (4.4)}$$

Here the value of mean

$$\mu = a + \sqrt{\frac{\pi b}{4}} \qquad \text{... (4.5)}$$

and Variance,

$$\sigma^2 = \frac{b\,(4-\pi)}{a} \qquad \text{... (4.6)}$$

Rayleigh noise is generated due to

- Range imaging

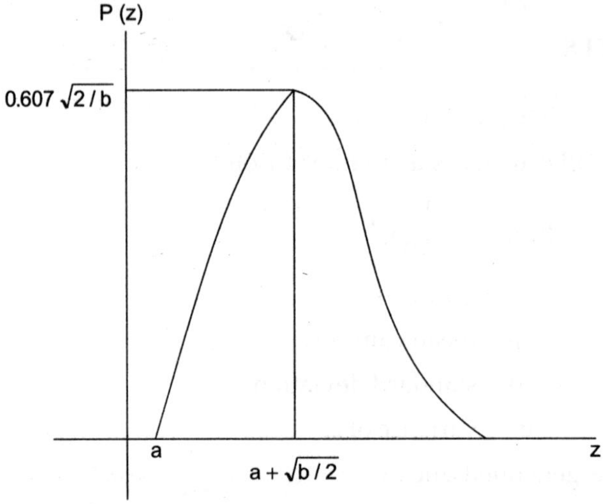

Fig. 4.3 *Rayleigh noise.*

(*c*) **Exponential Noise :** The PDF is given by

$$P(z) = \begin{cases} ae^{-az} & \text{for} \quad z \geq 0 \\ 0 & \text{for} \quad z < 0 \end{cases} \quad \text{... (4.7)}$$

mean given by

$$\mu = \frac{1}{a} \quad \text{... (4.8)}$$

Variance given by

$$\sigma^2 = \frac{1}{a^2} \quad \text{.. (4.9)}$$

Its application is laser imaging.

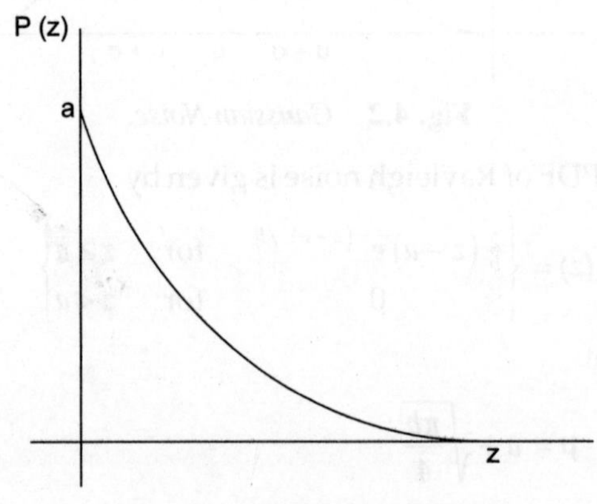

Fig. 4.4 *Exponential Noise.*

(*d*) **Uniform Noise :** The PDF of uniform noise is given by

$$P(z) = \begin{cases} \frac{1}{b-a} & \text{if } a \le z \le b \\ 0 & \text{otherwise} \end{cases} \quad \text{... (4.10)}$$

Mean value is given by

$$\mu = \frac{a+b}{2} \quad \text{... (4.11)}$$

Variance given by $\sigma^2 = \frac{(b-a)^2}{12}$ ... (4.12)

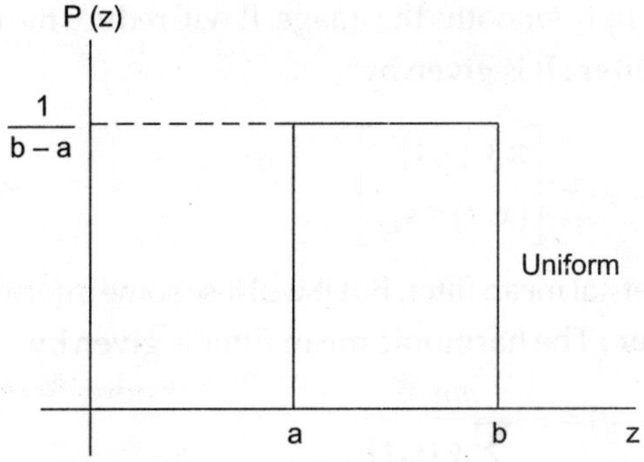

Fig. 4.5 *Uniform noise.*

(*e*) **Impulse (Salt and pepper noise) :** The PDF of impulse noise is given by

$$P(z) = \begin{cases} P_a & \text{for } z = a \\ P_b & \text{for } z = b \\ 0 & \text{otherwise} \end{cases} \quad \text{... (4.13)}$$

4.4 RESTORATION IN PRESENCE OF NOISE

As we know that

$$g(x, y) = H(x, y) * f(x, y) + \eta(x, y) \text{ (by equation 4.1)}$$

If we take degradation factor = unity

$$g(x, y) = f(x, y) + \eta(x, y) \quad \text{... (4.14)}$$

Now we apply spatial filtering that is applicable only when the noise is additive. Now if we want to detect the signal in presence of noise, we have to use filters. Different types of filters are :

1. **Mean Filters :**
   (*a*) Arithmetic mean filter
   (*b*) Geometric mean filter
   (*c*) Harmonic mean filter
   (*d*) Contra harmonic mean filter.
2. **Order-Statistics Filter :**
   (*a*) Median Filter
   (*b*) Max and Min filter
   (*c*) Mid-point filter
   (*d*) Alpha-trimmed mean filter.
3. **Adaptive Filter :**
   (*a*) Adaptive local noise reduction filter.
   (*b*) Adaptive median filter.

Now we will discuss one by one.

4.4.1 Mean Filter

(*a*) **Arithmetic Mean Filter :** The arithmetic mean filtering process computes the average value of the corrupted image $g(x, y)$ in the area defined by window s_{xy}.

$$\hat{f}(x, y) = \frac{1}{mn} \sum_{(s,t) \in s_{xy}} g(s, t) \qquad \text{... (4.15)}$$

Arithmetic filtering simply smooths the image. It will reduce the noise but blurring is increased.

(*b*) **Geometrical Mean Filter :** It is given by

$$\hat{f}(x, y) = \left[\begin{matrix} \pi\, g(s, t) \\ (x, t) \in s_{xy} \end{matrix} \right]^{\frac{1}{mn}} \qquad \text{... (4.16)}$$

It is better than arithmetical mean filter. But it will lose some information of image during filtering.

(*c*) **Harmonic Mean Filter :** The harmonic mean filter is given by

$$\hat{f}(x, y) = \frac{mn}{\sum_{(s,t) \in s_{xy}} g(s, t)} \qquad \text{... (4.17)}$$

It deals with gaussian noise.

(*d*) **Contra Harmonic Filter :**

It is given by $$\hat{f}(x, y) = \frac{\sum_{(s,t) \in s_{xy}} g(s, t)^{Q+1}}{\sum_{(s,t) \in s_{xy}} g(s, t)^{Q}} \qquad \text{... (4.18)}$$

where, Q = order of filter

for Q = positive value = filter for pepper noise.

Q = negative value = filter for salt noise.

4.4.2 Order Statistical Filters

(*a*) **Median Filter :** In this type of filter, the pixel value is replaced by median value of gray levels of neighbourhood pixels.

Here,

$$\hat{f}(x, y) = \underset{(s,t) \in s_{xy}}{\text{median}} \{g(s, t)\} \qquad \text{... (4.19)}$$

It is good for polar and bipolar impulse noise.

(*b*) **Max-Min Filter :** The median filter represents the 50th percentile of a ranked set of Number In case of Max, for 100th percentile of a Ranked set of Number.

$$\hat{f}(x, y) = \max_{(s,t) \in s_{xy}} \{g(s, t)\} \qquad \text{... (4.20)}$$

that is good for pepper noise. It will find the brightest point in image. Again in case of Min, for 0th percentile of a ranked set of Number.

$$\hat{f}(x, y) = \min_{(s,t) \in s_{xy}} \{g(s, t)\} \quad \text{... (4.21)}$$

that is good for salt noise.

It will find the darkest point of image.

(*c*) **Mid-point filter :** This is the average of Max and Min.

$$\hat{f}(x, y) = \frac{1}{2}\left[\max_{(s,t) \in s_{xy}} \{g(s, t)\} + \min_{(s,t) \in s_{xy}} \{g(s, t)\}\right] \quad \text{... (4.22)}$$

This is good for gaussian white noise.

(*d*) **Alpha-trimmed mean filter :** Suppose that if we delete the $\frac{d}{2}$ lowest and $\frac{d}{2}$ highest gray levels values of $g(s, t)$ in the s_{xy}. Then $g_r(s, t)$ remaining image will have $(mn - d)$ pixels and average of these pixels are called alpha-trimmed mean filter.

$$\hat{f}(x, y) = \frac{1}{mn - d} \sum_{(s,t) \in s_{xy}} g_r(s, t) \quad \text{... (4.23)}$$

If $d = 0$, it will act as arithmetic mean filter.

If $d = \dfrac{(mn - 1)}{2}$; it will act as a median filter.

4.4.3 Adaptive Filter

The filters discussed till now process the image without concerning image characteristics from one pixel to another pixel.

Now we design a filter, called adaptive filter whose behavior changes based on statistical characteristics of image inside the filter region s_{xy}.

(*a*) **Adaptive local noise reduction filter :** The simplest method to calculate the noise performance is to calculate the mean and variance.

- By calculation of means, we get the average gray level in that region.
- by calculation of variance, we get average contrast in the region.

Now apply our rectangular window s_{xy} in a region where we have to calculate mean and variance, now take '4' quantities

(*a*) $g(x, y)$, the value of noise image at (x, y)

(*b*) σ_n^2 = the noise variance that causes to convert $f(x, y)$ into $g(x, y)$.

(*c*) σ_L^2 = the local variance of s_{xy}.

(*d*) m_L = local mean of pixels in s_{xy}.

Now we design the filter of the behavior that follows the following characteristics :-

1. If σ_n^2 is zero, the filter should return simply the value of $g(x, y)$. Because at that case,

$$g(x, y) = f(x, y) \text{ at Noise} = 0. \quad \text{... (4.24)}$$

2. If local variance > variance of noise σ_n^2, the filter should return very close to $g(x, y)$.
3. If the two variances are equal, we want to filter to return to the arithmetic mean value of

pixels in s_{xy}. This condition occurs when local area has same properties as whole image. The overall noise will be reduced simply by averaging.

So by following the above properties, we have finally :

$$\hat{f}(x, y) = g(x, y) - \frac{\sigma_n^2}{\sigma_L^2}\left[g(x, y) - m_L\right] \quad \text{... (4.25)}$$

The only condition $\sigma_n^2 > \sigma_L^2$ will make this equation non-linear.

To avoid this condition, allow to this we will get negative pixel values. After that apply gray level shifting (but we will loose the dynamic range of image).

(*b*) **Adaptive Median Filter :**

- Simple median filter can not be good for impulse error. But adaptive median filter works good for impulsive noise.
- During this process also, it will preserve the details of image.
- Here the size of s_{xy} can also be varied according to situation.

Now, consider the following notation :

z_{min} = minimum gray level value in s_{xy}.

z_{max} = maximum gray level value in s_{xy}.

z_{med} = median of gray level in s_{xy}.

z_{xy} = gray level at coordinate (x, y)

s_{max} = maximum allowed size of s_{xy}.

So adaptive median filter algorithm works in two levels, denoted level A and level B, as follows

Level A : $A1 = z_{med} - z_{min}$

$A2 = z_{med} - z_{max}$

If $A1 > 0$ AND $A2 < 0$, Go to level B.

else increase the window size.

If window size $\leq s_{max}$ repeat level A else output z_{xy}.

Level B : $B1 = z_{xy} - z_{min}$

$B2 = z_{xy} - z_{max}$

If $B1 > 0$ AND $B2 < 0$ output z_{xy} else output z_{med}.

Basic purpose of algorithm :

1. Remove the salt and pepper (impulse) noise.
2. To provide smoothing of other noise that may not be impulsive.
3. To reduce distortion such as excessive thinning 'or' thickening of object boundaries.

z_{min} and z_{max} refers to the impulse noise.

Result and Analysis of Algorithm :

(*a*) The purpose of level A is to find whether median value z_{med} is an impulse '*or*' not.

If the condition, $z_{min} < z_{med} < z_{max}$ holds, then z_{med} cannot be impulsive. If this condition is satisfied, the algorithm will go at level B ; to check if the center point of window, z_{xy}, it self an impulse.

(*b*) If the condition

$$B_1 > 0 \text{ and } B_2 < 0 \text{ is true}$$

then $z_{min} < z_{xy} < z_{max}$ holds and again z_{xy} cannot be impulse noise. At this condition, algorithm will provide output = z_{xy}.

But if,

$$B_1 > 0 \text{ and } B_2 < 0 \text{ is false.}$$

Then filter will provide the output z_{med} (as this is not impulse proved in point '*a*') Because at this condition either $z_{min} = z_{xy}$

$$z_{xy} = z_{max}$$

(*c*) Again,

$$z_{min} < z_{med} < z_{max} \text{ does not hold.}$$

So the size of window will be increased and again repeat level A. If the max size of window has been arrived, then window will provide z_{xy}.

Every time one complete step is over and algorithm provides output, the window will be shifted at new location and repeats its process.

4.5 LINEAR-POSITION INVARIANT DEGRADATION : (POINT SPREAD FUNCTION)

(*a*) We know, for a degraded image

$$g(x, y) = H[f(x, y) + \eta(x, y) \quad \text{... (4.26)}$$

let us assume for noise $\eta(x, y) = 0$.

$$g(x, y) = H[f(x, y)] \quad \text{... (4.27)}$$

(*b*) By linear property :

$$H[af_1(x, y) + bf_2(x, y)] = aH[f_1(x, y)] + bH[f_2(x, y)] \quad \text{... (4.28)}$$

(*c*) By position invariant property :

$$H[f(x - \alpha, y - \beta)] = g(x - \alpha, y - \beta). \quad \text{... (4.29)}$$

(*d*) $f(x, y)$ can be expressed in terms of a continuous impulse function.

$$f(x, y) = \int_{-\infty}^{\infty}\int_{-\infty}^{\infty} f(\alpha, \beta) \,.\, \delta(x - \alpha, y - \beta) \,.\, d\alpha \,.\, d\beta \quad \text{... (4.30)}$$

again, $$g(x, y) = H[f(x, y)]$$

$$= H\left[\int_{-\infty}^{\infty}\int_{-\infty}^{\infty} f(\alpha, \beta) \,.\, \delta(x - \alpha, y - \beta) \,.\, d\alpha \,.\, d\beta\right]$$

'or' $$g(x, y) = \int_{-\infty}^{\infty}\int_{-\infty}^{\infty} H\left[f(\alpha, \beta)\, \delta(x - \alpha, y - \beta)\right] d\alpha \,.\, d\beta$$

as F(α, β) is independent of *x* and *y*

(*e*) so $$g(x, y) = \int_{-\infty}^{\infty}\int_{-\infty}^{\infty} f(\alpha, \beta) \,.\, H\left[\delta(x - \alpha, y - \beta)\right] d\alpha \,.\, d\beta \quad \text{... (4.31)}$$

Again, $H[\delta(x - \alpha, y - \beta)] = h(x, \alpha, y, \beta)$ ... (4.32)

is called the impulse response of '*H*'.

In optics, the impulse becomes a point of light and h (x, α, y, β) is commonly referred to as the point spread function (PSF). It is called point spread function as optical fiber system has blurred a point in some degree.

(*f*) So,
$$g(x, y) = \int_{-\infty}^{\infty}\int_{-\infty}^{\infty} f(\alpha, \beta)\, h(x, \alpha, y, \beta)\, d\alpha \,.\, d\beta \qquad \text{... (4.33)}$$

Again by time invarient property

$$g(x, y) = \int_{-\infty}^{\infty}\int_{-\infty}^{\infty} f(\alpha, \beta)\, h(x-\alpha, \beta-y)\, d\alpha \,.\, d\beta \qquad \text{... (4.34)}$$

'or' with noise
$$g(x, y) = \int_{-\infty}^{\infty}\int_{-\infty}^{\infty} f(\alpha, \beta)\,.\, h(x-\alpha, \beta-y)\, d\alpha \,.\, d\beta + \eta(x, y) \qquad \text{... (4.35)}$$

That is again the general equation for degradation of image.

4.6 ESTIMATION OF THE DEGRADATION FUNCTION

There are three ways to estimate the degradation function for use in image restoration.

(*a*) Observation

(*b*) Experimentation and

(*c*) Mathematically.

To estimate the image by use of degradation function is called blind deconvolution because the actual degradation factor can never be calculated correctly.

4.6.1 Estimation by Image Observation

- This is the way where we calculate the degradation function H (x, y) by image itself.
- Take a particular part of image that has very less blurring and also very simple (suppose has a object and background).
- Now we make a sub image with the help of this image that has very less blurring.
- Suppose the

  Sub image $= \hat{f}_s(x, y) = F_s(u, v)$

  the image part $= g_s(x, y) = G_s(u, v)$

  Then we have degradation factor

  $$H_s(u, v) = \frac{G_s(u, v)}{F_s(u, v)} \qquad \text{... (4.36)}$$

  Simple now calculate shape and frequency spectrum of $H_s(u, v)$,.
- We will apply this $H_s(u, v)$ now for whole image assuming that H (u, v) is position invariant (so same for whole image).

4.6.2 Estimation by Experimentation

- If we have similar equipments in lab to those equipments that caused the error / blurring in image, we can produce the same blurred image at laboratory as we have received.

- Now for that system take the input as impulse input and calculate $H_s(u, v)$ so that output $G_s(u, v)$ is same as blurred image we have received.

$$H_s(u, v) = \frac{G_s(u, v)}{A} \quad \text{... (4.37)}$$

As $\quad F_s(u, v) = A$ (constant) for impulse input.

so simply vary the value of A and get desired $H_s(u, v)$.

4.6.3 Estimation by Modeling

Suppose that we assume that image has been blurred by uniform linear motion between the image and the sensor during image acquisition.

(*a*) $f(x, y)$ is a going planner motion $x(t_0)$ and $y(t_0)$ in the 'x' and 'y' direction respectively.

So, $$g(x, y) = f[x - x_0(t), y - y_0(t)] \quad \text{... (4.38)}$$

(*b*) If shutter opening time is 'T', then complete image is given by

$$g(x, y) = \int_0^T f[x - x_0(t), y - y_0(t)] . dt \quad \text{... (4.39)}$$

(*c*) To calculate

$$G(u, v) = \int_{-\infty}^{\infty}\int_{-\infty}^{\infty} g(x, y) . e^{-j2\pi(ux+vy)} . dx . dy \quad \text{... (4.40)}$$

So $$G(u, v) = \int_{-\infty}^{\infty}\int_{-\infty}^{\infty} \left[\int_0^T f[x - x_0(t), y - y_0(t)] . e^{-j2\pi(ux+vy)} . dx . dy . dt\right]$$

Rearranging the equation

$$G(u, v) = \int_0^T \left[\int_0^{\infty}\int_0^{\infty} f[x - x_0(t), y - y_0(t)] e^{-j2\pi(ux+vy)} . dx . dy . dt\right]$$

$$= \int_0^T F(u, v) . e^{-j2\pi[ux_0(t)+vy_0(t)]} . dt$$

$$G(u, v) = F(u, v) \int_0^T e^{-j2\pi[ux_0(t)+vy_0(t)]} . dt \quad \text{... (4.41)}$$

(*d*) So we have

$$H(u, v) = \int_0^T e^{-j2\pi[ux_0(t)+vy_0(t)]} . dt$$

$$G(u, v) = F(u, v) . H(u, v) \quad \text{... (4.42)}$$

Thus, we can calculate the value of H (u, v) for a image.

4.7 PERIODIC NOISE REDUCTION BY FREQUENCY DOMAIN FILTERING

We have already discussed the low pass and high pass filters for image enhancement. Now we will discuss more specialized bandreject and bandpass filters as a tool of periodic noise reduction '*or*' removal.

Bandreject and Bandpass Filters

As the name suggests ; Bandreject filter rejects a particular band about the origin of the fourier transform. An ideal bandreject filter is given by expression :

$$H(u,v) = \begin{cases} 1 & \text{if} \quad D(u,v) < D_0 - \frac{W}{2} \\ 0 & \text{if} \quad D_0 - \frac{W}{2} \le D(u,v) \le D_0 + \frac{W}{2} \\ 1 & \text{if} \quad D(u,v) > D_0 + \frac{W}{2} \end{cases}$$

where $$D(u,v) = \left[u^2 + v^2\right]^{\frac{1}{2}} \qquad \text{... (4.43)}$$

W = Width of Band

D_0 = Radial.

Similarly a butterworth filter of order 'n' is given by

$$H(u,v) = \frac{1}{1 + \left[\dfrac{D(u,v).W}{D^2(u,v) - D_0^2}\right]^{2n}} \qquad \text{... (4.44)}$$

and a gaussian bandreject filter is given by

$$H(u,v) = 1 - e^{-\frac{1}{2}\left[\frac{D^2(u,v) - D_0^2}{D(u,v).W}\right]^2} \qquad \text{... (4.45)}$$

In Figure 4.6, all three plots has been drawn.

As we know that,

Bandpass filter = 1 − bandreject filter.

Thus all bandpass filters can be realized.

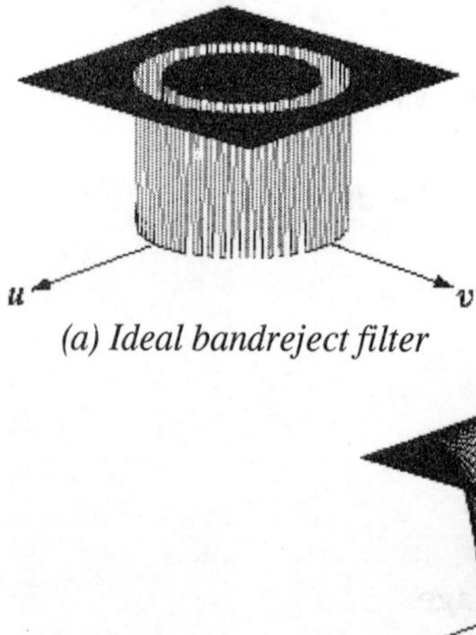

(a) *Ideal bandreject filter*

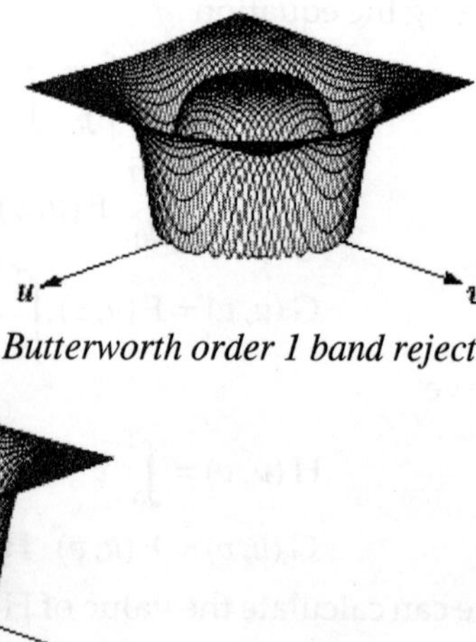

(b) *Butterworth order 1 band reject filter*

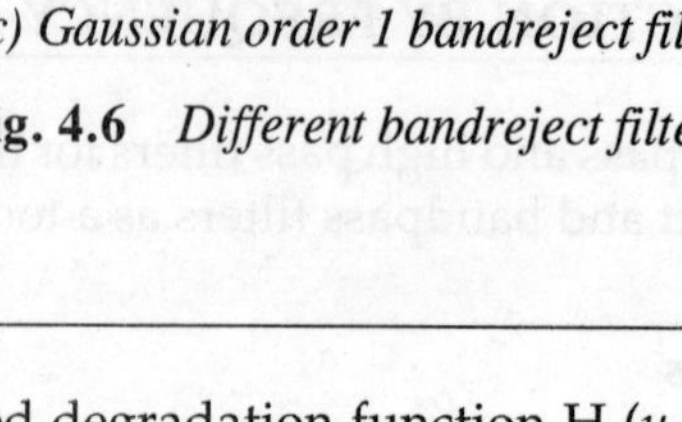

(c) *Gaussian order 1 bandreject filter*

Fig. 4.6 *Different bandreject filters.*

4.8 INVERSE FILTERING

- Till now we have calculated degradation function H (u, v) by any one of the methods explained previously.

- By applying that H (u, v), we should get $\hat{F}$ (u, v) as image that is recovered and very close to F (u, v) (real image) by formula.

$$\hat{F}(u,v) = \frac{G(u,v)}{H(u,v)} \qquad \text{... (4.46)}$$

But $\quad G(u,v) = H(u,v)\,F(u,v) + N(u,v)$

So

$$\hat{F}(u,v) = F(u,v) + \frac{N(u,v)}{H(u,v)} \qquad \text{... (4.47)}$$

So it should be cleared that even if we have calculated H (u, v), we can not calculate $\hat{F}$ (u, v) as N (u, v) is random and is not known. If H (u, v) = 0 equation is of no use.

Equation 4.46 shows inverse filtering, but as we have seen equation 4.47 direct inverse filtering is not possible.

Thus now, we have to calculate

- H (u, v) by any one method discussed previously.
- We have to calculate the statistical characteristics of Noise N (u, v).

So many methods are possible one of them is minimum mean square error (wiener) filtering.

4.9 MINIMUM MEAN SQUARE ERROR FILTERING (WIENER FILTERING)

- Our main objective is to find an estimated $\hat{f}$ of the uncorrupted image f such that the mean square value of error between them is minimized. This error measurement is given by

$$e^2 = E\left\{\left(f - \hat{f}\right)^2\right\} \qquad \text{... (4.48)}$$

- If we assume that
  - → Noise and image are uncorrelated
  - → One 'or' the other has zero mean.
  - → Gray levels in the estimate are a linear function of degraded image. Then, we get

$$\hat{f}(u,v) = \left[\frac{H^*(u,v)\,.\,S_f(u,v)}{S_f(u,v)\,|H(u,v)|^2 + S_\eta(u,v)}\right] G(u,v) \qquad \text{... (4.49)}$$

where $\quad H^*(u,v)$ = complex-conjugate of $H(u,v)$

$$= \left[\frac{H^*(u,v)}{|H(u,v)|^2 + \dfrac{S_\eta(u,v)}{S_f(u,v)}}\right] G(u,v)$$

$$\hat{F}(u,v) = \left[\frac{1}{H(u,v)} \frac{|H(u,v)|^2}{\left\{ |H(u,v)|^2 + \dfrac{S_n(u,v)}{S_f(u,v)} \right\}} \right] G(u,v) \qquad \text{... (4.50)}$$

Equation 4.50 shows the wiener filter.

Now even if $H(u,v) = 0$; equation is valid.

Now as $S_n(u,v)$ and $S_f(u,v) =$ constant.

So,

$$\frac{S_n(u,v)}{S_f(u,v)} = k \qquad \text{... (4.51)}$$

So equation 4.50 becomes.

$$\hat{F}(u,v) = \left[\frac{1}{H(u,v)} \frac{|H(u,v)|^2}{|H(u,v)|^2 + k} \right] G(u,v) \qquad \text{... (4.52)}$$

So by adjusting '*k*' we can desired image $\hat{F}(u,v)$.

Summary

1. Basic purpose of image restoration is also to improve the quality of image as in image enhancement.
2. But the image restoration is an objective analysis where we draw the mathematical model of image degradation different types of noise and then try to remove that. In image enhancement, we simply apply hit and trial method for improving look of an image.
3. For degradation of an image, there may be different types of Noise such as Gaussian Noise, uniform noise, exponential noise, salt and pepper noise etc.
4. For removal of noise, we can apply mean filtering, order-statistics filter and adaptive filter.
5. For restoration purpose, we have to calculate degradation factor by observation, experimentation and mathematical analysis.

Review Questions

1. Draw the image degradation model.
2. Differentiate between image restoration and image enhancement.
3. What are the different noise model ? How will you remove the noise in an image ?
4. What is point spread function ?
5. How does periodic noise is removed using frequency domain filtering?
6. What do you understand by inverse filtering ? What is the disadvantage of this filter and how can it be removed ?

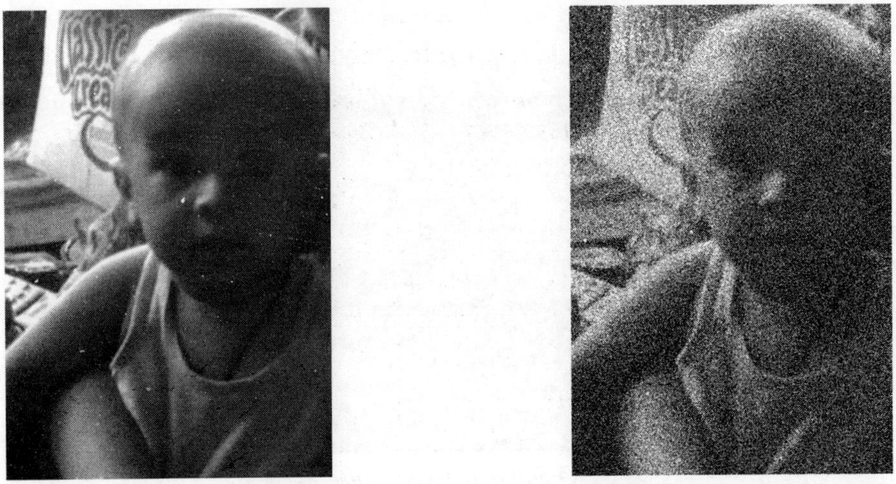

Test Image 4.1 *Uniform noise (43.02 %) added to original image.*

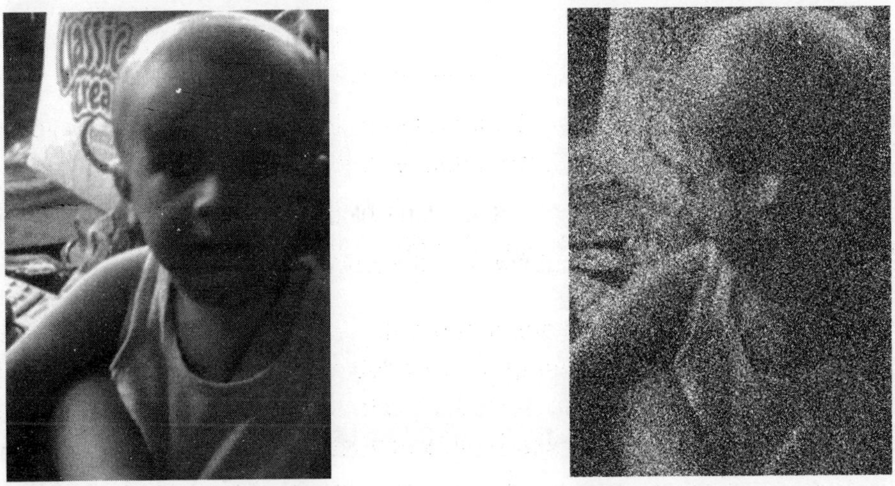

Test Image 4.2 *Gaussian noise (43.02 %) added to original image.*

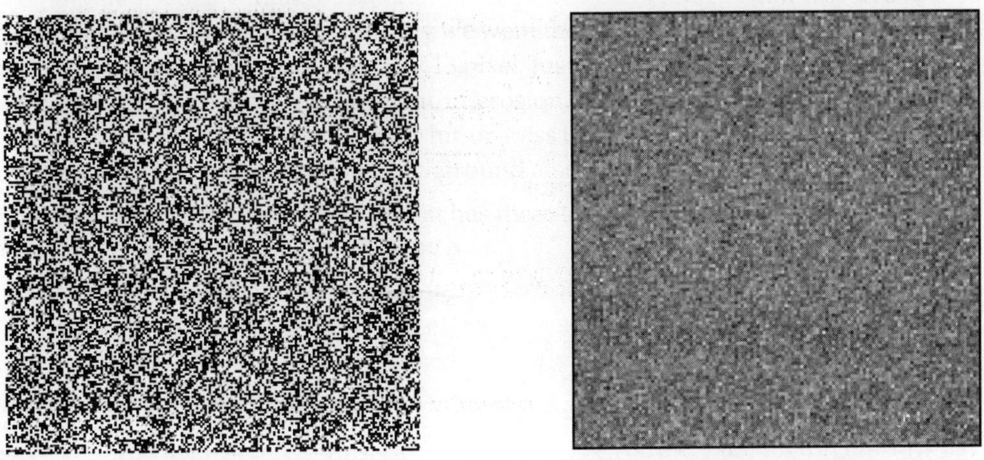

(a) Uniform noise *(b) Gaussian noise*

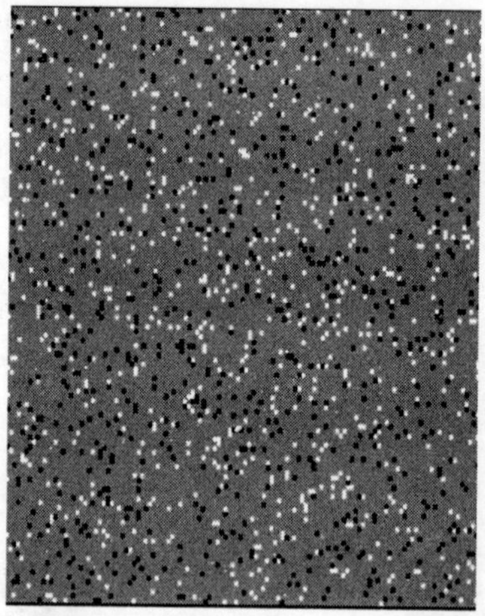

(c) Salt and peeper noise

Test Image 4.3 *Different noise models.*

5

CHAPTER

COLOR IMAGE PROCESSING

5.1 INTRODUCTION

Till now we have discussed the gray level images where a pixel value at any image point can be represented by a single-valued function with a range of 0 to 255 in a 8-bit system. Image may be multivalued also by making more than measurement at a point. These types of images can be grouped into two major types:

1. **Multi-spectral :** As the name suggests, measurement corresponds to different spectral bands of frequencies (*'or'* wavelength) of electromagnetic wave. For example, color imaging.
2. **Multi Model :** The measurement of different physical properties of any single object *'or'* its parts are concept of multi-model imaging. Different sensors are employed to extract multi-model characteristics. For example, X-ray, CT-Scan, MRI, etc.

Now here we will study multi-spectral-color imaging in detail.

5.2 ADVANTAGES OF COLOR IMAGE PROCESSING

(*i*) By color image processing we can identify object easily.

(*ii*) Human can discern thousands of colors shades and intensities, compared to only two dozen shades of gray.

5.3 CATEGORIES OF COLOR IMAGE PROCESSING

(*a*) **Full color processing :** In this method, we acquire color image directly by TV Cameras, *'or'* color scanner.

(*b*) **Pseudo-color processing :** In this category, we assign a color to a particular monochrome intensity *'or'* range of intensities.

5.4 COLOR FUNDAMENTALS

Three basic quantities are used to describe the quality of a chromatic light source:

(*a*) **Radiance :** Radiance is the total amount of energy that flows from light source. It is measured in watts.

(*b*) **Luminance :** Luminance gives the measure of energy that a observer perceives from the source. It is measured in lumens.

(*c*) **Brightness :** It is a subjective descriptor that is practically impossible to measure.

5.5 PRIMARY COLORS

Experimentally it has been seen that 6-7 million cones in human eyes can be divided into three basic sensing categories, corresoponding roughly to red, green and blue.

65% cons — sensitive for red.
33% cons — sensitive for green and
2% cons — sensitive for blue.

Due to this sensitivity of human eyes with respect to colors. Red, green and blue are the primary colors.

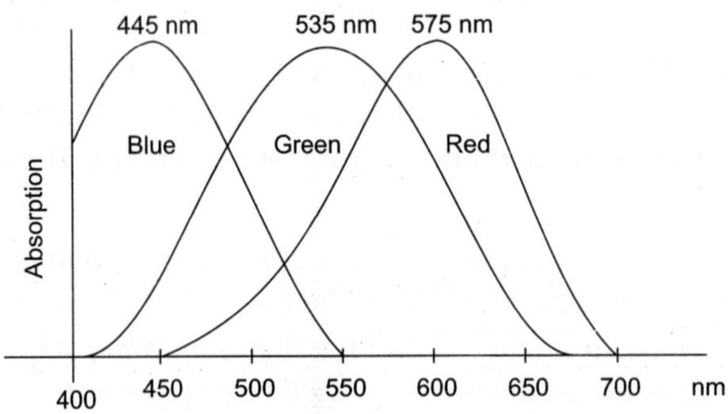

Fig. 5.1 *Primary color spectrum.*

5.6 SECONDARY COLOR

Primary colors can be added to get secondary colors of light.

Magenta — Red + Blue
Cyan — Green + Blue
Yellow — Red + Green

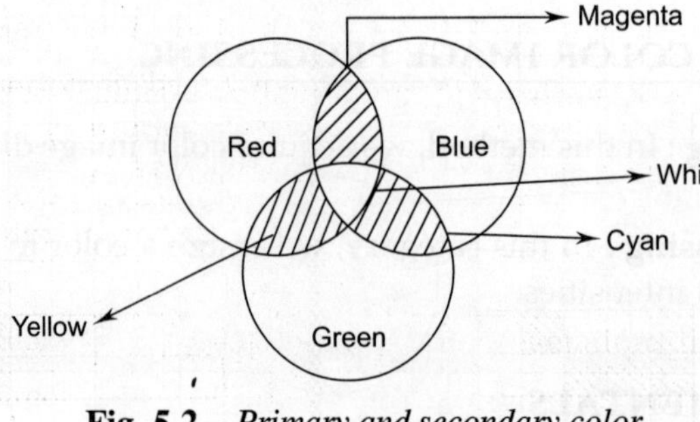

Fig. 5.2 *Primary and secondary color.*

5.7 PRIMARY AND SECONDARY COLORS FOR PIGMENTS

Just opposite to the simple technique.

→ Primary color — Magenta, cyan, yellow

→ Secondary color — Red, blue and green.

5.8 CHARACTERISTICS THAT ARE USED FOR DIFFERENTIATING DIFFERENT COLORS

(*a*) **Brightness :** It is notation for intensity. It cannot be practically measured.

(*b*) **Hue :** Dominant wavelength in a mixture of light waves.

(*c*) **Saturation :** It gives the measurement of degree to which pure light is diluted by white light.

$$\text{Saturation} \propto \frac{1}{\text{White light added}}$$

Pure color has high saturation and pink color means mixed color has less saturation.

Hue + saturation = called chromaticity.

5.9 COLOR MODELS

The purpose of color model is to facilitate the specification of colors in some standard, generally accepted way.

Thus in color model, we use coordinate system so that each color can be represented by a point.

These are different types of color models we can choose any one according to our requirement.

(*a*) **RGB Model :** Used for color model and broad class of color models corners.

(*b*) **CMY *'or'* CMYK Model :** Used for color printing.

(*c*) **HSI Model :** Used for human description and interpretation of colors. It decouples the colors and gray scales in an image.

5.9.1 The RGB-Color Model

In this model, we use cartesian coordinate system for presentation of color.

(*a*) RGB are at three points at corners and at basic scale.

(*b*) Magenta, yellow and cyan are at three remaining points at corner.

(*c*) Black is situated at origin and White is situated at the farest point. The line joining black and white shows gray scale.

(*d*) All other colors are inside the cube in the form of points and are defined by vectors extending from origin.

(*e*) **Pixel depth :** Number of pixels used to represent a pixel is called pixel depth.

In general application, we require 8 bits for presenting a color.

Thus, for RGB, we needs = 8 × 3 = 24 Bits

So total number of colors = 2^{24}

= 16, 777, 216.

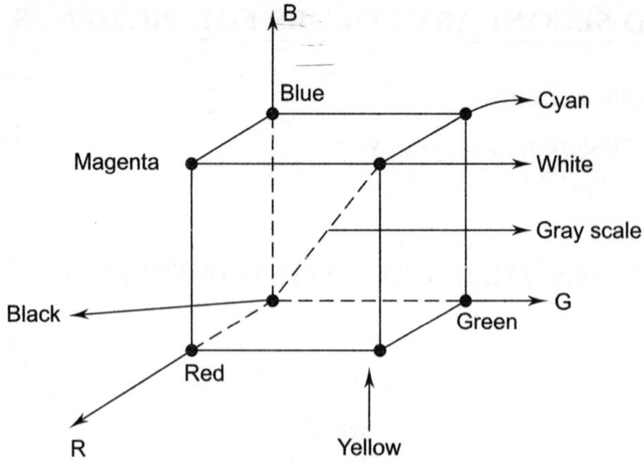

Fig. 5.3 *The RGB model in co-ordinate system.*

(*f*) But this large number of colors are practically not usable that why we use only 256 colors. *"The set of colors that can be used in stead of whole colors is called subset of colors.* ***That is also called safe RGB colors".***

5.9.2 The CMY and CMYK Color Model

Alternatively colors can be represented by secondary colors (*'or'* primary colors of pigment).

By RGB, we can get CMY by

$$\text{CMY} = \begin{bmatrix} 1 \\ 1 \\ 1 \end{bmatrix} - \begin{bmatrix} R \\ G \\ B \end{bmatrix}$$

This is generally used for color printing. But the output color black is muddy black that's why we add black in this model, so called CMYK color model.

5.9.3 HSI Color Model

"HSI model decouples the color and gray levels. It is the model that will provide information about image that is easily described and interpreted".

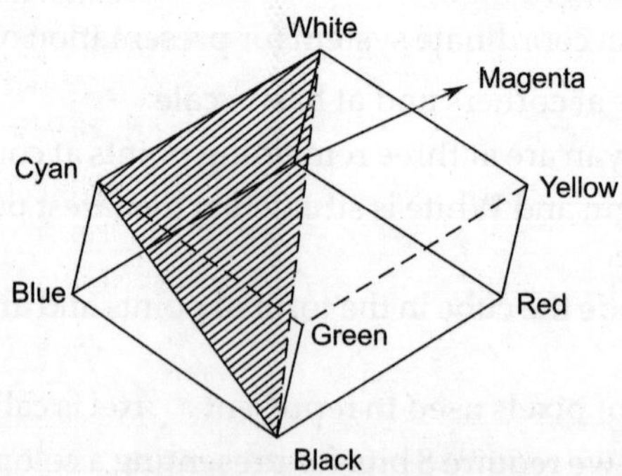

Fig. 5.4 *HSI color model.*

Here we can see a cube that has a axis connecting black and white points called intensity axis. If we want to calculate the intensity of any color ; we will draw the plane perpendicular to intensity axis and containing that color point.

→ In this plane, the saturation will increase, if the distance from the intensity axis has been increased.

→ This plane will contain same hue at every point. To get different hue, we have to rotate the plane at verticle axis.

Now to calculate the hue at any point, just see the different representation of color model as given below :

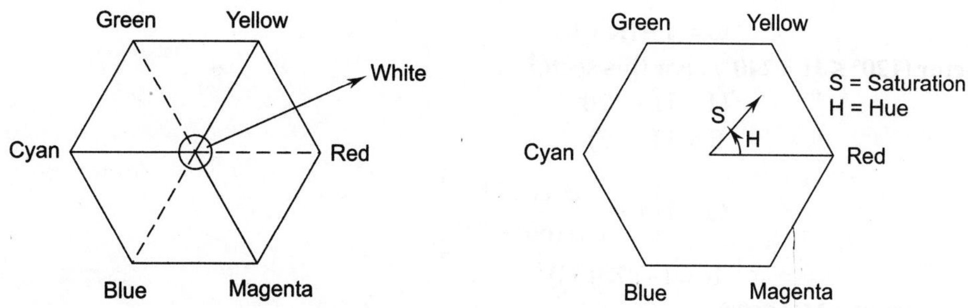

Fig. 5.5 *Hue color model and calculation of H and S.*

By this figure, it should be clear that angle between primary colors is 120° and also the angle between secondary colors is 120°. Now we have taken red color as reference and hue increases counter clock wise from there.

Saturation is calculated by the distance from reference point.

5.10 CONVERSIONS BETWEEN COLOR MODELS

5.10.1 Converting Colors from RGB to HSI

Given an image in RGB color formate, the H components of each RGB pixel is obtained by equations:

$$H = \begin{cases} \theta & \text{if} \quad B \le G \\ 360° - \theta & \text{if} \quad B > G \end{cases} \qquad \text{... (5.1)}$$

With

$$\theta = \cos^{-1}\left\{ \frac{\frac{1}{2}[(R-G)+(R-B)]}{\left[(R-G)^2+(R-B)(G-B)\right]^{\frac{1}{2}}} \right\} \qquad \text{... (5.2)}$$

The saturation component is given by

$$S = 1 - \frac{3}{(R+G+B)}[\min(R, G, B)] \qquad \text{... (5.3)}$$

Finally, the intensity component is given by

$$I = \frac{1}{3}(R+G+B) \qquad \text{... (5.4)}$$

It is assumed that RGB values have been normalized to range [0, 1] and angle θ has been measured w.r.t. red axis of HSI space.

5.10.2 Converting colors from HSI to RGB

RG sector ($0° \leq H \leq 120°$) : When H is in this sector, the RGB components are given by equation

$$B = I(1 - S)$$

$$R = I\left[1 + \frac{S \cos H}{\cos(60° - H)}\right] \quad \text{... (5.5)}$$

$$G = 1 - (R + B).$$

GB Sector ($120° \leq H < 240°$) : For this sector,

$$H = H - 120°$$

Now,

$$R = I(1 - S)$$

$$G = I\left[1 + \frac{S . \cos H}{\cos(60° - H)}\right] \quad \text{... (5.6)}$$

$$B = 1 - (R + G)$$

BR Sector ($240° \leq H \leq 360°$) :

$$H = H - 240°$$

Now,

$$G = I(1 - S)$$

$$B = I\left[1 + \frac{S . \cos H}{\cos(60° - H)}\right] \quad \text{... (5.7)}$$

$$R = 1 - (G + B)$$

5.11 PSEUDO COLOR IMAGE PROCESSING

"In this process, we simply assign a color to a gray level that's why called false coloring 'or' Pseudo-color image processing".

5.11.1 Intensity Slicing

One of the most popular technique is intensity slicing and then color coding.

Now take image a 3-D function. Now place a parallel plain to the coordinate plane of image.

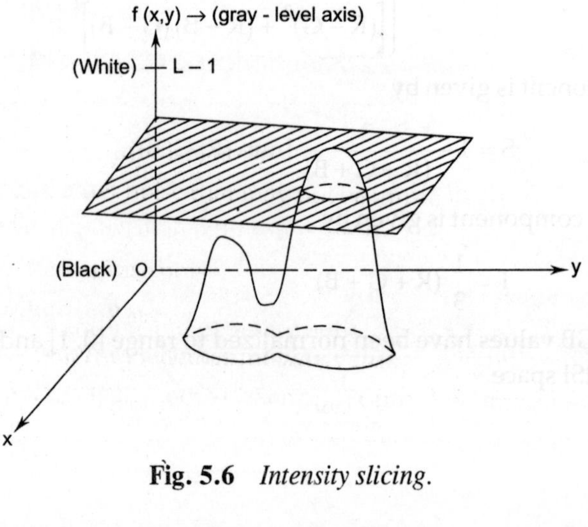

Fig. 5.6 *Intensity slicing.*

Now we may assign two different colors ; if the gray levels are above then plane, we will assign one color. If gray level below then plane, we will assign second color . The gray level at the plane itself, that can be assigned arbitrary any color out of these two colors.

If we want to take more than one color, we can move parallel plane up and down parallely.

We can represent the slicing technique by the following figure :

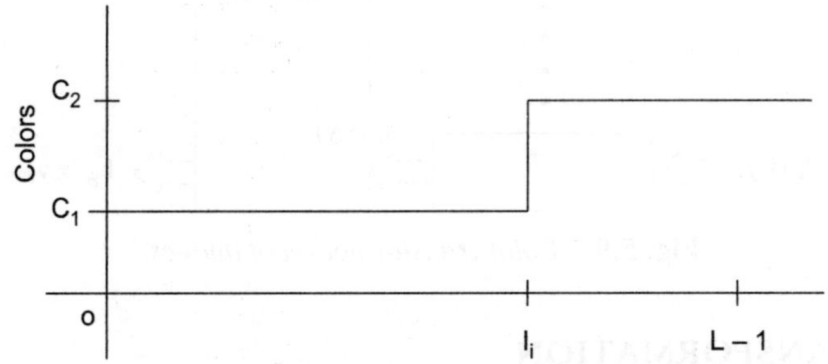

Fig. 5.7 *Representation of intensity slicing.*

5.11.2 Grey Level to Color Transformation

One possible and easy method of color transformation is that gray levels of an image are fed separately to red, green and blue transformations and then fed these three colors to different channels of color television monitor. Now by these channels of color television, we used to generate composite image.

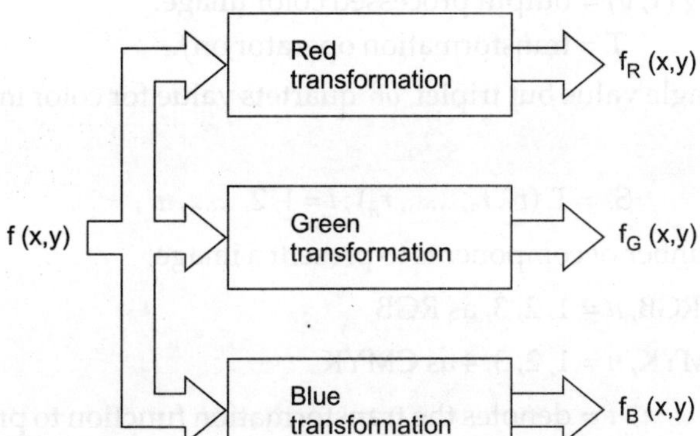

Fig. 5.8 *Color transformation of an image.*

"Note that this transformation is a function of gray levels only, not the positions of gray levels".

Color slicing is a special case of this transformation but this technique provides smooth, non-linear flexible functions of transformation.

The technique discussed just till now is applied to single image, but some time it is required to transform a number of images in a single composite signal. Then we follow the following transformation :

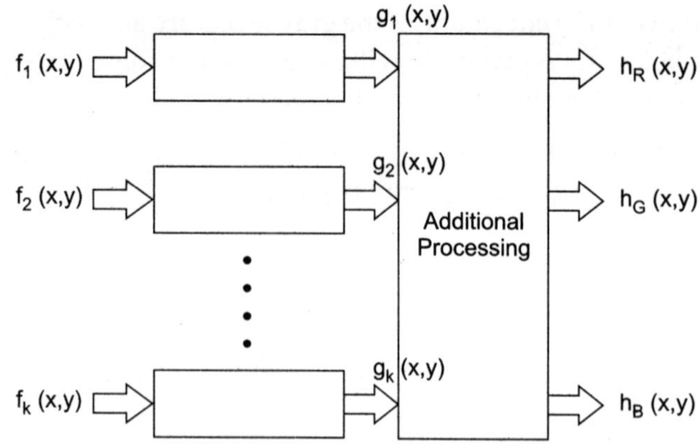

Fig. 5.9 *Color transformation of images.*

5.12 COLOR TRANSFORMATION

"In this transformation, we will discuss the process of all the components of color image within single color model". (till now we have discussed in the form of RGB, HSI and CMYK).

5.12.1 Formulation

We know for transformation of an image

$$g(x, y) = T[f(x, y)] \quad \text{... (5.8)}$$

Now $f(x, y)$ = color image

and $g(x, y)$ = output processed color image.

and T = transformation operator on f.

Now $f(x, y)$ is not a single value but triplet *'or'* quartets value for color image.

We again know that

$$S_i = T_i(r_1, r_2, ..., r_n) \,;\, i = 1, 2, ..., n \quad \text{... (5.9)}$$

Here n denotes the number of components to present a image.

For RGB, n = 1, 2, 3, as RGB

for CMYK, n = 1, 2, 3, 4 as CMYK ... (5.10)

i = denotes the transformation function to produce a S_i.

In general if we want to

(*a*) modify the intensity of image

$$g(x, y) = kf(x, y) \qquad 0 < k < 1 \quad \text{... (5.11)}$$

(*b*) By HSI color model, this modification can be done by

$$s_3 = kr_3 \quad \text{... (5.12)}$$

and $s_2 = r_2$ and $s_1 = r_1$ only r_3.

Component will be modified.

(*c*) In RGB color model, this modification can be done by

$$s_i = kr_i, i = 1, 2, 3. \quad \text{... (5.13)}$$

All these components can be modified.

(*d*) In CMY, this modification can be done by

$$s_i = kr_i + (1 - k) \qquad i = 1, 2, 3, \ldots \qquad \ldots (5.14)$$

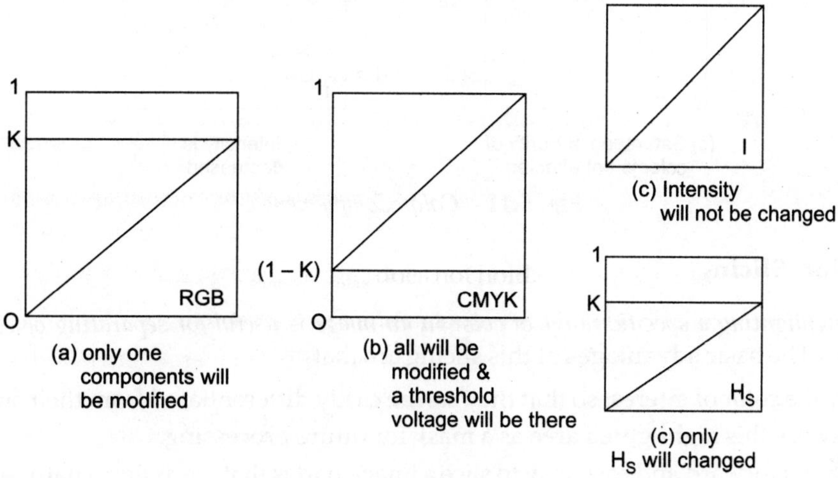

Fig. 5.10 *Color transformation*

5.12.2 Color Complement

"The hues directly opposite one another on the color circle are called complements to each other". This transformation is used for image enhancement in color image processing.

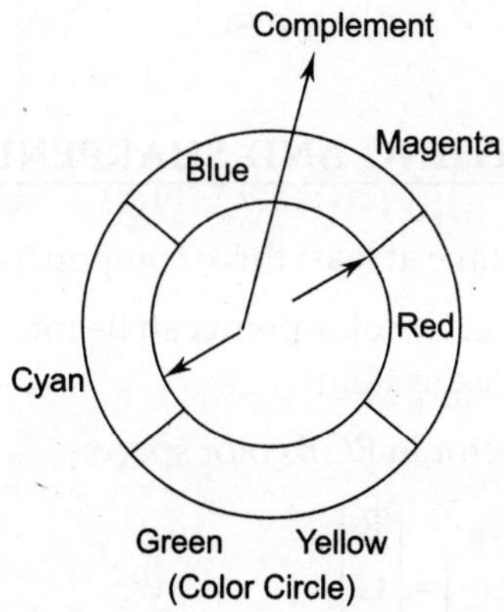

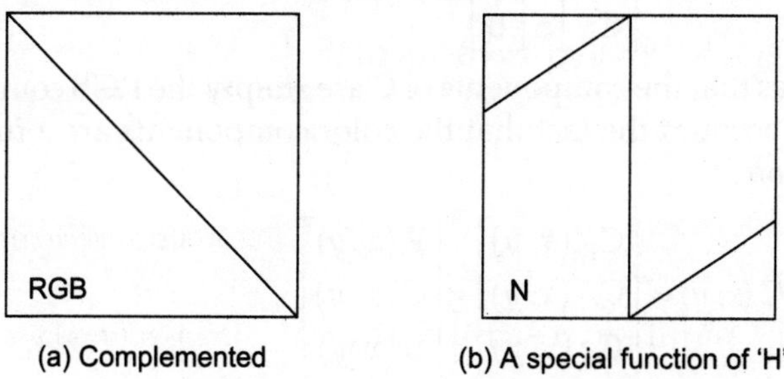

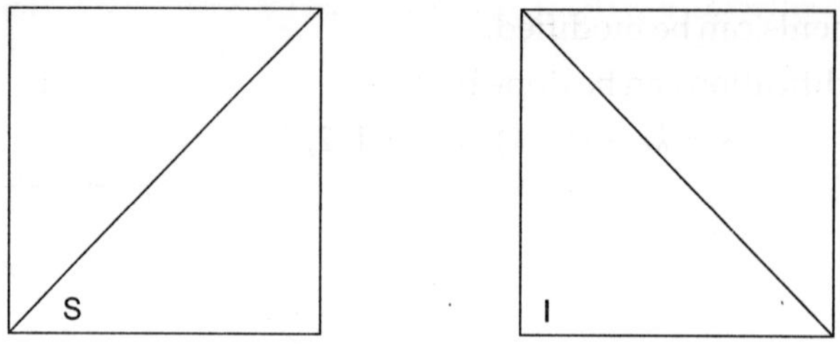

(c) Saturation or purity of color is not affected (d) Intensity is decreased

Fig. 5.11 *Color Complement.*

5.12.3 Color Slicing

"Some time highlighting a specific range of color in an image is useful for separating objects from their surroundings". The basic advantages of this slicing are that

(*a*) display the color of interest so that they can be easily differentiated from their surrounding.

(*b*) We may use this highlighted area as a mask for future processing.

A very straight forward and easy way to slice a image part is that we assign a natural color for the image part that is not of our interest. So,

$$s_i = \begin{Bmatrix} 0.5 & \text{if} & \left[\left| r_j - a_j \right| > \frac{w}{2} \right]_{i \leq j \leq n}^{i=1,2,\ldots\ldots,n} \\ r_i & ; & \text{otherwise} \end{Bmatrix} \quad \ldots (5.15)$$

where w = width of window (cube) of RGB.

This natural color is middle gray 'r' (0.5, 0.5, 0.5).

5.13 COLOR IMAGE SMOOTHING AND SHARPENING

As we know that full-color images have at least three components so color pixels are vectors.

For example, in the RGB system, each color point can be interpreted as a vector extending from origin to that point in RGB co-ordinate system.

Let 'C' represents an arbitrary vector in RGB color space.

$$C = \begin{bmatrix} C_R \\ C_G \\ C_B \end{bmatrix} = \begin{bmatrix} R \\ G \\ B \end{bmatrix} \quad \ldots (5.16)$$

This equation indicates that the components of C are simply the RGB components of color image at a point. We take into account the fact that the color components are a function of co-ordinates (x, y) by using the notation :

$$C(x, y) = \begin{bmatrix} C_R(x, y) \\ C_G(x, y) \\ C_B(x, y) \end{bmatrix} = \begin{bmatrix} R(x, y) \\ G(x, y) \\ B(x, y) \end{bmatrix} \quad \ldots (5.17)$$

For an image of size $M \times N$, there are MN such vectors, $C(x, y)$, for $x = 0, 1, 2, \ldots\ldots, M-1$ and $y = 0, 1, 2, \ldots\ldots, N-1$.

So now you can easily understand the figure given below. So *"we can apply gray scale image processing here also. But now this technique has to be applied to each component separately"*.

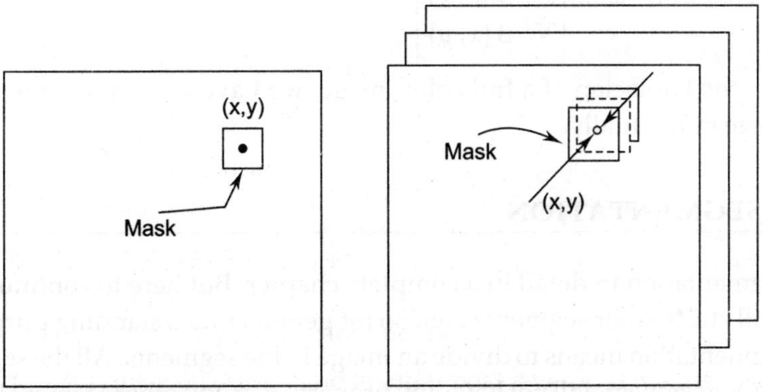

Fig. 5.12 *Mask applied on color image*

Now after clearing these facts, now we can apply spatial filtering for color image smoothing and sharpening.

5.13.1 Color Image Smoothing

Gray level smoothing can be viewed as a spatial filtering operation in which the coefficients of filtering mask are all 1's. As the mask is slide across the image, each pixel is replaced by the average of the pixels in the neighbourhood. Thus image is smoothed. As discussed at the beginning, this concept can be extended to the full color image also means same process has to be done on each color component of color image separately. *"One basic difference between gray scale image processing and color image processing is that now we have to work with vectors"*.

Let s_{xy} denotes the set of co-ordinates defining a neighbourhood centered at (x, y) in an RGB color image. The average of the RGB component vectors in that neighbourhood is

$$\bar{C}(x, y) = \frac{1}{k} \sum_{(x,y)\in s_{xy}} C(x, y) \qquad \text{... (5.18)}$$

Again in the form of vector :

$$\bar{C}(x, y) = \begin{bmatrix} \frac{1}{k} \sum\limits_{(x,y)\in s_{xy}} R(x, y) \\ \frac{1}{k} \sum\limits_{(x,y)\in s_{xy}} G(x, y) \\ \frac{1}{k} \sum\limits_{(x,y)\in s_{xy}} B(x, y) \end{bmatrix} \qquad \text{... (5.19)}$$

5.13.2 Color-Image Sharpening

Recalling the sharpening of gray-scale images, the color image sharpening is done by Laplacian. For vector analysis, we know that the Laplacian of a vector is defined as vector whose components are equal to Laplacian of individual scalar components of the input vectors. In the RGB color system,

$$\nabla^2 [C(x,y)] = \begin{bmatrix} \nabla^2 R(x,y) \\ \nabla^2 G(x,y) \\ \nabla^2 B(x,y) \end{bmatrix} \quad \text{... (5.20)}$$

So the compute the Laplacian of a full color image, we have to compute the Laplacian of each component of image individually.

5.14 COLOR SEGMENTATION

We will study segmentation in detail in a complete chapter. But here to continue the color image processing, we will study color segmentation. So for general understanding purpose, let us define segmentation. Segmentation means to divide an image in the segments. All the segments are totally separated means. One segment will not have any property that any other segment has. But in a single segment, all the pixels will have same qualities. Segmentation of an image can be done by two methods:

1. By finding similarities between pixels and arranging them in a single segment (with all similarities).
2. By finding differences between pixels and arranging them in different segments according to their differences.

Now we will study segmentation in color images.

5.14.1 Segmentation in RGB Images

Suppose that, our objective is to segment objects of a specific color range in a RGB image. We have given a set of sample color points that represents the colors of our interested color range. By that set of colors, we simply estimate the '*average*' color that we want to segment. Let this average color be denoted by RGB vector '*a*'.

Now our purpose is to compare the each RGB pixel of our image with this average value.

One of the simplest way to find the similarities between both is Euclidean distance. Let z denote an arbitrary point in RGB space.

The Euclidean distance between 'z' and 'a' is given by

$$\begin{aligned} D(z,a) &= \| z-a \| \\ &= [(z-a)^T (z-a)]^{1/2} \\ &= [(z_R-a_R)^2 + (z_G-a_G)^2 + (z_B-a_B)^2]^{1/2} \end{aligned}$$

where the subscripts R, G and B, denote the RGB components of vectors a and z. We say that z is similar to a if the distance between them is less than specified threshold D_0.

Summary

1. In gray level images, image is a single valued function ; but there are other methods of imaging in which image are multi-valued function such as multispectral and multimodel.
2. Example of multispectral is color imaging.
3. By color imaging, human being easily can identify the objects.

4. Color imaging is categorized in two categories : Full color imaging where we directly deals with color images. In second category, called pseudo-color imaging, gray-level images are converted into color images.
5. To describe the chromatic (color) light source ; we describe three factors called radiance, luminance and brightness.
6. To differentiate different color ; we describe brightness, hue and saturation.
7. Binary colors are red, green and blue. Secondary colors are made up of combining primary colors. Secondary colors are magenta, gyan and yellow.
8. For eyes pigment, primary colors are magenta, cyan and yellow and secondary colors are red, blue and green.
9. RGB, CMY (CMYK) and HSI model are some standard models for color imaging.
10. As in case of gray-level images ; we can smooth *'or'* sharp the color images. But now same process has to be done on three planes.

Review Questions

1. What are primary colors and secondary color in color imaging ? How are they defined ?
2. Describe the RGB color model ? How are these color can be converted to HSI color model ?
3. Describe HSI color model. How will you calculate hue and saturation from this model ?
4. What is pseudo-color-image processing ? How does a gray image convert into color image ?
5. What do you understand by color slicing ?
6. Describe
   (*a*) color imaging smoothing
   (*b*) color imaging sharpening.
7. Describe color image segmentation.

Experimental Results of different DIP Processes

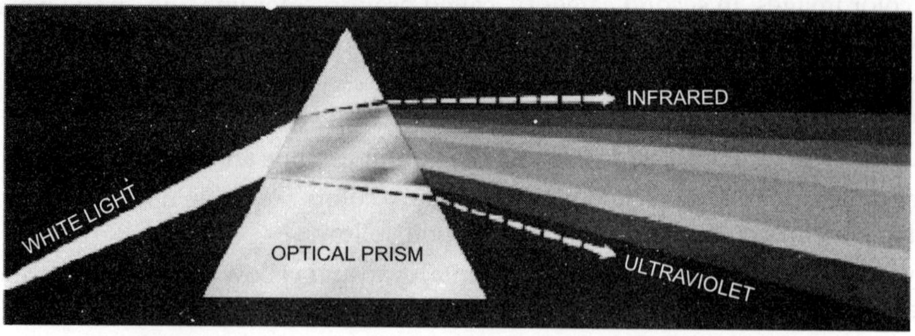

Test Figure 5.1 *Color Spectrum of white light after through the optical prism.*

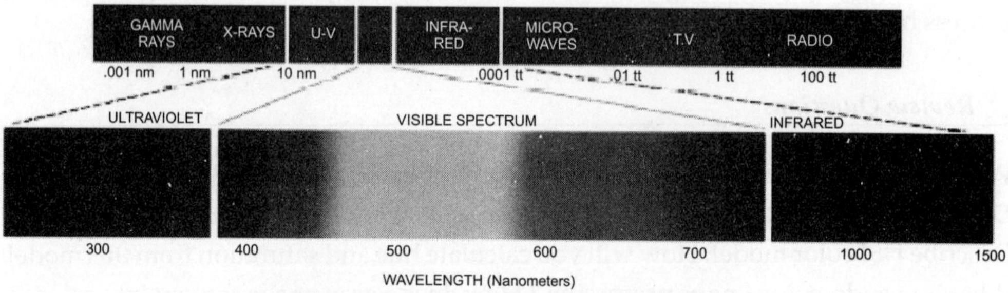

Test Figure 5.2 *Electromagnetic Spectrum of light.*

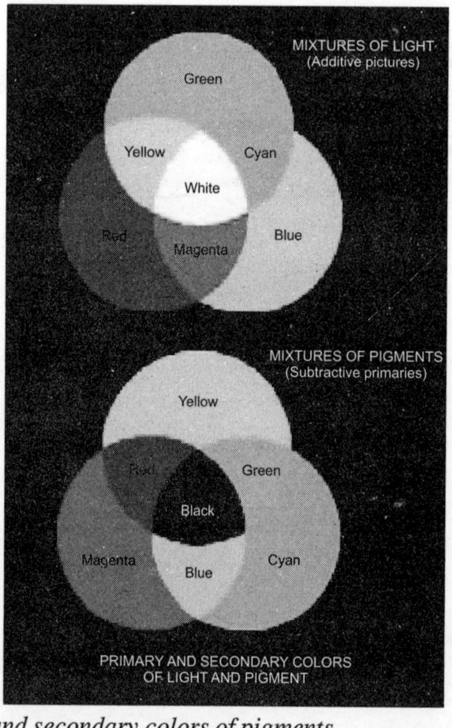

Test Figure 5.3 *Primary and secondary colors of pigments*

Primary Colors: *Red, Green, Blue*

Secondary Colors: *Magenta (Red + Blue), Cyan (Green + Blue), Yellow (Red + Green)*

Test Figure 5.4 *RGB Color model*

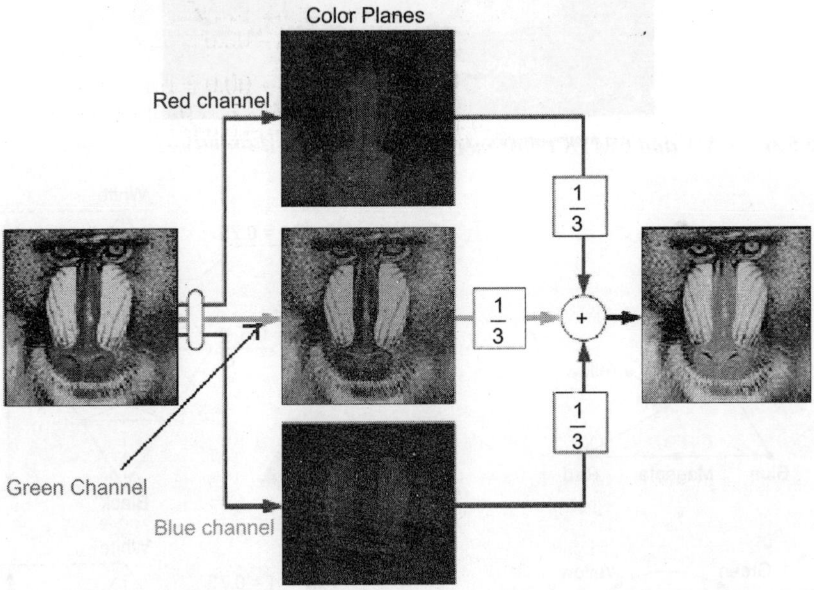

Test Figure 5.5 *Generation of RGB colors (A color image consists of three different color channels red, green and blue)*

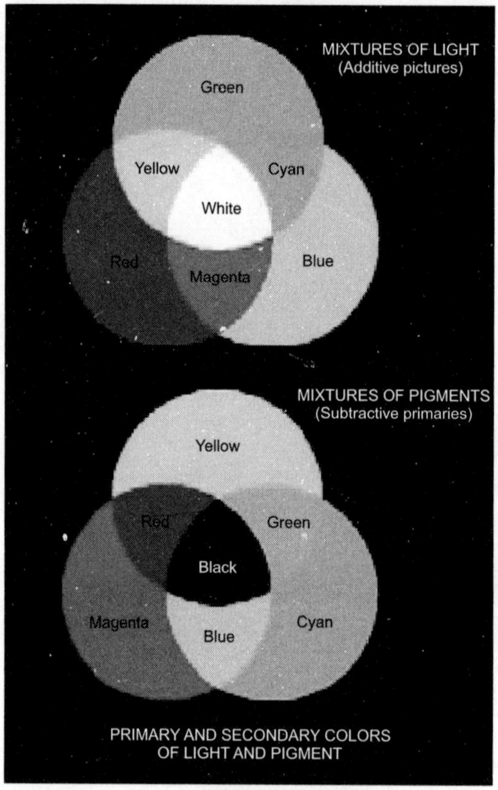

Test Figure 5.6 *CMY and CMYK color models*

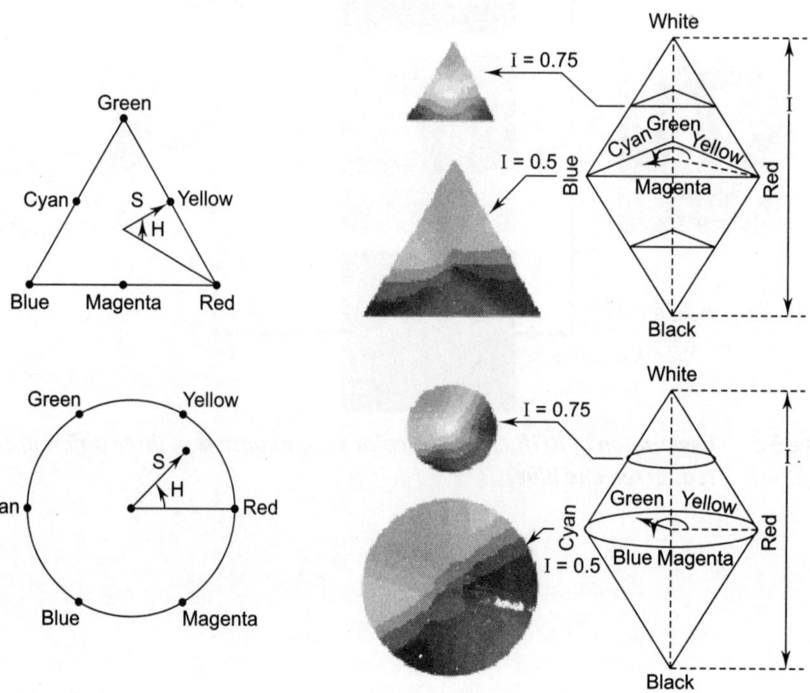

Test Figure 5.7 *HIS color models*

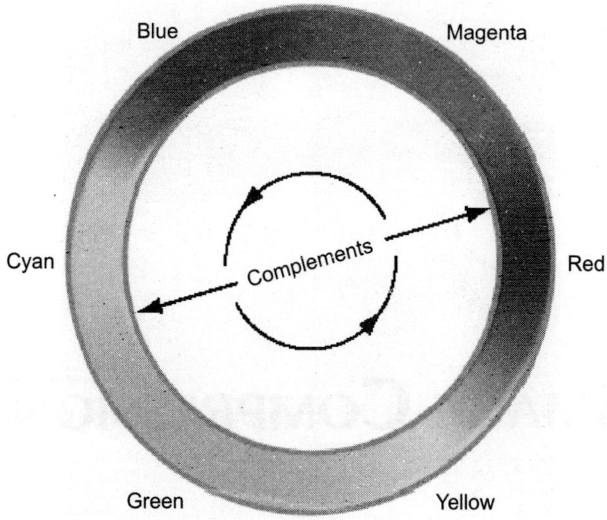

Test Figure 5.8 *Color circle and complement colors*

6

CHAPTER

Image Compression

6.1 INTRODUCTION

The data transmission and storage is very expensive. Generally, as we know that for presentation of digital data, we use encoding. By the encoding process also, we have very large amount of data (in comparison to original data). Thus, the overall consideration is :

1. To save the transmission bandwidth for transmission of data (In our case image).
2. To save the space for storage of image/data.

For that purpose, we use compression techniques. *"By compression, we mean to compress the data for easy transmission and easy storage of data. By decompression means, again converting the compressed data into original data again".*

Now we will start the specific discussion in respect to image processing.

6.2 MATHEMATICAL ANALYSIS

The term 'data compression' refers to the process of reducing the amount of data required to represent a given quantity of information.

"A data that is not relevant to represent any information is called data redundancy".

Data redundancy is the center issue in digital image compression.

If n_1 and n_2 denote the number of information carrying units in two data sets that represent the same information, the relative redundancy R_D of the first data set can be defined as :

$$R_D = 1 - \frac{1}{C_R} \qquad \text{... (6.1)}$$

where $C_R = \text{Compression Ratio} = \frac{n_1}{n_2}$

(*a*) Now if

$$n_1 = n_2$$

$$C_R = 1$$

$$R_D = 0$$

that represents that first data has no redundant information.

(*b*) If $n_2 << n_1$

So, $C_R = \frac{n_1}{n_2}$

$C_R \rightarrow \infty$

So, $R_D \rightarrow 1$

That represents highly redundant data and high compression can be done.

(*c*) If $n_2 >> n_1$

So, $C_R = \frac{n_1}{n_2}$

$C_R \rightarrow 0$

So, $R_D \rightarrow -\infty$

It means now second data is larger in comparison to original one. Now first of all, we will study data redundancy.

6.3 TYPES OF DATA REDUNDANCIES

In digital image processing, we have three basic types of redundancies :

(*a*) Coding redundancies.
(*b*) Inter pixel redundancies.
(*c*) Psychovisual redundancies.

6.3.1 Coding Redundancy

"If the gray levels of an image are coded in a way that uses more code symbol than absolutely necessary to represent each gray level, the resulting image is said to be code redundancy".

If we draw the histogram of an image, we see that

$$P_r(r_k) = \frac{n_k}{n} \quad \text{...(6.2)}$$

n_k = Number of time of k pixel occurrence

n = Number of total pixel.

Probability of occurrence of kth pixel.

We get a diagram ; that will show that a particular gray level has P probability of occurrence.

"Generally, the code redundancy is present when the codes assigned to set of events have not been selected to take full advantage of the probabilities of the event".

By natural coding, we assign the equal number of bits for symbols of high probability and less probability results in code redundancy. It is better to assign less (fewer) bits for more probable gray level and assign more bits for less probable gray level. That will provide image compression. This method is called variable length coding.

6.3.2 Inter-pixel Redundancy

"The only disadvantage of coding redundancy is that it would not provide the correlation between the pixels".

For correlation of pixels, we need to analysis the structural 'or' geometrical analysis of codes.

See the Fig. 6.1 given below

(*a*) Figure '*a*' and '*b*' shows to identical histogram having three denominating range of gray levels.

(*b*) Now if we apply the variable length coding, we get code redundancy and for both images, we get similar code pattern.

(*c*) Now if we draw the autocorrelation function

$$A(\Delta n) = \frac{T}{N - \Delta n} \sum_{y=0}^{N-1-\Delta n} f(x, y) f(x, y + \Delta n) \quad \text{... (6.3)}$$

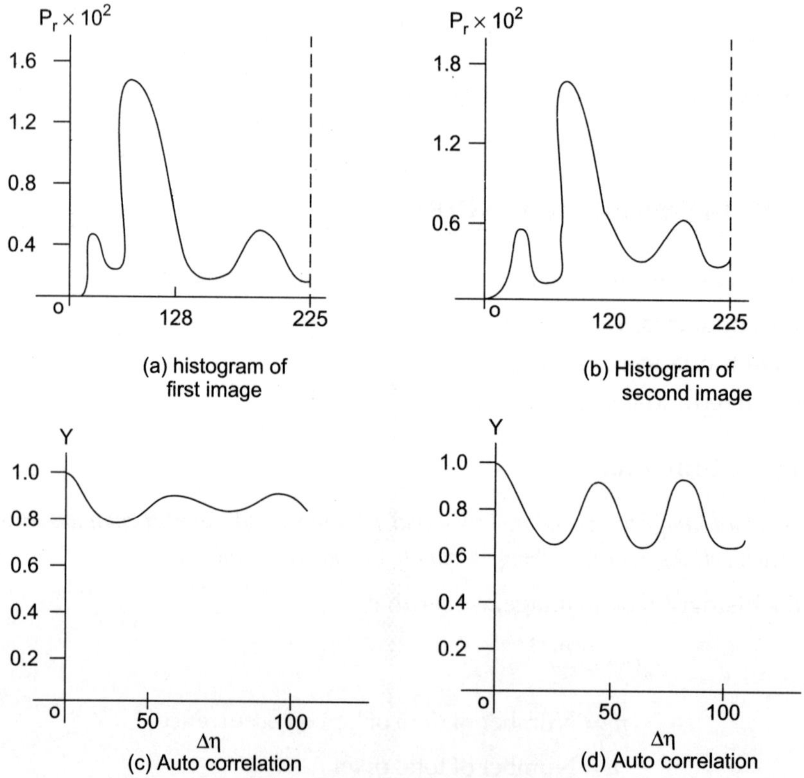

Fig. 6.1 *Interpixel redundancy.*

Now we see that there is dramatic difference between the shape of functions for image '*d*' we have very high correlation between pixels of image. *"Because the value of any given pixel can be reasonably predicted from the value of its neighbours, the information carried by individual pixels is relatively small. That is called interpixel redundancy"*. In order to reduce the interpixel redundancy in an image, the 2D pixel array are normally used for human viewing and interpretation must be transformed into more efficient format.

Simple example is that to code the difference between the successive pixels and send.

This type of transformation is generally reversible and called mapping.

6.3.3 Psychovisual Redundancy

(*a*) We should note the brightness of a region does not depend upon only the reflection made by region. It also depends upon eye.

"Certain informations simply has less relative importance than other information in normal visual processing. This information is said to be psychovisually redundant". It can be eliminated without significantly impairing the quality of image perception.

(*b*) Unlike coding and interpixel redundancy, psychovisual redundancy is associated with real *'or'* quantifiable visual information. Its elimination is possible only because the information itself is not essential for normal visual processing.

Since the elimination of psychovisually redundant data results in a loss of quantitive information. It is commonly referred to as quantization. Quantization results is lossy data compression.

6.4 IMAGE COMPRESSION MODEL

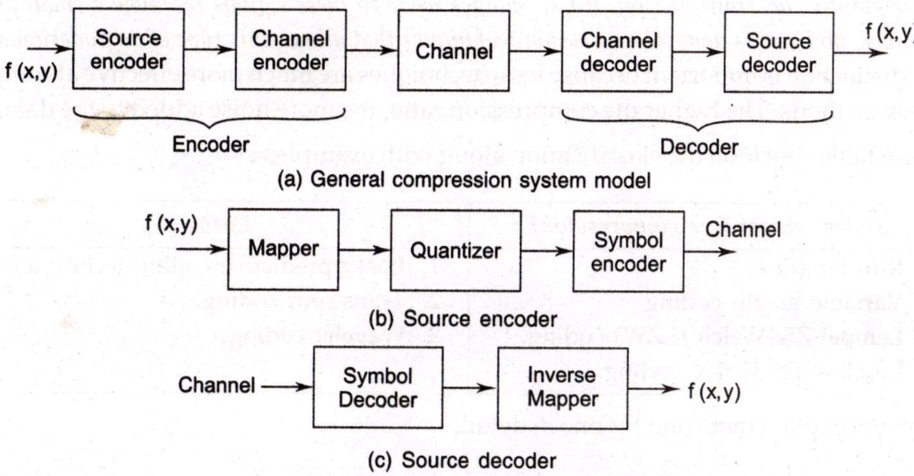

Fig. 6.2 *Image compression model.*

Figure *'a'* shows the basic block diagram for image compression system.

(*a*) **Source Encoder and Decoder:**

- The source encoder is responsible for reducing *'or'* eliminating any coding, interpixel *'or'* psychovisual redundancy in the input image.
- In the first stage of the source coding process, the mapper transforms the input data into a format designed to reduce interpixel redundancies in the input image.
- In the second stage of source encoding process, we use quantizer. Definitely quantizer will reduce the efficiency of mapper. But it is required to reduce psychovisual reduandcies.
- In the third and final stage, we use symbol encoder that will use the fixed *'or'* variable length coding to the quantizer output.

It should be clear that all these three stages are present in every model—it is not compulsory.

- If we want error free coding, then quantizer part will be omitted.

In predict compression system,

Quantizer + Mapper = Single Block.

(*b*) **Channel Encoder and Decoder :**

Channel encoder increases the noise immunity of the source encoder's output.

Encoder and decoder are designed to reduce the impact of channel noise by inserting a controlled form of redundancy in to source encoded data.

6.5 COMPRESSION STRATEGIES

The compression methods have been classified as either lossless *'or'* lossy.

"A lossless technique means that the restored data file is identical to the original. This is absolutely necessary for many types of data". For example : executable code, word processing files, tabulated numbers etc. You can not afford to misplace even a single bit of this type of information.

"In comparison, data files that represent images and other acquired signals do not have to be kept in perfect condition for storage 'or' transmission. If the changes made to these signals resemble a small amount of additional noise, no harm is done. Compression techniques that allows this type of degradation are called lossy". The distinction is important because lossy techniques are much more effective at compression than lossless methods. The higher the compression ratio, the more noise added to the data.

Following table conclude the classification along with examples :

Lossless (Error-free compression)	*Lossy*
1. Run-length 2. Variable length coding 3. Lempel-Ziv-Welch (LZW) coding. 4. Lossless predictive coding.	1. Lossy predictive coding techniques. 2. Transform coding. 3. Wavelet coding.

Now we will explain them one-by-one in detail.

6.6 LOSSLESS (ERROR FREE COMPRESSION)

6.6.1 Run-Length Encoding

Data files frequently contain the same character repeated many times in a row. For example, text files use multiple spaces to separate sentences, indent paragraphs, format tables and charts, etc. Digitized *signals* can also have runs of the same value, indicating that the signal is not changing. For instance, an image of the nighttime sky would contain long runs of the character or characters representing the black background. Likewise, digitized music might have a long run of zeros between songs. Run-length encoding is a simple method of compressing these types of files. Let us take one example given below—

Orginal — — — — — — —

Run-Lenth — — — — — — —

Example given illustrates run-length encoding for a data sequence having frequent runs of *zeros*. Each time a zero is encountered in the input data *two* values are written to the output file. The first of these values is a zero, a flag to indicate that run-length compression is beginning. The second value is the number of zeros in the run. If the average run-length is longer than two, compression will take place. On the other hand, many single zeros in the data can make the encoded file larger than the original.

Many different run-length schemes have been developed. For example, the input data can be treated as individual bytes, or groups of bytes that represent something more elaborate, such as floating point numbers. Run-length encoding can be used on only *one* of the characters (as with the *zero* above), *several* of the characters, or *all* of the characters.

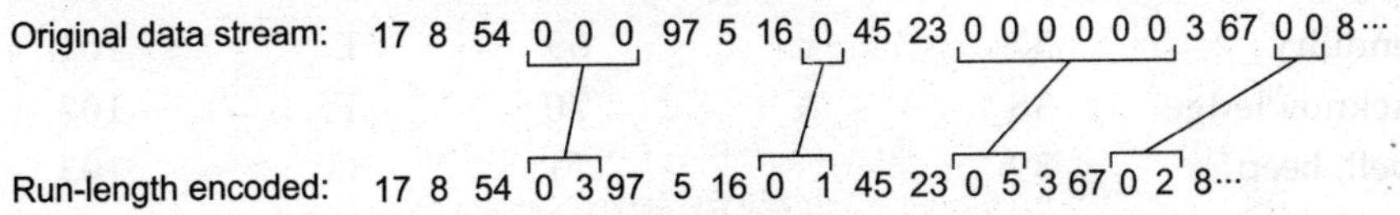

Fig. 6.2(a)

6.6.2 Variable Length Coding (Huffman Coding)

This method is named after D.A. Huffman, who developed the procedure in the 1950s. Figure 6.3 shows a histogram of the byte values from a large ASCII file. More than 96% of this file consists of only 31 characters : the lower case letters, the space, the comma, the period, and the carriage return. This observation can be used to make an appropriate compression scheme for this file. To start, we will assign each of these 31 common characters a five bit binary code : 00000 = "a", 00001 = "*b*", 00010 = "*c*", etc. This allows 96% of the file to be reduced in size by $\frac{5}{8}$. The last of the five bit codes, 11111, will be a flag indicating that the character being transmitted is not one of the 31 common characters. The next eight bits in the file indicate what the character is, according to the standard ASCII assignment. This results in 4% of the characters in the input file requiring 5 + 8 = 13 bits. The

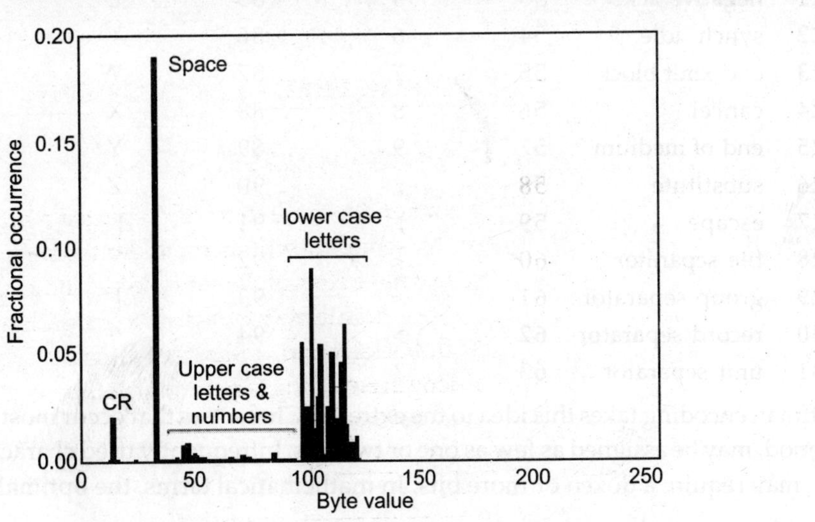

Fig. 6.3 *Histogram of text. The most common characters are the lower case letters, the space and carriage return.*

idea is to assign frequently used characters fewer bits, and seldom used characters more bits. In this example, the average number of bits required per original character is : $0.96 \times 5 + 0.04 \times 13 = 5.32$. In other words, an overall compression ratio of : 8 bits / 5.32 bits, or about 1.5 : 1.

Table 6.1 ***ASCII codes***

<table>
<tr><td>0</td><td>null</td><td>32</td><td>space</td><td>64</td><td>@</td><td>96</td><td>.</td></tr>
<tr><td>1</td><td>start heading</td><td>33</td><td>!</td><td>65</td><td>A</td><td>97</td><td>a</td></tr>
<tr><td>2</td><td>start of text</td><td>34</td><td>"</td><td>66</td><td>B</td><td>98</td><td>b</td></tr>
<tr><td>3</td><td>end of text</td><td>35</td><td>#</td><td>67</td><td>C</td><td>99</td><td>c</td></tr>
<tr><td>4</td><td>end of xmit</td><td>36</td><td>$</td><td>68</td><td>D</td><td>100</td><td>d</td></tr>
<tr><td>5</td><td>enquiry</td><td>37</td><td>%</td><td>69</td><td>E</td><td>101</td><td>e</td></tr>
<tr><td>6</td><td>acknowledge</td><td>38</td><td>&</td><td>70</td><td>F</td><td>102</td><td>f</td></tr>
<tr><td>7</td><td>bell, beep</td><td>39</td><td>'</td><td>71</td><td>G</td><td>103</td><td>g</td></tr>
<tr><td>8</td><td>backspace</td><td>40</td><td>(</td><td>72</td><td>H</td><td>104</td><td>h</td></tr>
<tr><td>9</td><td>horz. tab</td><td>41</td><td>)</td><td>73</td><td>I</td><td>105</td><td>i</td></tr>
<tr><td>10</td><td>line feed</td><td>42</td><td>*</td><td>74</td><td>J</td><td>106</td><td>j</td></tr>
<tr><td>11</td><td>vert. tab, home</td><td>43</td><td>+</td><td>75</td><td>K</td><td>107</td><td>k</td></tr>
<tr><td>12</td><td>form feed, cls</td><td>44</td><td>,</td><td>76</td><td>L</td><td>108</td><td>l</td></tr>
<tr><td>13</td><td>carriage return</td><td>45</td><td>-</td><td>77</td><td>M</td><td>109</td><td>m</td></tr>
<tr><td>14</td><td>shift out</td><td>46</td><td>.</td><td>78</td><td>N</td><td>110</td><td>n</td></tr>
<tr><td>15</td><td>shift in</td><td>47</td><td>/</td><td>79</td><td>O</td><td>111</td><td>o</td></tr>
<tr><td>16</td><td>data line esc</td><td>48</td><td>0</td><td>80</td><td>P</td><td>112</td><td>p</td></tr>
<tr><td>17</td><td>device control 1</td><td>49</td><td>1</td><td>81</td><td>Q</td><td>113</td><td>q</td></tr>
<tr><td>18</td><td>device control 2</td><td>50</td><td>2</td><td>82</td><td>R</td><td>114</td><td>r</td></tr>
<tr><td>19</td><td>device control 3</td><td>51</td><td>3</td><td>83</td><td>S</td><td>115</td><td>s</td></tr>
<tr><td>20</td><td>device control 4</td><td>52</td><td>4</td><td>84</td><td>T</td><td>116</td><td>t</td></tr>
<tr><td>21</td><td>negative ack.</td><td>53</td><td>5</td><td>85</td><td>U</td><td>117</td><td>u</td></tr>
<tr><td>22</td><td>synch. idle</td><td>54</td><td>6</td><td>86</td><td>V</td><td>118</td><td>v</td></tr>
<tr><td>23</td><td>end xmit block</td><td>55</td><td>7</td><td>87</td><td>W</td><td>119</td><td>w</td></tr>
<tr><td>24</td><td>cancel</td><td>56</td><td>8</td><td>88</td><td>X</td><td>120</td><td>x</td></tr>
<tr><td>25</td><td>end of medium</td><td>57</td><td>9</td><td>89</td><td>Y</td><td>121</td><td>y</td></tr>
<tr><td>26</td><td>substitute</td><td>58</td><td>:</td><td>90</td><td>Z</td><td>122</td><td>z</td></tr>
<tr><td>27</td><td>escape</td><td>59</td><td>;</td><td>91</td><td>[</td><td>123</td><td>{</td></tr>
<tr><td>28</td><td>file separator</td><td>60</td><td><</td><td>92</td><td>\</td><td>124</td><td>|</td></tr>
<tr><td>29</td><td>group separator</td><td>61</td><td>=</td><td>93</td><td>]</td><td>125</td><td>}</td></tr>
<tr><td>30</td><td>record separator</td><td>62</td><td>></td><td>94</td><td>^</td><td>126</td><td>~</td></tr>
<tr><td>31</td><td>unit separator</td><td>63</td><td>?</td><td>95</td><td>_</td><td>127</td><td>del</td></tr>
</table>

Huffman encoding takes this idea to the extreme. Characters that occur most often, such the space and period, may be assigned as few as one or two bits. Infrequently used characters, such as : !, @, #, $ and %, may require a dozen or more bits. In mathematical terms, the optimal situation is reached when the number of bits used for each character is proportional to the logarithm of the character's probability of occurrence.

A clever feature of Huffman encoding is how the variable length codes can be packed together. Imagine receiving a serial data stream of ones and zeros. If each character is represented by eight bits, you can directly separate one character from the next by breaking off 8 bit chunks. Now consider a Huffman encoded data stream, where each character can have a variable number of bits. How do you separate one character from the next ? The answer lies in the proper selection of the Huffman codes that enable the correct separation. An example will illustrate how this works.

Figure 6.4 shows a simplified Huffman encoding scheme. The characters A through G occur in the original data stream with the probabilities shown. Since the character A is the most common, we will represent it with two bits, the code : 00. The next most common character B, receives two bits, the code : 01. This continues to the least frequent character, G, being assigned four bits, 1111. As shown in this illustration, the variable length codes are restored into eight bit groups, the standard for computer use (Process of coding has been discussed in example).

When uncompression occurs, all the eight bit groups are placed end-to-end to form a long serial string of ones and zeros. Look closely at the encoding table of Fig. 6.4 and notice how each code consists of two parts : a number of zeros before a one, and an optional binary code after the one. This allows the binary data stream to be separated into codes without the need for delimiters or other marker between the codes. The uncompression program looks at the stream of ones and zeros until a valid code is formed, and then starting overlooking for the next character. The way that the codes are formed insures that no ambiguity exists in the separation.

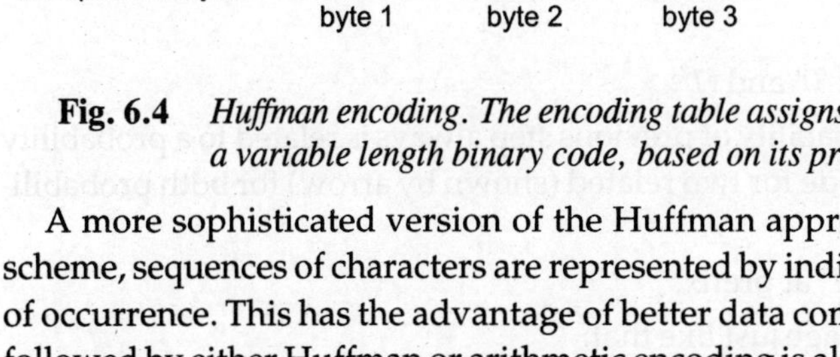

Example Encoding Table

Letter	Probability	Huffman code
A	.154	00
B	.010	01
C	.072	010
D	.063	110
E	.059	011
F	.015	0111
G	.011	1111

Fig. 6.4 *Huffman encoding. The encoding table assigns each of the seven letters used in this example a variable length binary code, based on its probability of occurrence.*

A more sophisticated version of the Huffman approach is called **arithmetic encoding**. In this scheme, sequences of characters are represented by individual codes, according to their probability of occurrence. This has the advantage of better data compression, say 5-10%. Run-length encoding followed by either Huffman or arithmetic encoding is also a common strategy. As you might expect, these types of algorithms are very complicated, and usually left to data compression specialists.

To implement Huffman or arithmetic encoding, the compression and uncompression algorithms must agree on the binary codes used to represent each character (or groups of characters). This can be handled in one of two ways. The simplest way is to use a predefined encoding table that is always the same, regardless of the information being compressed. More complex schemes use encoding optimized for the particular data being used. This requires that the encoding table be included in the compressed file for use by the uncompression program. Both methods are common.

Example : *Find the Huffman coding for given seven letters along with probability of occurrence.*

Letters = Probability

B = 0.110

A = 0.154

G = 0.011

D = 0.063

E = 0.059

C = 0.072

F = 0.015

Solution. Process for calculating Huffman coding :

1. Arrange the letters according to descending order of probability of occurrence.

   A = 0.154

   B = 0.110

   C = 0.072

   D = 0.063

   E = 0.059

   F = 0.015

   G = 0.011.

2. Now add lowest two and get new probability (combined of F and G) and place that new probability at appropriate place according to descending order.
3. We left at last only two probabilities because we need binary coding that has only two symbols '1' and '0'.
4. Now start coding :
   (*a*) For last two probabilities assign '0' and '1'.
   (*b*) Now follow the arrows. The probability of previous step always is related to a probability of next step. Just put the same code for two related (shown by arrow) for both probabilities.
   (*c*) Again for last two ; put '0' and '1' at prefix.
   (*d*) Proceed till last (1st reduction) stage just like that.
5. We will see that we will get more binary digits for less probable data and less binary digits for high probable data.

   The advantages is that the letter / symbol occurring again and again will now take less bits for representation (and symbol / letter occurring less very take more binary bits) so automatically total required bits will be decreased.

A = 0.154	0.154
B = 0.110	0.110
C = 0.072	0.072
D = 0.063	0.063
E = 0.059	0.059
F = 0.015	0.026
G = 0.011	

We have added lowest two probability (0.015 + 0.011) = 0.026 and placed that in descending order.

Repeat step (2) till only two probabilities are left.

Letters	Ist Reduction	IInd Reduction	IIIrd Reduction	IVth Reduction	Vth Reduction	VIth Reduction
A	0.154	0.154	0.154	0.154	0.195	0.289
B	0.110	0.110	0.110	0.135	0.154	0.195
C	0.072	0.072	0.085	0.110	0.135	
D	0.063	0.063	0.072	0.085		
E	0.059	0.059	0.063			
F	0.015	0.026				
G	0.011					

	Ist Reduction		IInd Reduction		IIIrd Reduction		IVth Reduction		Vth Reduction		VIth Reduction	
A	0.154	00	0.154	00	0.154	00	0.154	00	0.195	1	0.289	0
B	0.110	01	0.110	01	0.110	01	0.135	10	0.154	00	0.195	1
C	0.072	010	0.072	010	0.085	11	0.110	01	0.135	10		
D	0.063	110	0.063	110	0.072	010	0.085	11				
E	0.059	011	0.059	011	0.063	110						
F	0.015	0111	0.026	111								
G	0.011	1111										

Final codes

6.6.3 Arithmetic Coding

Now we will study arithmetic coding in detail. Basically *unlike the Huffman coding, arithmetic coding does not provide one-to-one correspondence between source symbol and code words. In arithmetic coding, an entire sequence of source symbols ('or' message) is assigned a single arithmetic code word.* The code word itself defines an interval of real numbers between '0' and '1'.

The basic advantages of arithmetic coding are that :

1. When applied to independent and identical distributed sources, the compression of each symbol is probably optimal.
2. It is effective in a wide range of situations and compression ratios.
3. It simplifies automatic modeling of complex sources, yielding near-optimal *'or'* significantly improved compression for sources that are not independent and identically distributed.

But there are some disadvantages also due to which arithmetic codes are getting less popularity such as:

1. Some time, they are very complex for coding and decoding.
2. Patents covered the most efficient implementation. Royalties and fear of patent infringement discouraged arithmetic coding in commercial products.
3. Efficient implementations were difficult.

But by recent technological developments ; all disadvantages have been handled.

Algorithm Overview :

Given :

An alphabet with symbols $S_0, S_1, ..., S_n$ where each symbol has a probability of occurrence of P_0, $P_1, ..., P_n$ such that $\sum P_i = 1$. Since $\sum P_i = 1$, we can represent each probability, P_i, as a unique non-overlapping range of values between *'0'* and *'1'*.

Now let us suppose that we have an alphabet *'a'*, *'b'*, *'c'*, *'d'* and *'e'* with probabilities of occurrence of 30%, 15%, 25%, 10% and 20%. (In other words 0.30, 0.15, 0.25, 0.10 and 0.20). So now we choose the following range assignments to each symbol based on its probability :

Symbol	Probability	Range
a	0.30	[0.00, 0.30)
b	0.15	[0.30, 0.45)
c	0.25	[0.45, 0.70)
d	0.10	[0.70, 0.80)
e	0.20	[0.80, 1.00)

where square brackets '[' mean that adjacent number is included and parenthesis '(' mean that adjacent number is excluded.

To assign a particular range, just put the maximum limit of previous range as current minimum limit and for current maximum limit of a particular range, just add all previous probabilities. For example, for range of alphabet *'c'* ;

minimum unit = 0.45 (max. limit of *'b'*)

max. limit = 0.30 + 0.15 + 0.25 = 0.70.

Encoding using arithmetic coding

By assigning each symbol its own unique probability range, it is possible to encode a single symbol by its range. Using this approach we could encode a string (a stream of symbols) as a series of probability range. For that purpose we should use the following process:

lower bound = '0'

upper bound = '1'

So for other symbols encoding

current range = upper bound – lower bound

upper bound = lower bound + (current range × upper bound of new symbol)

lower bound = lower bound + (current range × lower bound of new symbol). ...(6.4)

Now let us take example :

For our example just take to encode a string *'ace'* using range giving in table.

Start with lower and upper bounds of '0' and '1' respectively.

Now applying the process just discussed.

Encode *'a'*.

current range = 1 – 0 = 1

upper bound = 0 + (1 × 0.30) = 0.30

lower bound = 0 + (1 × 0.00) = 0.00

Encode *'c'*.

current range = 0.30 – 0.00 = 0.30

upper bound = 0.00 + (0.30 × 0.70) = 0.210

lower bound = 0.0 + (0.30 × 0.45) = 0.135.

Encode *'e'*

current range = 0.210 – 0.135 = 0.075

upper bound = 0.135 + (0.075 × 1.00) = 0.210

lower bound = 0.135 + (0.075 × 0.80) = 0.195.

So string *'ace'* may be encoded by any one value within probability range [0.195, 0.210)

Decoding using arithmetic coding

For decoding of a string we will have an encoded output. Starting from that we should follow the following steps :

1. **Given :** Encoded value = Encoded input.
2. Now just identify the symbol containing encoded value within its range.
3. Now as we have seen in encoding for *'c'* we have encoding process that has effect of *'a'*. Also in encoding of *'e'*, we have effect of *'a'* and *'c'* both so for decoding, we have to remove the effect of all symbols. For that

   Current range = upper bound of new symbol – lower bound of new symbol.

   Encoded value = (Encoded value – lower bound of new symbol) ÷ current range. ...(6.5)

For example, for same example as discussed above, we have to decode a three symbol string encoded as 0.20.

Decoding of first symbol starts with search of the range in which 0.20 lies that is [0.00, 0.30). So, 0.20 lies within [0.00, 0.30)

0.20 encodes *'a'*.

Now to remove the effect of *'a'* ;

$$\text{Current range} = (0.30 - 0.00) = 0.30$$

$$\text{Encoded value} = (0.20 - 0.0) \div 0.30 = 0.67$$

Now for decoding of second symbol 0.67 lies with in [0.45, 0.70) 0.67 encodes *'c'*.

Removing the effect of *'c'*.

$$\text{Current range} = 0.70 - 0.45 = 0.25$$

$$\text{Encoded value} = (0.67 - 0.45) \div 0.35$$

$$= 0.68.$$

Decoding of third symbol

0.88 lies within [0.80, 1.00)

0.88 encodes *'e'*.

Thus encoded string was *'ace'* that is the result of decoding.

6.6.4 LZW Compression

LZW compression is named after its developers, A. Lempel and L. Ziv, with later modifications by Terry A. Welch. It is the foremost technique for general purpose data compression due to its simplicity and versatility. Typically, you can expect LZW to compress text, executable code, and similar data files to about one-half their original size. LZW also performs well when presented with extremely redundant data files, such as tabulated numbers, computer source code, and acquired signals. Compression ratios of 5 : 1 are common for these cases.

LZW compression is always used in GIF image files, and offered as an option in TIFF and PostScript.

LZW compression uses a **code table,** as illustrated in Table 6.2. A common choice is to provide 4096 entries in the table. In this case, the LZW encoded data consists entirely of 12 bit codes, each referring to one of the entries in the code table. Uncompression is achieved by taking each code from the compressed file, and translating it through the code table to find what character or characters it represents. Codes 0-255 in the code table are always assigned to represent single bytes from the input file. For example, if only these first 256 codes were used, each byte in the original file would be converted into 12 bits in the LZW encoded file, resulting in a 50% larger file size. During uncompression, each 12 bit code would be translated via the code table back into the single bytes. Of course, this wouldn't be a useful situation.

Table 6.2 ***Example Code Table***

	code number	translation
identical code	0000	0
	001	1
	⋮	⋮
	0254	254
	0255	255
unique code	0256	245 201 4
	0257	243 245
	⋮	⋮
	4095	*xxx xxx xxx*

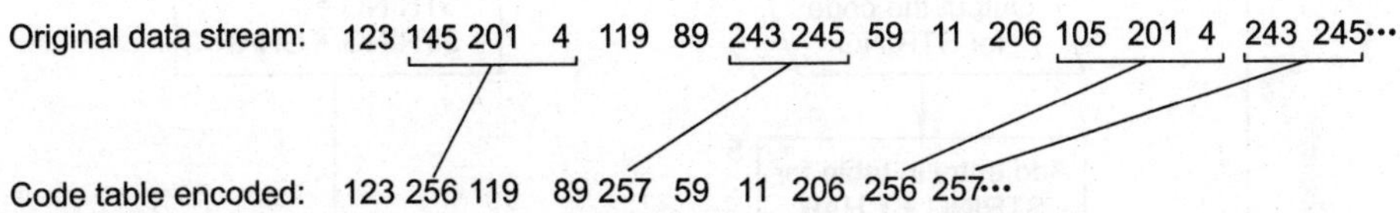

The LZW method achieves compression by using codes 256 through 4095 to represent *sequences* of bytes. For example, code 523 may represent the sequence of three bytes : 231 124 234. Each time the compression algorithm encounters this sequence in the input file, code 523 is placed in the encoded file. During uncompression, code 523 is translated via the code table to recreate the true 3 byte sequence. The longer the sequence assigned to a single code, and the more often the sequence is repeated, the higher the compression achieved.

Although this is a simple approach, there are two major obstacles that need to be overcome : (1) how to determine what sequences should be in the code table, and (2) how to provide the uncompression program the same code table used by the compression program. The LZW algorithm exquisitely solves both these problems.

When the LZW program starts to encode a file, the code table contains only the first 256 entries, with the remainder of the table being blank. This means that the first codes going into the compressed file are simply the single bytes from the input file being converted to 12 bits. As the encoding continues, the LZW algorithm identifies repeated sequences in the data, and adds them to the code table. Compression starts the second time a sequence is encountered. The key point is that a sequence from the input file is not added to the code table until it has already been placed in the compressed file as individual characters (codes 0 to 255). This is important because it allows the uncompression program to *reconstruct* the code table directly from the compressed data, without having to transmit the code table separately.

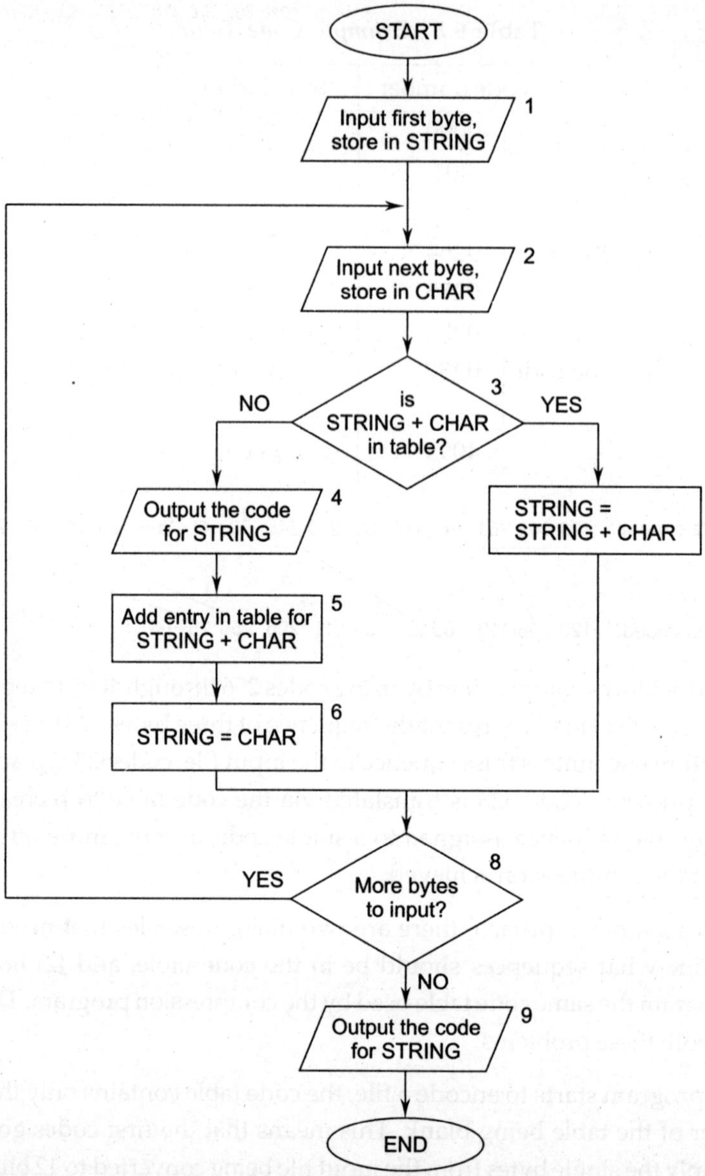

Fig. 6.5 *LZW compression flowchart. The variable, CHAR, is a single byte. The variable, STRING, is a variable length sequence of bytes. Data are read from the input file (box 1 and 2) as single bytes, and written to the compressed file (box 4) as 12 bit codes. Table 6.3 shows an example of this algorithm.*

Figure 6.5 shows a flowchart for LZW compression. Table 6.3 provides the step-by-step details for an example input file consisting of 45 bytes the ASCII text string ; *the/rain/in/Spain/falls/mainly/on/the/plain.* When we say that the LZW algorithm reads the character "*a*" from the input file, we mean it reads the value : 01100001 (97 expressed in 8 bits), where 97 is "*a*" in ASCII. When we say it writes the character "*a*" to the encoded file, we mean it writes : 000001100001 (97 expressed in 12 bits).

Table 6.3 ***LZW example. This shows the compression of the phrase : the/rain/in/Spain/falls/mainly/on/the/plain/.***

	CHAR	STRING + CHAR	In Table?	Output	Add to Table	New STRING	Comments
1	t	t				t	first character no action
2	h	th	no	t	256 = th	h	
3	e	he	no	h	257 = he	e	
4	/	e/	no	e	258 = e/	/	
5	r	/r	no	/	259 = /r	r	
6	a	ra	no	r	260 = ra	a	
7	i	ai	no	a	261 = ai	i	
8	n	in	no	i	262 = in	n	
9	/	n/	no	n	263 = n/	/	
10	i	/i	no	/	264 = /i	i	
11	n	in	yes (262)			in	first match found
12	/	in/	no	262	265 = in/	/	
13	S	/S	no	/	266 = /S	S	
14	p	Sp	no	S	267 = Sp	p	
15	a	pa	no	p	268 = pa	a	
16	i	ai	yes (261)			ai	matches ai, ain not in table yet
17	n	ain	no	261	269 = ain	n	ain added to table
18	/	n/	yes (263)			n/	
19	f	n/f	no	263	270 = n/f	f	
20	a	fa	no	f	271 = fa	a	
21	l	al	no	a	272 = al	l	
22	l	ll	no	l	273 = ll	l	
23	s	ls	no	l	274 = ls	s	
24	/	s/	no	s	275 = s/	/	
25	m	/m	no	/	276 = /m	m	
26	a	ma	no	m	277 = ma	a	
27	i	ai	yes (261)			ai	matches ai
28	n	ain	yes (269)			ain	matches longer string, ain
29	l	ainl	no	269	278 = ainl	l	
30	y	ly	no	l	279 = ly	y	
31	/	y/	no	y	280 = y/	/	
32	o	/o	no	/	281 = /o	o	
33	n	on	no	o	282 = on	n	
34	/	n/	yes (263)			n/	
35	t	n/t	no	263	283 = n/t	t	
36	h	th	yes (256)			th	matches th, the not in table yet

37	e	the	no	256	284 = the	e	the added to table
38	/	e/	yes			e/	
39	p	e/p	no	258	285 = e/p	p	
40	l	pl	no	p	286 = pl	l	
41	a	la	no	l	287 = la	a	
42	i	ai	yes (261)			ai	matches ai
43	n	ain	yes (269)			ain	matches longer string ain
44	/	ain/	no	269	288 = ain/	/	
45	EOF	/		/			end of file, output STRING

The compression algorithm uses two variables : *CHAR* and *STRING*. The variable, *CHAR*, holds a single character, *i.e.*, a single byte value between 0 and 255. The variable, *STRING*, is a variable length string, *i.e*, a group of one or more characters, with each character being a single byte. In box 1 of Fig. 6.5, the program starts by taking the first byte from the input file, and placing it in the variable, *STRING*. Table 6.3 shows this action in line 1. This is followed by the algorithm looping for each additional byte in the input file, controlled in the flow diagram by box 8. Each time a byte is read from the input file (box 2), it is stored in the variable, *CHAR*. The data table is then searched to determine if the concatenation of the two variables, *STRING + CHAR*, has already been assigned a code (box 3).

If a match in the code table is not found, three actions are taken, as shown in boxes 4, 5 and 6. In box 4, the 12 bit code corresponding to the contents of the variable, *STRING*, is written to the compressed file. In box 5, a new code is created in the table for the concatenation of *STRING + CHAR*. In box 6, the variable, *STRING*, takes the value of the variable, *CHAR*. An example of these actions is shown in lines 2 through 10 in Table 6.3, for the first 10 bytes of the example file.

When a match in the code table is found (box 3), the concatenation of *STRING + CHAR* is stored in the variable, *STRING*, without any other action taking place (box 7). That is, if a matching sequence is found in the table, no action should be taken before determining if there is a *longer* matching sequence also in the table. An example of this is shown in line 11, where the sequence : *STRING + CHAR* = in, is identified as already having a code in the table. In line 12, the next character from the input file, it is added to the sequence, and the code table is searched for : *in/.* Since this longer sequence is not in the table, the program *adds* it to the table, outputs the code for the shorter sequence that is in the table (code 262), and starts over searching for sequences beginning with the character, /. This flow of events is continued until there are no more characters in the input file. The program is wrapped up with the code corresponding to the current value of *STRING* being written to the compressed file (as illustrated in box 9 of Fig. 6.5 and line 45 of Table 6.3).

A flowchart of the LZW uncompression algorithm is shown in Fig. 6.6. Each code is read from the compressed file and compared to the code table to provide the translation. As each code is processed in this manner, the code table is updated so that it continually matches the one used during the compression. However, there is a small complication in the uncompression routine. There are certain combinations of data that result in the uncompression algorithm receiving a code that does not yet exist in its code table. This contingency is handled in boxes 4, 5 and 6.

Only a few dozen lines of code are required for the most elementary LZW programs. The real difficulty lies in the efficient management of the code table. The brute force approach results in large memory requirements and a slow program execution. Several tricks are used in commercial LZW programs to improve their performance. For instance, the memory problem arises because it is not known beforehand how long each of the character strings for each code will be. Most LZW programs handle this by taking advantage of the redundant nature of the code table. For example, look at line 29 in Table 6.3, where code 278 is defined to be *ainl*. Rather than storing these four bytes, code 278 could be stored as : *code 269 + l*, where code 269 was previously defined as ain in line 17. Likewise, code 269 would be stored as : *code 261 + n*, where code 261 was previously defined as *ai* in line 7. This pattern always holds : every code can be expressed as a previous code plus one new character.

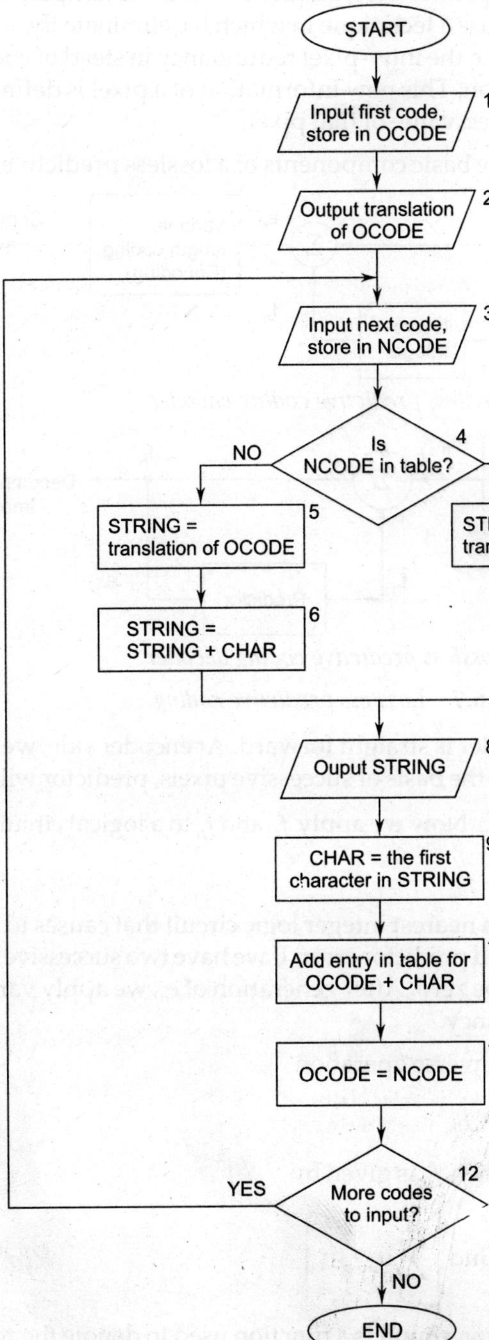

Fig. 6.6 *LZW uncompression flowchart. The variables, OCODE AND NCODE (oldcode and newcode), hold the 12 bit codes from the compressed file, CHAR holds a single byte, STRING holds a string of bytes.*

The execution time of the compression algorithm is limited by searching the code table to determine if a match is present.

6.6.5 Lossless Predictive Coding

Till now we have discussed the compression techniques in which decomposition of image into bit pattern is required. But now we discuss a technique in which we eliminate the interpixel redundancies of closely spaced pixels. To reduce the inter-pixel redundancy in stead of coding pixels directly. We apply coding to a new information. This new information of a pixel is defined as the difference between the actual pixel and predicted value of that pixel.

Figure (6.7) given below shows the basic components of a lossless predictive coding system.

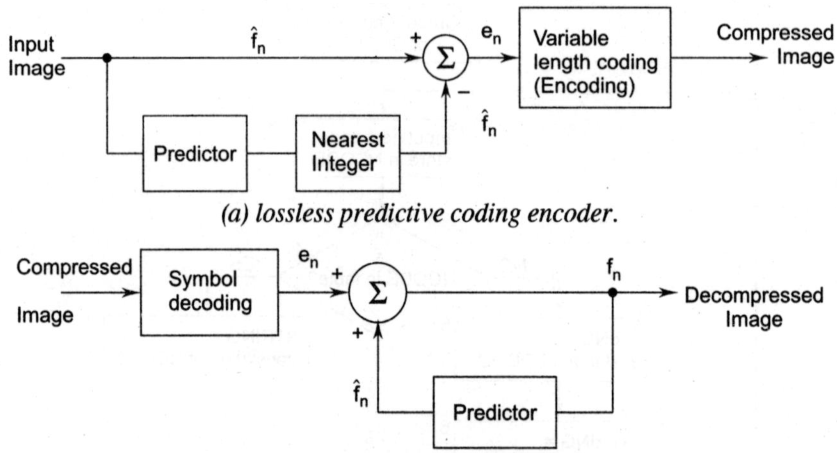

(a) lossless predictive coding encoder.

(b) Lossless predictive coding decoder.

Fig. 6.7 *Lossless predictive coding.*

Explanation of encoder and decoder is straight forward. At encoder side, we have predictor. We apply successive pixels of image. On the basis of successive pixels, predictor will generate an anticipated value $\hat{f}_n$ for the current pixel f_n. Now we apply $\hat{f}_n$ and f_n to a logical circuit that will generate.

$$e_n = f_n - \hat{f}_n \qquad \text{... (6.6)}$$

After predictor, we have applied a nearest integer logic circuit that causes to round-off the value generated by predictor. e_n is also called predictor error. If we have two successive pixels equal (means interpixel redundancy) then e_n will be zero. After generation of e_n, we apply variable length coding that will remove the coding redundancy.

At the decoder side performs the inverse operation

$$f_n = e_n + \hat{f}_n \qquad \text{... (6.7)}$$

If predictor is a linear predictor, then $\hat{f}_n$ is given by

$$\hat{f}_n = \text{round}\left[\sum_{i=1}^{m} \alpha_i f_{n-i}\right] \qquad \text{... (6.8)}$$

where m is the order of linear predictor, round is a function used to denote the rounding *'or'* nearest integer operation. α_i are the prediction coefficients where $i = 1, 2, \ldots\ldots, m$.

If we want to write the equation of $\hat{f}_n$ for 1-D image, then

$$\hat{f}_n(x, y) = \text{round}\left[\sum_{i=1}^{m} \alpha_i f(x, y-i)\right] \quad \text{... (6.9)}$$

So prediction $\hat{f}(x, y)$ is a function of the previous pixels on the current line alone.

In 2-D-images, the prediction is a function of previous pixels in a left-to-right, top-to-bottom scan of an image. In 3-D case, it is based on these pixels and the previous pixels of preceeding frames.

6.7 LOSSY COMPRESSION

As discussed previously, by lossless compression techniques, we get error free compression. But due to error free/lossless compression techniques, we get very low compression ratio. On the other hand there are a number of applications in which some error is tolerable, then we apply lossy compression. By the lossy compression, we may get compression ratio some time more than 100 : 1 in comparison to lossless compression that provides compression nearly 3 : 1 only. Now we will study lossy compression techniques in detail.

6.7.1 Lossy Predictive Coding

We have already discussed the lossless predictive coding. Here we have drawn the block diagram of lossy predictive coding. Here we have drawn the block diagram of lossy predictive coding system as shown in Fig. 6.8. The practical difference between lossless predictive coding and lossy predictive coding system is that we use quantizer in the case of lossy compression system.

The examples of such type of coding are – DPCM (Differential Pulse Code Modulation) and DM (Delta Modulation)

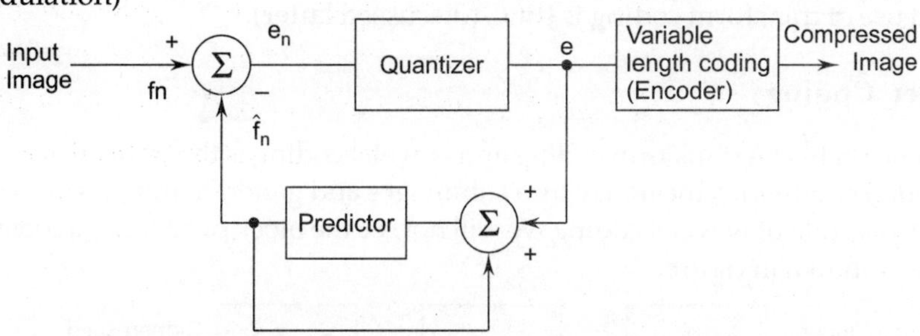

(a) Lossy predictive coding-encoder

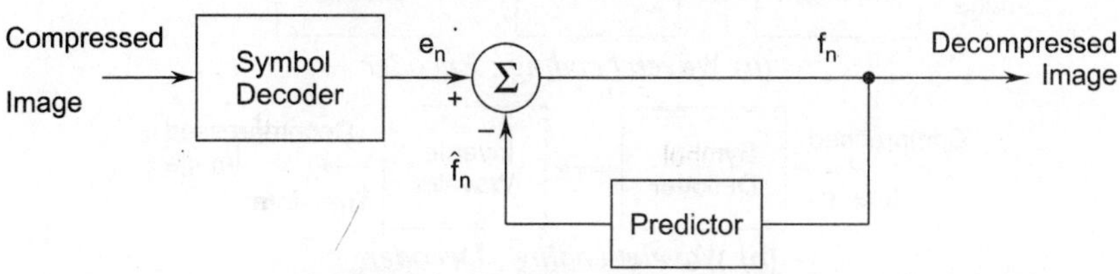

(b) Lossy predictive coding-decoder.

Fig. 6.8 *Lossy predictive coding.*

6.7.2 Transform Coding

Transform coding is a technique in which we apply compression on the transform of an image. In transform coding, a reversible, linear transform (such as fourier transform) is used to map the image into set of transform co-efficients. These transform coefficients are then quantized and coded.

Basic block diagram of transform coding has been drawn in figure 6.9.

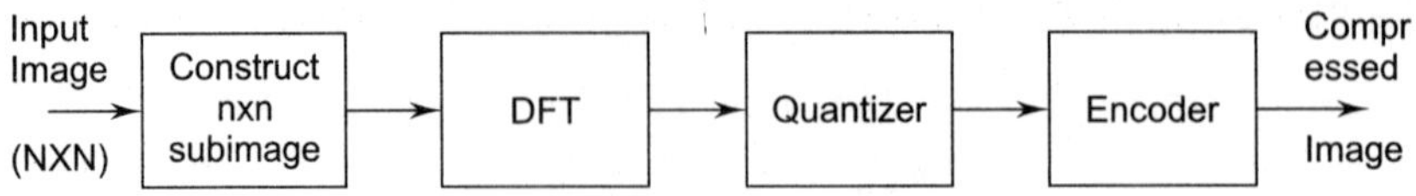

(a) Transform Coding-Encoder

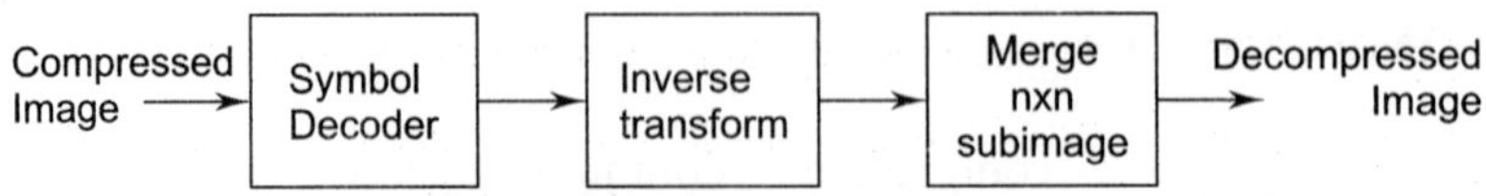

(b) Transform Coding-Decoder.

Fig. 6.9 *Transform Coding*

Let us discuss the basic steps of encoding using transform coding.

1. First of all an N × N input image is subdivided into subimages of size $n \times n$. During the subdivision of an image into subimages it should be cared that correlation (redundancy) between adjacent subimages is reduced to minimum level. Most popular subimage sizes are 8×8 and 16×16. Thus image has been converted into small pack of information that are easy to process.
2. Now by transformation (Fourier transform in case of digital signal is referred as discrete fourier transform, DFT) we generate transformation coefficient by the subimages.
3. By quantization process, generally we remove the redundant information.
4. Now apply variable length coding for reducing coding redundancy.

   The good use of transform coding is JPEG (discussed latter).

6.7.3 Wavelet Coding

The only difference between transform coding and wavelet coding is the transform function wavelet transform function subdivides the image into subimages and generate transform coefficients. That why in the block diagram of wavelet coding we will not see the block of subimage construction. Block diagram has been shown in figure.

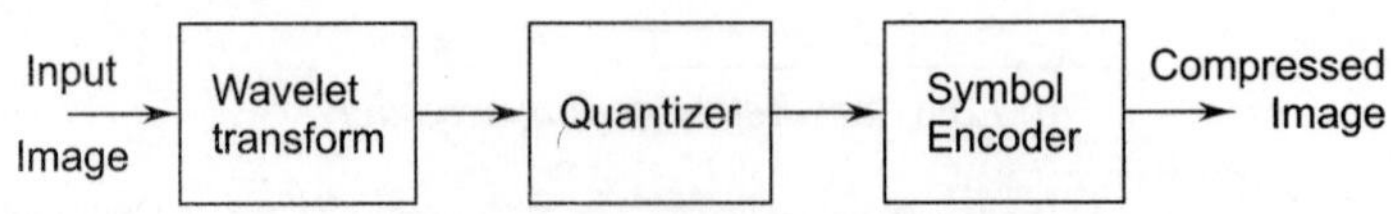

(a) Wavelet coding : Encoder

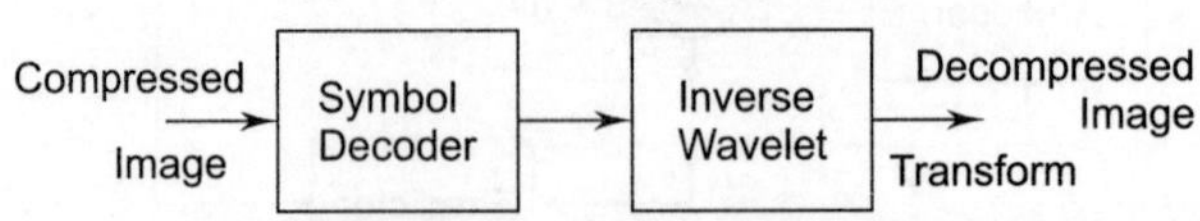

(b) Wavelet coding : Decoder.

Fig. 6.10 *Wavelet Coding.*

6.8 IMAGE COMPRESSION STANDARDS

After discussion of lossless and lossy compression models, we can study the different image compression standard that use these basic techniques for compression. We will study in detail the standards as given below :

1. JPEG
2. MPEG
3. GIF

Let us start with JPEG.

6.8.1 JPEG

Many standards of lossy compression have been developed. One of them is JPEG that is based on transform compression. JPEG is named after its origin, the joint photographers experts group. Now we discuss JPEG in detail.

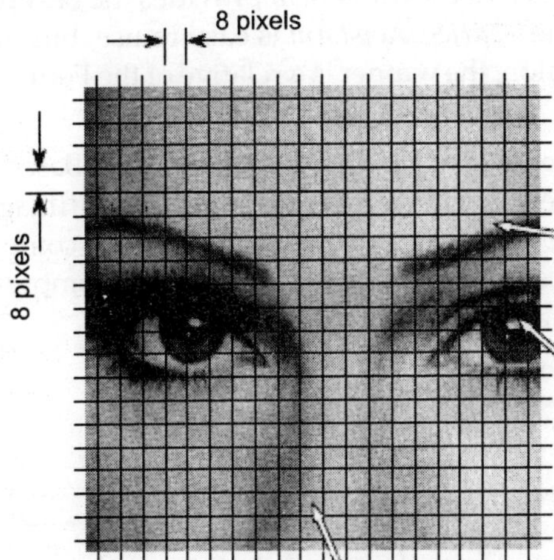

231	224	224	217	217	203	189	196
210	217	203	189	203	224	217	224
196	217	210	224	203	203	196	189
210	203	196	203	182	203	182	189
203	224	203	217	196	175	154	140
182	189	168	161	154	126	119	112
175	154	126	105	140	105	119	84
154	98	105	98	105	63	112	84

42	28	35	28	42	49	35	42
49	49	35	28	35	35	35	42
42	21	21	28	42	35	42	28
21	35	35	42	42	28	28	14
56	70	77	84	91	28	28	21
70	126	133	147	161	91	35	14
126	203	189	182	175	175	35	21
49	189	245	210	182	84	21	35

154	154	175	182	189	168	217	175
154	147	168	154	168	168	196	175
175	154	203	175	189	182	196	182
175	168	168	168	140	175	168	203
133	168	154	196	175	189	203	154
168	161	161	168	154	154	189	189
147	161	175	182	189	175	217	175
175	175	203	175	189	175	175	182

Fig. 6.11 *JPEG image division. JPEG transform compression starts by breaking the image into 8 × 8 groups, each containing 64 pixels. Three of these 8 × 8 groups are enlarged in this figure, showing the values of the individual pixels, a single byte value between 0 and 255.*

Transform compression is based on a simple premise : when the signal is passed through the Fourier (or other) transform, the resulting data values will no longer be equal in their information carrying roles. In particular, the low frequency components of a signal are more important than the high frequency components. Removing 50% of the bits from the high frequency components might remove, say, only 5% of the encoded information.

As shown in Fig. 6.11, JPEG compression starts by breaking the image into 8 × 8 pixel groups. The full JPEG algorithm can accept a wide range of bits per pixel, including the use of color information. In this example, each pixels is a single byte, a gray scale value between 0 and 255. These 8 × 8 pixel groups are treated independently during compression. That is, each group is initially represented by 64 bytes. After transforming and removing data each group is represented by, say, 2 to 20 bytes. During uncompression, the inverse transform is taken of the 2 to 20 bytes to create an approximation of the original 8 × 8 group. These approximated groups are then fitted together to form the uncompressed image. Why use 8 × 8 pixel groups instead of, for instance, 16 × 16 ? The 8 × 8 grouping was based on the maximum size that integrated circuit technology could handle at the time the standard was developed. In any event, the 8 × 8 size works well, and it may or may not be changed in the future.

Many different transforms have been investigated for data compression, some of them invented specifically for this purpose. For instance, the *Karhunen-Loeve* transform provides the best possible compression ratio, but is difficult to implement. The *Fourier transform* is easy to use, but does not provide adequate compression. After much competition, the winner is a relative of the Fourier transform, the Discrete Cosine Transform (DCT).

Figure 6.12 (*a*) and (*b*) show the key processing steps, which are the Heart of the DCT-Based modes of Operation. These figures illustrate the special case of single-components; Gray scale image compression. Image samples color image compression can then be approximately regarded as compression of multiple grayscale images, which are either compressed entirely one at a time, or are compressed by alternately Interleaving 8 × 8 sample blocks from each In turn.

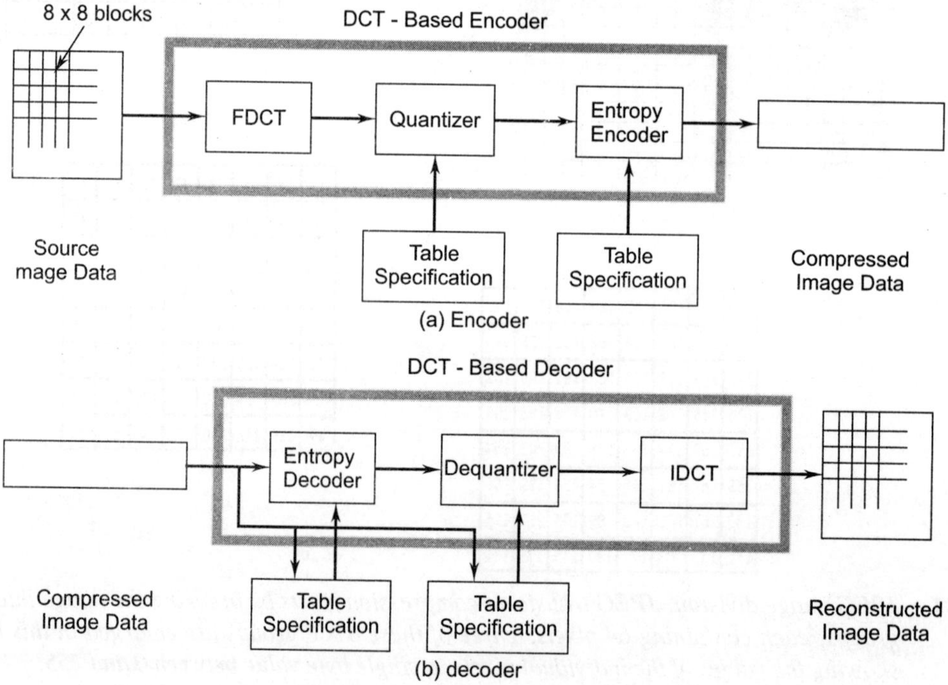

6.12 *JPEG compression method.*

Just as the Fourier transform uses sine and cosine waves to represent a signal, the DCT only uses cosine waves.

When the DCT is taken of an 8×8 group, it results in an 8×8 spectrum. In other words, 64 numbers are changed into 64 other numbers. All these values are *real*; there is no complex mathematics here. Just as in Fourier analysis, each value in the spectrum is the amplitude of a basis function. Figure 6.13 shows 6 of the 64 basis functions used in an 8×8 DCT, according to where the amplitude sits in the spectrum. The 8×8 DCT basis functions are given by :

$$b[x, y] = \cos\left[\frac{(2x+1)\,u\pi}{16}\right]\cos\left[\frac{(2y+1)\,v\pi}{16}\right] \qquad \text{... (6.10)}$$

The low frequencies reside in the upper-left corner of the spectrum, while the high frequencies are in the lower-right. The DC component is at [0, 0], the upper-left most value. The basis function for [0, 1], is one-half cycle of a cosine wave in one direction, and a constant value in the other. The basis function for [1, 0] is similar, just rotated by 90°.

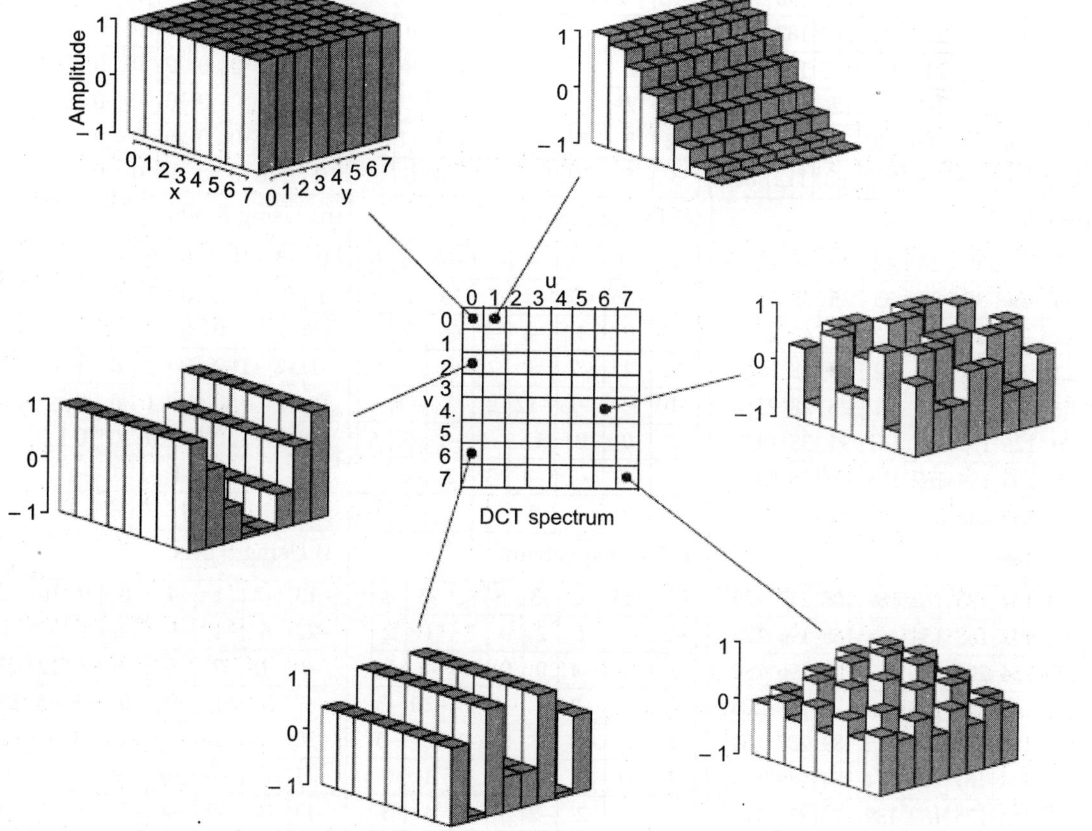

Fig. 6.13 *The DCT basis functions. The DCT spectrum consists of an 8×8 array, with each element in the array being an amplitude of one of the 64 basis functions. Six of these basic functions are shown here, referenced to where the corresponding amplitude resides.*

The DCT calculates the spectrum by correlating the 8×8 pixel group with each of the basis functions. That is, each spectral value is found by multiplying the appropriate basis function by the

8 × 8 pixel group, and then summing the products. Two adjustments are then needed to finish the DCT calculation (just as with the Fourier transform). First, divide the 15 spectral values in row 0 and column 0 by two. Second, divide all 64 values in the spectrum by 16. The inverse DCT is calculated by assigning each of the amplitudes in the spectrum to the proper basis function, and summing to recreate the spatial domain. No extra steps are required. These are exactly the same concepts as in Fourier analysis, just with different basis functions.

Figure 6.14 illustrates JPEG encoding for the three 8 × 8 groups identified in Fig. 6.11. The left column, Figures a, b and c, show the original pixel values. The center column, Figures d, e and f, show the DCT spectra of these groups.

Original Group

(a) Eyebrow

231	224	224	217	217	203	189	196
210	217	203	189	203	224	217	224
196	217	210	224	203	203	196	189
231	203	196	203	182	203	182	189
203	224	203	217	196	175	154	140
182	189	168	161	154	126	119	112
175	154	126	105	140	105	119	84
154	98	105	98	105	63	112	84

(b) Eye

42	28	35	28	42	49	35	42
49	49	35	28	35	35	35	42
42	21	21	28	42	35	42	28
21	35	35	42	42	28	28	14
56	70	77	84	91	28	28	21
70	126	133	147	161	91	35	14
126	203	189	182	175	175	35	21
49	189	245	210	182	84	21	35

(c) Nose

154	154	175	182	189	168	217	175
154	147	168	154	168	168	196	175
175	154	203	175	189	182	196	182
175	168	168	168	140	175	168	203
133	168	154	196	175	189	203	154
168	161	161	168	154	154	189	189
147	161	175	182	189	175	217	175
175	175	203	175	189	175	175	182

DCT Spectrum

(d) Eyebrow spectrum

174	19	0	3	1	0	-3	1
52	-13	-3	-4	-4	-4	5	-8
-18	-4	8	3	3	2	0	9
5	12	-4	0	0	-5	-1	0
1	2	-2	-1	4	4	2	0
-1	2	1	3	0	0	1	1
-2	5	-5	-5	3	2	-1	-1
3	5	-7	0	0	0	-4	0

(e) Eye spectrum

70	24	-28	-4	-2	-10	-1	0
-53	-35	43	13	7	13	1	3
23	9	-10	-8	-7	-6	5	-3
6	2	-2	8	2	-1	0	-1
-10	-2	-1	-12	2	1	-1	4
3	0	0	11	-4	-1	5	6
-3	-5	-5	-4	3	2	-3	5
3	0	4	5	1	2	1	0

(f) Nose spectrum

174	-11	-2	-3	-3	6	-3	4
-2	-3	1	2	0	3	1	2
3	0	-4	0	0	0	-1	9
-4	-6	-2	1	-1	4	-10	-3
1	2	-2	0	0	-2	0	-5
3	-1	3	-2	2	1	1	0
3	5	2	-2	3	0	4	3
4	-3	-13	3	-4	3	-5	3

Quantization Error

(g) Using 10 bit

0	0	0	0	-1	0	0	0
-1	0	0	0	0	0	0	-1
0	0	0	0	0	0	0	0
0	0	0	0	0	0	0	0
0	0	0	0	0	0	0	0
0	0	1	0	0	0	-1	0
0	0	0	0	0	0	0	0
0	0	0	0	0	0	0	0

(h) Using 8 bits

0	-3	-1	-1	0	0	0	-1
1	0	-1	-1	0	0	0	-1
-1	-2	1	0	0	0	-2	-2
-1	-2	-1	2	0	2	0	1
0	-2	1	0	0	1	0	0
0	-4	-1	0	0	0	0	0
0	-2	0	1	-1	-1	1	-1
-1	-3	1	1	1	-3	-2	-1

(i) Using 5 bits

-13	-7	1	4	0	0	10	-2
-22	6	-13	5	-6	2	-2	-13
-9	-15	0	-17	-8	8	12	25
-9	16	1	9	0	-5	-5	13
-20	-3	-13	-16	-19	-1	-4	-22
-11	6	-8	16	-9	-3	-7	6
-14	10	-9	-4	-18	3	3	-4
-13	19	12	9	8	5	-5	10

Fig. 6.14 *Examples of JPEG encoding. The left column shows three 8 × 8 pixel groups, the same ones shown in Fig. 6.11. The center column shows the DCT spectra of these three groups. The third column shows the error in the uncompressed pixel values resulting from using a finite number of bits to represent the spectrum.*

The right column, Figures (*g*), (*h*) and (*i*) shows the effects of reducing the number of bits used to represent each component in the frequency spectrum. For instance, (*g*) is formed by truncating each of the samples in (*d*) to ten bits taking the inverse DCT, and then subtracting the reconstructed image from the original. Likewise, (*h*) and (*i*) are formed by truncating each sample in the spectrum to eight and five bits, respectively. As expected, the error in the reconstruction increases as fewer bits are used to represent the data. As an example of this bit truncation, the spectra shown in the center column are represented with 8 bits per spectral value, arranged as 0 to 255 for the DC component, and – 127 to 127 for the other values.

The second method of compressing the frequency domain is to discard some of the 64 spectral values. As shown by the spectra in Fig. 6.14, nearly all of the signal is contained in the low frequency components. This means the highest frequency components can be eliminated, while only degrading the signal a small amount. Figure 6.15 shows an example of the image distortion that occurs when various numbers of the high frequency components are deleted. The 8 × 8 group used in this example is the eye image of Fig. 6.13. Figure (*d*) shows the correct reconstruction using all 64 spectral values. The remaining figures show the reconstruction using the indicated number of lowest frequency coefficients. As illustrated in (*c*), even removing three-fourths of the highest frequency components produces little error in the reconstruction. Even better, the error that does occur looks very much like random noise.

JPEG is good example of how several data compression schemes can be combined for greater effectiveness. The entire JPEG procedure is outlined in the following steps. First, the image is broken into the 8 × 8 groups. Second, the DCT is taken of each group. Third, each 8 × 8 spectrum is compressed by the above methods : reducing the number of bits and eliminating some of the components. This takes place in a single step, controlled by a quantization table. Two examples of quantization tables are shown in Fig. 6.16. Each value in the spectrum is divided by the matching value in the quantization table, and the result rounded to the nearest integer. For instance, the upper-left value of the quantization table is one, resulting in the DC value being left unchanged. In comparison, the lower-right entry in (*a*) is 16, meaning that the original range of – 127 to 127 is reduced to only – 7 to 7. In other words, the value has been reduced in precision from eight bits to four bits. In a more extreme case, the lower-right entry in (*b*) is 256, completely eliminating the spectral value.

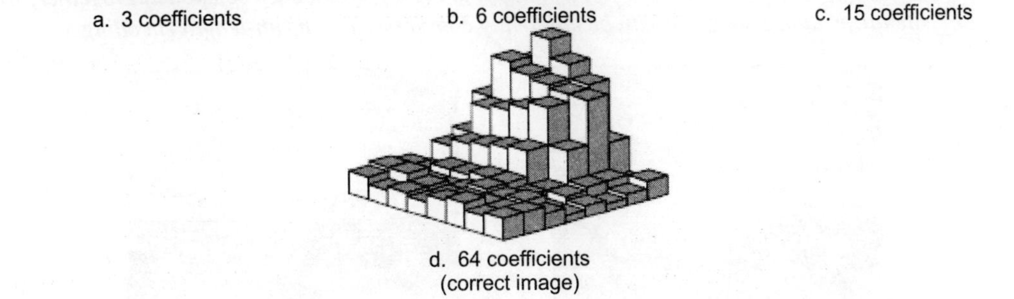

Fig. 6.15 *Example of JPEG reconstruction. The 8 × 8 pixel group used in this example in the eye in Fig. 6.11. As shown, less than $\frac{1}{4}$ of the 64 values are needed to achieve a good approximation to the correct image.*

(a) Low compression

1	1	1	1	1	2	2	4
1	1	1	1	1	2	2	4
1	1	1	1	2	2	2	4
1	1	1	1	2	2	4	8
1	1	2	2	2	2	4	8
2	2	2	2	2	4	8	8
2	2	2	4	4	8	8	16
4	4	4	4	8	8	16	16

(b) High compression

1	2	4	8	16	32	64	128
2	4	4	8	16	32	64	128
4	4	8	16	32	64	128	128
8	8	16	32	64	128	128	256
16	16	32	64	128	128	256	256
32	32	64	128	128	256	256	256
64	64	128	128	256	256	256	256
128	128	128	256	256	256	256	256

Fig. 6.16 *JPEG quantization tables. These are two example quantization tables that might be used during compression. Each value in the DCT spectrum is divided by the corresponding value in the quantization table, and the result rounded to the nearest integer.*

In the fourth step of JPEG encoding, the modified spectrum is converted from an 8×8 array into a linear sequence. The serpentine pattern shown in Fig. 6.17 is used for this step, placing all of the high frequency components together at the end of the linear sequence. This groups the zeros from the eliminated components into long runs. The fifth step compresses these runs of zeros by run-length encoding. In the sixth step, the sequence is encoded by either Huffman or arithmetic encoding to form the final compressed file.

The amount of compression, and the resulting loss of image quality, can be selected when the JPEG compression program is run. Figure 6.18 shows the type of image distortion resulting from high compression ratios. With the 45 : 1 compression ratio shown, each of the 8×8 groups is represented by only about 12 bits. Close inspection of this image shows that six of the lowest frequency basis functions are represented to some degree.

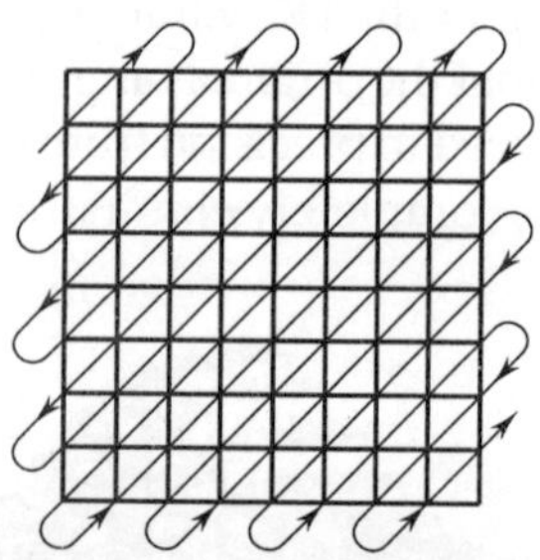

Fig. 6.17 *JPEG serial conversion. A serpentine pattern used to convert the 8×8 DCT spectrum into a linear sequence of 64 values. This places all of the high frequency components together, where the large number of zeros can be efficiently compressed with run-length encoding.*

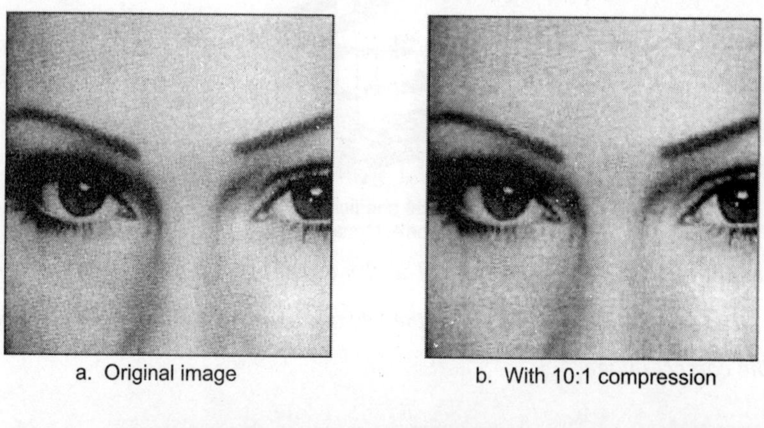

a. Original image

b. With 10:1 compression

c. With 45:1 compression

Fig. 6.18 *Example of JPEG distortion. Figure (a) shows the original image, while (b) and (c) shows restored images using compression ratios of 10 : 1 and 45 : 1, respectively. The high compression ratio used in (c) results in each 8 × 8 pixel group being represented by less than 12 bits.*

Why is the DCT better than the Fourier transform for image compression ? The main reason is that the DCT has one-half cycle basis functions, *i.e.,* S [0, 1] and S [1, 0]. As shown in Fig. 6.13, these gently slope from one side of the array to the other. In comparison, the lowest frequencies in the Fourier transform form *one complete cycle.* Images nearly always contain regions where the brightness is gradually changing over a region. Using a basis function that matches this basic pattern allows for better compression.

6.8.2 MPEG (Moving Picture Export Group)

There are now two MPEG standards, MPEG-1 and MPEG-2.

The MPEG-1 standard was developed in response to industry needs for an efficient way of storing and retrieving video information on digital storage media. One inexpensive medium is the CD-ROM which can deliver data at approximately 1.2Mbps, the MPEG-1 standard was subsequently aimed at this data rate, in fact the data rate is variable and all decoders must be able to decode at rates up to 1.856Mbps. Although the standard was developed with CD-ROM in mind, other storage and transmission media can include DAT, Winchester Disk, Optical Disk, ISDN and LAN. It is also important to say that it is common for double speed CD-ROMs to be used nowadays and it is generally accepted that any MPEG-1 decoder system should be able to decode at up to 3 Mbps.

The MPEG-2 standard was developed to support the need for Digital Video Broadcasting. The standard has been generally accepted for Digital TV systems, compressing fully intelaced TV resolution pictures to a bitrate up to around 20Mbps.

A version of MPEG-2 will also be used for the next generation of HDTV systems.

Two other relevant international standards were also being developed during the work of the MPEG committee : H.261 by CCITT aimed at telecommunications applications and ISO 10918 by the ISO JPEG committee aimed at the coding of still pictures. Elements of both standards were incorporated into the MPEG standard, but subsequent development work by the committee resulted in coding elements found in neither.

Some of the participants in the MPEG committee include : INTEL, BELLCORE, DEC, IBM, JVC Corp, PHILIPS CE, SGS-THOMSON, TCE, SONY Corp, NEC Corp and MATSUSHITA IEC. These may not be the most important members of the committee but it gives an indication of the relevant importance of the MPEG standard.

6.8.2.I MPEG-1

Although the MPEG-1 standard is quite flexible, the basic algorithms have been tuned to work well at data rates from 1 to 1.5 Mbps, at resolutions of about 350 by 250 Pixels at picture rates of up to 25 or 30 pictures per second. MPEG-1 codes progressively-scanned images and does not recognise the concept of interface, interfaced source video must be converted to a non interface format prior to encoding. The format of the coded video allows forward play and pause, typical coding and decoding methods allow random access, fast forward and reverse play and pause, typical coding and decoding methods allow random access, fast forward and reverse play also, the requirements for these functions are very much application dependent and different encoding techniques will include varying levels of flexibility to account for these functions.

Compression of the digitised video comes from the use of several techniques : Sub sampling of the chroma information to match the human visual system, differential coding to exploit spatial redundancy, motion compensation to exploit temporal redundancy, Discrete Cosine Transform (DCT) to match typical image statistics, quantization, variable length coding, entropy coding and use of interpolated pictures.

Algorithm Structure and Terminology

The MPEG hierarchy is arranged into layers (Fig. 6.19). This layered structure is designed for flexibility and management efficiency, each layer is intended to support a specific function i.e., the sequence layer specifies sequence parameters such as picture size, aspect ratio, picture rate, bit rate etc., whereas the picture layer defines parameters such as the temporal reference and picture type. This layered structure improves robustness and reduces susceptibility to data corruption.

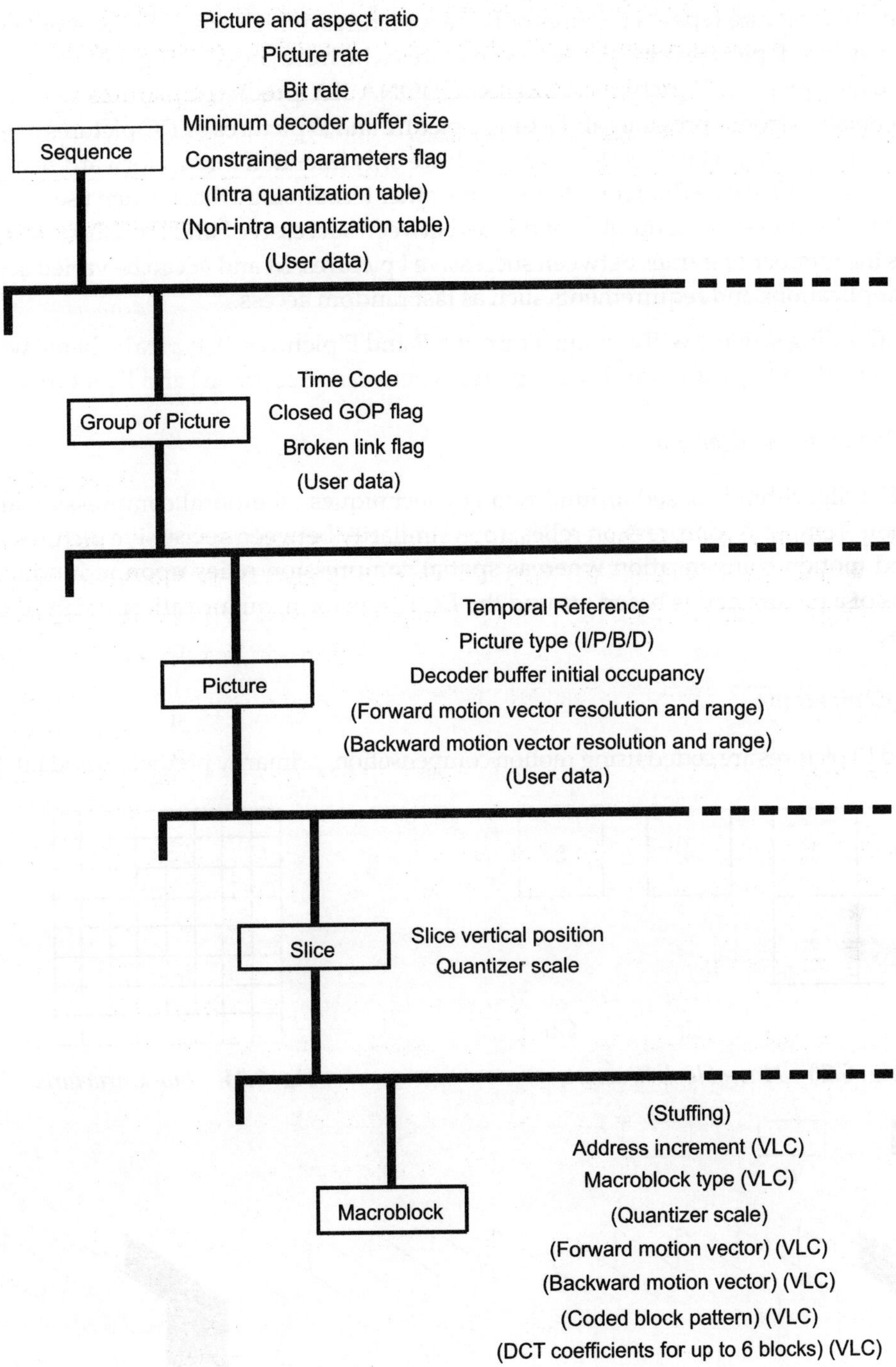

Fig. 6.19 *MPEG bistream hierarchy.*

For convenience of coding, macroblocks are divided into six blocks of component Pixels - four luma and two chroma (Cr and Cb) (Figure 6.20) Blocks are the basic coding unit and the DCT is applied at this block level. Each block contains 64 component Pixels arranged in an 8×8 array (Figure 6.21).

There are four picture types : I pictures or INTRA pictures, which are coded without reference to any other pictures ; P pictures or PREDICTED pictures which are coded using motion compensation from a previous picture ; B pictures or BIDIRECTIONALLY predicted pictures which are coded using interpolation from a previous and a future picture and D pictures or DC pictures in which only the low frequency component is coded and which are only intended for fast forward search mode. B and P pictures are often called Inter pictures. Some other terminology that is often used are the terms M and N, M + 1 represents the number of frames between successive I and P pictures whereas N + 1 represents the number of frames between successive I pictures. M and N can be varied according to different applications and requirements such as fast random access.

A typical coding scheme will contain a mix of I, P and B pictures. A typical scheme will have an I picture every 10 to 15 pictures and two B pictures between successive I and P pictures (Fig. 6.22).

MPEG-1 Compression Algorithm

The MPEG-1 algorithm is based around two key techniques : temporal compression and spatial compression. Temporal compression relies upon similarity between successive pictures using prediction and motion compensation whereas spatial compression relies upon redundancy within small areas of a picture and is based around the DCT transform, quantization and entropy coding techniques.

Temporal Compression

Inter (B and P) pictures are coded using motion compensation, primarily prediction and interpolation.

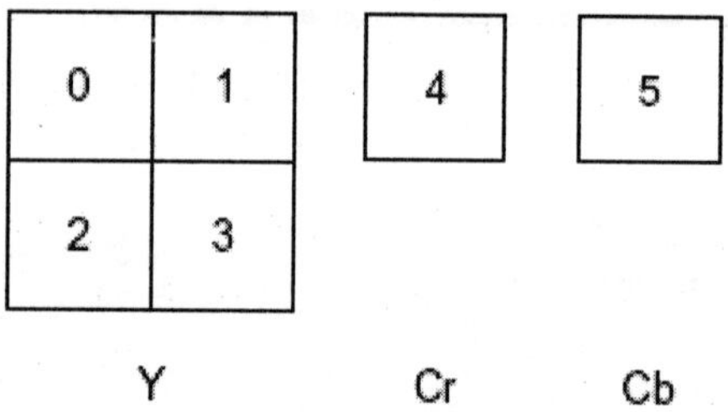

Fig. 6.20 *Macroblock structure*

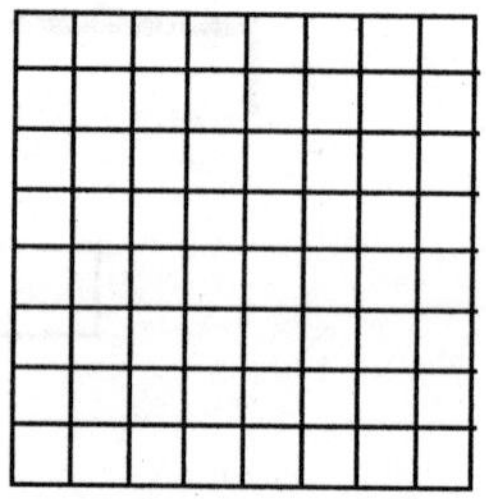

Fig. 6.21 *Block structure.*

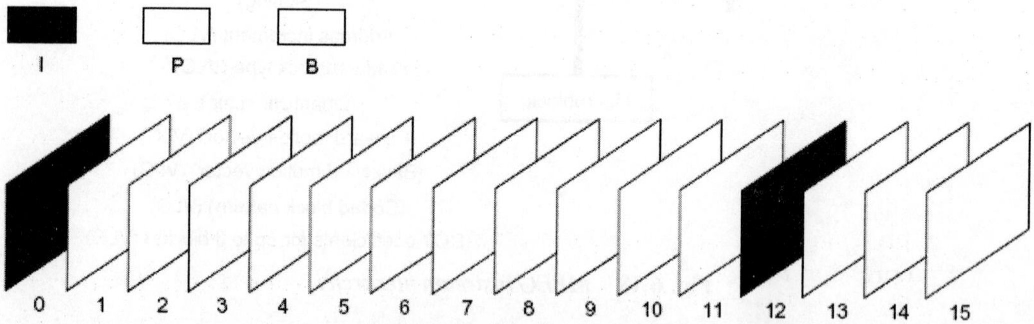

Fig. 6.22 *Typical sequence of pictures in display order.*

Prediction

The predicted picture is the previous picture modified by motion compensation. Motion vectors are calculated for each macroblock. The motion vector is applied to all four luminance blocks in the macro block. The motion vector for both chrominance blocks is calculated from the luma vector. This technique relies upon the assumption that within a macroblock the difference between successive pictures can be represented simply as a vector transform (*i.e.*, there is very little difference between successive pictures, the key difference being in position of the Pixels) (Fig. 6.23).

Interpolation

Interpolation (or bidirectional prediction) generates high compression in that the picture is represented simply as an interpolation between the past and future I or P pictures (again this is performed on a macroblock level).

Pictures are not transmitted in display order but in the order in which the decoder requires them to decode the bitstream (the decoder must of course have the reference picture (s) before any interpolated or predicted pictures can be decoded).

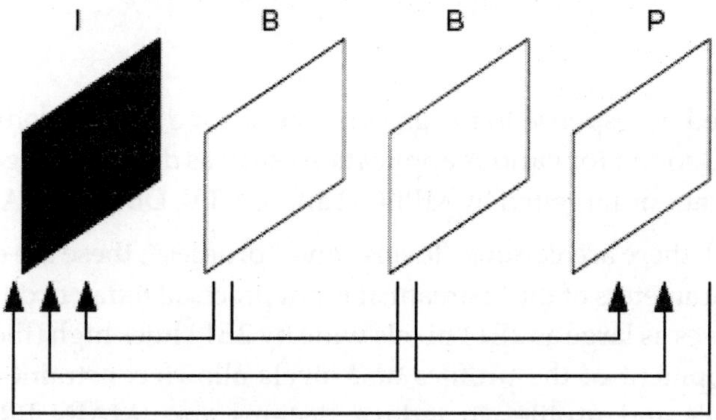

Fig. 6.23 *Make up of I, B and P pictures.*

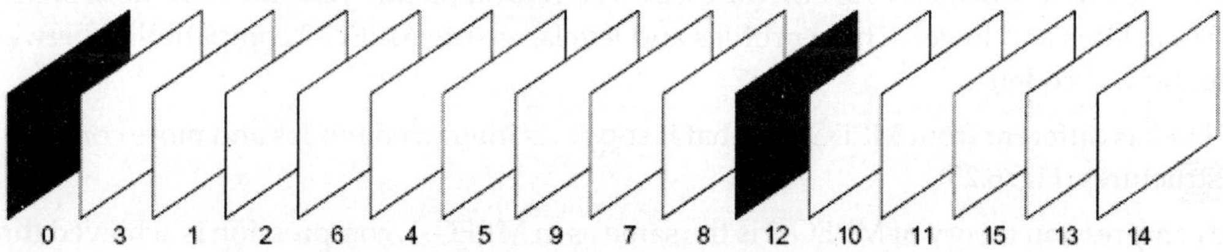

Fig. 6.24 *Typical sequence of pictures in transmission order.*

Spatial Compression

The spatial compression techniques are similar to those of JPEG, DCT, Quantization and entropy coding. The compression algorithm takes advantage of the redundancy within each block (8 × 8 Pixels).

The resulting compressed datastream is made up of a combination of spatial and temporal compression techniques which best suit the type of picture being compressed. Decoding is controlled through the use of MPEG system codes which are put into the data stream explaining how to reconstruct specific areas of picture - as shown in Fig. 6.19.

Through a combination of techniques, MPEG-1 compression is designed to give good quality (typically similar or better quality to VHS) images from such storage media as CD-ROM. The quality is however, dependent upon the type of picture compressed and the level of redundancy within the sequence coded. Picture quality will also depend upon how well the sequence has been coded and which features are required - For Example : For fast random access, N will tend towards zero hence the quality of compression will deteriorate, if random access is not required then the number of P and B frames can increase, hence increasing the potential quality. The standard does not specify a method of compression but a syntax for the compressed data, this allows for differing compression techniques depending upon differing requirements. The decoding techniques are defined due to the nature of the compressed data stream.

This method allows for true flexibility in coding whilst retaining the format and hierarchy ensuring compatibility in the datastream and hence uniform readability.

6.8.2.2 MPEG-2

MPEG-2 was developed in response to the growing need for a generic coding method of moving pictures and associated sound for various applications such as digital storage media and TV broadcasting. The key applications targetted by MPEG-2 are : CATV, DBS and DAB.

Within the standard, there are various "levels" and "profiles", these are essentially a set of constraints imposed on parameters of the bistream, it is not practical today to develop systems with the ability to decode pictures as large as 2E14 pixels wide by 2E14 lines high (these sizes are within the standard). The development of the profiles and levels allows constrained MPEG-2 compatible systems, the key levels and profiles in todays systems are : MAIN PROFILE@MAINLEVEL (MP@ML), MAINPROFILE@LOWLEVEL (MP@LL), SIMPLE PROFILE@MAIN LEVEL (SP@ML) and SIMPLE PROFILE@LOW LEVEL (SP@LL). The typical picture resolution of these images are $720 \times 576 \times 30$fps and lower. These profiles and levels, ensure MPEG-2 compatibility between all decoders and encoders.

MPEG-2 is different from MPEG-1 in that it supports interfaced modes and more complex sampling structures (Fig. 6.25).

The compression theory of MPEG-2 is the same as in MPEG-1, compression is achieved through the same techniques.

The inclusion of fields (*i.e.*, interlaced frames) in MPEG-2 means that the Prediction modes in MPEG-2 are far more complex than in MPEG-1, it is here where most of the differences lie.

Relevant MPEG-2 Modes are as follows :

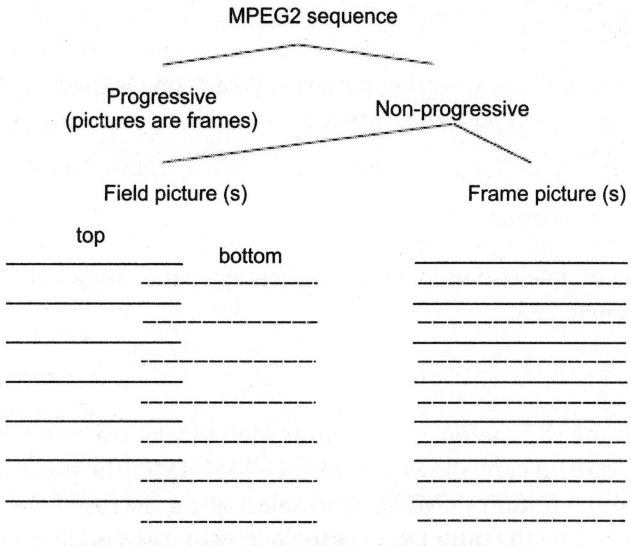

Fig. 6.25 *Frame pictures and field pictures.*

Field Prediction

With field prediction, the predictors in each field are independent. In a P frame picture with field prediction, the prediction is from two fields of the most recently decoded I- or P-frame. Picture prediction of a B- frame picture requires up to 4 vectors. The predictions for each field are formed by averaging the forward and backward predictors.

Dual-prime Prediction

This prediction mode is applicable to sequences in which there are no B-pictures. Only one vector, plus a small differential vector, is sent with every macroblock. All necessary vectors are derived from these.

Extended Motion Vector Range

In MPEG-1 the maximum motion vector range is – 1024 to 1023 for full-pel resolution, and – 512 to 511.5 for half-pel resolution. MPEG-2 specifies a maximum range of – 2048 to 2047.5 at half-pel resolution ; full-pel resolution is not defined. MPEG-2 specifies a vertical range of – 128 to 127.5 and horizontal range of – 1024 to 1023.5

Frame/Field DCT Coding

The luminance part of macroblock data may be reordered before the IDCT is performed on the blocks. The frame ordering is the same as that used in MPEG-1.

Concealment Motion Vectors

The option exits in MPG-2 to transmit motion vectors with intra macroblocks. This additional information is intended to be used when data is lost due to errors in the bitstream. In this case the lost macroblocks are reconstructed as if they were skipped macroblocks in a forward predicted field or frame. The motion vectors are those which have been stored by the decoder in the previous row of macroblocks.

Alternative Zig-Zag Scan

MPEG-2 allows two zig-zag block scanning patterns. Which one is used is specified in the picture layer of the bistream. The second pattern is intended to maximise the run lengths of blocks containing data from a single field.

Increased DCT Coefficient Precision

MPEG-2 decoders must be able to handle DCT coefficients in the range – 2047 to 2048 (12 bits). The range in MPEG-1 is – 256 to 255.

Alternative Intra VLCs

The precision to which the DC coefficients of intracoded blocks are coded can be changed every picture. Values of 8, 9 or 10 bits are allowed in MPEG-2 MP@ML (the precision is fixed at 8 bits in MPEG-1). There is also the option in MPEG-2 to select at the picture layer an alternative, more efficient, VLC table for coding the intra DCT coefficients. This selection is independent of the intra DC precision selection.

Non-Linear Quantizer Scale Mapping

Two mappings are defined between the 5-bit quantizer scale code transmitted in the bistream and the actual quantizer scale. The first mapping is linear, as in MPEG-1. The alternative mapping is non-linear and is designed to give a finer control of quantizer scale when the values are low. Which mapping is used is defined at the picture layer of the bistream.

Alternative IDCT Mismatch Control

The coefficients at the input to the IDCT are modified in order to avoid certain patterns of data.

This operation reduces the mismatch of outputs between different IDCT implementations, specifically in the encoder and decoder. In MPEG-1 the dequantized AC coefficients are forced to be odd before saturation. In MPEG-2 all of the coefficients of a block are summed after the saturation stage. If this sum even, the last coefficient is changed by 1.

Pan-Scan

Information is transmitted in the bistream which defines the dimensions and location of the displayable region within the encoded picture. The position of this window can be changed every field. This feature is useful, for example, when displaying part of a 16/9-format coded picture on a 4/3-format display. The MPEG-2 standard does not specify what should be done with this information, since it affects the display and not the decoding process.

6.8.3 GIF-Graphic Interchange Format Compression

- GIF uses basic form of file compression (Lempel Zev Welch, or LZW) that squeezes out inefficiencies in the data storage without losing data or distorting the image, basically limiting the color palette to 256 or less colors depending on the image and settings.

- The LZW compression scheme is best at compressing images with large fields of homogeneous color.
- It is less efficient at compressing complicated pictures with many colors and complex textures.

Improving GIF Compression

- The strategy is to reduce the number of colors in your GIF image to the minimum number necessary and to remove stray colors that are not required to represent the image.
- A GIF graphic cannot have more than 256 colors but it can have fewer colors, down to the minimum of two (black and white).
- Images with fewer colors will compress more efficiently under LZW compression.

Interlaced GIF

- The conventional (non-interlaced) GIF graphic downloads one line of pixels at a time from top to bottom, and browsers display each line of the image as it gradually builds on the screen.
- In interlaced GIF files the image data is stored in a format that allows browsers that support interlaced GIFs to begin to build a low-resolution version of the full-sized GIF picture on the screen while the file is downloading.
- "fuzzy-to-sharp" animated effect of interlacing is visually appealing.
- most important benefit of interlacing is that it gives the reader a preview of the full area of the picture while the picture downloads into the browser.
- Interlacing is best for larger GIF images
- Interlacing is a poor choice for small GIF graphics such as navigation bars, buttons, and icons.
- Small graphics will load onto the screen much faster if you keep them in conventional (non-interlaced) GIF format.
- Interlacing has no significant effect on the file size of GIF graphics.

Transparent GIF

- Unlike JPEGs GIFs support transparency.
- Transparency works best with simple diagrammatic graphics.

Animated GIF

- The GIF file format allows you to combine multiple GIF images into a single file to create animation.
- There are a number of drawbacks to this functionality.
- The GIF format applies no compression between frames, so if you are combining four 30-kilobyte images into a single animation, you will end up with a 120 KB GIF file.
- The load is lightened somewhat by the fact that animated GIF files stream to the user, so the frames load and play even before the entire file is downloaded.
- Another drawback of GIF animations is that they are an imposition and a potential distraction.
- There are no interface controls for this file format, GIF animations play whether you want them to or not.

- If looping is enabled, the animations play again and again and again.
- GIF animations are rarely used in a meaningful way, and generally distract readers from the main content of the page.
- If you are using GIF animation as content—to illustrate a concept or technique where animation is really required—use the technique sparingly.

Summary

1. Image compression stands for compression of image by reducing (removing) redundant information from image.
2. The purpose of image compression is to reduce the storage space and requirement of bandwidth for transmission of image.
3. Redundancy can be off three types—coding redundancy, inter-pixel redundancy 'and' psychovisual redundancy.
4. There are two types of compression strategies :
   (*a*) lossless (error free) compression (*b*) lossy (error) compression.
   Lossy compression technique provides more compression in comparison to lossless compression.
5. Lossless compression techniques are run length coding, variable length coding, LZW coding and lossless predictive coding.
6. Lossy compression techniques are lossy predictive coding, transform coding and wavelet coding.
7. Lossless coding is applied to those data in which we need accuracy such as executable codes. Lossy coding is applied where loss in tolerable - such as image.
8. These are different compression standard such as JPEG (Joint Photographers Expert Group), MPEG (Moving Picture Expert Group) and GFF (Graphic Interchange Format).

Review Questions

1. What do you understand by image compression ? What is Redundant data ?
2. What do you understand by image data redundancy ?
3. Draw the image compression model and describe the work of each block.
4. Write short notes on :
   (*a*) Variable length coding ; and
   (*b*) LZW coding.
5. Write short notes on :
   (*a*) Lossy predictive coding ; and
   (*b*) Lossless predictive coding and compare both.
6. Describe :
   (*a*) JPEG (*b*) MPEG.
7. What is the compression technique used in JPEG ; explain ?

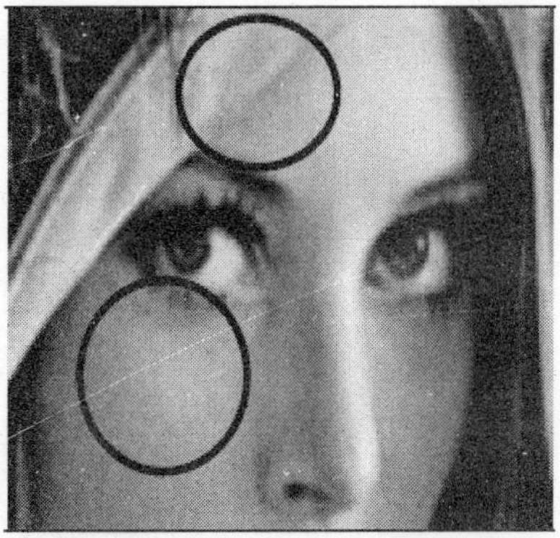

Original Image (769 KB)

.gif (127 KB)

.gif (98 KB)

JPEG (342 KB)

JPEG (55 KB)

Test Image 6.1 *Image compressed by different standards (Compare the circled areas for comparison)*

CHAPTER 7

MORPHOLOGICAL IMAGE PROCESSING

7.1 INTRODUCTION

Morphological basically is a biological word that stands for structure and forms of animals and plant that is always useful for representation and basic information about animals and plants.

"In the field of image processing mathematical morphology is a tool that is useful for representation and description of region shapes such as boundary, skeletons and the convex hull".

The roots of morphology are in set theory. Here we are concern with binary images only. Then a set of black pixels ('or' only set of white pixels also) in a binary image is a complete morphological description of the image. In binary images, the sets are called the members of 2-D integer space z^2 where each element of a set is a tuple (2-D vector). So before starting the morphological image processing, let us discuss about the basics of set theory.

7.2 BASIC CONCEPT OF SET THEORY

1. Let A be a set in z^2. If $a = (a_1, a_2)$ is a element of A, then we write

$$a \in A \qquad \text{... (7.1)}$$

2. Similarly, if a is not an element of A, we write

$$a \notin A \qquad \text{... (7.2)}$$

3. The set with no elements is called the null 'or' empty set and is denoted by the symbol ϕ.
4. If we write the expression

$$C = \{w \mid w = -d, \text{ for } d \in D\} \qquad \text{... (7.3)}$$

We means that set 'C' is the set of elements, w, such that 'w' is formed by multiplying each of the two co-ordinates of all elements of set 'D' by – 1.

5. If every element of set 'A' is also an element of another set 'B', then A is said to be a subset of 'B'. It is denoted by

$$A \subseteq B \qquad \text{... (7.4)}$$

6. The union of two sets 'A' and 'B' is denoted by

$$C = A \cup B \qquad \text{... (7.5)}$$

It means new set 'C' will have all the elements of set A and set B.

7. The intersection of two sets 'A' and 'B' is represented by

$$C = A \cap B \qquad \text{... (7.6)}$$

Thus set 'C' will have all the elements that are common in set 'A' and set 'B'.

8. Two sets 'A' and 'B' are called mutually exclusive, if both do not have any common element. It can be represented by

$$A \cap B = \phi \qquad \text{... (7.7)}$$

9. The complement of a set 'A' is the set of elements that should not be in 'A'.

$$A^C = \{w \mid w \notin A\} \qquad \text{... (7.8)}$$

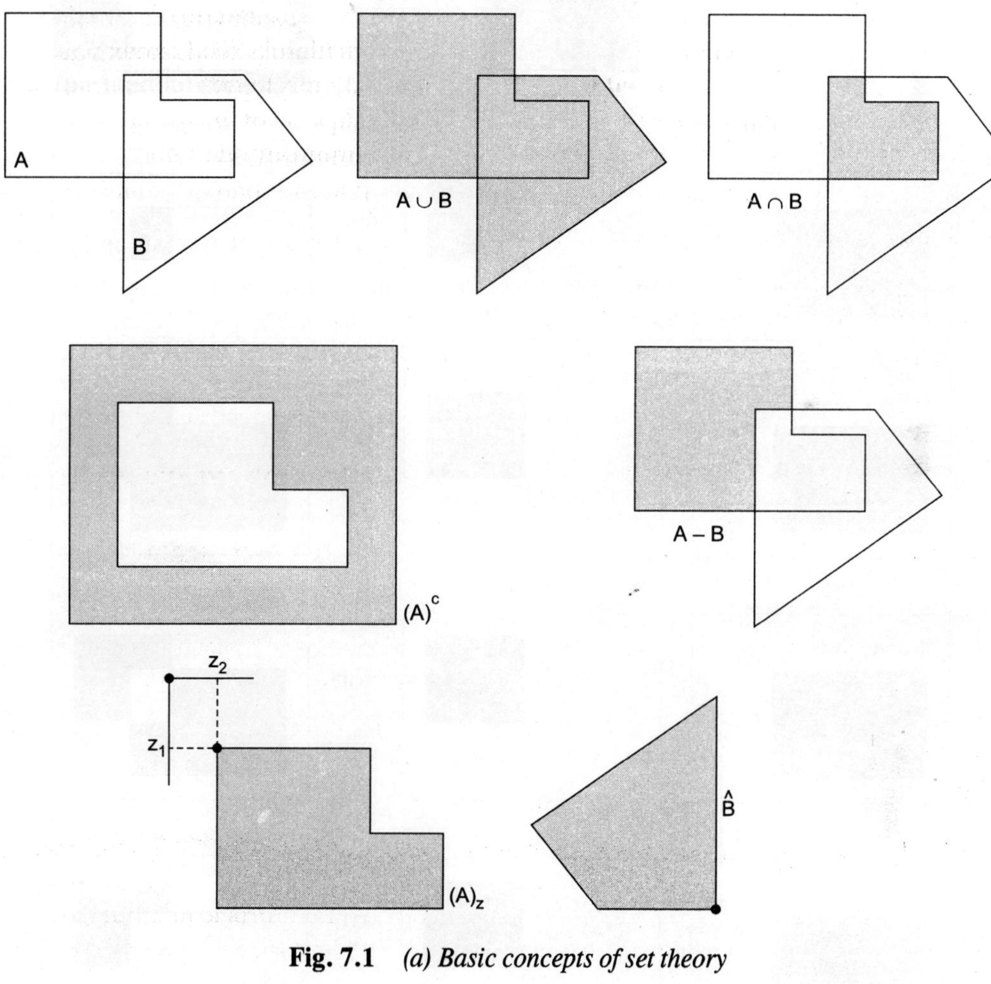

Fig. 7.1 *(a) Basic concepts of set theory*

10. The difference of two sets A and B is denoted by A – B. It is defined by

$$A - B = \{w \mid w \in A, w \notin B\} = (A \cap B)^C \quad \dots (7.9)$$

The difference set belongs to A, it means it may have the elements of 'A' but can not have the elements of 'B'.

11. The reflection of set B can be represented by $\hat{B}$. It is defined by

$$\hat{B} = \{w \mid w = -b \text{ for } b \in B\} \quad \dots (7.10)$$

12. The translation of set 'A' by point $z = \{z_1, z_2\}$ is denoted by $(A)_z$. It is defined as

$$(A)_z = \{c \mid c = a + z, \text{ for } a \in A\} \quad \dots (7.11)$$

All the set theory laws discussed till now have been drawn in figure 7.1 also.

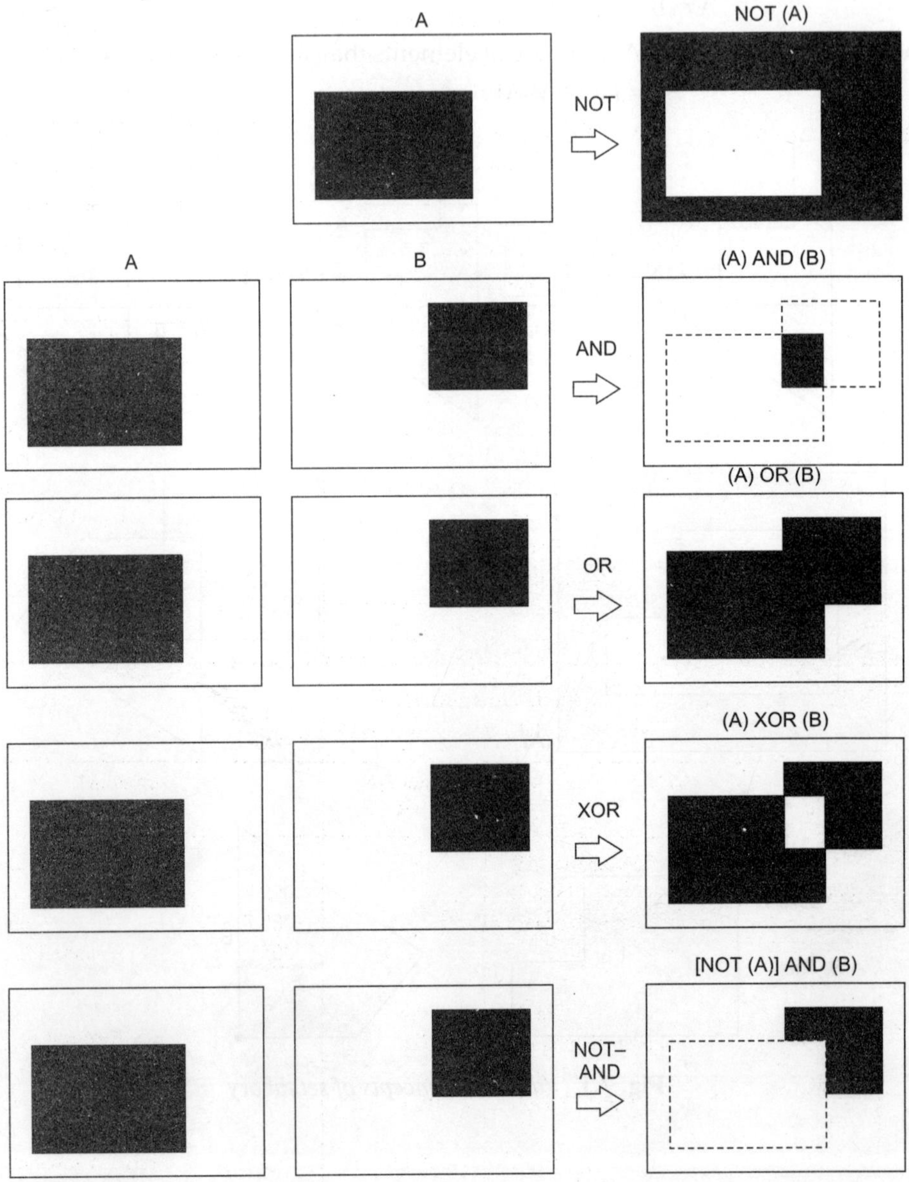

Fig. 7.1 *(b) Basic Logical Function*

7.3 LOGIC OPERATIONS INVOLVING BINARY IMAGES

Before applying different logic operations of binary on binary image, we just revise the important logic operations in the form of table as given below :

Table No. 7.1 *Logical Operation*

A	B	Not A $(\overline{A})$	A AND B (A . B)	A OR B (A + B)	AX – ORB A ⊕ B
0	0	1	0	0	0
0	1	1	0	1	1
1	0	0	0	1	1
1	1	0	1	1	0

Here student should remember that by using AND, 'OR' and 'NOT' we can implement further different logics. For example,

$$\text{A X–NOR B } (A \odot B) = \text{NOT } [A \oplus B] \quad \text{... (7.12)}$$

All the operations have been shown by figures. Here black indicates that the binary image pixel is '1' and white indicates that the binary image pixel is '0'.

By figure it should be clear that

1. A ANB B (A . B) and $A \cap B$ can be used interchangeably.
2. A or B (A + B) and $A \cup B$ can be used interchangeably.

   If students remember, these functions have been already been discussed in Chapter 2.

7.4 DILATION AND EROSION

Dilation and Erosion are the fundamentals of morphological processing. Let us discuss them in detail.

7.4.1 Dilation

With A and B as sets in z^2 (means binary image) ; the dilation of A by B, denoted by $A \oplus B$, is defined as

$$A \oplus B = \left\{ z \mid (\hat{B})_z \cap A \neq \phi \right\} \quad \text{... (7.13)}$$

Equation shows that *"first of all obtain reflection of B about origin and then shift this reflection by z. Then dilation of A by B is set of all displacements z such that $\hat{B}$ and A overlap by at least one element"*. Thus based on above interpretation equation can be rewritten in the form

$$A \oplus B = \left\{ z \mid \left[(\hat{B})_z \cap B \right] \subseteq A \right\} \quad \text{... (7.14)}$$

Set 'B' is referred as structuring element.

Here Fig. 7.2 (*a*) shows the simple set, A and the structuring element B. The Black dot denotes the origin of the element.

As the structuring element 'B' is symmetric with reference to its origin, the reflection of 'B' is same as B itself. The dashed line shows the reference and solid line shows the limit beyond which further displacements of the origin of $\hat{B}$ by z will cause the $\left\{ (\hat{B})_z \cap A \right\}$ = Null (that is not desirable condition).

Thus, all points inside the boundary shows the dilation of A by B. Next figure 7.2 (*b*) shows the next example of dilation of A by B.

Application of dilation is for bridging gaps of character due to poor resolution. Example has been shown in Fig. 7.2 (*b*).

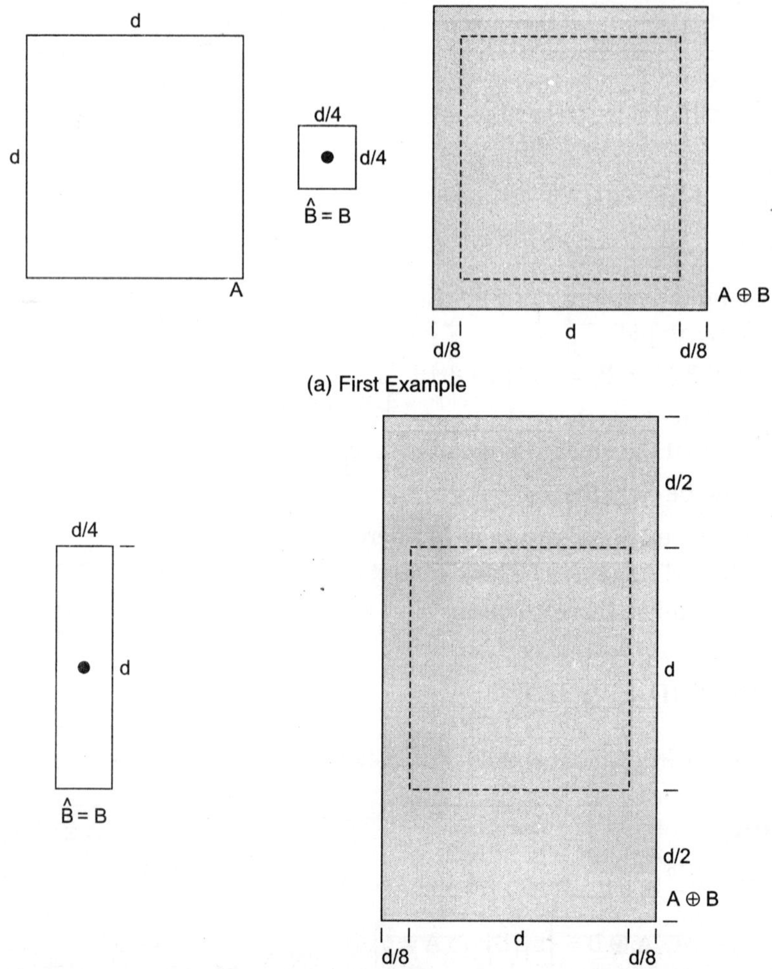

(a) First Example

(b) Second Example

Fig. 7.2 *Dilation Process.*

7.4.2 Erosion

For sets A and B in z^2 (means binary image) the erosion of A by B, denoted by A ⊖ B, is defined as

$$A \ominus B = \{z \mid (B)_z \subseteq A\} \quad \text{... (7.15)}$$

Equation shows that "*the erosion of A by B is set of all points z such that B, shifted by z is contained in A*".

Again we can discuss the same examples in Fig. 7.3 (*a*) as in case of dilation. Again dashed line shows the reference. The boundary of the shaded region shows the limit beyond which further displacement of origin of B will cause the condition that will not satisfy the desired condition. Next figure 7.3 (*b*) shows the next example of erosion.

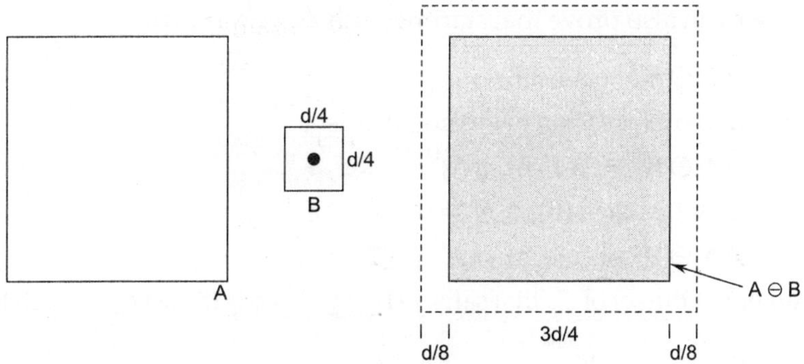

(a) First Example

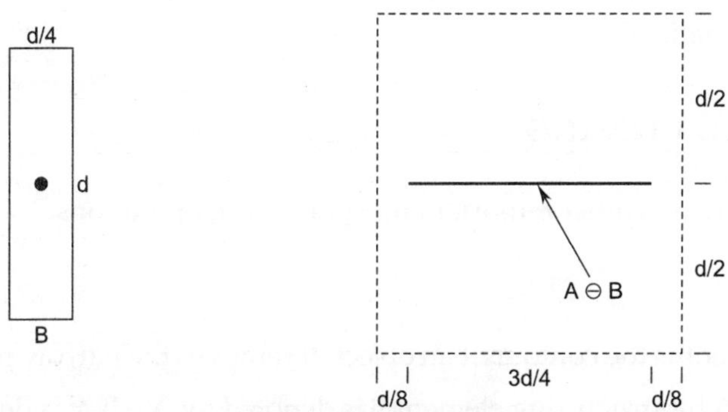

(b) Second Example

Fig. 7.3 *Erosion.*

The main application of erosion is for eliminating irrelevant size detail from an binary image suppose that we have the following example in which we have an binary image that has squares of size 1, 3, 5, 7, 9 and 15 pixels on the side. Now we want to remove all the squares except the largest one (that is of size 15-pixels). So now for erosion, just choose the structuring element of size bigger than the squares we want to eliminate and smaller than the squares we want to save. Just for our example justified size is 13. Thus, we choose the structuring element of size 13 × 13 pixels. After erosion, the result has been shown in Fig. 7.4 (*b*).

Fig. 7.4 *Application of Erosion.*

7.4.3 Relation Between Dilation and Erosion

By examples and discussion it should be cleared that *"dilation and erosion are dual with respect to set complementation and reflection to each other. Dilation expands an image and erosion shrinks the image"*.

Mathematically we can also prove that starting with

$$(A \ominus B)^C = A^C \oplus \hat{B} \qquad \text{... (7.16)}$$

to prove that start with the expression of erosion that is

$$(A \ominus B)^C = \{z \mid (B)_z \subseteq A\}^C \qquad \text{... (7.17)}$$

If $(B)_z$ is contained in set A, then $(B)_z \cap A^C = \phi$, then

$$(A \ominus B)^C = \{z \mid (B)_z \cap A^C = \phi\}^C \qquad \text{... (7.18)}$$

But the complement of the set of z's that satisfy $(B_z) \cap A^C = \phi$ is the set of z's such that $(B)_z \cap A^C \neq \phi$. Thus,

$$(A \ominus B)^C = \{z \mid (B)_z \cap A^C \neq \phi\} = A^C \oplus \hat{B} \qquad \text{... (7.19)}$$

That is the proved relation.

7.5 OPENING AND CLOSING

Opening and closing are two other important morphological operations.

7.5.1 Opening

Opening generally smooths the contour of an object. It removes the narrow peaks of image.

The opening of set A by structuring element B is denoted by A o B. It is defined by the following equation

$$A \circ B = (A \ominus B) \oplus B \qquad \text{... (7.20)}$$

Thus, the "*opening A by B is the erosion of A by B, followed by a dilation of the result by B*".

Equation can be written in another form also, according to that

$$A \circ B = \cup \{(B)_z \mid (B)_z \subseteq A\} \qquad \text{... (7.21)}$$

Where U {.} denotes the union of all the sets inside the braces. Equation states that the opening of A by B is obtained by taking the union of all translates of B that fits into A.

By this second equation, the geometrical interpretation of opening operation can easily be described. We can view structuring element '*B*' as a flat '*rolling ball*'. The boundary of A o B is then established by the points in B that reaches the farthest into the boundary of A as B is rolled around the inside of this boundary. The operation has been shown below in Fig. (7.5).

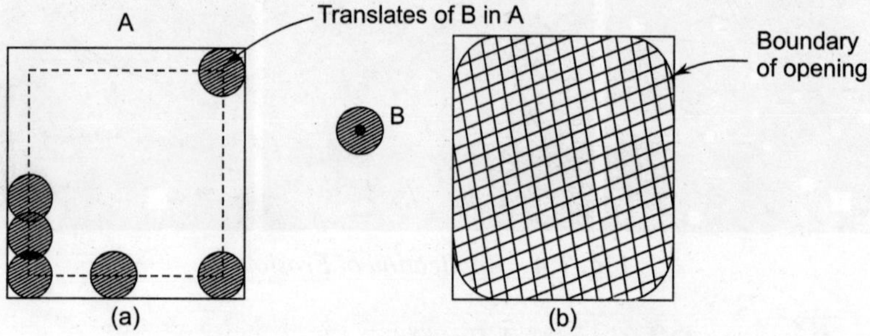

(a) Structuring element 'B' inside the inner boundary of 'A'.
(b) Complete opening.

Fig. 7.5 *Opening Process.*

7.5.2 Closing

Closing also tends to smooth sections of contours. But opposite to opening, it generally fuses narrow breaks and long thin gulfs. It eliminates small holes and fills gaps in contour.

Closing of set 'A' by structuring element 'B' is denoted by $A \bullet B$. It is given by the following formula:

$$A \bullet B = (A \oplus B) \ominus B \quad \text{... (7.22)}$$

So we can say the *"closing of A by B is simply dilation of A by B followed by the erosion of the result by B. Again"* just like dilation and erosion ; opening and closing are duals of each other with respect to set complementation and reflection. Thus, geometric representation of closing is same as opening. But now the structuring element is rolled outside boundary of A. The process has been drawn below

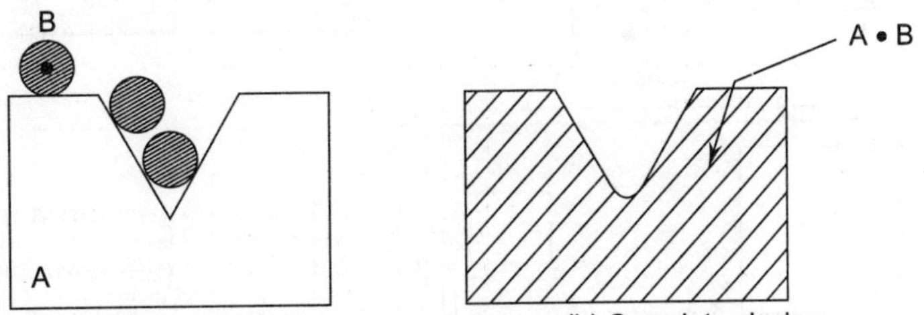

(a) Structuring element rolling on the outer boundary of A

(b) Complete closing

Fig. 7.6 *Closing process*

7.5.3 Relation between Opening and Closing

"As stated earlier that opening and closing are duals of each other with respect to set complementation and reflection". That is

$$(A \bullet B)^C = (A^C \circ \hat{B}) \quad \text{... (7.23)}$$

7.6 HIT-OR-MISS TRANSFORMATION

It is a basic tool that is used for shape detection. If you remember the example of erosion in which we have a binary image that contains a squares of shape 1, 3, 5, 7, 9 and 15 and we have to remove the squares of size 1, 3, 5, 7 and 9 pixels and only we went the square of 15-pixel size to be there. Then we have used a structuring element of size 13 × 13 pixel. Just by this example, we can say that by erosion also we can detect a particular shape. But in erosion, we detect shape without considering the background matches. Now we will use the hit-or-miss transformation for finding a particular location of shape with the consideration of background also.

Let us suppose that we have a set 'A' that has three shapes ('or' subsets) denoted by X, Y and Z. Our objective is to find the location of shape X.

To find the location of shape 'X' we may use the erosion as discussed above ; so we may apply the following expression :

$$A * B = (A \ominus B_1) \cap (A^C \ominus B_2) \quad \text{... (7.24)}$$

where $\otimes$ represents the hit - or - miss transformation.

Here $(A \ominus B_1)$ = simply represents the erosion of A with object itself to find the location of X so $B_1 = X$.

$$(A \ominus B_1) = (A \ominus X) \quad \text{... (7.25)}$$

Without considering the background.

But if we want to consider the background also then, in stead of A ; we have to consider A^C. Simultaneously we have to use a window that encloses the 'X' for showing the local background of 'X' itself. Then local background of X = $(w - X) = B_2$ and total background of 'A' can be given by (w.r.t. X) = $A^C \ominus B_2$. The whole process has been shown in Figure (7.7) given.

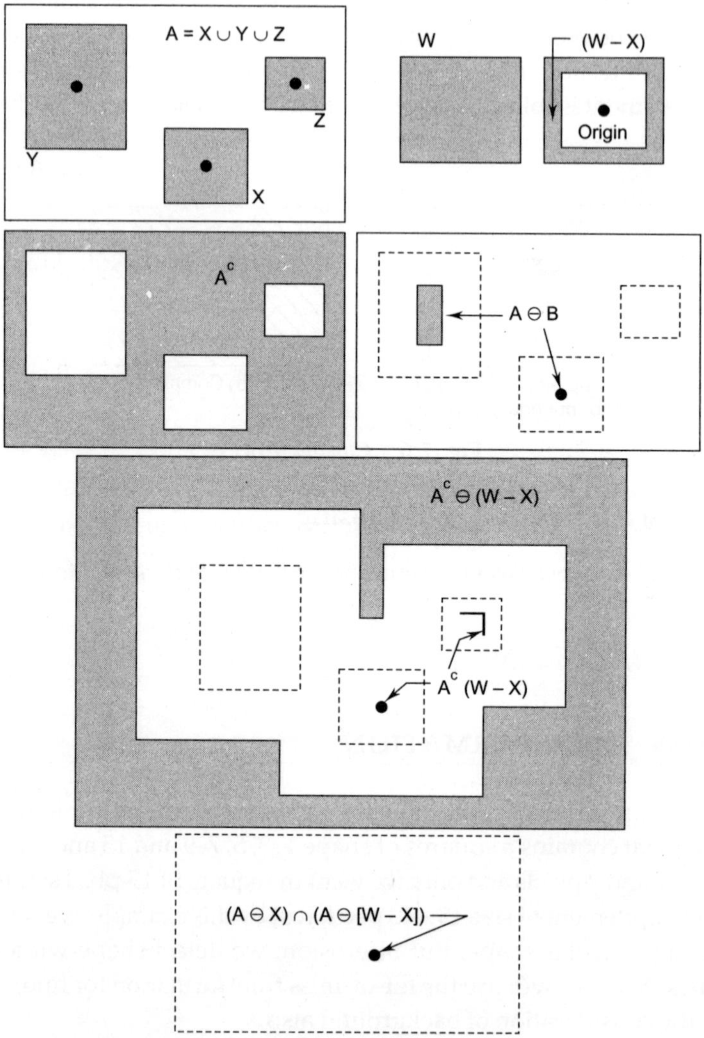

Fig. 7.7 *Hit 'or' Miss Transformation.*

7.7 BASIC MORPHOLOGICAL ALGORITHM

At the beginning of chapter itself, it has been cleared that the basic use of morphological processing in the field of image processing is to extract the image components that are useful for image representation and description. So now we will study the morphological algorithms that are useful for extracting image components such as boundaries, connected components, the convex hull and skeleton of a region.

7.7.1 Boundary Extraction

The boundary of A is denoted by β (A). It can be obtained by first eroding 'A' by 'B' and then performing the set difference between A and its erosion. That is

$$\beta(A) = A - (A \ominus B) \quad \text{... (7.26)}$$

Where B is a suitable structuring element.

The figure 7.8 shows the process of boundary extraction.

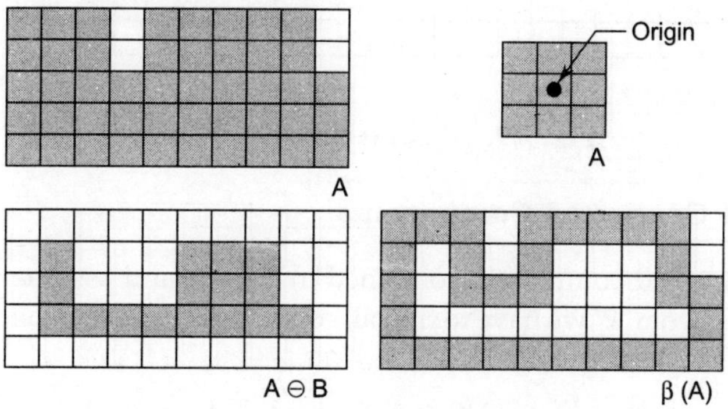

Fig. 7.8 *Process of boundary extraction.*

7.7.2 Region Filling

This algorithm is used for region filling. Here we use the dilation, complementation and intersections. Here if we see the given figure ; A denotes a set containing a subset. Here we begin with a point P inside the boundary and now we will fill entire region with 1's. The process can be represented by

$$X_k = (X_{k-1} \oplus B) \cap A^C, k = 1, 2, 3, \quad \text{.... (7.27)}$$

where X_0 = P and B is symmetrical structuring element as shown in Fig. 7.9.

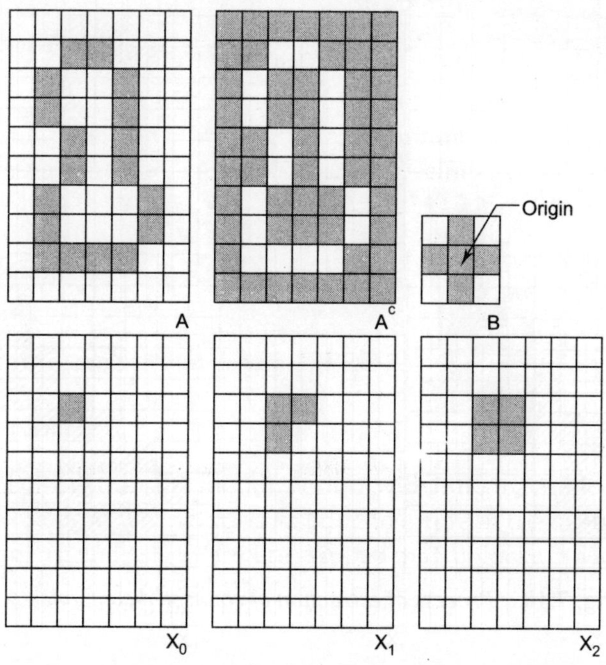

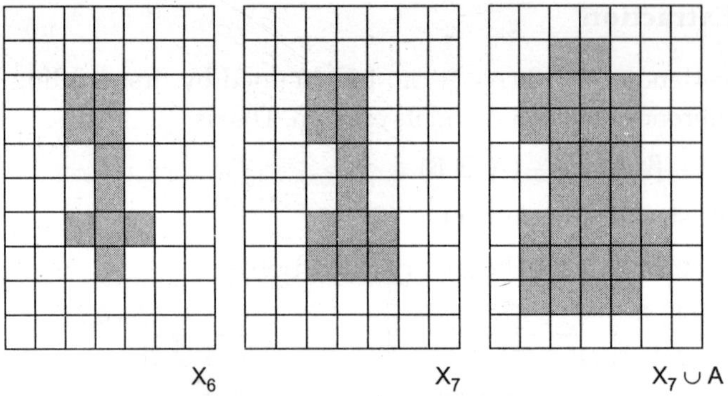

Fig. 7.9. *Process of region filling.*

7.7.3 Extraction of Connected Components

Let Y represents a connected component contained in a set A and assume that a point P of Y is known. Now by starting from 'P' we have to find all component 'Y'. Then following expression will find the elements of Y.

$$X_k = (X_{k-1} \oplus B) \cap A \qquad k = 1, 2, 3, \qquad \text{... (7.28)}$$

where X = P and B is a suitable structuring element. We see that equation is same as used for region filling but now in stead of A^C, we have used A. Figure 7.10 given below shows the whole process.

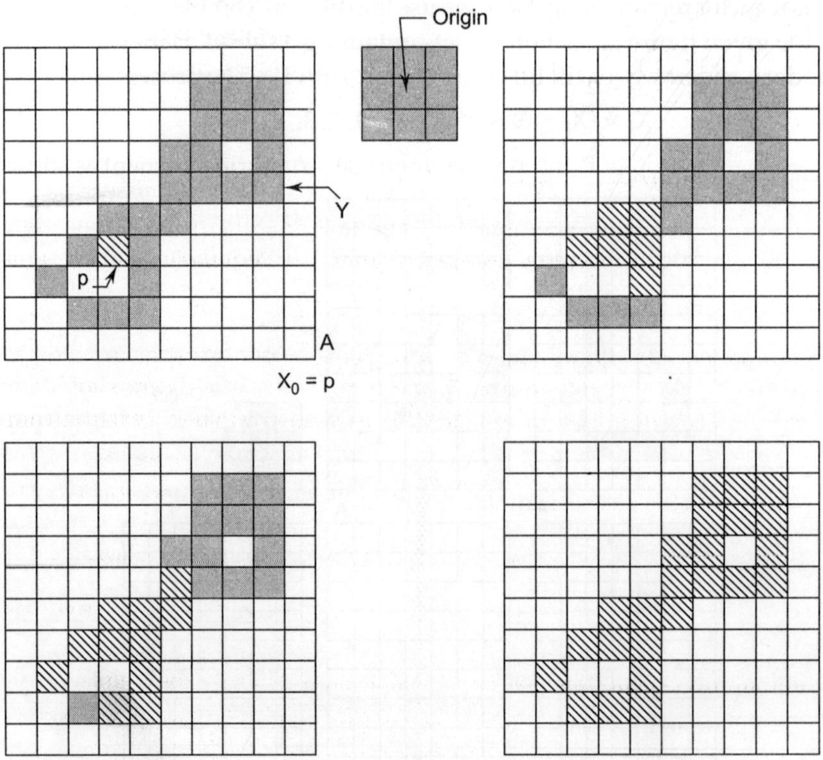

Fig. 7.10 *Process of extraction of connected components.*

7.7.4 Convex Hull

A set 'A' is said to be convex if the straight line segment joining any two points in A lies entirely within A. The convex hull H of an arbitrary set 'S' is the smallest convex set containing 'S'. Now we will discuss a simple morphological algorithm for obtaining the convex hull C (A) of a set A.

Let B^i, where $i = 1, 2, 3, 4$ represents the four structuring elements in Fig. 7.11. The procedure consists of implementing the equation :

$$X_k^i = (X_{k-1} * B^i) \cup A \qquad \text{... (7.29)}$$

where $\quad i = 1, 2, 3, 4$ and $k = 1, 2, 3, \ldots$

& $\quad X_o^i = A.$

Now let $D^i = X^i_{\text{conv}}$, where subscript *"conv"* indicates convergence in the sense that $X_k^i = X_{k-1}^i$, then convex Hull of A is

$$C(A) = \bigcup_{i=1}^{4} D^i \qquad \text{... (7.30)}$$

Inwords,

1. Simply apply hit-'or'-miss transform to A with B^1 as

   $$k = 1 \,;\, X_1^i = (X_0 * B^i) \cup A$$

   for $\quad i = 1 \,;\, X_1^1 = (X_0 * B^1) \cup A$

   and then perform union with A and call the result D^1.
2. Again repeat (1) with B^2 and call the result D^2.
3. By same process ; calculate D^3 and D^4,.
4. After calculating D^1, D^2, D^3 and D^4 ; calculate the union of D^1, D^2, D^3 and D^4. That will be convex hull.

The given shows the whole process as discussed. Here one thing should be considered that X shows don't care. This means that a structuring element is said to have found a match in A if the 3-by-3 region of A under the structuring element mask at that location matches the pattern of the mask.

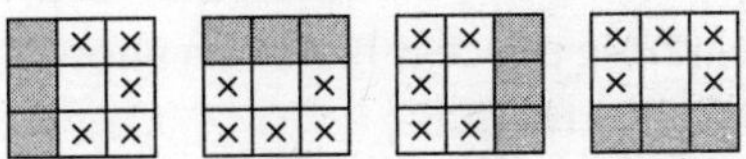

$B^1 \quad B^2 \quad B^3 \quad B^4$

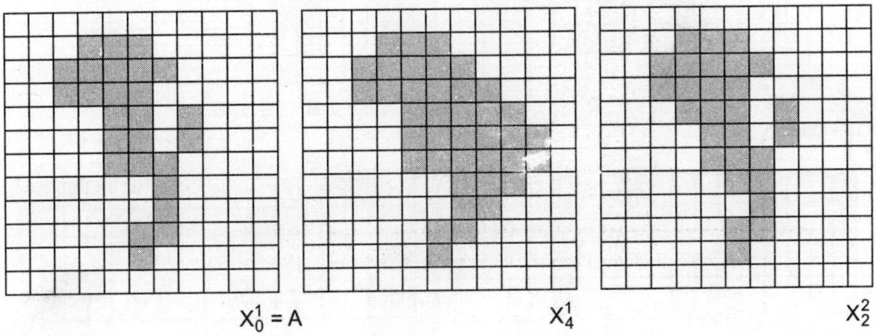

$X_0^1 = A \qquad X_4^1 \qquad X_2^2$

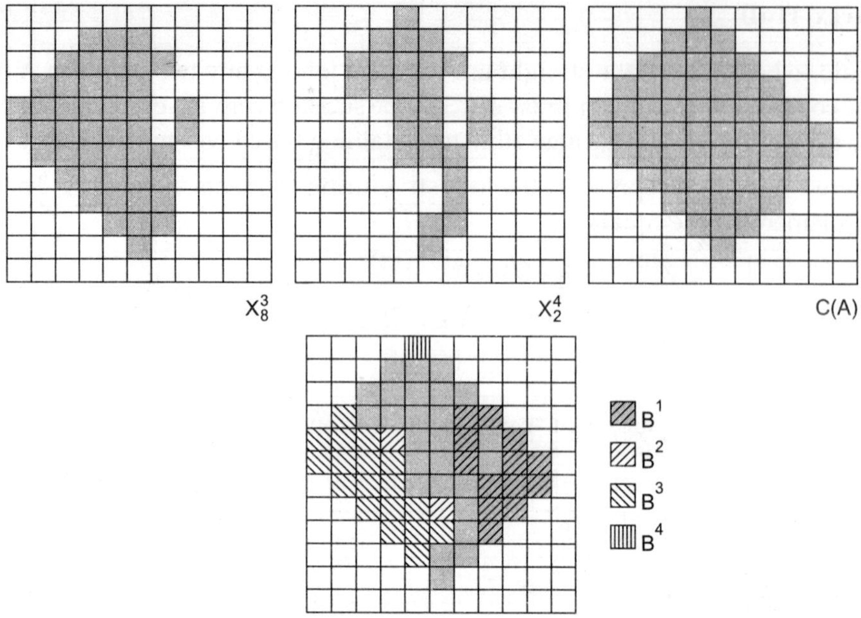

Fig. 7.11 *Process of convex null.*

7.7.5 Thinning

The thinning of a set 'A' by a structuring element is denoted by $A \otimes B$. It is given in form of hit or miss transform that is

$$A \otimes B = A - (A * B)$$
$$= A \cap (A * B)^C \qquad \text{... (7.31)}$$

A more useful expression for thinning A symmetrically is based on a sequence of structuring elements:

$$\{B\} = \{B^1, B^2, B^3, \ldots\ldots, B^n\} \qquad \text{... (7.32)}$$

Where B^i is the rotated version of B^{i-1}. Now by using this concept again,

$$A \otimes \{B\} = ((\ldots\ldots((A \otimes B^1) \otimes B^2) \ldots) \otimes B^n) \qquad \text{... (7.33)}$$

The process is to thin A by one pass with B^1, then thin this result with one pass B^2 and so on until A is thinned with one pass B^n. The whole process has been shown in Fig. 7.12. Here thinning starts with B^1 and goes on till the thinning occurs to B^8.

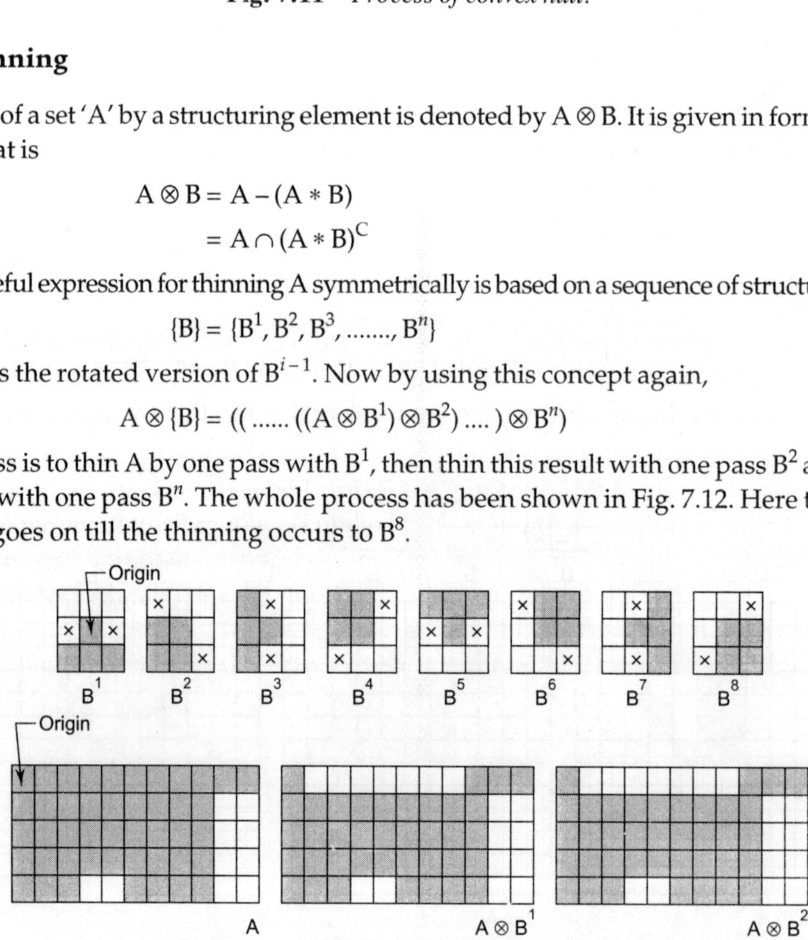

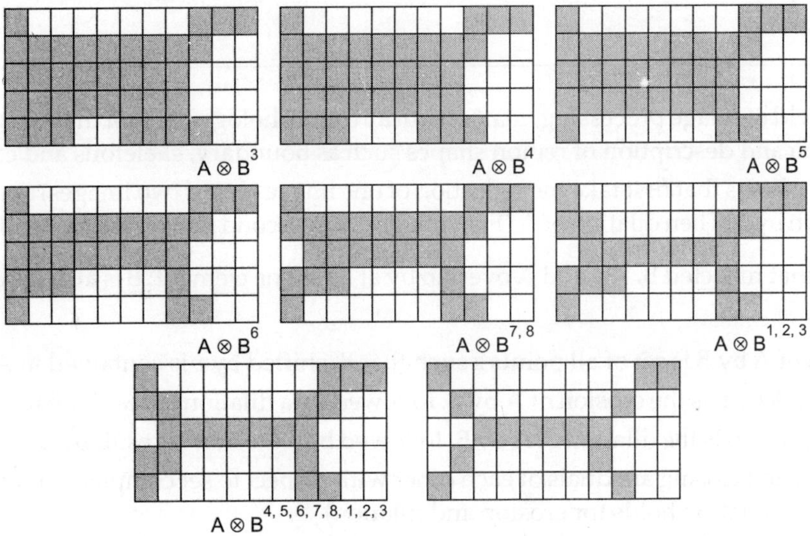

Fig. 7.12 *Process of thinning.*

7.7.6 Thickening

Simply the thickening process is dual to that of thinning. It is defined by the expression :-

$$A \odot B = A \cup (A * B) \qquad \text{... (7.34)}$$

As in thinning ; thickening can be defined as a sequential operation

$$A \odot \{B\} = ((...... ((A \odot B^1) \odot B^2 ...) \odot B^n) \qquad \text{... (7.35)}$$

The structuring element is same as used for thinning process. But now, '1' is replaced by '0' and '0' is replaced by '1'. The whole process has been shown in Figure 7.13 given below :

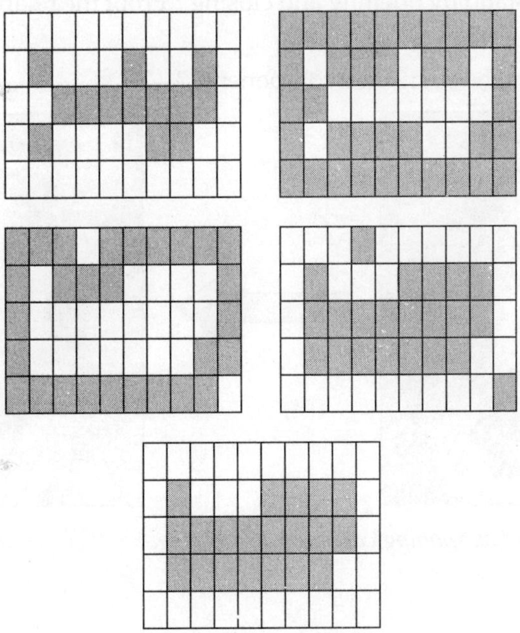

Fig. 7.13 *Process of thickening.*

Summary

1. In the field of image processing, mathematically morphology is a tool that is useful for representation and description of region shapes such as boundary, skeletons and convex hull.
2. Dilation shows that first take the reflection of one image (out of two images) and then shift his reflection by Z. Then dilation of A (First image) by B (second image) is a set of all displacement Z such that reflected B. $(\hat{B})$ and A overlap by at least one element. B is also called structuring element.
3. Erosion of A by B is set of all points z such that B, shifted by z is contained in A.
4. Opening A by B is the erosion of A by B, followed by a dilation of result by B.
5. Closing A by B is the dilation of A by B, followed by a erosion of result by B.
6. Opening and closing are duals of each other with respect to set complementation and reflection (same relation holds for erosion and dilation)
7. Hit 'or' Miss is a general tool used for shape detection.
8. Basic morphological algorithms are boundary extraction, Region filling, extraction of connected components, convex hull, thinning, thickening. All these are based on basic functions of morphological image processing.

Review Questions

1. What do you understand by morphological image processing ?
2. What do you understand by dilation and erosion ? Proof the relation between them.
3. What do you understand by opening and closing ? Proof the relation between them.
4. Describe thinning and thickening.
5. How may you extract the connected components ?

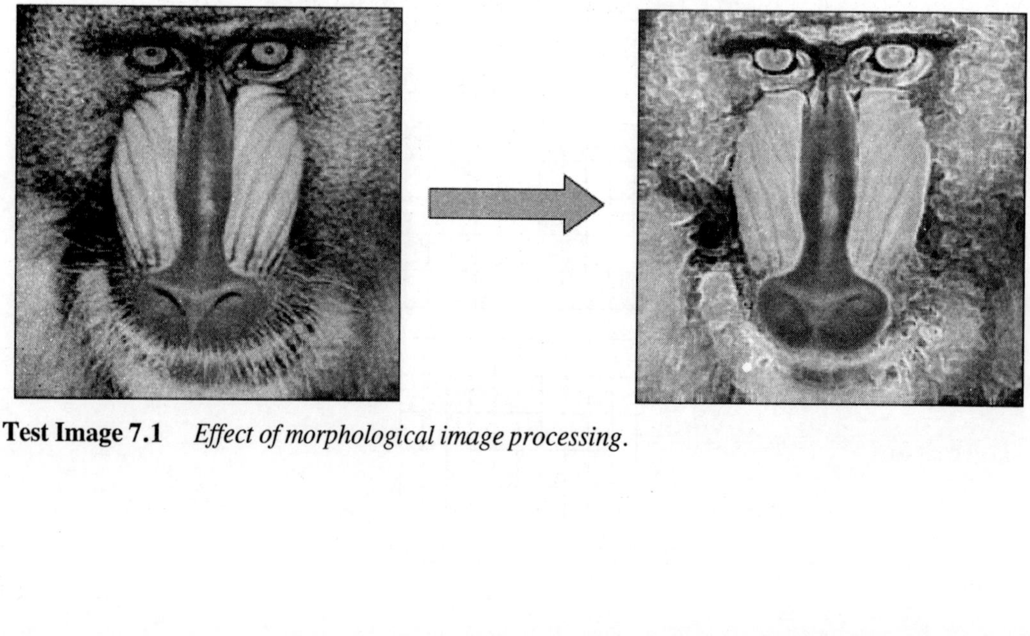

Test Image 7.1 *Effect of morphological image processing.*

8

CHAPTER

IMAGE REGISTRATION

8.1 INTRODUCTION

A problem of aligning two or more different images of the same scene, acquired from different viewpoints, at different times and/or with different kind of imaging sensors, arises frequently in many research areas dealing with image processing or analysis.

"The process of aligning the images and compensating for the differences caused by different acquisition conditions is called image registration". An example of registering two images taken from different viewpoints is presented in Fig. 8.1.

(a) (b) (c)

Fig. 8.1 *Image registration of reference (a) and sensed image (b) using similarity transform. Registration result (c) shows sensed image overlaid over reference image after applying the resulting similarity transform.*

Image registration algorithms appear in every image analysis task where additional information is required and gained from combination of various image data sources. Image registration is heavily used in remote sensing, computer vision and medical imaging research areas.

8.2 IMAGE REGISTRATION IN THEORY

8.2.1 Definition

"Image registration can be defined as determination of one-to-one mapping between the coordinates in one image space and those in another, such that points in two image spaces that correspond to the same scene point

are mapped to each other". In case of image to scene registration, image coordinates are mapped to the corresponding points in the scene.

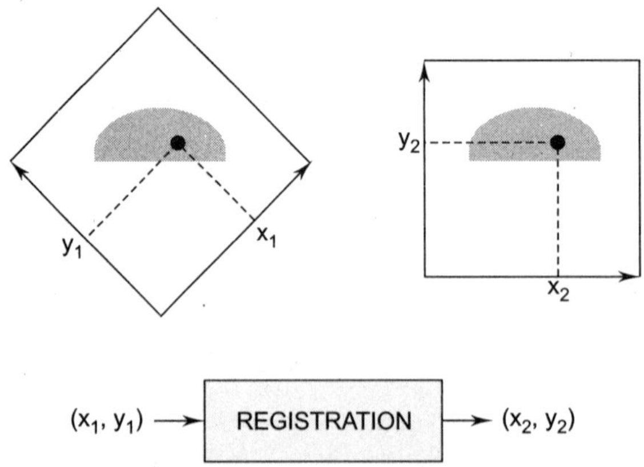

Fig. 8.2 *Image registration*

Thus the registration problem is to find the optimal spatial transformation that matches the images, either for the purpose of determining the parameters of matching transformation or to expose the differences between the images.

An example of 2D image registration is presented in Fig. 8.2 where two images of the same object are presented, image 1, frequently called the sensed image, with spatial coordinates x_1,y_1 and image 2, the reference image, with coordinates x_2,y_2. The images differ in two obvious ways. The orientation of the object is different in the two images and a part of the object is missing in image 2. Image 1 has been rotated so that the object appears in the same orientation in both images in order to emphasize the difference in orientation of image spaces relative to the object. The images are obviously taken from different viewpoints. The difference in shape could be the result of object deformation through time, in case the images are acquired at different times, or the result of different physical properties of that part of the object introduced to the image due to different sensor types. The goal of image registration is now to define the mapping from coordinates x_1,y_1 in the sensed image to the coordinates x_2,y_2 in the reference image such that they correspond to the same physical points in the scene. One of these points is represented in Fig. 8.2 by a black dot. A small exception is image to scene registration, where coordinates x_2,y_2 would directly represent the coordinates of the physical space of the scene.

8.2.2 Methodology

The diversity of images to be registered and various possible types of degradations make image registration a complex process where single universal method seems to be still far from reality. There exist numerous image registration approaches, more or less specific to the task at hand. Nevertheless the majority of the image registration methods consists and can be viewed as a combination of the following four distinctive components :

- Feature space
- Search space or transformation model
- Similarity metric
- Search strategy

The feature space represents the information in the images that will be used for image matching. Search space or transformation model is the class of transformations that are capable of aligning the images for matching. The search strategy decides how to choose the next transformation from this space, to be tested in the search for the optimal transformation. The similarity metric determines the relative merit for each test. Search continues according to the search strategy until a transformation is found whose similarity measure is satisfactory.

8.3 GEOMETRICAL TRANSFORMATION MODEL

8.3.1 Plane-to-Plane Transform Model

An important constituting part of each image registration method is the transformation model. The model defines the geometric misalignment between the images that can be compensated for. By adjusting the parameters of this model, we look for the transformation that overlays one image over another and the selected features become optimally aligned. The transformation model parameter space is therefore the search space in which we look for optimal solution using the selected similarity metric and optimization method.

Since available geometric transformations between the images are constrained by the transformation model, we have to be careful to choose a model that reflects expected variations between the two images. The model has to be general enough to handle all expected variations that might occur, up to the acceptable approximation error.

There exist several transformation models, basically differing in the complexity of the transformation, *i.e.*, degrees of freedom of the model, and in the scope of their influence. Fig. 8.3 presents different examples of 2-D transformations. Global transformation model applies to the whole image in the same fashion while for local transformations parameters vary across the image.

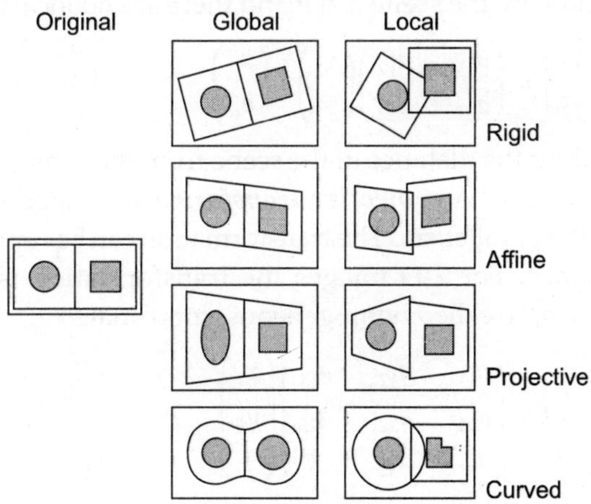

Fig. 8.3 *2D transformation models.*

8.3.2 Mapping

8.3.2.1 *Global mapping models*

'The transformation is called global when it applies to the entire image'. This means that a change in any of the transformation parameters influences the transformation of the image as a whole. The transformation can be rigid, affine, projective or curved.

Rigid transformation preserves the distance of any two points in the first image, when they are mapped onto the second image. Rigid transformation can be decomposed into translation, rotation and (mirror) reflection. Equation equation 8.1 presents rigid transform of mapping 2-D point (x_1,y_1) from sensed image into point (x_2,y_2) in the reference image. The transformation for higher dimensional images follows the same principle.

$$\begin{pmatrix} x_2 \\ y_2 \end{pmatrix} = s \cdot \begin{pmatrix} \cos\varphi & \mp\sin\varphi \\ \sin\varphi & \pm\cos\varphi \end{pmatrix} \begin{pmatrix} x_1 \\ y_1 \end{pmatrix} + \begin{pmatrix} a_x \\ a_y \end{pmatrix} \quad \text{...(8.1)}$$

In equation 8.1, φ denotes the rotation angle and (a_x,a_y) the translation vector. Scaling factor s is unity in this case. If uniform scaling factor is not equal to 1, the new transformation is called similarity transformation or shape-preserving mapping. As the name indicates, angles and curvatures in the image are preserved.

Slightly more general but still linear model is an ***affine transformation***, defined by equation 8.2. The transformation consists of linear transformation, a real-valued matrix with elements a, and a translation, vector (a_x,a_y). Property of affine transformation is that it maps straight lines onto straight lines and preserves parallelism. An example of such transformation is for instance non-uniform scaling and shearing. It can be used to register images taken from different viewpoints, assuming the distance from the camera to the scene is large in comparison to the size of the scanned area, the camera is perfect pin-hole camera, the scene is flat and there are no local image deformations.

$$\begin{pmatrix} x_2 \\ y_2 \end{pmatrix} = \begin{pmatrix} a_{11} & a_{12} \\ a_{21} & a_{22} \end{pmatrix} \begin{pmatrix} x_1 \\ y_1 \end{pmatrix} + \begin{pmatrix} a_x \\ a_y \end{pmatrix} \quad \text{...(8.2)}$$

When assumption regarding the distance of the scene from the camera is not valid, the transformation can be further generalized. A ***projective transformation*** maps straight lines into straight lines, but does not preserve the parallelism. The transformation can be represented by a linear matrix in a higher dimensional space. For 2-D images the transformation is formulated in equation equation 8.3.w represents extra, so called homogeneous, coordinate.

$$\begin{pmatrix} u \\ v \\ w \end{pmatrix} = \begin{pmatrix} a_{11} & a_{12} & a_{13} \\ a_{21} & a_{22} & a_{23} \\ a_{31} & a_{32} & 1 \end{pmatrix} \begin{pmatrix} x_1 \\ y_1 \\ 1 \end{pmatrix} \quad \text{...(8.3)}$$

$$\begin{pmatrix} x_2 \\ y_2 \end{pmatrix} = \begin{pmatrix} \dfrac{u}{w} \\ \dfrac{v}{w} \end{pmatrix}$$

The most general form of transformation is called ***curved transform,*** which may map straight line onto a curve among others. A well known class of curved transformations are the transformations of polynomial type. For 2-D images, a polynomial transformation is presented in equation 8.4, where *a* and *b* are parameters of the transformation that need to be determined.

$$x_2 = a_{00} + a_{10}x_1 + a_{01}y_1 + a_{20}x_1^2 + a_{11}xy + a_{02}y_1^2 + \ldots \qquad \ldots(8.4)$$
$$y_2 = b_{00} + b_{10}x_1 + b_{01}y_1 + b_{20}x_1^2 + b_{11}xy + b_{02}y_1^2 + \ldots$$

The order of the polynomial transformation depends on the trade-off between accuracy and cost of optimization. In practice, polynomials of up to third order are used. Because of their unpredictable behavior when the degree of the polynomial is high, they are only useful for low-frequency deformations.

The major limitation of global mapping models is the fact that they can not account for local geometric deformations between the images. In case we use salient point correspondence for image registration, global image transformation is determined as the one that on average, by using for instance least squares method, overlays the entire feature point pairs the most. Unfortunately this means that local deformations become spread throughout the entire image. This can be solved by computing local mapping models, which depend only on feature correspondences in local image neighbourhoods

8.3.2.2 Local Mapping Models

'*Global transformation is characterized by a single mapping transformation with one set of parameters independent of the position in the image. In contrast, local mapping transformation varies across different regions of the image, thus accounting for distortions which differ across the image*'. Considering that salient feature point correspondence is used as a base for registration, which is mostly the case when using local mapping models, the transformation in each part of the image is influenced only by the feature point matches sufficiently close or their influence is weighted by their proximity. Local methods are therefore more powerful and can handle distortions that global methods can not. Of course, there is the trade-off between the power of such methods and their computational complexity.

Class of techniques most commonly used to account for local geometrical distortions by salient feature point matching is ***piece-wise interpolation***. Here a spatial mapping transformation is calculated for each image coordinate by interpolating between certain set of matched coordinate values of corresponding feature points. For N corresponding feature points in 2-D image, two bivariate functions are constructed to map the coordinates, while taking on the desired values at feature points, as in equation 8.5.

$$x_{i2} = F_x(x_{i1}, y_{i1}) \qquad i = 1, \ldots, N \qquad \ldots(8.5)$$
$$y_{i2} = F_y(x_{i1}, y_{i1})$$

Methods applied must be designed for irregularly scattered feature points. A general spline approach to piece-wise interpolation is frequently used. This requires the selection of a set of basis functions and a set of constraints to be satisfied such that solving a system of linear equations will specify the interpolating function. The spline surface is presented in equation 8.6, where B_i represents the basis functions and V_i the feature points, *i.e.*, x_{i2} or y_{i2} from equation 8.5. S can represent either of the two coordinates, x_2 or y_2, in 2-D case.

$$S(x_1, y_1) = \sum_i V_i B_i(x_1, y_1) \qquad \ldots(8.6)$$

The basis function are mostly constructed using low-order polynomials, for which the coefficients are computed using constraints derived by satisfying end conditions and various orders of spatial continuity.

In the simplest case, a weighted sum of neighbouring points is computed where the weights are related inversely with the distance, as in linear interpolation. This approach is called ***inverse distance weighted interpolation***. Similar concept is used in local weighted-mean method, where a polynomial of degree n is found for each feature point which fits its n-1 nearest feature points. A point in the registered image is then computed as the weighted mean of all these polynomials, where the weights correspond to the distance to each of the feature points and are choosen such that they guarantee smoothness everywhere. An alternative to these methods is to determine the set of neighbouring feature points by some partitioning of the image, such as triangulation. The mapping transformation is then computed for each point in the image from interpolation of vertices of the image patch to which it belongs.

Although these methods compute local interpolation values, they may or may not use all the feature points in the calculation. If they use all points, they are generally more complex and may not be suitable for large feature point sets. However, since global information might be important, several local mapping methods, *i.e.*, methods which look for local registration transformation, employ parameters computed from global information.

All local methods presented so far can be categorized as curved transformations. Local rigid, affine or projective transforms are very rare in literature. Sometimes local rigid transformation can appear embedded in local curved transformation, or it can be used for registration problems that are intrinsically locally rigid. For instance registering rigidly individual bones of patient's skeleton can be solved by splitting the image into subsections meeting rigid constraints. Special care has to be taken to prevent transformation discontinuities.

In comparison to the global methods presented in the previous section, the optimization of local methods is much more complex. Because the parameters of the transformation depend on the location in the image, a separate calculation is performed for parameters of each sub-region, using global or local feature alignment and in the meantime considering certain global constrains, related to consistency of transformation for instance. Furthermore, local methods are heavily dependent on accurate match of corresponding feature points, considering we use salient points as registration features. For instance they are very sensitive to missing feature point matches. The number of feature matches and their positioning in the image is of greate importance as well.

8.4 STEREO IMAGING

Stereo imaging can be better understood by human vision. Both of our eyes generate two intensity maps of the scene in our retinal plane. So we can say that "*one object is being viewed from two different positions. So these two images are registered and then we generate a single intensity image*". To convert two images into single image is called fusion of images.

Even though this registration and fusion mechanism is not fully understood. It is possible for us to recover the depth information of an object, which otherwise is lost in the case of single image.

So we can say that we have two objectives of stereo imaging:

1. Find the correspondence between the pair of stereo images. This correspondence can be achieved with the help of geometrical transformation and mapping (so many otherway are also possible).
2. After the correspondence between both stereo images, just try to find a single image.

No we will discuss some algorithm for finding correspondence between pairs of stereo images.

8.4.1 Algorithms to Establish Correspondence

Horn describes the establishment of correspondence as a problem of 'finding conjugate points'.

In case of our eyes ; left eyes and right eyes capture the image. Now for establishment the correspondence, the same entity in both versions of image is detected.

Now for finding establishment of correspondence between stereo images, two most important aspects of image functions can be used.

1. **Brightness pattern of image function :** This is gray level similarity based measurement between the pair of stereo images. This has been already covered under the topic transform model (geometrical and mapping) in previous section.
2. **Feature sets extracted from the image :** Such features could be different geometrical patterns embeded in image, for example, detection of corresponding edges, corner 'or' domain specific shapes in a pair of stereo images.

In the following section, we present one such features matching based approach.

8.4.2 Feature based Correspondence Approach

Let the transformation between the left eye image to that of right eye is given by

$$M_R = RM_L + T \qquad \text{... (8.7)}$$

M_R and M_L are the corresponding points in the right eye and left eye image respectively. R is the rotation matrix and T is translation vector. R and T are known through eye calibration (in case of camera, defined by camera calibration ; these are nothing but some practically defined constant).

Let us start the linear structure. Using above equation, a line segment of the left eye image L is projected into right eye image R. The steps for matching this linear structure with the corresponding segment of the right eye image as follows :

1. First of all divide an entire image space into smaller sub-image regions so that the search space for any projected feature is reduced.
2. Let f_P be the projected feature on the image R, as in our example it is a linear structure projected from left eye L.
   The neighbours of projected line and their distances are tabulated. The distance measure could be Euclidean distance between middle points of line segments.
   In comparison Euclidean distance, Mahalanobis distance plays good role in case of eyes.
   For a pair of feature sets S_1 and S_2, the Mahalanobis distance is given by

$$D(S_1, S_2) = (S_1 - S_2)^t (A_1 + A_2)^{-1} (S_1 - S_2) \qquad \text{... (8.8)}$$

   Where A_1 and A_2 are the covariance matrixes for feature sets S_1 and S_2 respectively.

3. Now for each pair of match, we calculate confidence factor. The confidence factor is given by

$$C = \frac{D(S_1, S_3) - D(S_1, S_2)}{D(S_2, S_3)} \quad \text{... (8.9)}$$

The smaller magnitude of confidence factor implies that there is an ambiguity in matching and the correspondence between the candidates are rejected even if the nearest neighbours are close to the projected candidate.

Thus we find the establishment of correspondence.

8.4.3 Algorithms to Recover Path

Let us assume that the correspondence is established between the stereo image pair. Let the disparity between two cameras are $2d$. *Disparity is the distance of separation between the left and right camera.* Here two images of the point P (x, y, z) are formed at $(x + d)$ and $(x - d)$ location along x-axis.

If 'f' is the focal length of pin-hole camera system and x_l and x_r are the left and right camera images respectively

$$x_l = \frac{(x-d)f}{f-z} \text{ and}$$

$$x_r = \frac{(x+d)f}{f-z} \quad \text{... (8.10)}$$

Equivalently,

$$z = f - \frac{2df}{x_r - x_l} \quad \text{... (8.11)}$$

Thus, the depth of object could be recovered once the correspondence between both the images has been established.

Summary

1. The process of aligning the images and compensating for the differences caused by different acquisition condition is called image registration.
2. For image registration, basic methodology has four steps—feature space, search space, similarity matrix and search strategy.
3. Stereo imaging means a same image has been acquired by two cameras at different positions.

Review Questions

1. What do you understand by image registration ?
2. What do you understand by local mapping and global mapping ?
3. What is stereo imaging ?

9 CHAPTER

FEATURE EXTRACTION AND IMAGE SEGMENTATION

9.1 INTRODUCTION

The discussion till now was concern with the image processing where input was an image and output was also an image.

Now on words, we will study different processes in which input signal is an image and output is the feature of images. The basic purpose of feature extraction from an image is to make easy the computer analysis and process of an image.

"A feature is defined as a function of one 'or' more measurements, the values of some quantifiable property of an object, computed so that it quantifies some significant characteristics of object". One of the biggest advantages of feature extraction lies that it significantly reduces the information (in comparison to original image) to represent an image for understanding the content of image. Characteristics of an object is also called 'attribute' of feature of an object.

9.2 CLASSIFICATION OF FEATURES

Features can be categorized in different ways. But the most acceptable classification is discussed in this book.

Features can be catagorized in two categories :

1. **Low Level Features :** Low level features can be extracted directly from image.
2. **High Level Features :** High level features can not be extracted directly from an image. They must be based on low-level features.

For a good feature extraction process, the feature extraction should be invariance so that feature extraction is faithful and applicable for any position, location, size and scale variations.

Thus now onwards *'segmentation, representation and description and object / pattern recognition of an image are basic and different approaches for feature extraction ('or' attribute extraction) of an image'*. It should be clear to readers otherwise the correlation between these processes will be difficult.

9.3 FEATURES OF AN IMAGE

There may be a number of features of an image, but broadly features of an image are :

'point, edge, line region, and corner point' which will be discussed in this chapter.

For more fine study of an image, we may study the attributes of an image that will be studied in preceding chapters.

9.4 ATTRIBUTES OF FEATURES

There may be a number of attributes (characteristics) of features, but we are basically interested in the following attributes of feature.

9.4.1 Geometrical Attributes

Geometrical attribute of a feature may be orientation, length, curvature, area, perimeter, line, width, diameter, elongation, axes of symmetry, number/position of singular points.

9.4.2 Topological Attributes

Topological attributes of a feature may be above, left, adjacency, common end point, parallel, vertical, touch, overlap etc.

Now we will start with feature extraction of an image.

9.5 COMPLETE PROCESS OF FEATURE EXTRACTION

A complete process of feature extraction has three basic parts :

1. Image preprocessing ;
2. Desired feature extraction ; and
3. Invariant extraction.

By image preprocessing, we generally remove the noise from image. Due to noise generally we calculate false features of an image. For better feature extraction, we can adjust contrast and saturation level of an image also.

Now after preprocessing, we can extract the desired features of an image. But it is always desirable that extract the lines always before extracting the feature of an image.

The final step of feature extracting is to extract the features which are invariant so that those features are always useful because not changing with relation, location, position and size of an image.

9.6 IMAGE SEGMENTATION

Image segmentation subdivides an image into its constituent regions 'or' object. For higher level feature extraction, image segmentation is fundamental. For image segmentation, we depend upon features of an image such as point, line, edge and region.

Image segmentation is very important but difficult process because the accuracy of image segmentation defines the success 'or' failure of computerized analysis procedure of an image. Now let us discuss point, line, edge and region detection one by one in detail that will help us for segmentation of an image.

9.6.1 Point Detection

"Point detection is based on discontinuities in image. Our approach is based on abrupt change in intensity of an image". So these isolate points, whose intensity are changing abruptly, may be detected straight forward by using the following mask :

w_1	w_2	w_3
w_4	w_5	w_6
w_7	w_8	w_9

(a) General mask

–1	–1	–1
–1	8	–1
–1	–1	–1

(b) Mask for point detection.

Fig. 9.1 *Marks for point detection*

Recall that the general expression for response of a filter/mask is given by

$$R = w_1 z_1 + w_2 z_2 + \ldots\ldots + w_9 z_9$$

$$R = \sum_{i=1}^{9} w_i z_i \qquad \ldots (9.1)$$

where z_i is the gray level of the pixel associated with mask coefficient w_i. The response of the mask is defined with respect to its center location.

We say that a point has been detected at location on which mask is centered. If at the location the response of mask is greater than a particular predefined threshold.

$$|R| \geq T$$

T = Non negative predefined threshold value.

Recall that the sum of all coefficients of mask is always zero that will cause the response of mask zero if we have constant gray level (means we donot have any point). Point detection is a low level feature extraction.

9.6.2 Line Detection

"It is also based on abrupt change in intensity of gray level of image. It also reflects a discontinuity in image". For the line detection, we use the following mask :

Horizontal

–1	–1	–1
2	2	2
–1	–1	–1

+ 45°

–1	–1	2
–1	2	–1
2	–1	–1

Vertical

–1	2	–1
–1	2	–1
–1	2	–1

– 45°

2	–1	–1
–1	2	–1
–1	–1	2

Fig. 9.2 *Mask used for line detection.*

By moving first mask on the image, we can detect the one-pixel thick line in horizontal direction. The direction of line is simply decided by the coefficients of mask. The preferred direction of mask is weighted with a larger coefficients than others.

On the basis of above discussion, second, third and forth masks are for + 45°, vertical and – 45° lines respectively.

Now suppose that we have run all the masks on image and there are four responses R_1, R_2, R_3 and R_4. Suppose that at a particular point.

$$|R_1| > |R_j| \text{ where } j = 2, 3, 4 \text{ and } j \neq 1.$$

Then that point is associated with horizontal line. Thus we can decide, which point is associated with which line. Line detection is a low-level feature extraction.

9.6.3 Edge Detection

Edge detection is one of the most important phenomena in image processing.

9.6.3.1 *Introduction and Basics of Edge Detection*

Edge detection is also based on discontinuity measurement. It also shows the abrupt change in the intensity of gray levels.

"Edge can be defined as a set of connected pixels that lies in the boundary between two regions".

An ideal edge has been shown in figure. Here we see that a immediate transition of gray level has been shown. Technically

"An ideal edge is defined as a set of connected pixels each of which is located at an orthogonal step transition in gray level". Thus an ideal edge has an step type response.

But practically, edges cannot be sharp. Edges practically are blurred and degree of blurring depends upon many factors such as quality of the image acquisition system, the sampling rate and the illumination conditions under which the image is acquired. As a result edges are 'ramp like' profile as shown in Fig. 9.3. The key points are :

1. The slope of ramp is inversely proportional to degree of blurring in the edge. More blurring means less slope.
2. Blurred edges are always thick and sharp edges are always thin.

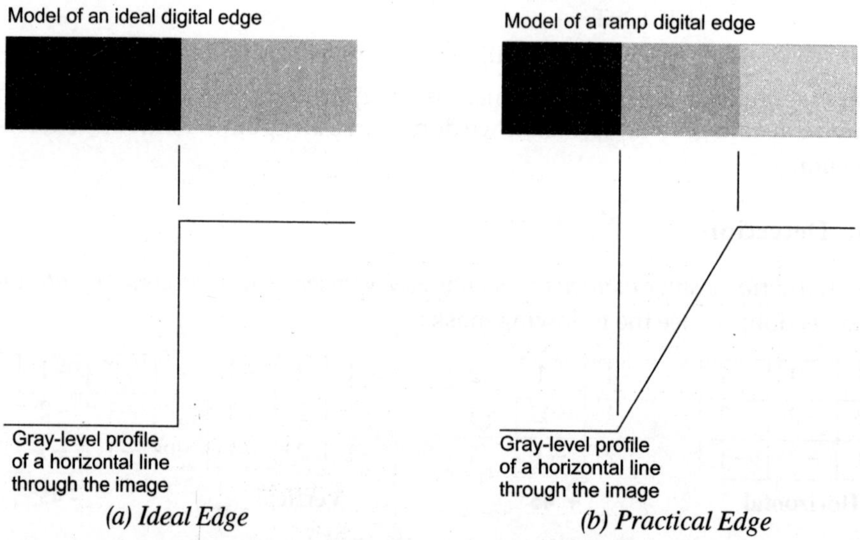

Fig. 9.3 *Model of ideal and practical edges*

9.6.3.2 *Edge Detector*

As discussed at the beginning of edge that edges are abrupt changes in the gray levels at the boundary of two regions, so we can use derivatives for the measurement of edges. As if there is no edge, means no change in intensity level, resultant derivative of image at that area will be zero. If derivative shows some value means, there is a possibility of edges. Here in the figure 9.4 we have drawn the first derivative and second derivative of an practical edge. We may describe as follow :

1. As we know that ramp is given by

$$g(t) = r(t) = t \quad \text{... (9.2)}$$

So first derivative will be :

$$\frac{dg(t)}{dt} = \frac{dr(t)}{dt} = 1 \quad \text{... (9.3)}$$

Thus for edge (means gray level transition) always shows a constant first derivative and for constant gray levels.

$$g(t) = r(t) = \text{constant} \quad \text{... (9.4)}$$

$$\frac{dg(t)}{dt} = \frac{dr(t)}{dt} = 0 \quad \text{... (9.5)}$$

First derivative will be zero thus by first derivative, the presence of edge is decided.

2. Now take the second derivative from first derivative. Here we see that we get positive second derivative for edge at dark side and negative second derivative for edge at white side. Thus by second derivative we can find the edges situated at dark side and white side of image. (But if carefully, we are not absorbing the first derivative and second derivative of an edge, then by second derivative we can confuse about the presence of edge).

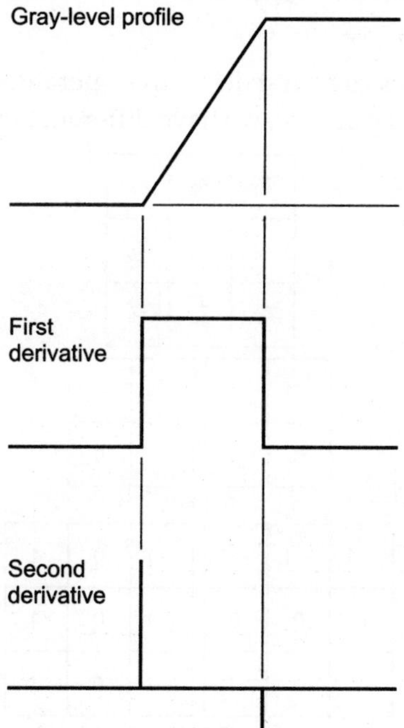

Fig. 9.4 *First and second derivatives of Edges.*

Now assume a line between positive second derivative and negative second derivative of edge ; then middle of this line shows the center of edge. Thus by second derivative of edge, we can locate the edge (This is called the zero crossing of edge also. Because detecting center means detecting the location where edge is crossing zero).

Till now we have discussed general properties of edge operators. But now we will discuss the specific qualities and practical way of calculating derivative of edges.

9.6.3.3 *First Derivative (Gradient Operator) of Edge*

First derivative is also called gradient of an signal mathematically. The gradient of an image $f(x, y)$ at location (x, y) is defined as the vector

$$\nabla f = \begin{bmatrix} G_x \\ G_y \end{bmatrix} = \begin{bmatrix} \frac{\partial f}{\partial x} \\ \frac{\partial f}{\partial y} \end{bmatrix} \qquad \text{... (9.6)}$$

(We know the gradient shows the maximum rate of change at any point)

Magnitude of this vector is defined as

$$\text{meg}\,(\nabla f) = \left[G_x^2 + G_y^2\right]^{\frac{1}{2}}$$

This quantity gives the max rate of change of $f(x, y)$ per unit distance in the direction of ∇f.

Let $\alpha(x, y)$ represent the angle of vector ∇f at (x, y), then this angle is given by

$$\alpha(x, y) = \tan^{-1}\left(\frac{G_y}{G_x}\right) \qquad \text{... (9.7)}$$

(angle is measured *w.r.t.* x axis)

But this all is only theoretical basics of first derivative operators of edge. Practically these can not be implemented on image. For that purpose, we have different types of masks.

z_1	z_2	z_3
z_4	z_5	z_6
z_7	z_8	z_9

– 1	0
0	1

0	– 1
1	0

Roberts

– 1	– 1	– 1
0	0	0
1	1	1

– 1	0	1
– 1	0	1
– 1	0	1

Prewitt

– 1	– 2	– 1
0	0	0
1	2	1

– 1	0	1
– 2	0	2
– 1	0	1

Sobel

Fig. 9.5 *Different matrices operators used for calculation of first derivative.*

(*a*) **roberts Cross-gradient operators :** Here we have drawn 3 × 3 area for image where $z_1, ..., z_9$ shows the pixel values. One of the simplest ways to implement the first-order partial derivative at point z_5 is to use the following roberts cross-gradient operators :

$$G_x = (z_9 - z_5)$$

and $$G_y = (z_8 - z_6) \quad ...(9.8)$$

But this is only 2 × 2 size mask. This is always avoided, to use this size mask because these masks do not have clear center.

(*b*) **Prewitt Operator :** Prewitt operator is performed using 3 × 3 mask. In this mask, the derivative in x direction is calculated by difference between first and third row of 3 × 3 mask.

$$G_x = (z_7 + z_8 + z_9) - (z_1 + z_2 + z_3) \quad ...(9.9)$$

Similarly the derivative in y direction is calculated by the difference between first and third columns of mask.

$$G_y = (z_3 + z_6 + z_9) - (z_1 + z_4 + z_7) \quad ...(9.10)$$

(*c*) **Sobel Operator :** Sobel operator is a slightly modified version of prewitt operator and given by

$$G_x = (z_7 + 2z_8 + z_9) - (z_1 + 2z_2 + z_3) \quad ...(9.11)$$

and $$G_y = (z_3 + 2z_6 + z_9) - (z_1 + 2z_4 + z_7) \quad ...(9.12)$$

here we have doubled center coefficient of mask for giving more importance for center point. Thus, the calculating G_x and G_y, we can apply

$$\text{meg}(\nabla f) = \left[G_x^2 + G_y^2\right]^{\frac{1}{2}}$$

$$\simeq |G_x| + |G_y| \quad ...(9.13)$$

That also provide good result of our interest.

9.6.3.4 *The Second Derivative (The Laplacian)*

Second derivative is also called Laplacian and defined by

$$\nabla^2 f = \frac{\partial^2 f}{\partial x^2} + \frac{\partial^2 f}{\partial y^2} \quad ...(9.14)$$

For 3 × 3 region, for isotropic rotation increment of 45°, it is given by

$$\nabla^2 f = 4z_5 - (z_2 + z_4 + z_6 + z_8) \quad ...(9.15)$$

and can be calculated by 3 × 3 mask given below :

0	–1	0
–1	4	–1
0	–1	0

Fig. 9.6 *(a) Implementation of equation.*

For isotropic rotational increment of 90°, it is given by

$$\nabla^2 f = 8z_5 - (z_1 + z_2 + z_3 + z_4 + z_6 + z_7 + z_8) \quad ...(9.16)$$

and can be calculated by 3 × 3 mask given below

−1	−1	−1
−1	8	−1
−1	−1	−1

Fig. 9.6 *(b) Implementation of equation.*

But "*Laplacian functions (second derivative) are not used in its real form because it has the following disadvantages*".

(*a*) More sensitive to noise

(*b*) It will provide double edges. So confusing some time for edge detection.

(*c*) It will not give the direction of edges.

But it is still useful due to the following advantages :

(*a*) to detect zero crossing means center of edge.

(*b*) to know what pixels are at black side area and what pixel are at white side area.

So we use Laplacian along with other smoothing functions to reduce the noise. Generally, Laplacian is used with gaussian function that is given by

$$h(r) = e^{\frac{-r^2}{2\sigma^2}} \qquad \text{... (9.17)}$$

where $r^2 = x^2 + y^2$ and σ = Deviation

Now to calculate Laplacian :

$$\nabla^2 h(r) = -\left[\frac{r^2 - \sigma^2}{\sigma^4}\right] . e^{-\frac{r^2}{2\sigma^2}} \qquad \text{... (9.18)}$$

This equation (2) is referred as

Laplacian of a Gaussian (LOG)

Now we can draw the original LOG diagram and its cross-section.

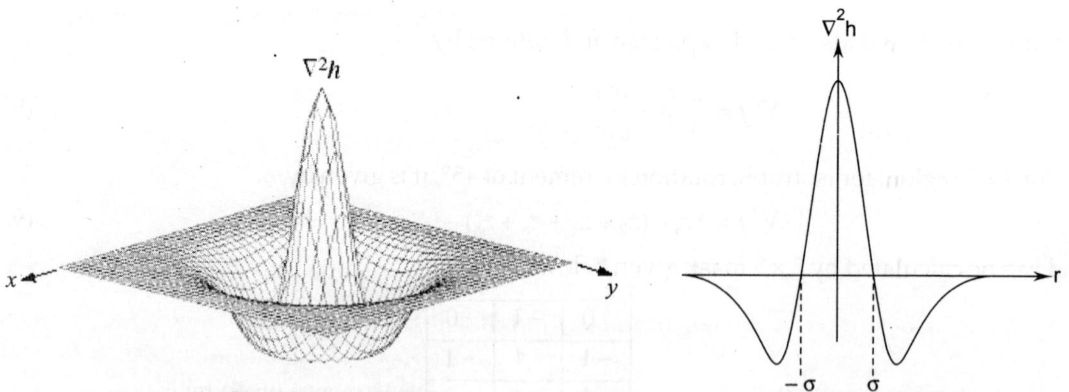

(a) (Real) image of LOG *(b) (Cross section)*

Fig. 9.7 *LOG*

It loops like Mexican hat

thats why is also called Mexican hat function.

We can also find the mask that will approximately represent the LOG function.

0	0	−1	0	0
0	−1	−2	−1	0
−1	−2	16	−2	−1
0	−1	−2	−1	0
0	0	−1	0	0

5×5

Fig. 9.8 *Implementation of LOG.*

It has '+ ve' high vlue at center and after that decreasing and at long distance '0' to get response

Convolution of Image with LOG = Convolution of image with Gaussian function and then calculating second derivative.

Thus, we have conclusion, that

(*a*) Due to Gaussian function, the smoothing function is there, that will reduce noise.

(*b*) By Laplacian function, we get zero-crossing function that will help to establish the location of edge.

Edge detection is also a low-level feature extraction.

9.7 EDGE LINKING

Edge detectors yield pixels in an image lie on edges. Our next step is to try to collect these pixels together into a set of edges. In other words, we may say that our aim is to replace many points on edges with a new edges. Basically, "*the need of edge linking is due to the following two reasons*".

1. Small pieces of edges may be missing.
2. Small edge segments may appear to be present due to noise where there is no real edge.

In general, edge linking methods can be classified into two categories :

(*a*) **Local Edge Linkers :** Where edge points are grouped to form edge by considering each point's relationship to any neighbouring edge points.

(*b*) **Global Edge Linker :** Where all edge points in the image plane are considered at the same time and sets of edge points are prepared.

Now we will study them in detail.

9.7.1 Local Edge Linker

One of the simplest approaches for linking edge points is :

1. Detect the edge points by one of the technique discussed above.
2. Now analyze the characteristics of pixels in a small neighbourhood (say 3×3 or 5×5) about every point (x, y) in image.

Now all the points (that has been analyzed) are similar according to a set of predefined criteria are linked forming an edge of pixels that shares those criteria.

Now we have to discuss the criteria of similarities in this type of analysis. The basic criteria is

1. The strength of the response of the gradient operator used to produce the edge pixel.
2. The direction of gradient vector.

For a particular point (x_0, y_0) ;

if strength of gradient = meg $[(\nabla f)(x_0 y_0)]$

Direction of gradient $= \alpha(x_0, y_0)$

For a point (x, y) at the edge, if

Strength of gradient $= \text{meg}\,[f(x, y)]$

Direction of gradient $= \alpha(x, y)$

Point (x_0, y_0) is said to similar to (x, y), if

$$\text{meg}\,[f(x, y) - \text{meg}\,[f(x_0, y_0)] \leq E \qquad \text{... (9.19)}$$

E = Non-negative threshold and

$$\alpha\,[f(x, y)] - \alpha\,[f(x_0, y_0)] \leq A \qquad \text{... (9.20)}$$

A = Non-negative angle threshold.

Thus (x_0, y_0) and (x, y) are linked together.

9.7.2 Global Edge Linkers

We will study the two methods of global edge linking :

1. Global edge linking by using Hough transform.
2. Global edge linking by using Graph-theoretical techniques.

9.7.2.1 Global Edge Linking by using Hough Transform

Suppose we have given n points in an image and we have to find whether these points are related to a single line 'or' not. One possible way is to draw the line equation between each pair of points and then see how many lines are very close to each other 'or' intersect to each other. Definitely this process is not good because we have to draw about n^2 line equations and n^3 comparisons for finding a result. One alternative approach is there called Hough transform for this purpose, we will discuss that here.

Let us suppose that we are looking for straight line in image. If we take a point (x', y') in the image, all lines which pass through that pixel have the form

$$y' = mx' + c \qquad \text{... (9.21)}$$

For varying values of m and c

$$y' = mx' + c$$

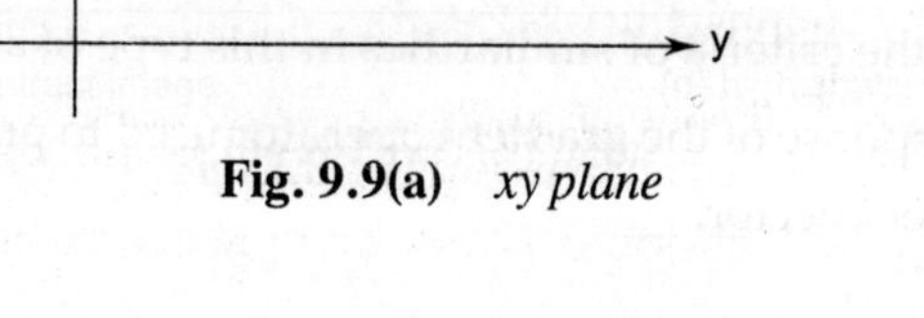

Fig. 9.9(a) *xy plane*

However this equation can be written as

$$c = -x'm + y' \quad \text{...} (9.22)$$

Now consider x' and y' to be constant and m and c as varying. This line can be drawn as given below :

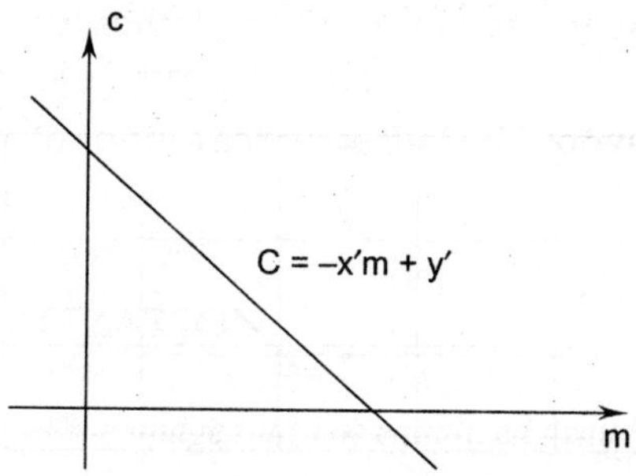

Fig. 9.9 *(b) Parameter space.*

Each different line through point (x', y') corresponds to one of points on this line in (m, c) space.

Now further proceed by considering two pixels p and q in (x, y) space which lies on the same line. Now we can draw all the possible lines through it are represented a single line in (m, c) space. Definitely, single line passing through these two pixels will be represented by two lines intersecting in (m, c) space.

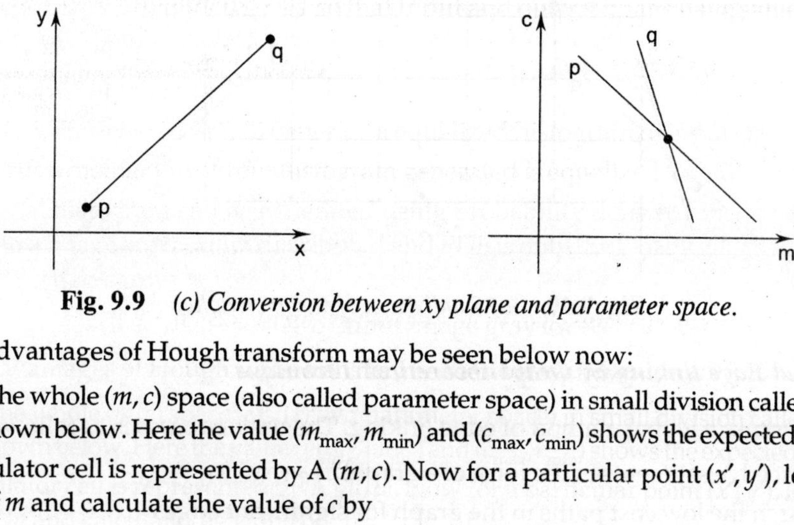

Fig. 9.9 *(c) Conversion between xy plane and parameter space.*

The main advantages of Hough transform may be seen below now:

1. Divide the whole (m, c) space (also called parameter space) in small division called accumulator cell as shown below. Here the value (m_{max}, m_{min}) and (c_{max}, c_{min}) shows the expected range of space.
2. Accumulator cell is represented by A (m, c). Now for a particular point (x', y'), let us select one value of m and calculate the value of c by
$$c = -x'm + y'.$$
Calculated value should be rounded off.
3. At initial state set
$$A(m, c) = 0$$
Now for every value of 'm', calculate the value of 'c' and subdivide A (m, c) one by one in the whole range as shown in Fig. 9.10 *(a)*.
4. To decide pixels to a part of line, just take the values of m and c ; if the value of m and c is with in one cell of space ; all the pixels are related to same line / edge.

The Hough transform can be implemented for normal representation of line also. The equation is given by

$$x \,.\, \cos\theta + y \sin\theta = \rho.$$

Here we have drawn the (x, y) plane representation of line along with parametric space (showing accumulator cells) in Fig. 9.10 (*b*).

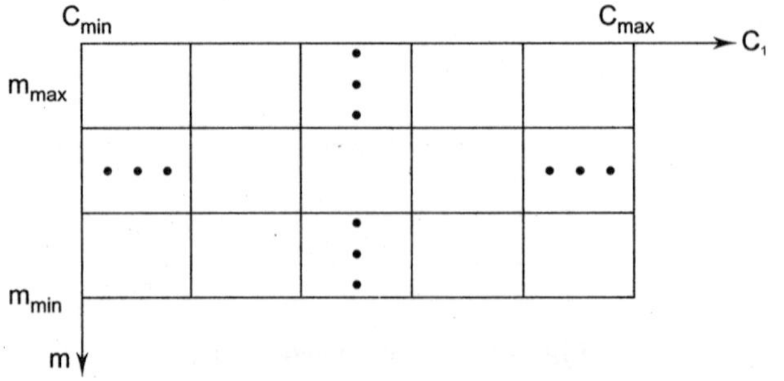

Fig. 9.10 *(a) Subdivision of parameter plane.*

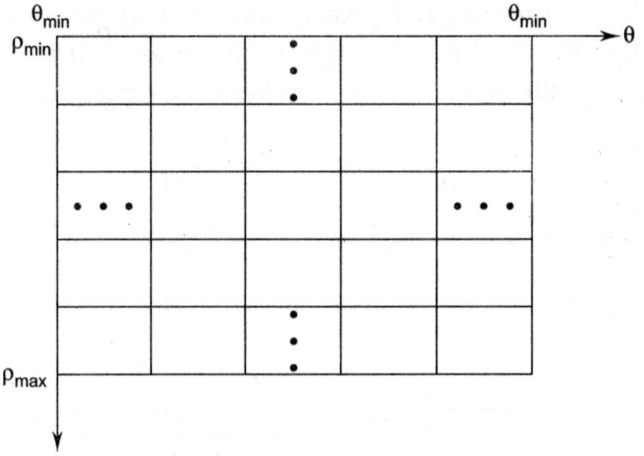

Fig. 9.10 *(b) Subdivision of parameter plane.*

9.7.2.2 *Global Edge linking by Graph-theoretical Technique*

Now we will discuss a global method of edge linking. The basic process is as following :

1. Represent edge segments in the form of a graph.
2. Now search the low cost paths in the graph for significant edges.

This approach is good for presence of Noise. But definitely time taking and complicated.

So, let us start with some basic definitions :

1. Graph G = (N, U) is a finite, non empty set of Nodes N, together with a set U of unordered pairs of distinct elements of N.
2. Each pair (n_i, n_j) of U is called an arc.
3. If arc is directed from node n_i to node n_j, then n_i is called parent node and n_j is called successor node.
4. Node is the first level (from where we have to start calculation) is called start 'or' root Node. Node at the last level (where we have to finish calculation) is called goal node.

5. Between two pixels p and q, the cost of path between these two pixels is defined by

$$C(p, q) = H - [f(p) - f(q)] \quad \text{...(9.23)}$$

H = Highest gray level in the image and

$f(p)$ = gray level of pixel p.

$f(q)$ = gray level of pixel q.

Now let us discuss one example as given below :

1. Start with node point between (1, 1) and (1, 2) that has cost

$$C(p, q) = H - [f(p) - f(q)]$$

H = Highest gray level = 7

$f(p)$ = gray level of (1, 1) = 5

$f(q)$ = gray level of (1, 2) = 6

So, $C = 7 - (5 - 6)$

$C = 8.$

Cost of remaining path can be calculated easily be same way.

Now from (1, 1), (1, 2), we have to go suppose (3, 1), (3, 2) and (3, 2) (3, 3)

Then **First Path :**

(1, 1), (1, 2) → (2, 1), (2, 2) → (3, 1), (3, 2).

Second Path :

(1, 1), (1, 2) → (2, 1), (2, 2) → (3, 2), (2, 2)
↓
(3, 2), (3, 3).

Third Path :

(1, 1), (1, 2) → (2, 2), (1, 2) → (2, 2), (2, 3)
↓
(3, 2), (3, 3)

Fourth Path :

(1, 1), (1, 2) → (2, 2), (1, 2) → (2, 2), (2, 3)
↓
(3, 1), (3, 2) ← (2, 2) (3, 2).

2. Start with node point between (1, 2) (1, 3).

First Path :

(1, 2) (1, 3) → (2, 2), (2, 3) → (3, 2), (3, 3)

Second Path :

(1, 2) (1, 3) → (2, 2) (2, 3) → (2, 2), (3, 2)
↓
(3, 1), (3, 2)

Third Path :

(1, 2), (1, 3) → (1, 2), (2, 2) → (2, 1), (2, 2)
↓
(3, 1), (3,2).

Fourth Path :

$$(1,2),(1,3) \rightarrow (1,2),(2,2) \rightarrow (2,1),(2,2)$$
$$\downarrow$$
$$(3,2),(3,3) \leftarrow (3,1),(2,2)$$

3. Thus the final graph can be plated as given below.

   Thus for all images from all possible root node to goal node graph is plotted. Now as we have seen that from a particular root node to goal node, more than one path can be possible. So only adopt minimum cost path and those pixels which are laying on that path concern to a single line / edge. Remember that total path cost = Addition of cost of total path followed between root to goal node.

   For example,

   Consider point ('↑') where between (1, 1) (1, 2) to (3, 1) (3, 2), there are two paths (First path and Fourth Path).

   So cost of first path ; by graph

   $$= 8 + 8 + 1 = 17.$$

   Cost of fourth path by graph

   $$= 8 + 6 + 0 + 1 + 1 = 16.$$

   So fourth path is looking longer than first path but has low cost so preferred one.

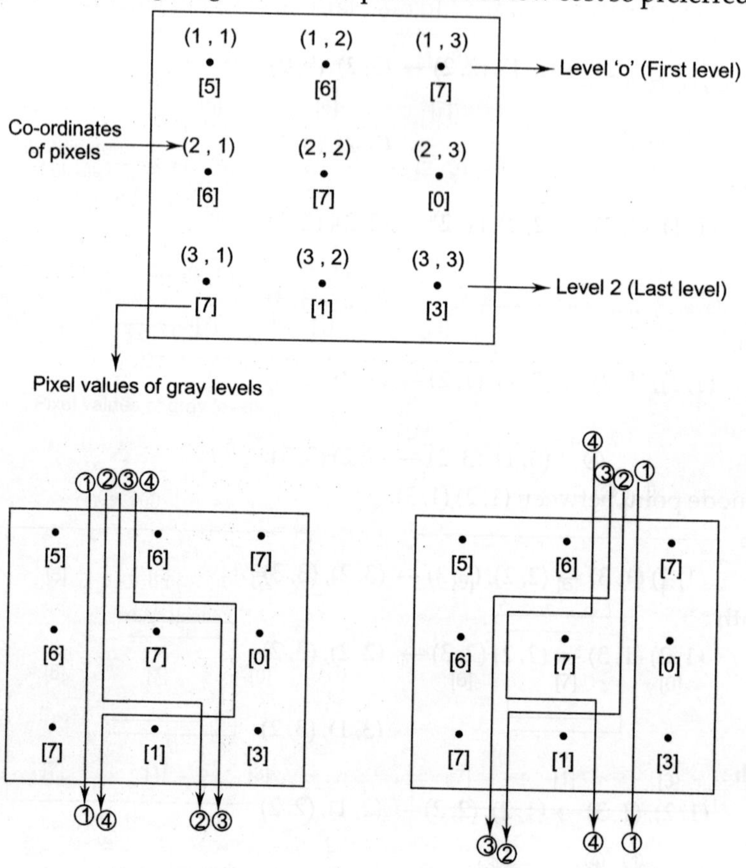

Fig. 9.11 *Graph theoretical technique.*

9.8 THRESHOLDING

Thresholding plays a very important role in segmentation. Thats why we will consider thresholding here in detail. Basically thresholding may be defined as :

1. Single level thresholding and
2. Multi level thresholding.

1. **Single level thresholding :** Suppose that an image $f(x, y)$ has light objects on a dark background. If we draw the histogram of this type of image, it will have two dominant modes of gray levels. One group near the zero point of histogram showing dark background and one group near the maximum point of histogram showing light object.

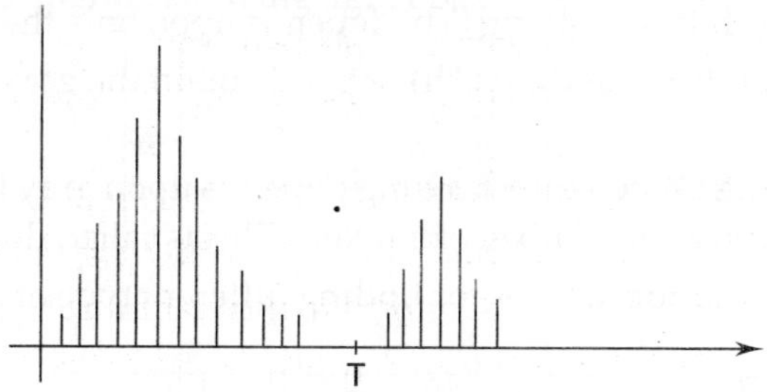

9.12 *Single Level Thresholding.*

So at any point (x, y). If

$f(x, y) > T$, it is called object and

$f(x, y) < T$, it is called background.

This is called single-level thresholding because we have separated information of an image by single threshold.

2. **Multilevel thresholding :** Now let us suppose that we have three dominant modes characterize the image histogram for two types of light objects and black background. This is called multilevel thresholding because we have used more than one threshold for separation of image information.

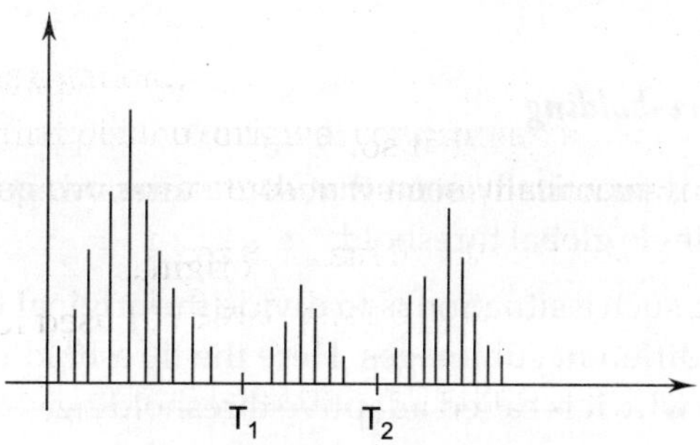

9.13 *Multilevel thresholding.*

Here multilevel thresholding classifies a point (x, y) as belonging to one object class if $T_1 < (x, y) \le T_2$. The point (x, y) is belonging to other object class if $f(x, y) > T_2$. The point (x, y) is belonging to background if $f(x, y) \le T_1$.

So we can say that thresholding itself is a fundamental of segmentation.

9.8.1 Types of Thresholding

So based on above discussion and practical analysis ; it is found that thresholding is a test function of

1. Spatial co-ordinates (x, y).
2. $f(x, y)$; gray level of point (x, y).
3. $P(x, y)$; some local property at point (x, y).

So it can be written as

$$\text{Th} = T[x, y, f(x, y), P(x, y)] \qquad ...(9.24)$$

So the basis of this function thresholding may be categorized as follows :

(*a*) **Global thresholding :** If thresholding (Th) depends upon only the gray levels of an image.

(*b*) **Local thresholding :** If thresholding (Th) depends upon the gray levels of image and some local properties also.

(*c*) **Adaptive thresholding :** When thresholding depends upon gray levels, local properties and spatial co-ordinates (position of pixels) of pixels. This is called dynamic thresholding.

Now we will study the basic approaches for finding different type of thresholding.

9.8.1.1 Global Thresholding

As we know that global thresholding depends upon only gray levels of an image. So,

1. Select an initial estimate of threshold, T.
2. Segment the image using T. This will produce two groups of pixels : G_1 group consisting of all pixels with gray level values > T and G_2 group consisting of all pixels with gray levels ≤ T.
3. Compute the average gray level values μ_1 and μ_2 for the pixels in regions G_1 and G_2.
4. Compute a new threshold value

$$T = \frac{1}{2}(\mu_1 + \mu_2)$$

5. Repeat steps 2 to 4 until the difference in T in successive iterations is smaller than a predefined parameter T_0.

9.8.1.2 Basic Adaptive Thresholding

Due to poor illumination, it is practically seen that some time, we get histogram that can not be partitioned effectively by a single global threshold.

An approach for handling such a situation is to divide the original image into subimages. Now use different thresholds for different subimages. Here the threshold used for each pixel depends upon location of pixels thats why it is called adaptive thresholding.

9.8.1.3 Local Thresholding

It can be easily seen that we may select good threshold if histogram peaks are tall, narrow, symmetric and separated by deep valleys. One approach for improving the shape of any histogram is to consider those pixels that lie on 'or' near the edges between object and background. As edges shows the abrupt changes in gray levels of pixels, definitely we will get deep valley, highly separated histograms. Here we depends upon the local property of image (edges) thats why called local thresholding.

9.8.1.4 Edge Detection by Using Local Thresholding

Recall that by gradient calculation of pixels, we can verify whether an edge is present or not. By calculation of Laplacian, we can decide whether a pixel of edge lies in dark side 'or' light side of an edge.

These two quantities can be used in thresholding also for detecting the edge. These two quantities may be used to form a three level image as follows :

$$S(x, y) = \begin{cases} 0 & \text{if} \quad \nabla f < T \\ + & \text{if} \quad \nabla f \geq T \quad \text{and } \nabla^2 f \geq 0 \\ - & \text{if} \quad \nabla f \geq T \quad \text{and } \nabla^2 f < 0 \end{cases} \quad \text{... (9.25)}$$

where symbol 0, + and – represent any three distinct gray levels. T is the threshold and ∇f (gradient) and $\nabla^2 f$ (Laplacian) are calculated at every point (x, y).

For a dark subject on a light background, the use of above equation generates :

(*a*) All the pixels that are not at edge are labeled '0'.

(*b*) All the pixels that are at the dark side of edge are labeled '+'.

(*c*) All the pixels that are at the light side of edge are labeled '–'.

The symbol '+' and '–' are reversed for light object on dark background.

9.9 REGION BASED SEGMENTATION

"Another way of extracting information from an image is to group pixels together into regions of similarities. Thus point, line and edge detection were based on discontinuities in an image on the other hand region based segmentation is based on basis of similarities".

In a 2D-image, we group pixels together according to the rate of change of their intensity over a region. For 3D-image, we group together pixels according to the rate of change of depth in image, corresponding to pixels laying on the same surface such as plane, cylinder, sphere etc. There are basically two main approaches to region based segmentation :

1. Region splitting and merging ; and
2. Region growing.

Now we will study these two techniques in detail one by one.

9.9.1 Region Splitting and Merging

The basic idea of image splitting to break the image into a set of disjoint regions which are coherent within themselves. The process can be defined as follows :

1. Initially take the image as a whole to be the area of interest.
2. Look at area of interest and decide if all pixels contained in the region satisfy some similarity constraint.
3. If 'TRUE' then the area of interest corresponds to a region of image.
4. If 'FALSE' then the area of interest is splitted into subareas (usually into four equal sub-areas) and now consider each of subareas as the area of interest in turn.
5. This process is continuously performed until no further splitting is possible. In the worst case the areas may be of just one pixel size.

This is also called divide and conquer 'or' top down method.

One thing should be handled carefully, if only a splitting schedule is used then the final segmentation would probably contain many neighbouring regions that have identical 'or' similar properties. Thus, a merging process is used after each split which compares adjacent regions and merges them if necessary. That's why it is called split and merging algorithm.

To illustrate the basic principle of these methods. Let us consider an imaginary image.

1. Let I denotes the whole image as shown in Fig. 9.14(*a*).

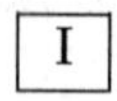

Fig. 9.14(*a*) *Test image.*

2. Suppose that all the pixels in I are not similar so we have to split the region I in four subregions.

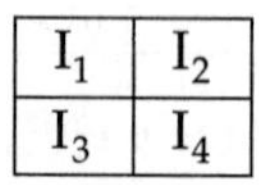

Fig. 9.14(*b*) *I^{st} splitting into subdivision.*

3. Assume that all pixels within region I_1, I_2 and I_3 respectively are similar but those in I_4 are not. So, I_4 is splitted again in four subregions.

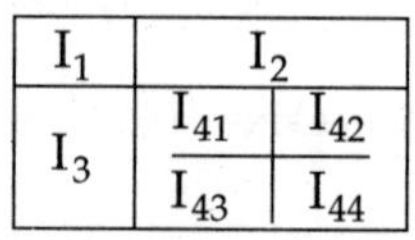

Fig. 9.14(*c*) *Further subdivisions.*

4. Suppose that after splitting, we found that I_{43} and I_{44} are found to be identical so we have to merge them again.

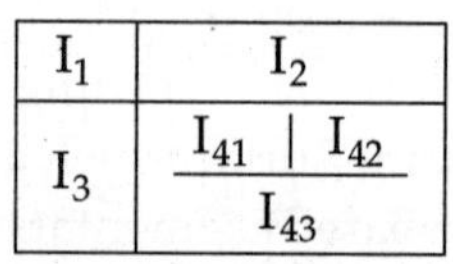

Fig. 9.14(*d*) *Merging of I_{43} and I_{44}.*

We can also show all the splitting process by a tree as given below :

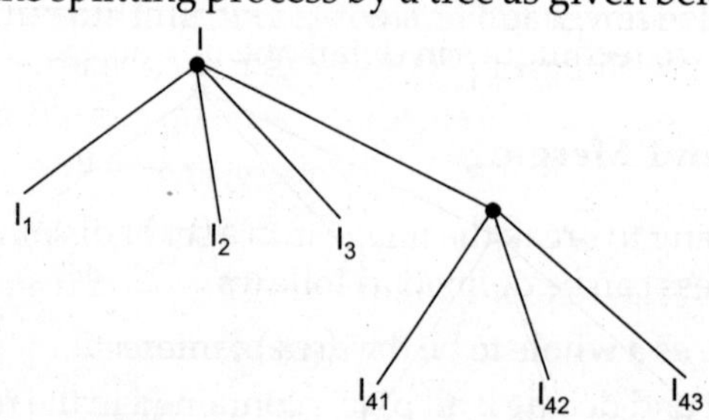

Fig. 9.14(*e*) *Quadtree of splitting and merging.*

It is also called quadtree.

9.9.2 Region Growing

Region growing approach is the opposite of the split and merge approach. The process can be defined as follows :

1. Start by choosing an arbitrary seed pixel and compare it with neighbouring pixels.

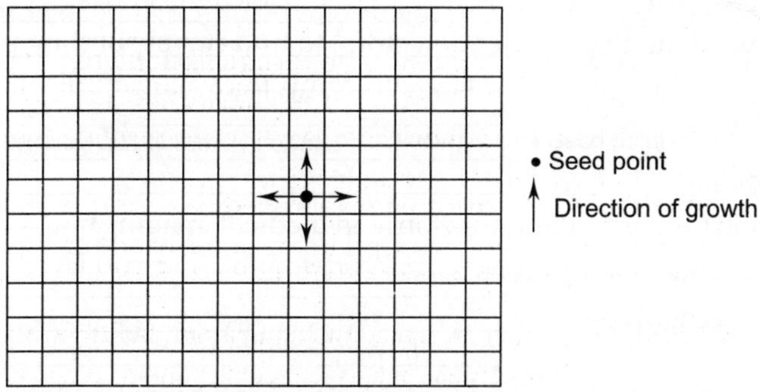

Fig. 9.15(*a*) *Ist stop of region growing.*

2. Region is grown from seed pixel by adding in neighbouring pixels that are similar, increasing the size of the region.

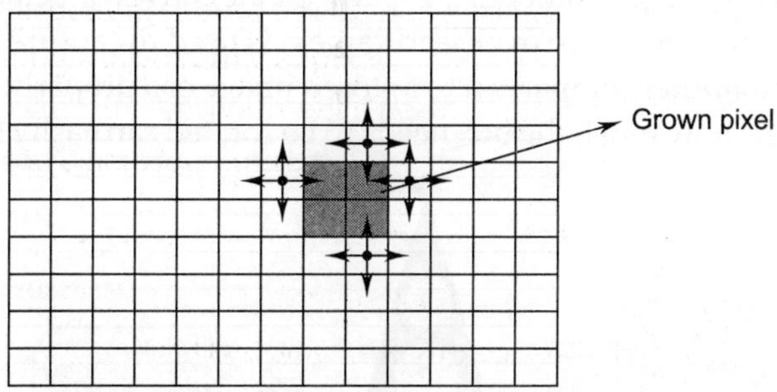

Fig. 9.15(*b*) *Further process of region growing.*

3. When the growth of one region stops we simply choose another seed pixel which does not yet belong to any region and start again.

This is revised until all possible regions are found. This is called bottom up.

The main disadvantages of this technique are :

1. Current region dominates the growth process.
2. Different choice of seeds may give different segmentation results.
3. Problem can secure if arbitrary choosen seed point lies on the edge.

To remove these disadvantages, we use 'simultaneous region growing' technique :

1. Similarities between regions are also considered.
2. At a time a single region is not allowed to finalized. A number of parallel regions are grown.
3. Process is difficult but many algorithms are available for easy implementation.

9.10 CORNER DETECTION

Introduction

"Corner points are points which are formed from two or more edges and edges usually define the boundary between two different objects or parts of the same object. Corners are those points where lines bend very sharply with high curvature. (These are another low-level feature that again can be extracted automatically from the image)". Many corner detectors have been developed and some of the more important ones.

9.10.1 Applications of Corner Detectors

The use of interest points (and thus corner detectors) to find corresponding points across multiple images is a key step in many image processing and computer vision applications. Some of the most notable examples are :

- stereo matching
- image registration (of particular importance in medical imaging)
- stitching of panoramic photographs
- object detection/recognition
- motion tracking
- robot navigation

Fig. 9.16 shows part of a hypothetical system to illustrate how a corner detector might be used in an automated assembly line. This assembly line fills triangle gift boxes with four different chocolates. However, the boxes must be positioned properly on the conveyor belt to ensure the chocolates are packed properly into the boxes. An overhead camera is used to capture a picture of each box as it passes under it and a computer compares it to a stored image of a properly aligned box. By finding the corners of each image, how much the box needs to be rotated can easily be computed.

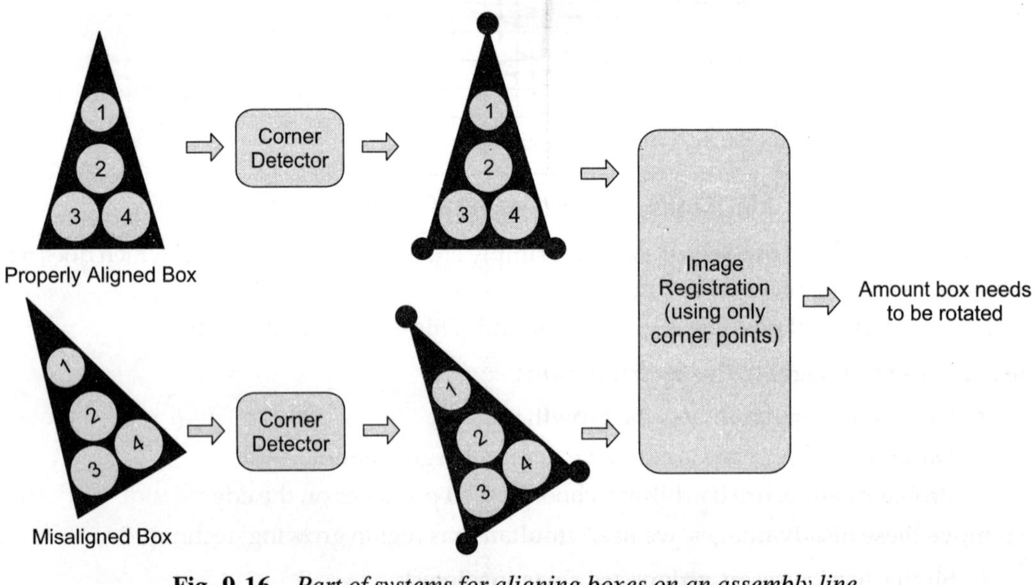

Fig. 9.16 *Part of systems for aligning boxes on an assembly line.*

9.10.2 Requirements of a Corner Detector

It is desirable for a corner detection to satisfy a number of criteria :

1. All *"true corners"* should be detected.
2. No *"false corners"* should be detected.
3. Corner points should be well localized.
4. Detector should have a high repeatability rate (good stability).
5. Detector should be robust with respect to noise.
6. Detector should be computationally efficient.

The detection of all true corners with no false corners is application (interpretation) dependent since there is no well-defined definition of a grayscale corner. However, in many images the corners are intuitively clear and such images can be used to evaluate the performance of different corner detectors.

Localization refers to how accurately the position of a corner is found. This is critical in applications requiring the precise alignment of multiple images (for example, in registration of medical images). In Fig. 9.17, the reported position of the corner is illustrated with a circle. The corner detector on the right has good localization whereas the corner detector on the left has poor localization. Although good localization is desirable for all applications, it is not critical for all applications (for example, an object detection algorithm may simply require the approximate location of all the object's corners).

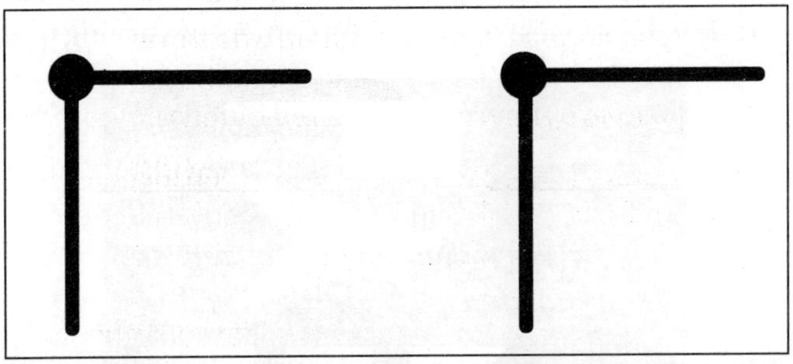

Fig. 9.17 *Illustration of good and poor localization, respectively.*

A corner detector that is robust against these transformations is said to have a **high repeatability** rate. The repeatability rate is the percentage of the total number of corner points which are repeated between two images. Fig. 9.18 shows a corner detector that fails to detect one of the triangle's corners after it is rotated, so has a repeatability rate of $\frac{2}{3}$ for this transformation.

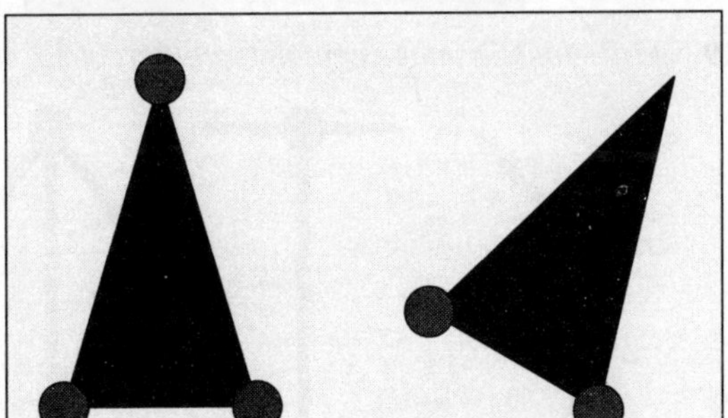

Fig. 9.18 *Corner detector failing to detect one of the triangle's corners after rotation.*

Since **noise** in images is unavoidable in most applications, a corner detector must be robust against it. The corner detector should not incorrectly identify noise as corner points and noise should have minimal affect on the localization ability of the detector.

Many applications require real-time processing so the corner detector must be **computationally efficient**. Such applications will often elect to use a simpler (and less robut or precise) corner detector in order to minimize the time spent finding the corner. Many corner detectors have been designed with this criteria in mind.

9.10.3 Evaluating and Comparing Corner Detectors

Each of the corner detectors are evalulated on an artificial test image containing different corner types and two real world images. It is important to remember that the intended application of the corner detector must be kept in mind when selecting a corner detector. For example, in an image alignment application the repeatability rate is critical, but detecting all true corners is of little importance as long as a sufficient number of interest points are available to allow accurate alignment of the images. However, in an object recognition application failing to detect a corner may result in a different description of the object being generate leading to a misclassification of the object.

The image in Fig. 9.19 contains many corner types (L-Junction, Y-Junction, T-Junction, Arrow-Junction, and X-Junction as depicted in Fig. 9.20 and is widely used to evaluate how a corner detector responds to each of these corner types. This test images also contains corners formed at a range of different grayscale values to test operation on corners of varying intensity.

Fig. 9.19 *Artificial test image containing different corner types.*

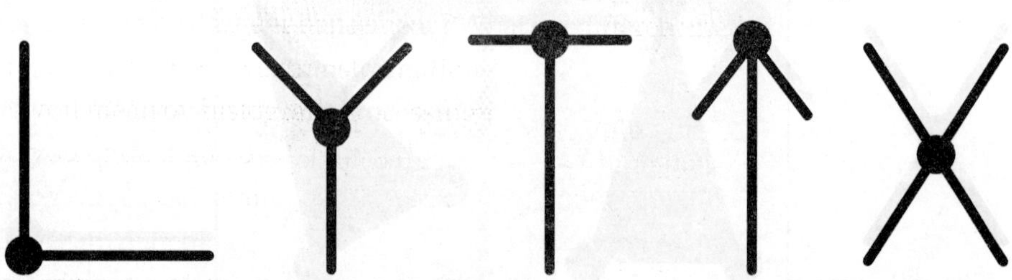

Fig. 9.20 *Example of L-junction, Y-junction, T-junction, Arrow-junction, and X-junction corner types.*

Since the majority of applications operate on real-world images, each of the corner detectors are evaluated on the two real images in Fig. 9.21. The *"block"* image tests the operation of the corner detectors on a real image where the location of the corners is intuitively clear, the background is uniform, and each object has a nearly uniform colour and texture. An image such as this, is representative of the type of images required in many assembly line or manufacturing type applications. The *"house"* image is a more difficult image due to the texture on the side and roof of the house and the presence of many different types of corners. This examples illustrates why a strict definition for a corner has not been established—it is unlikely different individuals would agree on exactly what parts of the image have a corner and would certainly not agree on the precise location of a given corner.

Fig. 9.21 *Real test images of a block and house scene.*

9.10.4 Background

Since the first corner detectors were developed in the late 1970's, dozens of corner detectors have been proposed. This section highlights a few of the more prevalent detectors in order to give the reader a feel for the variety of approaches that have been developed and to provide a historical context for the corner detectors discussed in this website. Perhaps most importantly, this sections illustrates that the seemingly simple problem of corner detection is still an open problem as no universally "good" corner detector exists. Fig. 9.22 shows a timeline of the corner detectors discussed in this section.

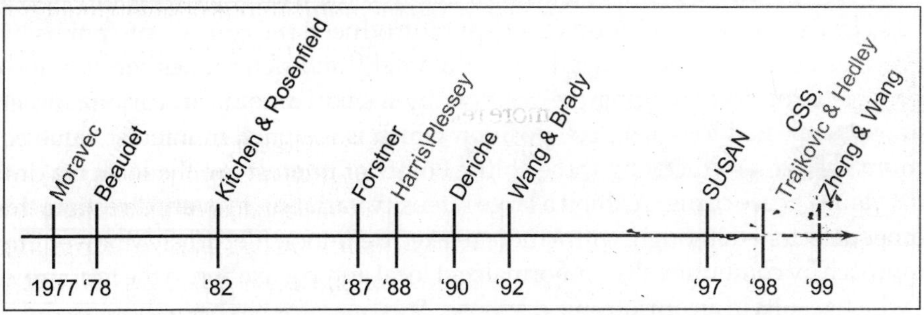

Fig. 9.22 *Timeline of select corner detectors.*

There is a significant number of different approaches for detecting corners. However, there are three main trends for detection of corners in gray scale images : **edge-relation methods, topology methods, and autocorrelation methods.**

Most of the corner detectors discussed here can be placed into one of these categories. However, it should be made clear that the classification is somewhat arbitrary as most of the detectors have multiple interpretations and thus could be classified in more than one way.

(*a*) ***Edge-Relation Methods***

Kitchen and Rosenfeld were the first to apply differential geometry operators to corner detection. They proposed a cornerness measure for each pixel based on the change of gradient direction (second-order derivatives) along an edge contour weighted by the local gradient magnitude. Corners are then identified by the local maximum of this measure, which can be done in a computationally efficient manner by applying non maximum suppression to the gradient magnitudes before weighting the second-order derivatives. This corner detector suffers from sensitivity as it relies on second-order derivative terms and has been shown to have a poor repeatability rate and localization.

A popular corner detector designed for motion estimation was proposed by Wang and Brady. They applied differential geometry operators to detect corners based on the measurement of surface curvature, but derived a simplified cornerness measure suitable for real-time applications while improving performance relative to the Kitchen and Rosenfield operator.

(*b*) ***Topology Methods***

Beaudet developed one of the first corner detectors and the insights gained from his approach are exploited by many other corner detectors. The Beaudet operator is a rotationally invariant measure of cornerness given by the determinant of the Hessian matrix. Since the Hessian matrix involves the computation of second-order derivatives this operator is sensitive to noise. In addition, it has been shown to be unstable in scale space. This approach can be viewed as looking for high curvature edges (*i.e.*, saddle points in the image surface) by calculating image Gaussian curvature (*i.e.*, the product of two principle curvatures).

Deriche extended Beaudet's operator by applying it at multiple scales. Lines are drawn between the corresponding corners at each scale and the intersection of these lines with the nearest zero crossing of the Laplacian image are defined as the position of the corner. This method improves the localization relative to the Beaudet approach, but the Deriche operator still suffers from sensitivity to noise.

(*c*) ***Autocorrelation Methods***

The Moravec operator is of importance as it inspired the widely used Plessey operator developed by Harris etal., and as Moravec's paper introduced the concept of "points of interest". His operator considers a local window in the image and determines the average change of intensity resulting from shifting the window by a small amount in various directions. This operation is repeated for each pixel position which is assigned in interest value equal to the minimum change produced by these shifts. Points of interest are the local maximum of the interest values. Since corners exhibit a large intensity variation in every direction, this operator is a corner detector—although, with a more relaxed definition for corner. Moravec implemented this approach by computing the un-normalized local autocorrelation in the four principle directions, which results in an anisotropic response. This operator has been shown to be sensitive to noise along strong edges because only the minimum intensity change is considered for each pixel position (as opposed to the variation between them).

Many of the weaknesses of the Moravec operator are addressed by the Plessey operator (often referred to as the Harris operator). Harris estimates the measure of local auto correlation using first-order derivatives which is suggested by performing an analytic expansion of the Moravec operator. The response is isotrpic as the variation of the autocorrelation over different orientations can be calculated from the principle curvatures of the local autocorrelation. The Plessey operator is generally considered the best operator with respect to detecting true corners, but has poor localization and is expensive to compute.

To address the computational complexity of the Plessey operator, Zheng and wang have proposed a computationally simplified cornerness measure justified by analyzing the Plessey operator and identifying the key aspects responsible for corner detection. As expected, this corner detector has slightly degraded performance in terms of detecting corners, but reduced the computational complexity and makes some additions to improve localization.

The Forstner operator uses a similar measure of cornerness to the Plessey operator (although, how this measure is calculated differs greatly) and uses local statistics to calculate the selection threshold. The result is better localization at the cost of increased computation. In practice, the Forstner operator is often used as it is easily extended to detect the center of circular features along with corners.

(*d*) ***Alternative Methods***

The Curvature Scale Space (CSS) operator detects corners by directly looking for local maxima of absolute curvature. That is, it detects corners using the intuitive notion of locating when the contour of an objects makes a sharp turn. The following is an outline of the steps involved in the CSS corner detector :

1. Extract the edge contours from the input image using any good edge detector (*e.g.*, Canny)
2. Fill small gaps in edge contours. When the gap forms a T-junction, mark it as a T-corner.
3. Compute curvature on the edge contours at a high scale.
4. The corner points are defined as the maxima of absolute curvature that are above a threshold value.
5. Track the corners through multiple lower scales to improve localization.
6. Compare T-corners to the other corners found using the CSS procedure and remove very close corners.

Experimental results indicate approximately 80% of the time is spent performing edge detection. Applications requiring faster corner detection can trade off other performance criteria for speed by using a simpler corner detector. Steps 2 and 6 corcern themselves with T-junctions in order to avoid assigning two corners to pixels which are close together. As illustrated in Fig. 9.23, as the contour is being followed it will pass by a T-junction twice and thus come across the same corner twice.

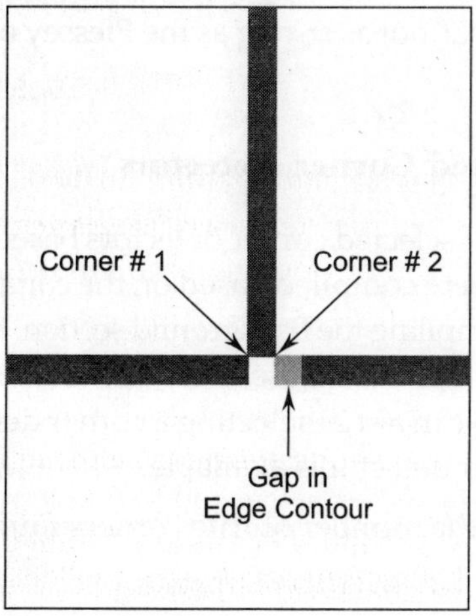

Fig. 9.23 *CSS operator detecting the same corner twice at a T-junction.*

A novel corner detector algorithm based on brightness comparisons within a circular mask is proposed by Smith and Brady. SUSAN (Smallest Univalue Segment Assimilating Nucleus) assumes that within a relatively small circular region pixels belonging to a given object will have relatively uniform brightness. The algorithm computes the number of pixels with similar brightness to the pixel at the center of the mask (the nucleus of the mask). These pixels are called the USAN (Univalue Segment Assimilating Nucleus) of the mask. Corners are detected by applying the mask to all pixels in the image and then finding the local minima in this new USAN map. Fig. 9.24 illustrates this circular mask applied to different positions of a black rectangle with the USAN. Notice that the USAN becomes smaller as it approaches an edge and this reduction is stronger at corners. SUSAN can thus be used for both line and edge detection. This corner detector is robust to noise (note that no spatial derivatives are computed), fast to compute, but only has an average repeatability rate.

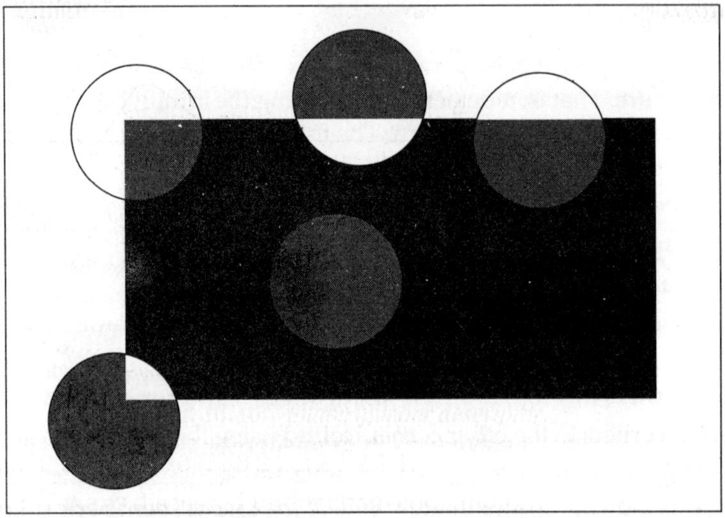

Fig. 9.24 *USAN For different circular masks on a uniform rectangle.*

Trajkovic and Hedley have proposed a corner detector that uses the same intuition used in the SUSAN operator. For a given point in the image, the variation in brightness along all lines passing through the point are considered. At corners the variation in brightness will be high for all lines. The repeatability rate of this algorithm is not as strong as the Plessey operator, but it is one of the fastest available corner detectors.

9.10.5 Comparison of Selected Corner Detectors

Table 9.1 provides a comparison of selected corner detectors based on the criteria given in the Introduction. The results of Table 9.1 were compiled based on the comparisons performed in along with the literature search done while compiling the Background section. It should be noted that no standard evaluation method has been developed for these criteria so results vary based on how the different criteria is tested. This comparison can aid in selecting a corner detector for a given application and emphasizes that no optimal corner detector is available.

Detection rate is a measure of the number of true corners found relative to the number of false detections and missed corners.

Table 9.1 ***Comparison of Selected Corner Detectors***

Operator	*Detection Rate*	*Localization*	*Repeatability Rate*	*Robustness to Noise*	*Speed*
Beaudet	Fair	Fair	Poor for scaling, good for affine transformations	Poor	Good
Moravec	Fair	Good	Fair	Fair	Good
Kitchen & Rosenfield	Fair	Fair	Fair	Fair	Poor
Forstner	Good	Good	Excellent for affine transformations, fair for scaling	Good	Poor
Plessey	Good	Good for L-junctions, poor for all other types	Excellent for affine transformations if isotropic gradient calculations are used, fair for scaling	Fair	Poor
Deriche	Fair	Good	Good	Poor	Good
Wang & Brady	Good	Good	Good	Fair	Good
SUSAN	Good	Bad for blurred images, very good otherwise	Good for scaling, poor for affine transformations	Excellent	Good
CSS	Good	Good	Excellent	Good	Highly dependent on edge detector used
Trajkovic & Hedley (4-neighbours)	Poor	Good	Fair (not rotationally invariant)	Poor	Excellent
Trajkovic & Hedley (8-neighbours)	Fair	Good	Fair+ (not rotationally invariant)	Good	Excellent
Zheng & Wang	Good	Good for L-junctions, fair for all other types	Excellent for affine transformations, fair for scaling	Fair	Fair

9.10.6 Corner Detection Algorithms

Three corner detection algorithms are explored in detail in this section. They have been chosen because they are historically significant, widely used, or well suited for a particular application (*i.e.*, real-time). In addition, all these detectors can be considered interest point corner detectors as they assign a measure of cornerness to all pixels in an image. The majority of corner detectors fall into this interest point category, although how they calculate the cornerness measure varies significantly as discussed in the Background section. This is in contrast to corner detectors which find corners by tracing the contours of objects and look for local maxima of absolute curvature or approaches using morphological operators.

The following corner detection algorithms are considered here :

- Moravec (1977)
- Harris/Plessey (1988)
- Trajkovic and Hedley (4-Neighbours) (1998)
- Trajkovic and Hedley (8-Neighbours) (1998)

All of these algorithms follow the same general steps for detecting corners. Fig. 9.25 shows a flowchart of these steps :

1. ***Apply Corner Operator :*** This step takes as input the image and typically a few parameters required by the corner operator. For each pixel in the input image, the corner operator is applied to obtain a *cornerness measure* for this pixel. The cornerness measure is simply a number indicating the degree to which the corner operator believes this pixel is a corner. Interest point corner detection algorithms differ on how the corner operator makes this measurement, but all algorithms consider only pixels within a small window centered on the pixel a measurement is being made for. The output of this step is a *cornerness map*. Since for each pixel in the input image the corner operator is applied to obtain a cornerness measure, the cornerness map has the same dimensions as the input image and can by thought of as a processed version of the input image.
2. ***Threshold Cornerness Map :*** Interest point corner detectors define corners as local maximum in the cornerness map. However, at this point the cornerness map will contain many local maximum that have a relatively small cornerness measure and are not true corners. To avoid reporting these points as corners, the cornerness map is typically thresholded. All values in the cornerness map below the threshold are set to zero. Choosing the threshold is application dependent and often requires trial and error experimentation. The threshold must be set high enough to remove local maximum that are not true corners, but low enough to retain local maximum at true corners. In practice there is rarely a threshold value that will remove all false corners and retain all true corners so a trade-off must be made based on the requirements of the application.
3. ***Non-maximal Suppression :*** The thresholded cornerness map contains only non-zero values around the local maximums that need to be marked as corner points. To locate the local maxima, *non-maximal suppression* is applied. For each point in the thresholded cornerness map, non-maximal suppression sets the cornerness measure for this point to zero if its cornerness measure is not larger than the cornerness measure of all points within a certain distance. After non-maximal suppression is applied, the corners are simply the non-zero points remaining in the cornerness map.

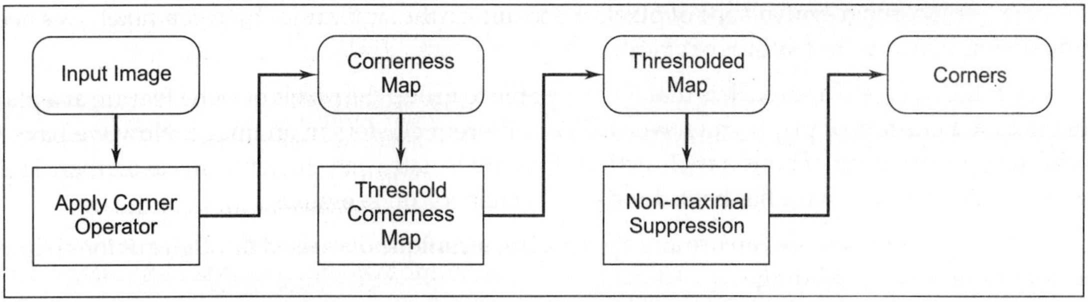

Fig. 9.25 *Flowchart for interest point corner detectors.*

The results of applying each of these steps is illustrated in Fig. 9.28.

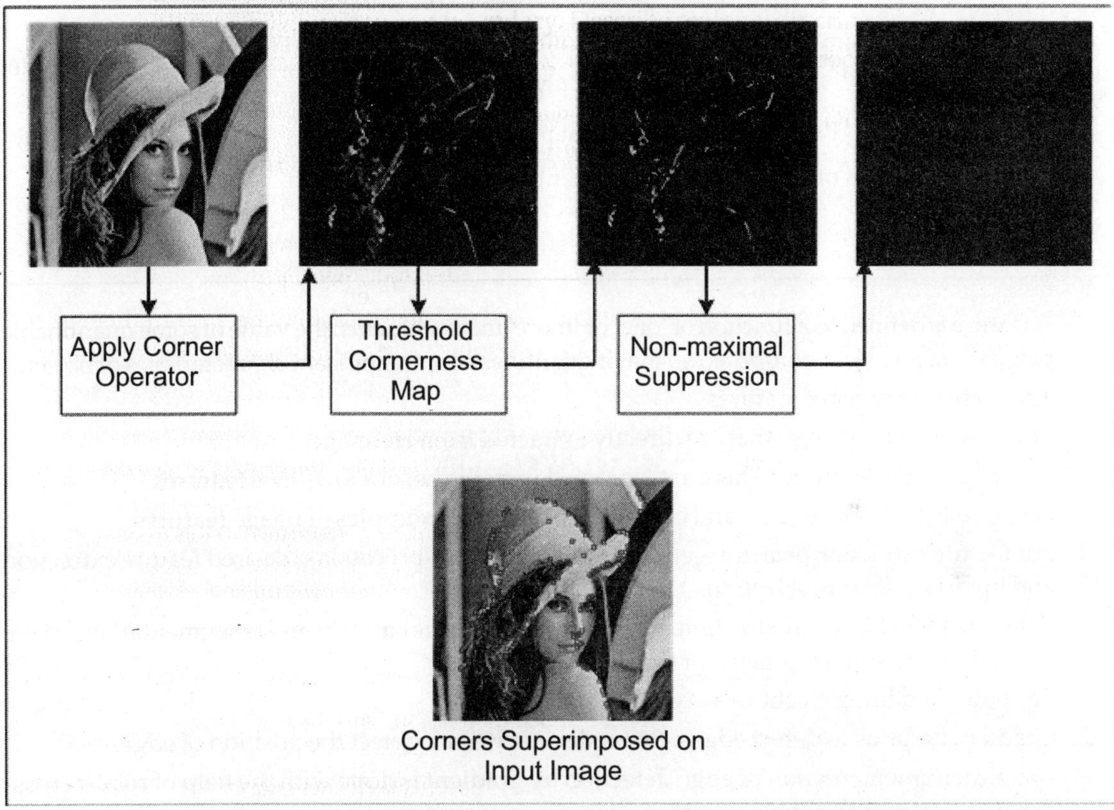

Fig. 9.26 *Example of steps in a typical interest point corner detector.*

9.11 PIXEL BASED APPROACH

At last of our discussion, we will conclude with pixel based approaches for image segmentation.

An image contains various regions corresponding to different objects. These objects contain pixels. So we can say that :

1. A group of pixel is called object.
2. A region always contains same type of objects 'or' pixels.

A object will contain similar type of pixels. So to decide the similarities between pixels, we need comparisons between the features of object.

So a straight forward approach is that if we are able to group the pixels of same feature at a place (that is called clusters of pixel) ; then we will get different clusters in an image. Now we have to decide a appropriate set of boundary functions that can isolate each cluster from each other. Thus, we can say that whole image has been divided into clusters 'or' segments.

For boundary function, we can use any appropriate technique discussed through out the chapter. Just for example - thresholding.

Suppose that there exists a threshold 't' such that feature values of all pixels that actually belong to region of first type are less than 'or' equal to 't' and gray level of all pixels that actually belongs to region of second type are greater than 't'. In this case, the segmented image is obtained as

$$b(r,c) = \begin{cases} 1 & \text{if} \quad P(r,c) \leq t \\ 0 & \text{if} \quad P(r,c) > t \end{cases} \qquad \text{... (9.26)}$$

Where $P(r, c)$ = Feature value at pixel (r, c).

Thus, it is nothing but other wording / representation of segmentation.

Summary

1. A feature is defined as a function of 'one' or 'more' measurements, the value of some quantifiable property of an object, computed so that it quantifies some significant characteristics of object.
2. There are two types of features :
   (*i*) Low-level features : that are directly extracted from an image.
   (*ii*) High-level features : There are extracted with the help of low-level features.
3. Points, edges, lines, regions and corner points are the examples of image features.
4. For feature extraction of an image. We follow image pre-processing, desired feature extraction and invariant feature selection.
5. For higher level feature extraction, image segmentation is basic. In image segmentation, image is divided into small segments of same features.
6. For point and line detection ; we use special marks.
7. Gradient helps us to detect edges. By Laplacian, we can detect the position of edge.
8. Practical implementation of edge detection by gradient is done with the help of robert cross-gradient, prewitt and sobel operator.
9. To avoid the disadvantages of Laplacian, we use Laplacian of Gaussian (LOG).
10. Edge linking is done to link small pieces of edges and to avoid the false edges.
11. By thresholding, we may divide image into different segments. Thresholding may local, global 'or' adaptive based on process of thresholding.
12. Region is defined as a group of pixels having same features. Region detection is done with the help of splitting and merging and region growing techniques.
13. Corner points are made up of two 'or' more edges. Corner points generally lies on the boundary of two different objects (also as a part of object).

Review Questions

1. What do you understand by features and feature extraction in digital image processing ?
2. Define point and line detection.
3. What are different edge detectors ? Compare them.
4. What do you understand by edge linking ? Discuss global edge linking methods.
5. What do you understand by thresholding ? How may an edge be detected using thresholding ?
6. Define region splitting and merging.
7. What are corner points ? Define corner point detectors.

CHAPTER 10

Object Representation and Description

10.1 INTRODUCTION

Till now we have extracted the features 'or' attributes of an image by segmentation and other processes. Our basic purpose of feature extraction is to make useful image for different processes and purposes.

But till now we have only raw data. These extracted feature and attributes are of no uses for computer and other machines. For that purpose we use descriptors which makes image ready for recognition.

It is possible that the raw data extracted from image can be applied directly to descriptor. But it is better to use representation before description. By representation, compactness of an image is increased.

So let us start with representation and then study descriptors.

10.2 REPRESENTATION

As described earlier *"after segmentation, we can apply the image directly for descriptor, but if we are using representation, that will increase compactness of image"*.

For representation of an image, we may use different techniques some of them are as given below:

1. Chain codes.
2. Polygonal approximation.

Now we will study them in detail.

10.2.1 Chain Codes

Chains codes are used to represent a boundary by a connected sequence of a straight line segments of specific length and directions. Typically this representation is based on 4 'or' 8 connectivity of the segment.

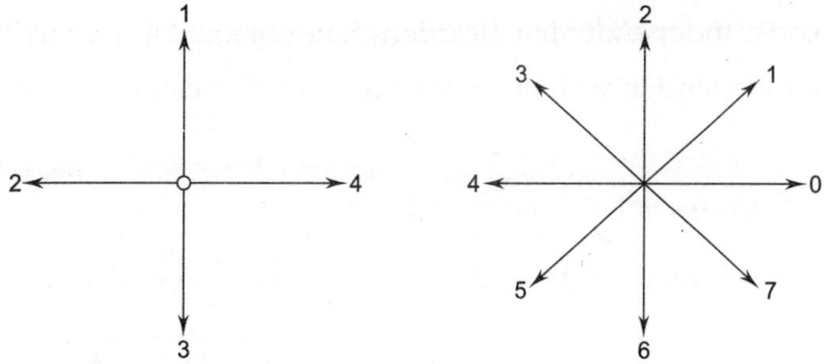

(a) 4 – Directional (b) 8 – Directional

Fig. 10.1 *Direction of chain code.*

Now simply,

1. Divide each segment of image in small grids with equal spacing in x and y direction.
2. Now decide a direction, say clockwise and according to Fig. (*a*) assign codes for every pixel (x, y).

But the basic disadvantage of this chain code is that :

1. The resulting chain of codes tends to be quite long.
2. Any small change in boundary due to noise 'or' any other disturbance, code will be changed and this new code will have no relation with the real image boundary.

To avoid this type of problems, we resample the boundary by selecting a large grid spacing as shown below :

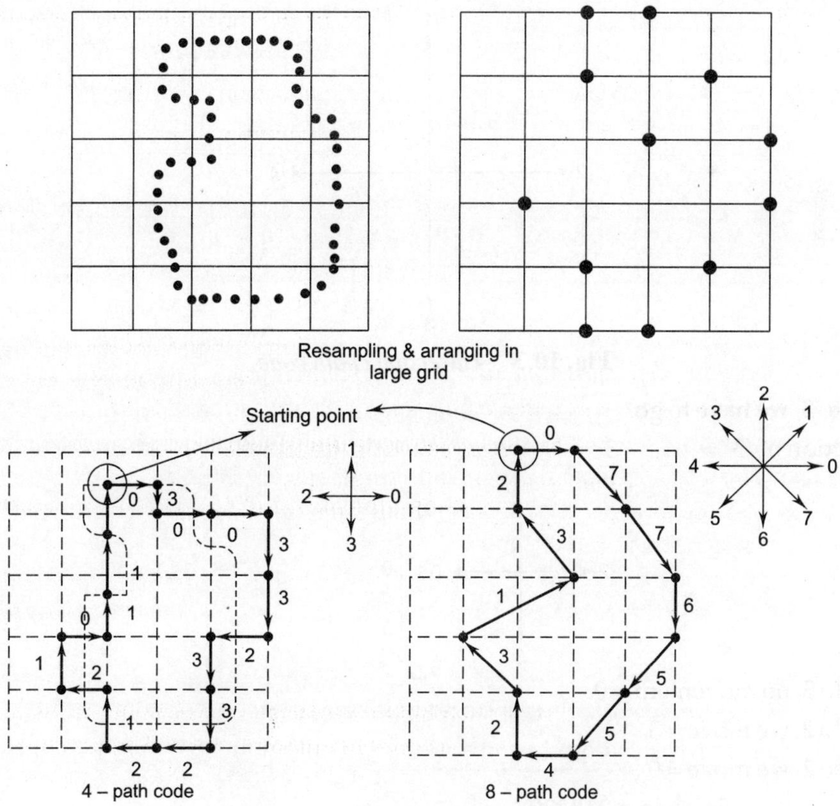

Fig. 10.2 *Chain coding by using grid.*

We can make the codes independent to direction change also.

To make direction independence chain codes, we send first difference chain codes in stead of codes itself.

Codes = 1 0 1 0 3 3 2 2

to make first difference code just count the changes (direction changes) and write that

(*a*) for 1 to 0, we have to go in direction of 3 = 3.

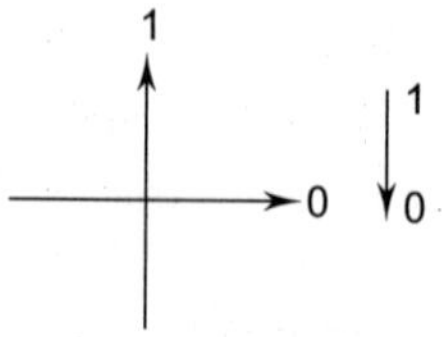

(*b*) from 0 to 1, we have to go in direction of 1 = 1.

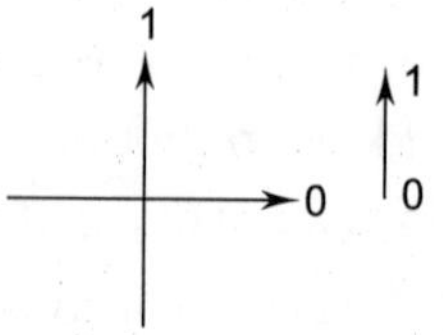

(*c*) from 1 to 0, we have to go in direction of 3 = 3

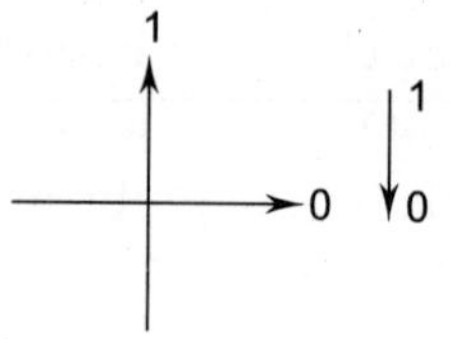

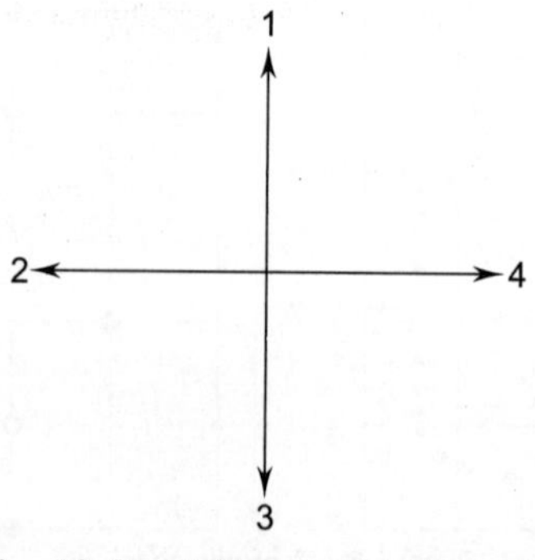

Fig. 10.3 *4 direction chain code.*

(*d*) from 0 to 3, we have to go.

In direction of '3' = 3

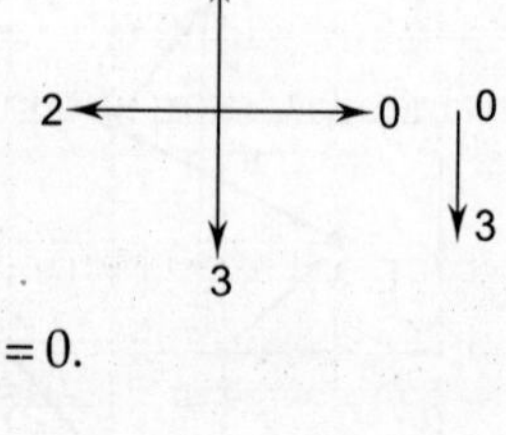

(*e*) from 3 to 3, no movement = 0.

(*f*) from 3 to 2, we move = 3

(*g*) from 2 to 2, we move = 0

So code = 313330

10.2.2 Polygonal Approximation

A digital boundary can be approximated by a polygon.

Our main purpose is to convert a boundary shape into fewest possible polygon segments.

10.2.2.1 Minimum Perimeter Polygons

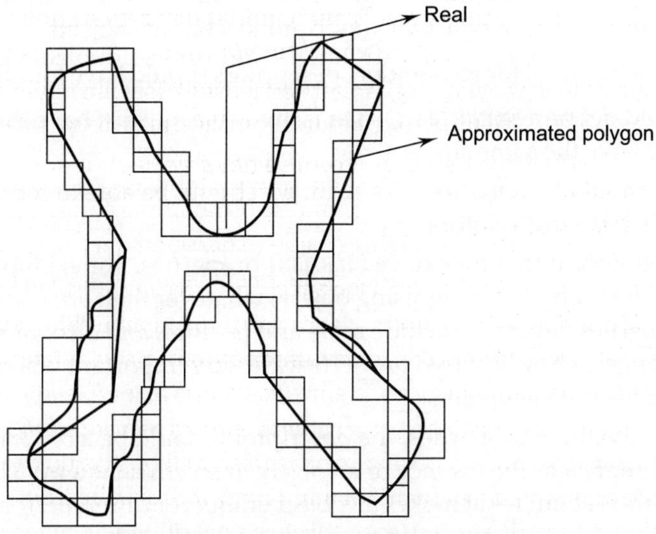

Fig. 10.4 *Minimum perimeter polygon.*

Here just assume that image segment is rubber band. As it will sink, automatically the rubber band will get a shape of polygon.

The rubber band if taking the shape of walls of cell ; then the error between the real image and approximation = $\sqrt{2}d$

d = minimum possible distance between two pixels.

10.2.2.2 Splitting Techniques

In this technique, we split the boundary segment using any criterian.

Just take an example that we decide a boundary segment. Now we draw a line between two points of segment. Now criteria is that we should split the boundary segment in such a way that we cover the maximum distance (perpendicular) from drawn line. See the process below by image.

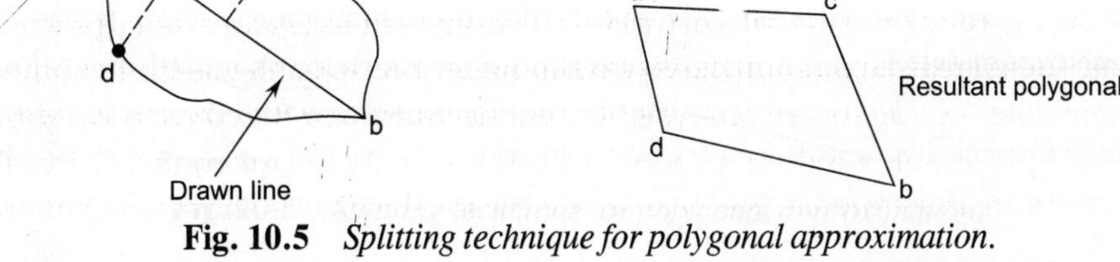

Fig. 10.5 *Splitting technique for polygonal approximation.*

10.3 OBJECT DESCRIPTION

10.3.1 Introduction

"Objects are represented as a collection of pixels in an image. Thus, for purposes of recognition we need to describe the properties of groups of pixels". The description is often just a set of numbers called the object's *descriptors*. From these, we can compare and recognise objects by simply matching the descriptors of objects in an image against the descriptors of known objects.

However, in order to be useful for recognition, descriptors should have four important properties:

1. First, they should define a *complete set*. That is, two objects must have the same descriptors if and only if they have the same shape.
2. Secondly, they should be *congruent*. As such, we should be able to recognise *similar* objects when they have *similar* descriptors.
3. Thirdly, it is convenient that they have *invariant* properties. For example, *rotation* invariant descriptors will be useful for recognising object ; whatever their *orientation*. Other important invariance properties naturally include scale and position and also invariance to affine and perspective changes. These last two properties are very important when recognising objects observed from different viewpoints.
4. In addition to these three properties, the descriptors should be a *compact* set. Namely, a descriptor should represent the essence of an object in an efficient way. That is, it should only contain information about what makes an object unique, or different from the other objects.

The quantity of information used to describe this characterisation should be less than the information necessary to have a complete description of the object itself.

Unfortunately, there is no set of complete and compact descriptors to characterise general objects. Thus, the best recognition performance is obtained by carefully selected properties. As such, the process of recognition is strongly related to each particular application with a particular type of object. In this chapter, we present the characterisation of objects by two forms of descriptors : *Region* and *shape* descriptors.

10.3.2 Boundary Descriptions

10.3.2.1 Boundary and Region

"A region usually describes contents (or interior points) which are surrounded by a boundary (or perimeter) which is often called the region's contour. The form of the contour is generally referred to as its shape. A point can be defined to be on the boundary (contour) if it is part of the region and there is at least one pixel in its neighbourhood that is not part of the region". The boundary itself is usually found by contour following: we first find one point on the contour and then progress round the contour either in a clockwise direction, or anti-clockwise, finding the nearest (or next) contour point.

In order to define the interior points in a region and the points in the boundary, we need to consider neighbouring relationships between pixels. These relationships are described by means of *connectivity* rules. There are two common ways of defining connectivity : 4-*way* (or 4-neighbourhood) where only immediate *neighbours* are analysed for connectivity ; or 8-*way* (or 8-neighbourhood) where all the eight pixels surrounding a choosen pixel are analysed for connectivity. These two types of connectivity are illustrated in Fig. 10.6. In this figure, the pixel is shown in light grey and its neighbours in dark grey. In 4-way connectivity, Fig. 10.6 (*a*), a pixel has four neighbours in the directions north, east, south and west, its immediate neighbours. The four extra neighbours in 8-way connectivity, Fig. 10.6 (*b*), are those in the directions north east, south east, south west and north west, the points at the *corners*.

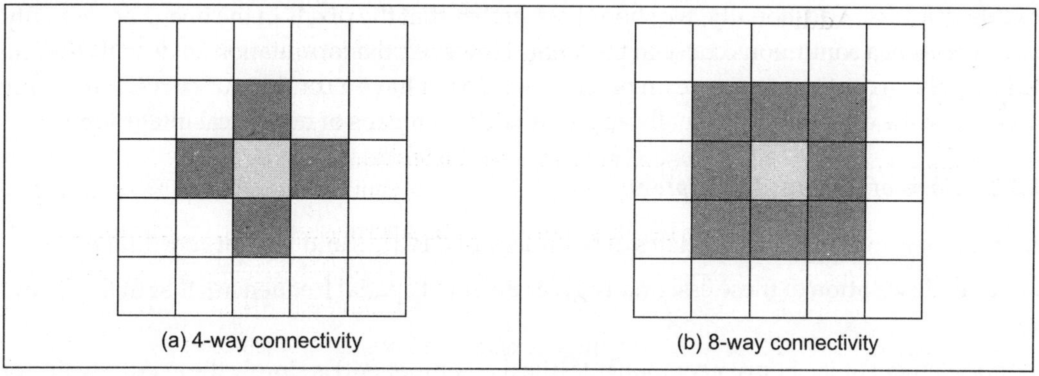

Fig. 10.6 *Main types of connectivity analysis.*

A boundary and a region can be defined using both types of connectivity and they are always *complementary*. That is, if the boundary pixels are connected in 4 way, then the region pixels will be connected in 8-way and vice versa. This relationship can be seen in the example shown in Fig. 10.7. In the example in this figure, the boundary is shown in dark grey and the region in light grey. We can observe that for a diagonal boundary, the 4-way connectivity gives a staircase boundary whereas 8-way connectivity gives a diagonal line formed from the points at the corners of the neighbourhood. Notice that all the pixels that form the region in Fig. 10.7 (*b*) have 8-way connectivity, whilst the pixels in Fig. 10.7 (*c*) have 4-way connectivity. This is complementary to the pixels in the border.

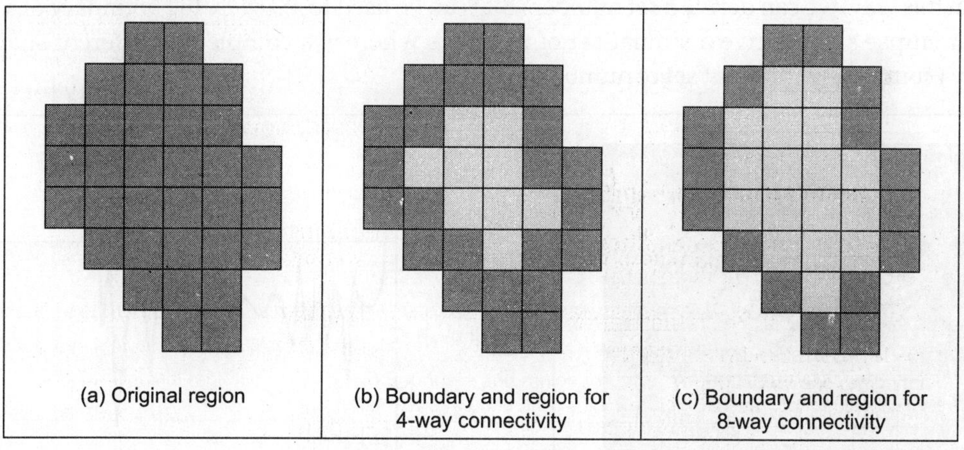

Fig. 10.7 *Boundaries and regions.*

Fourier Descriptors

Fourier descriptors allow us to bring the power of Fourier theory to shape description. The main idea is to characterize a contour by a set of numbers that represent the frequency content of a whole shape. Based on frequency analysis we can select a *small* set of numbers (the Fourier coefficients) that describe a shape rather than any noise (*i.e.*, the noise affecting the spatial position of the boundary pixels). The general recipe to obtain a Fourier description of the curve involves two main steps. First, we have to define a representation of a curve. Secondly, we expand it using Fourier theory.

It is important to notice that although a curve in an image is composed of discrete pixels, Fourier descriptors are developed for continuous curves. This is convenient since it leads to a discrete set of Fourier descriptors. Additionally, we should remember that the pixels in the image are actually the sampled points of a continuous curve in the scene. However, the formulation leads to the definition of the integral of a continuous curve. In practice, we do not have a continuous curve, but a sampled version. Thus, the expansion is actually approximated by means of numerical integration.

10.3.2.2 Basis of Fourier Descriptors

In the most basic form, the co-ordinates of boundary pixels are x and y point coordinates.

A Fourier description of these essentially gives the set of spatial frequencies that fit the boundary points.

The *first* element of the Fourier components (the d.c. component) is simply the average value of the x and y co-ordinates, giving the co-ordinates of the center point of the boundary, expressed in complex form. The *second* component essentially gives the radius of the circle that best fits the points. Accordingly, a circle can be described by its zero- and first-order components (the d.c. component and first harmonic). The *higher* order components increasingly describe detail, as they are associated with higher frequencies.

This is illustrated in Fig. 10.8. Here, the Fourier description of the ellipse in Fig. 10.8 (a) is the frequency components in Fig. 10.8 (b), depicted in logarithmic form for purposes of display. The Fourier description has been obtained by using the ellipse boundary points' co-ordinates. Here we can see that the low order components dominate the description, as to be expected for such a smooth shape. In this way, we can derive a set numbers that can be used to *recognise* the boundary of a shape: a similar ellipse should give a similar set of numbers whereas a completely different shape will result in a completely different set of numbers.

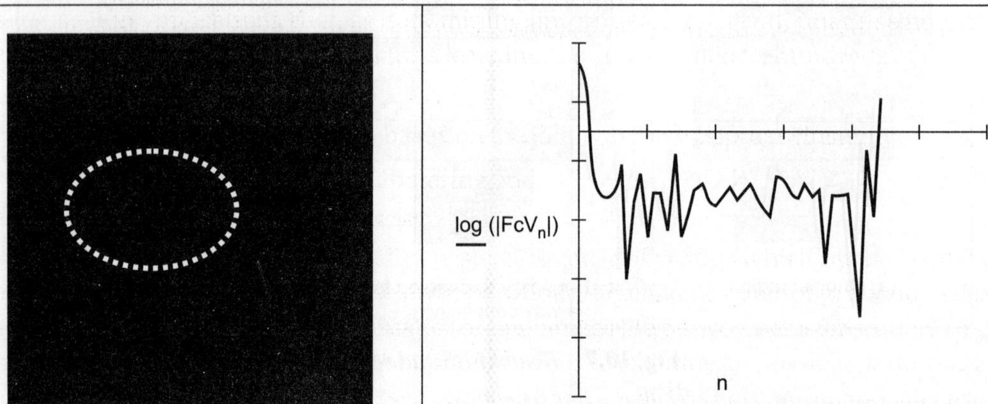

(a) Original ellipse (b) Fourier components

Fig. 10.8 *Basic fourier descriptor.*

We do, however, need to check the result. One way is to take the descriptors of a circle, since the first harmonic should be the circle's radius. A better way though is to *reconstruct* the shape from its descriptors, if the reconstruction matches the original shape then the description would appear correct. Naturally, we can reconstruct a shape from this Fourier description since the descriptors are *regenerative.* The zero-order component gives the position (or origin) of a shape. The ellipse can be reconstructed by adding in all spatial components, to extend and compact the shape along the x and *y* axes, respectively. By this inversion, we return to the original ellipse. When we include the zero and first descriptor, then we reconstruct a circle, as expected, shown in Fig. 10.9 (*b*). When we include all Fourier descriptors the reconstruction, Fig. 10.9 (*c*), is very close to the original, Fig. 10.9 (*a*), with slight difference due to discretisation effects.

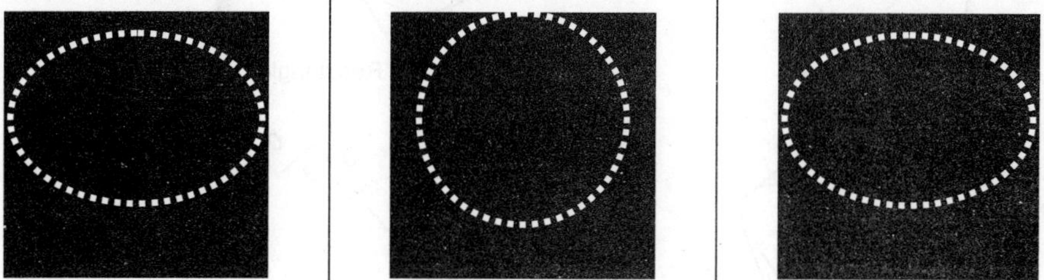

(a) Original ellipse | (b) Reconstruction by zero- and first-order components | (c) Reconstruction by all Fourier components

Fig. 10.9 *Reconstructing an ellipse from a Fourier description.*

But this is only an outline of the basis of Fourier descriptors, since we have yet to consider descriptors which give the same description whatever an object's position, scale and rotation. Here we have just considered an object's description that is achieved in a manner that allows for reconstruction. In order to develop practically useful descriptors, we shall need to consider more basic properties. As such, we first turn to the use of Fourier theory for shape description.

10.3.2.3 Shape Numbers

Another type of popular boundary descriptor is shape number.

"The shape number of a boundary based on the 4-directional code is defined as the first difference of smallest magnitude".

The order '*n*' of shape number is defined as the number of digits in its representation. Note that first difference is computed treating the chain codes as circular sequence. In practice, for a desired shape order, we find the rectangle of order *n*, suppose that we need of order 18, then it will be $n = 18$ subdivision in rectangles of 3×6 ; these small rectangles are also called grids. Now chain-code directions are aligned with these grids. Now just obtain chain code and use its first difference to compute the shape number.

Let us discuss one example, suppose that for $n = 18$, we have to find boundary description using shape number. So,

1. Basic rectangle of order $n = 18$; means a rectangle that is covering whole image with minimum perimeter.
2. Now divide this rectangle by $n = 18 = 3 \times 6$ rectangles.
3. Now align the chain codes direction with grids.
4. Find chain codes and shape number.

Whole process have been given below in figure.

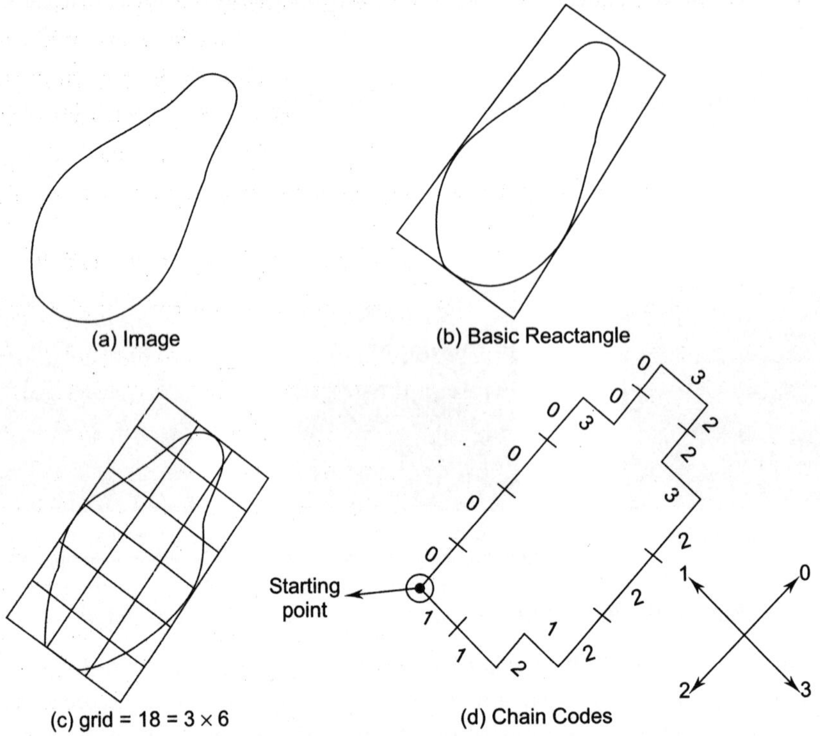

Fig. 10.10 *Shape number descriptor.*

Chain Code: 0 0 0 0 3 0 0 3 2 2 3 2 2 2 2 1 2 1 1.

Difference Code: Take as discussed under chain code topic.

We will get

3 0 0 0 3 1 0 3 3 0 1 3 0 0 3 1 3 0

Now shape number : Shape number is first difference of smallest distance. First difference is calculated by treating chain code as circular. So,

3 0 0 0 3 1 0 3 3 0 1 3 0 0 3 1 3 0

Circularly shifted

= 0 0 0 3 1 0 3 3 0 1 3 0 0 3 1 3 0 3

is the desired shape number.

10.3.3 Region Descriptors

So far, we have concentrated on descriptions of the perimeter, or boundary. The natural counterpart is to describe the region, or the area, by regional shape descriptors.

10.3.3.1 Basic Region Descriptors

A region can be described by considering scalar measures based on its geometric properties.

1. The simplest property is given by its size or area. In general, the area of a region in the plane is defined as

$$A(S) = \int_x \int_y I(x, y)\, dy\, dx \qquad \text{... (10.1)}$$

where I $(x, y) = 1$ if the pixel is within a shape, $(x, y) \in S$, and 0 otherwise. In practice, integrals are approximated by summations. That is,

$$A(S) = \sum_x \sum_y I(x, y)\, \Delta A \qquad \text{... (10.2)}$$

where ΔA is the area of one pixel. Thus, if $\Delta A = 1$, then the area is measured in pixels. Area changes with changes in scale. However, it is invariant to image rotation. Small errors in the computation of the area will appear when applying a rotation transformation due to discretisation of the image.

2. Another simple property is defined by the perimeter of the region. If $x(t)$ and $y(t)$ denote the parametric co-ordinates of a curve enclosing a region S, then the perimeter of the region is defined as

$$P(S) = \int_t \sqrt{x^2(t) + y^2(t)}\, dt \qquad \text{... (10.3)}$$

This equation corresponds to the sums of all the infinitesimal arcs that define the curve. In the discrete case, $x(t)$ and $y(t)$ are defined by a set of pixels in the image. Thus, equation (10.3) is approximated

$$P(S) = \sum_i \sqrt{(x_i - x_{i-1})^2 + (y_i - y_{i-1})^2} \qquad \text{... (10.4)}$$

where x_i and y_i represent the co-ordinates of the ith pixel forming the curve. Since pixels are organised in a square grid, then the terms in the summation can only take two values. When the pixels (x_i, y_i) and (x_{i-1}, y_{i-1}) are 4-neighbours (as shown in Fig. 10.6 (*a*)), the summation term is unity. Otherwise, the summation term is equal to 2. Notice that the discrete approximation in Equation 10.4 produces small errors in the measured perimeter. As such, it is unlikely that an exact value of $2\pi r$ will be achieved for the perimeter of a circular region of radius r.

3. Based on the perimeter and area it is possible to characterize the compactness of a region. Compactness is an oft-expressed measure of shape given by the ratio of perimeter to area. That is,

$$C(S) = \frac{4\pi A(s)}{P^2(s)} \qquad \text{... (10.5)}$$

In order to show the meaning of this equation, we can rewrite it as

$$C(S) = \frac{A(s)}{P^2(s)/4\pi} \qquad \text{... (10.6)}$$

Here, the denominator represents the area of a circle whose perimeter is P (S). Thus, compactness measures the ratio between the area of the shape and the circle that can be traced with the same perimeter. That is, compactness measures the efficiency with which a boundary encloses an area. For a circular region (Fig. 10.11 (*a*)) (This represents the maximum compactness value) Fig. 10.11 (*b*) and (*c*) show two examples in which compactness is reduced. If we take the perimeter of these regions and draw a circle with the same perimeter, then we can observe that the circle contains more area. This means that the shapes are not compact. A shape becomes more compact if we move region pixels far away from the centre of gravity of the shape to fill empty spaces closer to the centre of gravity. Note that compactness alone is not a good discriminator of a region ; low values of C are associated with involuted regions such as the one in Fig. 10.11 (*b*) and also with simple though highly elongated shapes. This ambiguity can be resolved by employing additional shape measures.

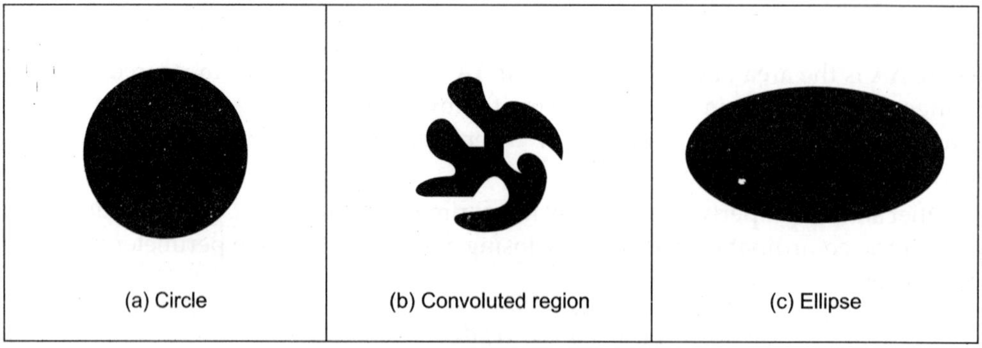

Fig. 10.11 *Examples of compactness.*

4. Another measure that can be used to characterise regions is dispersion.
Dispersion (irregularity) has been measured as the ratio of major chord length to area (Chen, 1995). A simple version of this measure can be defined as

$$I(S) = \frac{\pi \max (x_i - \bar{x})^2 + (y_i - \bar{y})^2}{A(S)} \quad \text{... (10.7)}$$

where (x, y) represent the co-ordinates of the centre of mass of the region. Notice that the numerator defines the area of the maximum circle enclosing the region. Thus, this measure describes the density of the region. An alternative measure of dispersion can actually also be expressed as the ratio of the maximum to the minimum radius. That is,

$$IR(S) = \frac{\max \sqrt{(x_i - \bar{x})^2 + (y_i - \bar{y})^2}}{\min \sqrt{(x_i - \bar{x})^2 + (y_i - \bar{y})^2}} \quad \text{... (10.8)}$$

This measure defines the ratio between the radius of the maximum circle enclosing the region and the maximum circle that can be contained in the region. Thus, the measure will increase as the region spreads. One *disadvantage* of the irregularity measures is that they are insensitive to slight *discontinuity* in the shape, such as a thin crack in a disk. On the other hand, these discontinuities will be registered by the earlier measures of compactness since the perimeter will increase disproportionately with the area.

10.3.3.2 Moments

Moments decribe a shape's *layout* (the arrangement of its pixels), a bit like combining area, compactness, irregularity and higher order descriptions together. Moments are a *global* description of a shape, accruing this same advantage as Fourier descriptors since there is an in-built ability to discern, and filter, noise. Further, in image analysis, they are *statistical moments*, as opposed to *mechanical* ones, but the two are analogous. For example, the mechanical moment of inertia describes the rate of change in momentum ; the statistical second-order moment describes the rate of change in a shape's area. In this way, statistical moments can be considered as a global region description. Moments for image analysis were again originally introduced in the 1960s (Hu, 1962) and an excellent and fairly up-to-date review is available (Prokop, 1992). Moments are actually often associated more with *statistical* pattern recognition than with *model-based* vision since a major assumption is that there is an *unoccluded* view of the target shape. Target images are often derived by thresholding, usually one of the optimal forms that can require a single object in the field of view. More complex applications, including handling occlusion, could presuppose *feature* extraction by some means, with a model to in-fill for the missing parts. However, moments do provide a global description with invariance properties and with the advantages of a compact description aimed to avoid the effects of noise. As such, they have proved popular and successful in many applications.

The *two-dimensional Cartesian moment* is actually associated with an order that starts from low (where the lowest is zero) up to higher orders. The moment of order p and q, m_{qp} of a function I (x, y), is defined as

$$m_{pq} = \int_{-\infty}^{\infty} \int_{-\infty}^{\infty} x^p y^q \, \mathrm{I}(x, y)\, dx\, dy \qquad \text{... (10.9)}$$

For discrete images, equation 10.9 is usually approximated by

$$m_{pq} = \sum_x \sum_y x^p y^q \, \mathrm{I}(x, y)\, \Delta \mathrm{A} \qquad \text{... (10.10)}$$

These descriptors have a uniqueness property in that if the function satisfies certain conditions, then moments of all orders exist. Also, and conversely, the set of descriptors uniquely determines the original function, in a manner similar to reconstruction via the inverse Fourier transform. However, these moments are descriptors, rather than a specification which can be used to reconstruct a shape. The zero-order moment, m_{00}, is

$$m_{00} = \sum_x \sum_y \mathrm{I}(x, y)\, \Delta \mathrm{A} \qquad \text{... (10.11)}$$

which represents the total mass of a function. Notice that this equation is equal to Equation (10.2) when I (x, y) takes values of zero and one. However, equation (10.11) is more general since the function I (x, y) can take a range of values. In the definition of moments, these values are generally related to density. The two first-order moments, m_{01} and m_{10}, are given by

$$m_{10} = \sum_x \sum_y x\mathrm{I}(x, y)\, \Delta \mathrm{A}\, ; m_{01} = \sum_x \sum_y y\mathrm{I}(x, y)\, \Delta \mathrm{A} \qquad \text{... (10.12)}$$

For binary images, these values are proportional to the shape's centre co-ordinates (the values merely require division by the shape's area). In general, the centre of mass (x, y) can be calculated from the ratio of the first-order to the zero-order components as

$$\bar{x} = \frac{m_{10}}{m_{00}}\, ; \bar{y} = \frac{m_{01}}{m_{00}} \qquad \text{... (10.13)}$$

10.3.4 Relationship

Till now we have discussed the descriptors that provide simple discription of an object. But the ultimate goal is not only to describe an object through its global features 'or' through features of each component. Our goal is also to find the inter-relationship between them. By using relational description, we can solve our purpose.

10.3.4.1 Relational Descriptor

"The main purpose of relational descriptor is that to find some rules for basic patterns in a region. And after finding some basic patterns in an image, we will describe the whole image by the relation between these basic patterns. These basic patterns are also called primitives of an image".

Let us take one example. Suppose that from an image segment, we have extracted the following basic pattern (primitives).

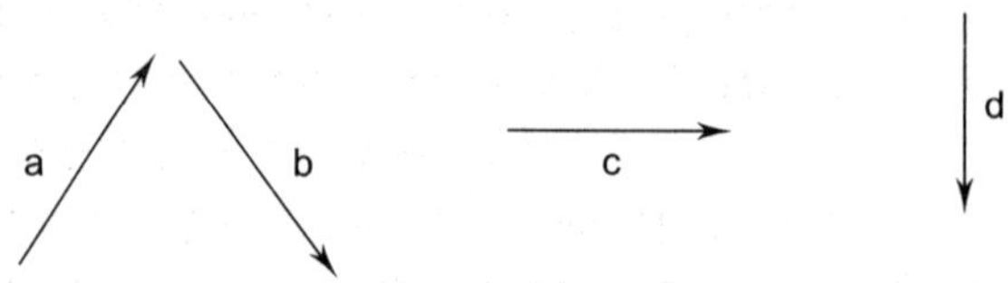

Fig. 10.12 *Extraction of Primitives.*

Now on the basis of the primitives extracted, we can now find the relationship between different features in image and also may develop the basic rules for them. For example, some other features of that image can be descripted by these features following some mathematical rules.

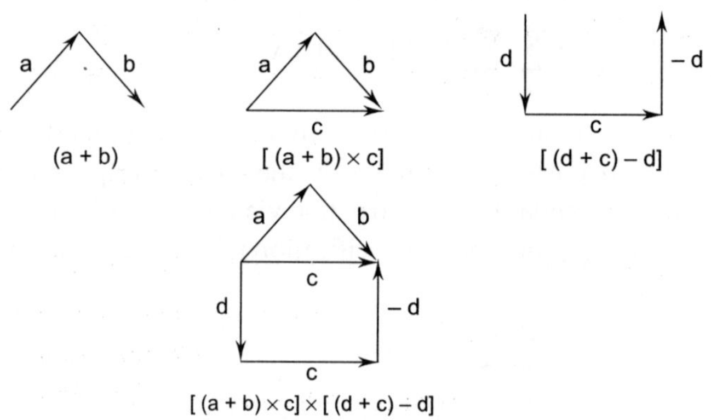

Fig. 10.13 *Description of shape on the basis of relation between primitive.*

Summary

1. After feature extraction, we get raw data of an image. To make them suitable for computer processing we need descriptors.
2. By representation ; we can get compact image before applying to descriptors.
3. For representation ; we may use different techniques ; but most useful are chain codes and polygonal approximation.
4. For description, we may depend upon the external shape of feature that is referred as boundary description we may also depend upon the internal properties of feature, called region description.
5. Basic boundary descriptors are Fourier descriptor and shape number.
6. Basic regional descriptors are areas of region, perimeter of region, compactness dispersion and moments etc.

7. Boundary and regional descriptors do not provide the relation between different features, for that purpose we use relational descriptors.
8. Relational descriptors extracts basic primitive from features first and then describe the features based on relation between these primitives.

Review Questions

1. What do you understand by representation of an image ?
2. Describe :
    1. Chain Codes
    2. Polygonal approximation methods of representation.
3. Differentiate between region and boundary. Describe regional descriptors.
4. What is the advantage to use relational descriptors ? Describe the process of description using relational descriptors.

11 CHAPTER

PATTERN/OBJECT RECOGNITION

11.1 INTRODUCTION

Automatic (machine) Pattern/object recognition, description, classification, and grouping of pattern/objects are important problems in a variety of engineering and scientific disciplines such as biology, psychology, medicine, marketing, computer vision, artificial intelligence, remote sensing and image processing.

11.2 DEFINITION

"Pattern/object recognition aims to classify data (pattern/objects) based on either a prior knowledge or on statistical information extracted from the pattern/objects. The pattern/objects to be classified are usually groups of measurements or observations, defining points in an appropriate multidimensional space. For example, a pattern/object could be a fingerprint image, a handwritten cursive word, a human face, or a speech signal".

11.3 PATTERN/OBJECT REORGANIZATION SYSTEM

A complete pattern/object recognition system consists of a sensor that gathers the observations to be classified or described ; feature extraction mechanism that computes numeric or symbolic information from the observations; and a classification or description scheme that does the actual job of classifying or describing observations, relying on the extracted features (See Fig. 11.1).

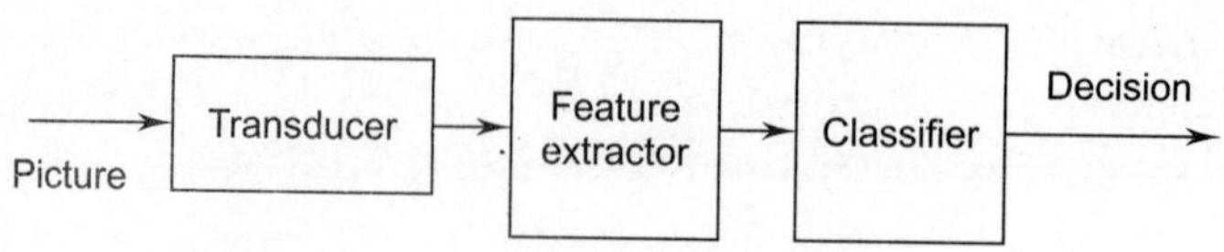

Fig. 11.1 *A pattern classification system.*

Table 11.1 *Examples of Pattern Recognition Applications*

Problem Domain	*Application*	*Input Pattern*	*Pattern Classes*
Bioinformatics	Sequence analysis	DNA/Protein sequence	Known types of genes/ pattern
Data mining	Searching for meaningful patterns	Points in multi-dimensional space	Compact and well-separated closers
Document classification	Internet search	Text document	Semantic categories (*e.g.*, business, sports, etc.)
Document image analysis	Reading machine for the blind	Document image	Alphanumeric characters, cards
Industrial automation	Printed circuit board inspection	Intensity or range image	Defective / non-defective nature of product
Multimedia database retrieval	Interent search	Video clip	Video generes. action, dialogue, etc.)
Biometric recognition	Personal identification	Face, iris, fingerprint	Authorized uses for access control
Remote sensing	Forecasting crop yield	Multispecial image	Land use categories, growth pattern of crops
Speech recognition	Telephone directory enquiry without operator assistance	Speech waveform	Spoken words

11.4 CLASSIFICATION

Given a pattern/object, its recognition/classification may consist of one of the following two tasks :

1. **Supervised classification** (*e.g.*, discriminant analysis) in which the input Pattern/object is identified as a member of a predefined class.
2. **Unsupervised classification** (*e.g.*, clustering) in which the pattern/object is assigned to a hitherto unknown class. Note that the recognition problem here is being posed as a classification or categorization task, where the classes are either defined by the system designer (in supervised classification) or are learned based on the similarity of pattern/objects (in unsupervised classification).

11.5 APPROACHES FOR PATTERN/OBJECT RECOGNITION

The four best-known approaches for pattern/object recognition are :

1. **Template matching**
2. **Statistical classification :** It includes methods based on Bayes decision rule, the maximum likelihood or density estimator. Three well-known methods are K-nearest neighbour (KNN), Parzen window classifier and branch-and bound methods (BnB).
3. **Syntactic or structural matching :** Examples are fisher's linear discriminant, multilayer perceptrons, decision tree and support vector machine and

4. **Neural networks.**

These models are not necessarily independent and sometimes the same pattern/object recognition method exists with different interpretations. Attempts have been made to design hybrid systems involving multiple models.

11.6 TEMPLATE MATCHING

One of the simplest and earliest approaches to pattern recognition is based on template matching. Matching is a generic operation in pattern recognition which is used to determine the similarity between two entities (points, curves, or shapes) of the same type. In template matching, a template (typically, a 2-D shape) or a prototype of the pattern to be recognized is available. The pattern to be recognized is matched against the stored template while taking into account all allowable pose (translation and rotation) and scale changes. The similarity measure, often a correlation, may be optimized based on the available training set.

Consider that we want to find the template of Fig. 11.2 (*b*) in the image of Fig. 11.2(*a*). The template is first positioned at the origin and then matched with the image to give a count which reflects how well the template matched that part of the image at that position.

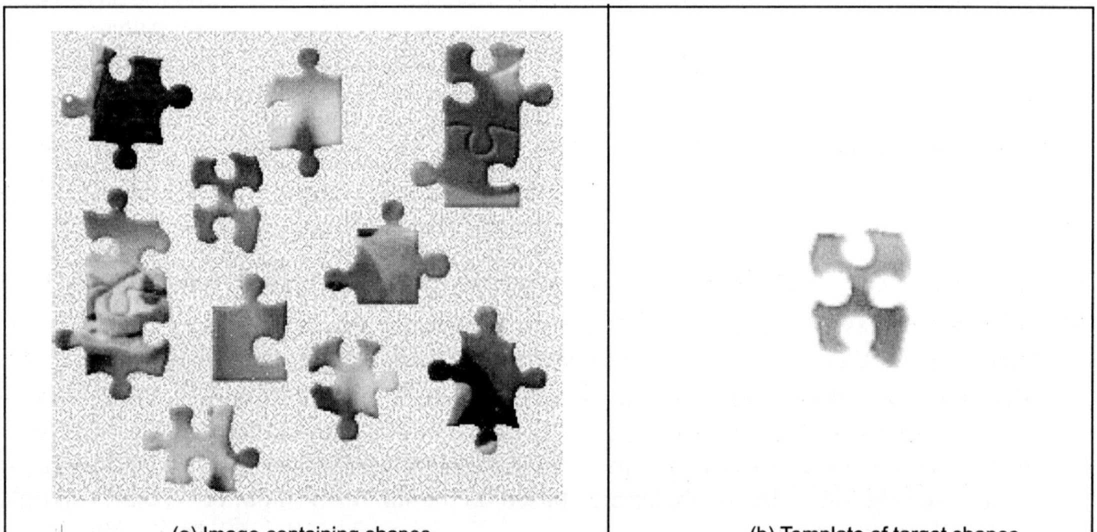

(a) Image containing shapes

(b) Template of target shapes

Fig. 11.2 *Illustrating template matching.*

The procedure is repeated for the entire image and the point which led to the best match, the maximum count, is deemed to be the point where the shape (given by the template) lies within the image.

Often, the template itself is learned from the training set. Template matching is computationally demanding, but the availability of faster processors has now made this approach more feasible. The rigid template matching mentioned above, while effective in some application domains, has a number of disadvantages. For instance, it would fail if the patterns are distorted due to the imaging process, viewpoint change, or large intra class variations among the patterns. Deformable template models or rubber sheet deformations can be used to match patterns when the deformation cannot be easily explained or modeled directly.

11.7 STATISTICAL PATTERN/OBJECT RECOGNITION SYSTEM

Statistical pattern/object recognition has been used successfully to design a number of commercial recognition systems. *"In statistical pattern/object recognition, a pattern/object is represented by a set of d features, or attributes, viewed as a d-dimensional feature vector. Well-known concepts from statistical decision theory are utilized to establish decision boundaries between pattern/object classes"*. The recognition system is operated in two modes : training (learning) and classification (testing) (see Fig. 11.3). The role of the preprocessing module is to segment the pattern/object of interest from the background, remove noise, normalize the pattern/object, and any other operation, which will contribute in defining a compact representation of the pattern/object. In the training mode, the feature extraction/selection module finds the appropriate features for representing the input pattern/objects and the classifier is trained to partition the feature space. The feedback path allows a designer to optimize the preprocessing and feature extraction/selection strategies. In the classification mode, the trained classifier assigns the input pattern/object to one of the pattern/object classes under consideration based on the measured features.

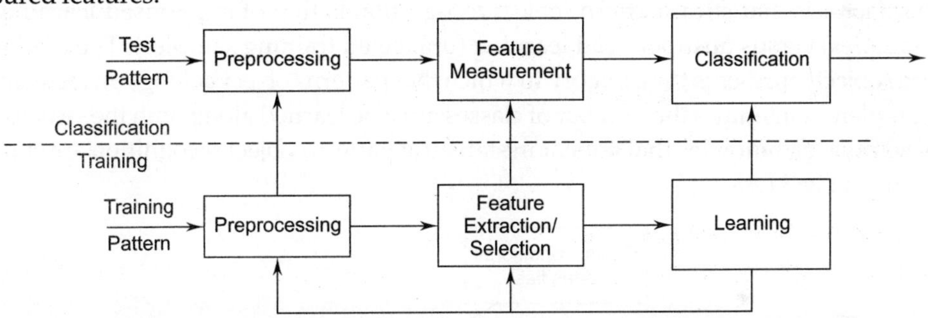

Fig. 11.3 *Block diagram of a statistical object recognition system.*

The decision making process in statistical pattern/object recognition can be summarized as follows : A given pattern/object is to be assigned to one of c categories. $w_1, w_2, \ldots\ldots, w_c \mid$ based on a vector of d feature values $x = (x_1, x_2, \ldots\ldots, x_d)$. The features are assumed to have a probability density or mass (depending on whether the features are continuous or discrete) function conditioned on the pattern/object class. Thus, a pattern/object vector x belonging to class w_i is viewed as an observation drawn randomly from the class-conditional probability function $p(x \mid w_i)$. A number of well-known decision rules, including the Bayes decision rule, the maximum likelihood rule (which can be viewed as a particular case of the Bayes rule), and the Neyman-Pearson rule are available to define the decision boundary. The optimal Bayes decision rule for minimizing the risk (expected value of the loss function) can be stated as follows : Assign input pattern/object x to class w_i for which the conditional risk

$$R(w_i \mid x) = \sum_{j=1}^{c} L(\omega_i, \omega_j) . P\left(\frac{\omega_j}{x}\right) \qquad \ldots (11.1)$$

is minimum, where $L(w_i, w_j)$ is the loss incurred in deciding w_i, when the true class is $w_j \mid$ and $P(w_j \mid x)$ is the posterior probability. In the case of the $\frac{0}{1}$ loss function, as defined in (11.2), the conditional risk becomes the conditional probability of misclassification.

For this choice of loss function, the Bayes decision rule can be simplified as follows (also called the maximum a posterior (MAP) rule) : Assign input pattern/object x to class w_i if

$$P(w_i \mid x) > P(w_j \mid x) \text{ for all } j \neq i. \qquad \text{... (11.2)}$$

Various strategies are utilized to design a classifier in statistical pattern/object recognition, depending on the kind of information available about the class-conditional densities. If all of the class-conditional densities are completely specified, then the optimal Bayes decision rule can be used to design a classifier. However, the class-conditional densities are usually not known in practice and must be learned from the available training pattern/objects. If the form of the class-conditional densities is known (*e.g.*, multivariate Gaussian), but some of the parameters of the densities (*e.g.*, mean vectors and covariance matrices) are unknown, then we have a parametric decision problem. A common strategy for this kind of problem is to replace the unknown parameters in the density functions by their estimated values, resulting in the so-called Bayes plug-in classifier. The optimal Bayesian strategy in this situation requires additional information in the form of a prior distribution on the unknown parameters. If the form of the class-conditional densities is not known, then we operate in a nonparametric mode. In this case, we must either estimate the density function (*e.g.*, Parzen window approach) or directly construct the decision boundary based on the training data (*e.g.*, k-nearest neighbour rule).

Another factor in statistical pattern/object recognition is that of supervised learning (labeled training samples) versus unsupervised learning (unlabeled training samples). The label of a training pattern/object represents the category to which that pattern/object belongs. In an unsupervised learning problem, sometimes the number of classes must be learned along with the structure of each class. The various dichotomies that appear in statistical pattern/object recognition are shown in the tree structure of Fig. 11.4.

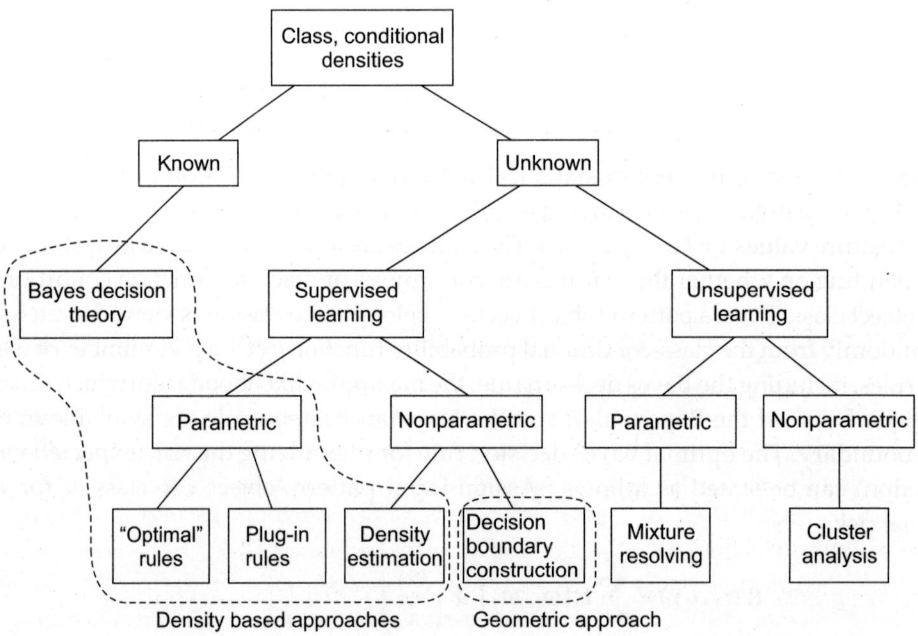

Fig. 11.4 *Various approaches in statistical pattern recognition.*

As we traverse the tree from top to bottom and left to right, less information is available to the system designer and as a result, the difficulty of classification problems increases. In some sense, most of the approaches in statistical pattern/object recognition (leaf nodes in the tree of Fig. 11.4) are attempting to implement the Bayes decision rule. The field of cluster analysis essentially deals with decision-making problems in the nonparametric and unsupervised learning mode. Further, in cluster analysis the number of categories or clusters may not even be specified ; the task is to discover a reasonable categorization of the data (if one exists). Cluster analysis algorithms along with various techniques for visualizing and projecting multidimensional data are also referred to as exploratory data analysis methods. Yet another dichotomy in statistical pattern/object recognition can be based on whether the decision boundaries are obtained directly (geometric approach) or indirectly (probabilistic density-based approach) as shown in Fig. 11.4. The probabilistic approach requires to estimate density functions first, and then construct the discriminant functions, which specify the decision boundaries. On the other hand, the geometric approach often constructs the decision boundaries directly from optimizing certain cost functions. We should point out that under certain assumptions on the density functions, the two approaches are equivalent. No matter which classification or decision rule is used, it must be trained using the available training samples. As a result, the performance of a classifier depends on both the number of available training samples as well as the specific values of the samples. At the same time, the goal of designing a recognition system is to classify future test samples which are likely to be different from the training samples. Therefore, optimizing a classifier to maximize its performance on the training set may not always result in the desired performance on a test set. The generalization ability of a classifier refers to its performance in classifying test pattern/objects which were not used during the training stage. A poor generalization ability of a classifier can be attributed to any one of the following factors :

1. The number of features is too large relative to the number of training samples (curse of dimensionality).
2. The number of unknown parameters associated with the classifier is large (*e.g.*, polynomial classifiers or a large neutral network), and
3. A classifier is too intensively optimized on the training set (over trained) ; this is analogous to the phenomenon of over fitting in regression when there are too many free parameters.

Overtraining has been investigated theoretically for classifiers that minimize the apparent error rate (the error on the training set).

11.7.1 Unsupervised Classification (Clustering)

In many applications of pattern/object recognition, it is extremely difficult or expensive, or even impossible, to reliably label a training sample with its true category. Consider, for example, the application of land-use classification in remote sensing. In order to obtain the ground truth information (category for each pixel) in the image, either the specific site associated with the pixel should be visited or its category should be extracted from a Geographical Information System. *"Unsupervised classification refers to situations where the objective is to construct decision boundaries based on unlabeled training data. Unsupervised classification is also known as data clustering which is a generic label for a variety of procedures designed to find natural groupings, or clusters, in multidimensional data, based on measured or perceived similarities among the pattern/objects. Category labels and other information about the source of the data influence the interpretation of the clustering, not the formation of the clusters".*

Unsupervised classification or clustering is a very difficult problem because data can reveal clusters with different shapes and sizes (see Fig. 11.5).

Fig. 11.5 *Clusters with different shapes and sizes.*

To compound the problem further, the number of clusters in the data often depends on the resolution (fine *vs.* coarse) with which we view the data. One example of clustering is the detection and delineation of a region containing a high density of pattern/objects compared to the background. A number of functional definitions of a cluster have been proposed which include :

1. Pattern/objects within a cluster are more similar to each other than are pattern/objects belonging to different clusters and
2. A cluster consists of a relatively high density of points separated from other clusters by a relatively low density of points.

Even with these functional definitions of a cluster, it is not easy to come up with an operational definition of clusters. One of the challenges is to select an appropriate measure of similarity to define clusters which, in general, is both data (cluster shape) and context dependent.

Cluster analysis is a very important and useful technique. The speed, reliability, and consistency with which a clustering algorithm can organize large amounts of data constitute overwhelming reasons to use it in applications such as data mining, information retrieval, image segmentation, signal compression and coding, and machine learning. As a consequence, hundreds of clustering algorithms have been proposed in the literature and new clustering algorithms continue to appear.

However, most of these algorithms are based on the following two popular clustering techniques:

1. **Iterative square-error partitional clustering and**
2. **Agglomerative hierarchical clustering.**

Hierarchical techniques organize data in a nested sequence of groups which can be displayed in the form of a dendrogram or a tree. Square-error partitional algorithms attempt to obtain that partition which minimizes the within-cluster scatter or maximizes the between-cluster scatter. To guarantee that an optimum solution has been obtained, one has to examine all possible partitions of the *n* d-dimensional pattern/objects into K clusters (for a given K), which is not computationally feasible. So, various heuristics are used to reduce the search, but then there is no guarantee of optimality.

Partitional clustering techniques are used more frequently than hierarchical techniques in pattern/object recognition applications, so we will restrict our coverage to partitional methods. Recent studies in cluster analysis suggest that a user of a clustering algorithm should keep the following issues in mind :

1. Every clustering algorithm will find clusters in a given dataset whether they exist or not ; the data should, therefore, be subjected to tests for clustering tendency before applying a clustering algorithm, followed by a validation of the clusters generated by the algorithm ;
2. There is no best clustering algorithm. Therefore, a user is advised to try several clustering algorithms on a given dataset. Further, issues of data collection, data representation, normalization, and cluster validity are as important as the choice of clustering strategy.

The problem of partitional clustering can be formally stated as follows :

Given n pattern/objects in a d-dimensional metric space, determine a partition of the pattern/objects into K clusters, such that the pattern/objects in a cluster are more similar to each other than to pattern/objects in different clusters. The value of K may or may not be specified.

A clustering criterion, either global or local, must be adopted. A global criterion, such as square-error, represents each cluster by a prototype and assigns the pattern/objects to clusters according to the most similar prototypes. A local criterion forms clusters by utilizing local structure in the data. For example, clusters can be formed by identifying high-density regions in the pattern/object space or by assigning a pattern/object and its k nearest neighbors to the same cluster. Most of the partitional clustering techniques implicitly assume continuous-valued feature vectors so that the pattern/objects can be viewed as being embedded in a metric space. If the features are on a nominal or ordinal scale, Euclidean distances and cluster centers are not very meaningful, so hierarchical clustering methods are normally applied.

In the following subsections, we briefly summarize the most popular approach to partitional clustering : square-error clustering.

11.7.1.1 *Square-Error Clustering*

The most commonly used partitional clustering strategy is based on the square-error criterion. *"The general objective is to obtain that partition which, for a fixed number of clusters, minimizes the square-error".*

Suppose that the given set of n pattern/objects in d dimensions has somehow been partitioned into K clusters $\{C_1, C_2, ..., C_k\}$ such that cluster C and n_k pattern/objects and each pattern/object is in exactly one cluster, so that $\sum_{i=1}^{j} n_k = n$. The mean vector, or center, of cluster C_k is defined as the centroid of the cluster, or

$$m^{(k)} = \left(\frac{1}{n_k}\right)\sum_{i=1}^{n_k} x_i^{(k)}, \qquad ...(11.3)$$

where $x_i^{(k)}$ | is the ith pattern/object belonging to cluster C_k. The-error for cluster C_k is the sum of the squared Euclidean distances between each pattern/object in C_k, and its cluster center $m^{(k)}$. This square-error is also called the within-cluster variation

$$e_k^2 = \sum_{i=1}^{n_k} \left(x_i^{(k)} - m^{(k)}\right)^{\mathrm{T}} \left(x_i^{(k)} - m^{(k)}\right) \quad \text{... (11.4)}$$

The square-error for the entire clustering containing K clusters is the sum of the within-cluster variations :

$$\mathrm{E}_{\mathrm{K}}^2 = \sum_{k=1}^{\mathrm{K}} e_k^2 . \quad \text{... (11.5)}$$

The objective of a square-error clustering method is to find a partition containing K clusters that minimizes $\mathrm{E}_{\mathrm{K}}^2 \big|$ for a fixed K. The resulting partition has also been referred to as the minimum variance partition. A general algorithm for the iterative partitional clustering method is given below.

Algorithm for iterative partitional clustering :

Step 1. Select an initial partition with K clusters. Repeat through 5 until the cluster membership stabilizes.

Step 2. Generate a new partition by assigning each pattern/object to its closest cluster center.

Step 3. Compute new cluster centers as the centroids of the clusters.

Step 4. Repeat steps 2 and 3 until an optimum value of the criterion function is found.

Step 5. Adjust the number of clusters by merging and splitting existing clusters or by removing small, or outlier, clusters.

The above algorithm, without step 5, is also known as the K-means algorithm. The details of the steps in the algorithm must either be supplied by the user as parameters or be implicitly hidden in the computer program. However, these details are crucial to the success of the program. A big frustration in using clustering programs is the lack of guidelines available for choosing K, initial partition, updating the partition, adjusting the number of clusters, and the stopping criterion.

The simple K-means partitional clustering algorithm described above is computationally efficient and gives surprisingly good results if the clusters are compact, hyper spherical in shape and well-separated in the feature space.

11.8 SYNTACTIC/STRUCTURAL OBJECT RECOGNITION SYSTEM

In many recognition problems involving complex pattern/objects, it is more appropriate to adopt a hierarchical perspective where a pattern/object is viewed as being composed of simple sub pattern/objects which are themselves built from yet simpler sub pattern/objects. "*The simplest/elementary sub pattern/objects to be recognized are called primitives and the given complex pattern/object is represented in terms of the interrelationships between these primitives*". In syntactic pattern/object recognition, a formal analogy is drawn between the structure of pattern/objects and the syntax of a language. The pattern/objects are viewed as sentences belonging to a language, primitives are viewed as the alphabet of the language, and the sentences are generated according to a grammar. Thus, a large collection of complex pattern/objects can be described by a small number of primitives and grammatical rules. The grammar for each pattern/object class must be inferred from the available training samples.

Structural pattern/object recognition is intuitively appealing because, in addition to classification, this approach also provides a description of how the given pattern/object is constructed from the primitives. This paradigm has been used in situations where the pattern/objects have a definite structure which can be captured in terms of a set of rules, such as EKG waveforms, textured images, and shape analysis of contours. The implementation of a syntactic approach, however, leads to many difficulties which primarily have to do with the segmentation of noisy pattern/objects (to detect the primitives) and the inference of the grammar from training data.

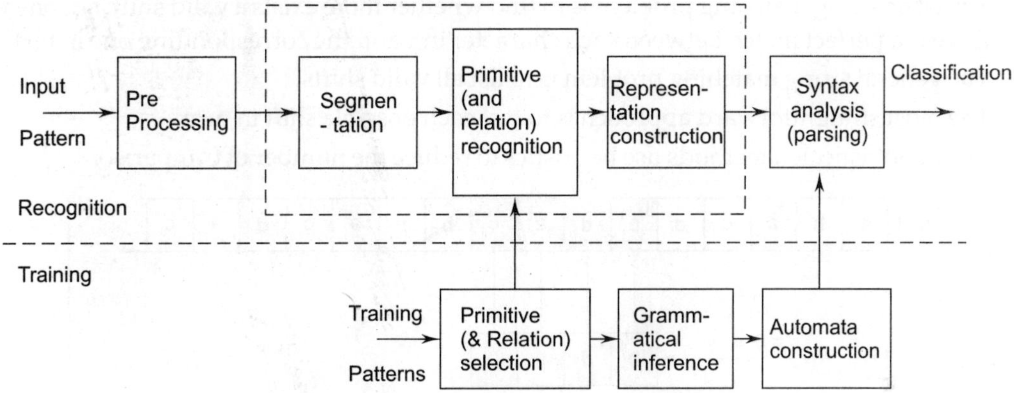

Fig. 11.6 *Block diagram of a syntactic pattern recognition system.*

A basic block diagram of a syntactic pattern recognition system is shown in Fig. 11.6. The system has two major parts : training and recognition. The training part consists of primitive (and relation) selection, grammatical inference, automata construction from the training patterns and recognition part consists of preprocessing, segmentation 'or' decomposition, primitive (and relation) recognition, construction of pattern representation and syntactic parsing analysis for the input testing system.

Then, recognition and classification are done using : Parsing (for formal grammars), Relational graph matching (for relational descriptions). We will study strings, grammatical methods, and graph-theoretical approaches.

11.8.1 Recognition with Strings

String elements are called characters (or letters, symbols). String representation of a pattern/object is also called a word. A particularly long string is denoted text. Any contiguous string that is part of another string is called a factor (or substring, segment) of that string.

Important pattern/object recognition problems that involve computations on strings include :

1. **String matching :** Given string x and text, determine whether x is a factor of text, and if so, where it appears.
2. **String edit distance :** Given two strings x and y, compute the minimum number of **basic operations** — character insertions, deletions and exchanges — needed to transform x into y.
3. **String matching with errors :** Given string x and text, find the locations in text where the *"distance"* of x to any factor of text is minimal.
4. **String matching with the *"don't care"* symbol :** This is the same as basic string matching but the special *"don't care"* symbol can match any other symbol.

11.8.1.1 *String Matching*

1. The most fundamental and useful operation in string matching is testing whether a candidate string *x* is a factor of text.
2. The number of characters in text is usually much larger than that in *x*, *i.e.*, | text | > | *x* |, where each discrete character is taken from an alphabet.
3. A shift, *s*, is an offset needed to align the first character of *x* with character number s + 1 in text.
4. The basic string matching problem is to find whether there exists a valid shift, *i.e.*, one where there is a perfect match between each character in *x* and the corresponding one in text.
5. The general string matching problem is to list all valid shifts.
6. The most straightforward approach is to test each possible shift in turn.
7. More sophisticated methods use heuristics to reduce the number of comparisons.

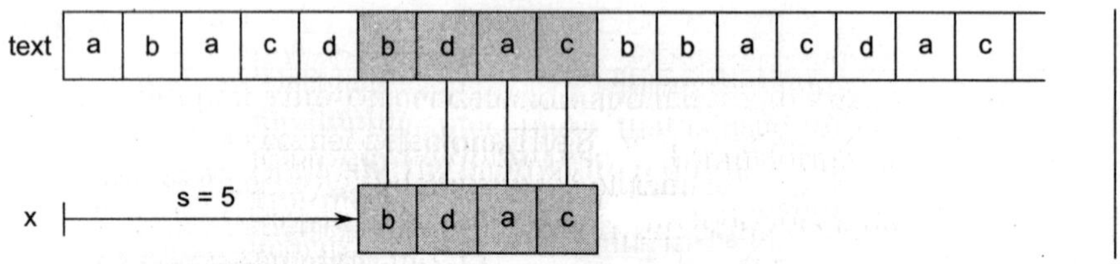

Fig. 11.7 *The general string matching problem is to find all shifts s for which the pattern/object x appears in text. Any such shift is called valid. In this example, x = "bdac00 is indeed a factor of text, and s = 5 is the only valid shift.*

11.8.1.2 *String Edit Distance*

1. The fundamental idea underlying pattern/object recognition using edit distance is based on the nearest neighbor algorithm.
2. We store a full training set of strings and their associated category labels.
3. During classification, a test string is compared to each stored string, a "distance" is computed, and the string is assigned the category label of the nearest string in the training set.
4. Edit distance between *x* and *y* describes how many of the following fundamental operations are required to transform *x* and *y*.

Substitutions : A character in *x* is replaced by the corresponding character in *y*.

Insertions : A character in *y* is inserted into *x*, thereby increasing the length of *x* by one character.

Deletions : A character in *x* is deleted, thereby decreasing the length of *x* by one character.

x	excused	source string
	exhused	substitute *h* for *c*
	exhaused	insert *a*
	exhausted	insert *t*
y	exhausted	target string

Fig. 11.8 *Transformation of x = "excused" to y = "exhausted" through one substitution and two insertions.*

11.8.1.3 String Matching with Errors

1. Given a pattern/object x and text, string matching with errors algorithm finds the shift for which the edit distance between x and a factor of text is minimum.
2. The algorithm for the string matching with errors problem is very similar to that for edit distance but some additional heuristics can reduce the computational burden.

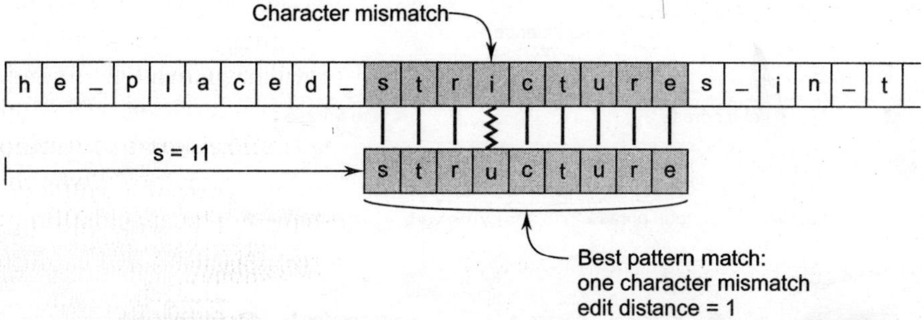

Fig. 11.9 *Finding the shift s for which the edit distance between x and an aligned factor of text is minimum. In this figure, the minimum edit distance is 1, corresponding to the character exchange u → i, and the shift s = 11 is the location.*

11.8.1.4 String Matching with "Don't Care"

1. String matching with the *"don't care"* symbol, Φ, is formally the same as basic string matching, but the Φ in either x or text is said to match any character.
2. The straightforward approach is to modify the string matching algorithm to include a condition for matching the *"don't care"* symbol.

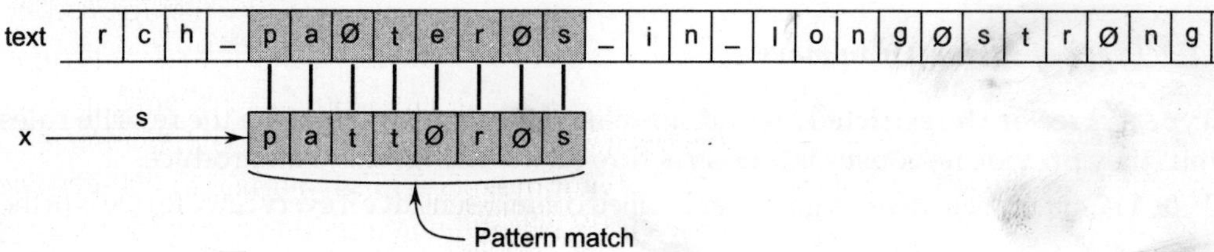

Fig. 11.10 *The problem of string matching with the "don't care" symbol is the same as the basic string matching except that the Φ symbol can match any character. The Figure shows the only valid shift.*

11.8.2 Grammatical Methods

"Grammars provide detailed models that underlie the generation of the sequence of characters in strings". For example, strings representing telephone numbers conform to a strict structure. Similarly, optical character recognition systems that recognize and interpret mathematical equations can use rules that constrain the arrangement of the symbols. In pattern/object recognition, we are given a sentence (a string generated by a set of rules) and a grammar (the set of rules), and seek to determine whether the sentence was generated by this grammar. Formally, a grammar consists of four components:

1. **Symbols :** Every sentence consists of a string of characters (or primitive symbols, terminal symbols) taken from an alphabet.
2. **Variables :** These are called the non terminal symbols (or intermediate symbols, internal symbols).
3. **Root symbol :** It is a special variable, the source from which all sequences are derived.

4. **Productions :** The set of production rules (or rewrite rules) specify how to transform a set of variables and symbols into other variables and symbols. For example, if A is a variable and c a terminal symbol, the rewrite rule $cA \rightarrow cc$ means that any time the segment cA appears in a string, it can be replaced by *cc*.

The language L (G) generated by a grammar G is the set of all strings (possibly infinite in number) that can be generated by G.

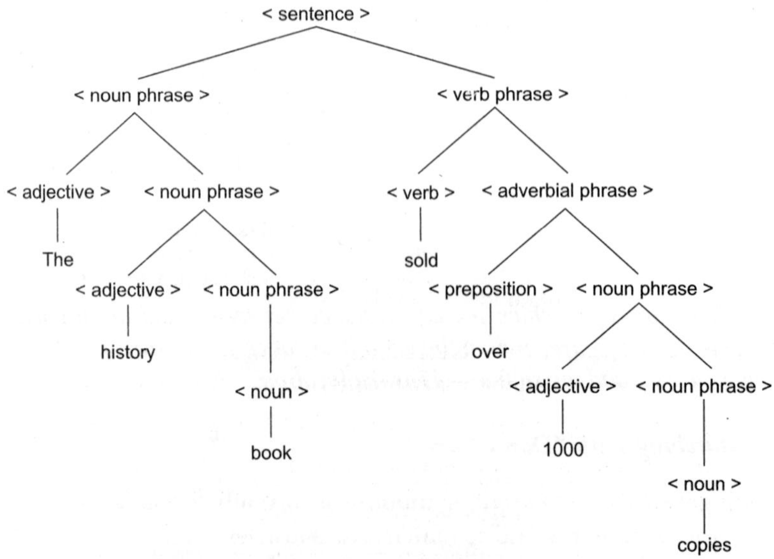

Fig. 11.11 *The derivation tree illustrates how a portion of English grammar can transform the root symbol into a particular sentence.*

11.8.2.1 Types of String Grammars

1. **Type 0 : Free or Unrestricted :** Free grammars have no restrictions on the rewrite rules, and thus they provide no constraints or structure on the strings they can produce.
2. **Type 1 : Context-Sensitive :** A grammar is called context-sensitive if every rewrite rule is of the form
$$\alpha I \beta \rightarrow \alpha x \beta \qquad \text{... (11.6)}$$
where α and β are any strings made up of intermediate and terminal symbols, I is an intermediate symbol and x is an intermediate or terminal symbol, *i.e.*, I can be rewritten as x in the context of α on the left and β on the right.
3. **Type 2 : Context-Free :** A grammar is called context-free if every production rule is of the form
$$I \rightarrow x \qquad \text{... (11.7)}$$
where I is an intermediate symbol, and x is an intermediate or terminal symbol, *i.e.*, there is no need for a context for the rewriting of I by x.
4. **Type 3 : Finite State or Regular :** A grammar is called regular if every rewrite rule is of the form
$$\alpha \rightarrow z\beta \quad \text{or} \quad \alpha \rightarrow z \qquad \text{... (11.8)}$$

where α and β are made up of intermediate symbols and z is a terminal symbol. The class of grammars of type i includes all grammars of type $i + 1$.

11.8.2.2 Recognition Using Grammars

Suppose we are given a test sentence x that was generated by one of c different grammars G1, G2, ..., Gc which can be considered as different models or classes. The test sentence x is classified according to which grammar could have produced it, or equivalently, the language L (G*i*) of which *x* is a member. Parsing is the inverse process that, given a particular *x*, finds a derivation in G that leads to *x*.

Bottom-up parsing starts with the test sentence *x*, and seeks to simplify it, so as to represent it as the root symbol. The basic approach is to use candidate productions backwards, *i.e.*, find rewrite rules whose right hand side matches part of the current string, and replace that part with a segment that could have produced it.

Top-down parsing starts with the root node and successively applies productions with the goal of finding a derivation of the test sentence *x*. Since it is rare that the sentence is derived in the first production attempted, it is necessary to specify some criteria to guide the choice of which rewrite rule to apply.

11.8.2.3 Examples of Pattern/object Description Using Grammars

Example No. 11.1.

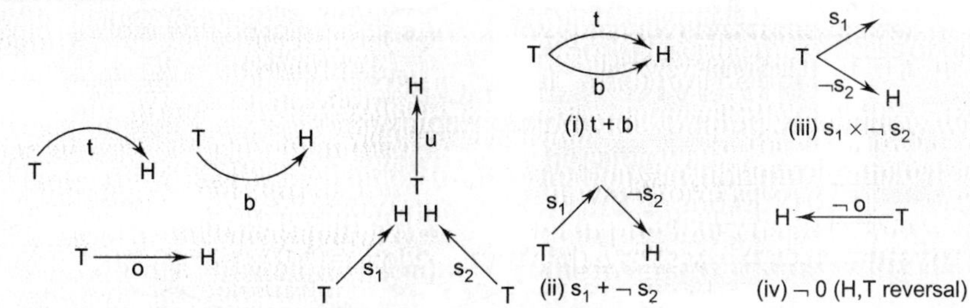

Fig. 11.12 *A 2-D line drawing picture description grammar with the set of terminal symbols {t, b, u, o, s, *, ¬, +} where + represents head to tail concatenation, *represents head-head and tail-tail attachment, and ¬ represents head and tail reversal. H represents heads of lines and T represents the tails.*

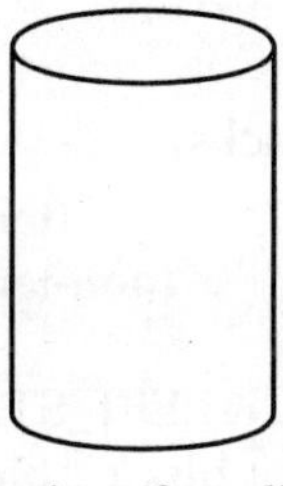

Cylinder → Top * Body
Top → t * b
Body → ¬ u + b + u
(alternate:)
Cylinder → t * b * (¬ u + b + u)

Fig. 11.13 *Representation of a cylinder using the line drawing picture description grammar.*

Example No. 11.2.

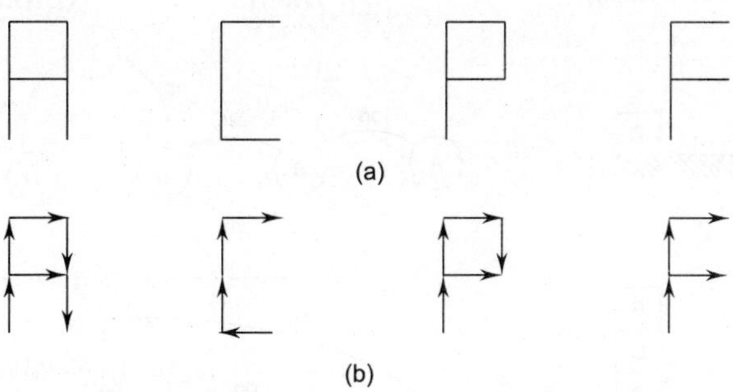

A = u + ((u + 0 + ¬ u).0) + ¬ u C = ¬ o + u + u + o P = u + ((u + 0 + ¬ u).0) F = u + (o × u) + o)

(c)

Fig. 11.14 *Representation of four characters using the line drawing picture description grammar. (a) Pattern data. (b) Primitive representation and interconnection. (Corresponding descriptions).*

Example No. 11.3

A grammar describing four blocks arranged in 2-block stacks :

V_T = {table, block, +, ↑} (terminal symbols)

V_N = {DESC, LEFT_STACK, RIGHT_STACK} (non-terminal symbols)

S = DESC ∈ V_N (root symbol)

P = {DESC → LEFT_STACK + RIGHT_STACK DESC → RIGHT_STACK

+ LEFT_STACK LEFT_STACK → block ↑ block ↑ table RIGHT_STACK → block ↑ block ↑ table} (production rules)

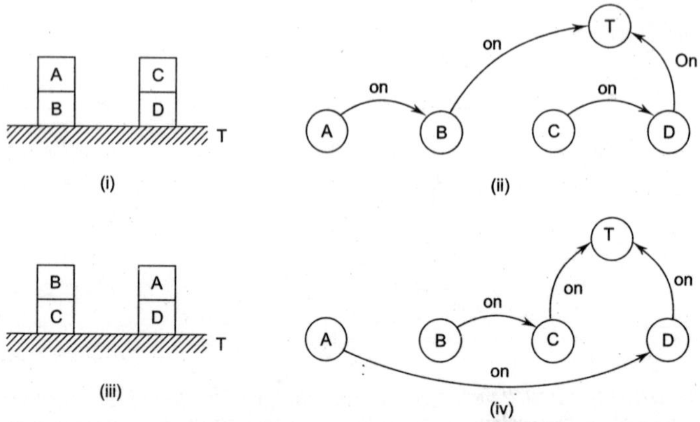

Fig. 11.15 *A grammar describing four blocks arranged in 2-block stacks. (i) An example. (ii) Graphical description corresponding to (i). (iii) Another example. (iv) Graphical description corresponding to (iii).*

Example No. 11.4

A grammar describing four blocks in 3-block and 1-block stacks

V_T = {table, block, +, ↑} (terminal symbols)

V_N = {DESC, LEFT_STACK, RIGHT_STACK} (non-terminal symbols)

S = DESC ∈ V_N (root symbol)

P = {DESC → LEFT_STACK + RIGHT_STACK LEFT_STACK + RIGHT_STACK → block ↑ table + block ↑ block ↑ block ↑ table LEFT_STACK + RIGHT_STACK → block ↑ block ↑ block ↑ table + block ↑ table} (product on rules)

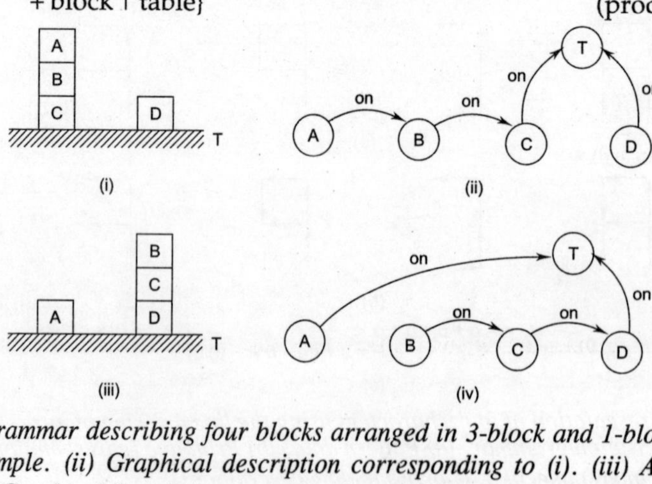

Fig. 11.16 *A grammar describing four blocks arranged in 3-block and 1-block stacks. (i) An example. (ii) Graphical description corresponding to (i). (iii) Another example. (iv) Graphical description corresponding to (iii).*

Example No. 11.5.

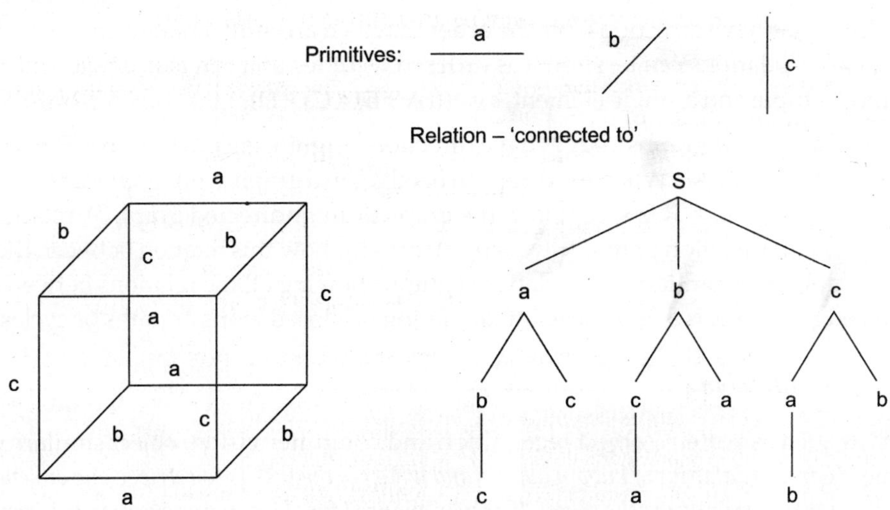

Fig. 11.17 *Tree grammar-based representation of a cube.*

Example No. 11.6.

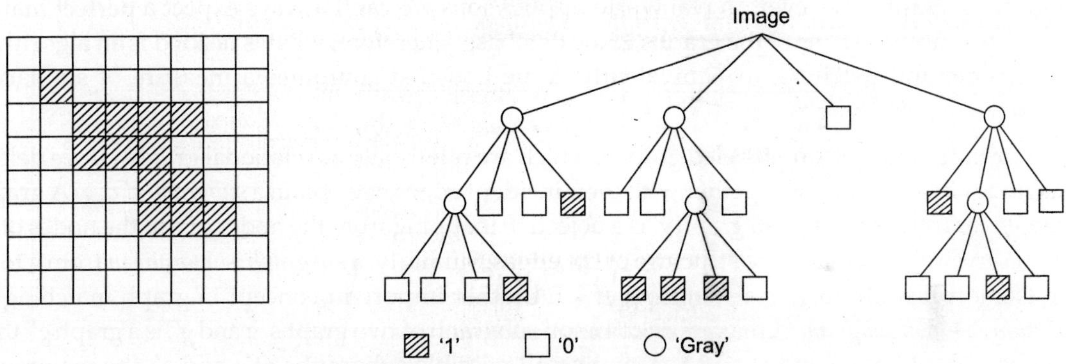

Fig. 11.18 *Guadtree representation of an 8 × 8 binary image.*

11.8.3 Graph-Theoretic Methods

11.8.3.1 Definitions

"Graphical alternatives for structural representations are natural extensions of higher dimensional grammars because graphs are valuable tools for representing relational information". A graph G = {N, R} is an ordered pair represented using :

1. a set of nodes (vertices), N,
2. a set of edges (arcs), $R \subseteq N \times N$.

A subgraph of G is itself a graph Gs = {Ns, Rs} where $Ns \subseteq N$ and Rs consists of edges in R that connect only the nodes in Ns. A graph is connected if there is a path between all pairs of its nodes. A graph is complete if there is an edge between all pairs of its nodes.

A relation from set A to set B is a subset of A × B. It is usually shown using a function $f: A \rightarrow B$ or $b = f(a)$. For example, the relation *"lies on"* can contain :

R = {(floor, foundation), (rug, floor), (chair, rug), (person, chair)}.

Note that relations have directions, *i.e.*, the order in which an entity appears in the pair is significant. Higher-order relations can be shown as ordered n-tuples that can also be viewed as ordered pairs of an $(n-1)$-tuple and a single element, *e.g.*, $(((A \times B) \times C) \times D)$.

In directional graphs (digraphs), edges have directional significance, *i.e.*, $(a, b) \in R$ means there is an edge from node a to node b. When the direction of edges in a graph is not important, *i.e.*, specification of either (a, b) or $(b, a) \in R$ is acceptable, the graph is an undirected graph. A relational graph represents a particular relation graphically using arrows to show this relation between the elements as a directed graph. A semantic net is a relational graph showing all the relations between its nodes using labeled edges. A tree is a finite acyclic (containing no closed loops or paths or cycles) digraph.

11.8.3.2 Graph Matching

In applications such as pattern/object recognition and computer vision, object similarity is an important issue. "*Given a database of known objects and a query, the task is to retrieve one or several objects from the database that are similar to the query. If graphs are used for object representation this problem turns into determining the similarity of graphs, which is generally referred to as graph matching*". Standard concepts in graph matching include graph isomorphism, sub graph isomorphism, and maximum common subgraph. However, in real world applications we can't always expect a perfect match between the input and one of the graphs in the database. Therefore, what is needed is an algorithm for error-tolerant matching, or equivalently, a method that computes a measure of similarity beetween two given graphs.

We consider directed and labeled graphs, which are referred to as relational graphs. If we delete some nodes from a graph g, together with their incident edges, we obtain a *subgraph* $g' \subseteq g$. A graph *isomorphism* from a graph g to a graph g' is a objective mapping from the nodes of g to the nodes of g' that preserves all labels and the structure of the edges. Similarly, a *subgraph isomorphism* from g to g' is an isomorphism from g to a subgraph of g'. Another important concept in graph matching is *maximum common subgraph*. A maximum common subgraph of two graphs, g and g', is a graph g'' that is a subgraph of both g and g' and has, among all possible subgraphs of g and g', the maximum number of nodes. Notice that the maximum common subgraph of two graphs is usually not unique. Graph isomorphism is a useful concept to find out if two objects are the same, up to invariance properties inherent to the underlying graph representation. Similarly, subgraph isomorphism can be used to find out if one object is part of another object, or if one object is present in a group of objects. Maximum common subgraph can be used to measure the similarity of objects even if there exists no graph or subgraph isomorphism between the corresponding graphs. Clearly, the larger the maximum common subgraph of two graphs is, the greater is their similarity. Real world objects are usually affected by noise such that the graph representation of identical objects may not exactly match. Therefore it is necessary to integrate some degree of error tolerance into the graph matching process. A powerful alternative to maximum common subgraph computation is *error-tolerant graph matching* using *graph edit distance*.

In its most general form, a graph *edit operation* is either a deletion, insertion, or substitution (*i.e.*, label change). Edit operations can be applied to nodes as well as to edges. The edit distance of two graphs, g and g', is defined as the shortest sequence of edit operations that transform g into g'. Obviously, the shorter this sequence is the more similar are the two graphs. Thus edit distance is suitable to measure the similarity of graphs. The sequence of edit operations that transform g into g'

implies an error-correcting mapping from the nodes of g to the nodes of g'. In practical applications, some edit operations may have more importance than others. Hence, very often *costs* are assigned to the individual edit operations. Typically, the more likely an edit operation is to occur the smaller is its cost. An assignment of costs to the individual edit operations is often called a *cost function*. Given a set of edit operations together with their costs, graph edit distance computation in its most general form means to find a sequence of edit operations that transform, with minimum cost, one of the given graphs into the other. Actually, graph isomorphism, subgraph isomorphism, and maximum common subgraph detection are all special instances of graph edit distance computation under special cost functions.

. Left f_1 be the confidence value of the label of a node in the first graph and f_2 be the cofidence value of a node with the same label in the second graph. The cost of node substitution is $| f_1 - f_2 |$ and the cost of node insertion or deletion is f_1.

Let g_1 be the confidence value of the label of an edge in the first graph and g_2 be the corresponding value for an edge in the second graph. The cost of edge substitution is $| g_1 - g_2 |$ and the cost of edge insertion or deletion is g_1.

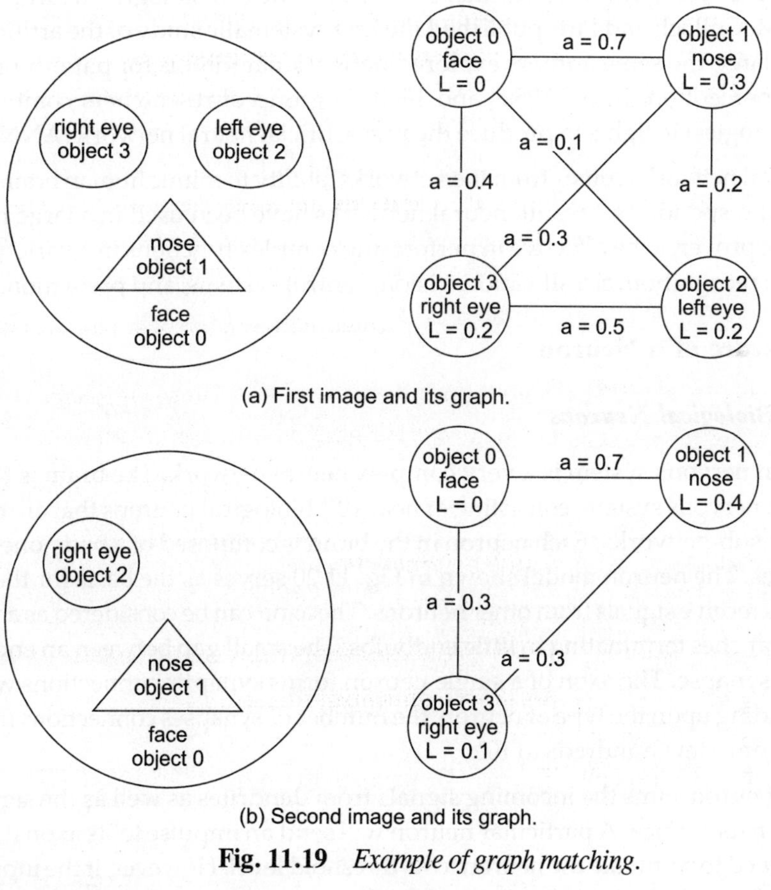

Fig. 11.19 *Example of graph matching.*

Node substitution:

1. object 0 in (*b*) with object 0 in (*a*) with cost $| 1.0 - 1.0 | = 0$
2. object 1 in (*b*) with object 1 in (*a*) with cost $| 0.4 - 0.3 | = 0.1$

3. object 2 in (*b*) with object 3 in (*a*) with cost $|0.1-0.2| = 0.1$

Edge substitution for these nodes :

$|0.7-0.7| = 0$, $|0.3-0.4| = 0.1$, $|0.3-0.3| = 0$

Node deletion : object 2 in (*a*) with cost 0.2

Edge deletion for this node : 0.5, 0.2, 0.1

Total cost of matching is $0.1 + 0.1 + 0.1 + 0.2 + 0.5 + 0.2 + 0.1 = 1.3$.

11.9 FUNDAMENTALS OF NEURAL NETWORKS

11.9.1 Introduction

For many decades, it has been a goal of science and engineering to develop intelligent machines with a large number of simple elements. References to this subject can be found in the scientific literature of the 19th century. During the 1940s, researchers desiring to duplicate the function of the human brain, have developed simple hardware (and later software) models of biological neurons and their interaction systems. McCulloch and Pitts published the first systematic study of the artificial neural network. Four years later, the same authors explored network paradigms for pattern recognition using a single layer perception. In the 1950s and 1960s, a group of researchers combined these biological and psychological insights to produce the first artificial neural network (ANN).

The interest in neural networks comes from the networks' ability to mimic human brain as well as its ability to learn and respond. As a result, neural networks have been used in a large number of applications and have proven to be effective in performing complex functions in a variety of fields. These include pattern recognition, classification, vision, control systems, and prediction.

11.9.2 Basic Structure of a Neuron

11.9.2.1 Model of Biological Neurons

In general, the human nervous system is a very complex neural network. The brain is the central element of the human nervous system, consisting of near 10^{16} biological neurons that are connected to each other through sub-networks. Each neuron in the brain is composed of a body one axon and multitude of dendrites. The neuron model shown in Fig. 11.20 serves as the basis for the artificial neuron. The dendrites receive signals from other neurons. The axon can be considered as a long tube, which divides into branches terminating in little endbulbs. The small gap between an endbulb and a dendrite is called a synapse. The axon of a single neuron forms synaptic connections with many other neurons. Depending upon the type of neuron, the number of synapses connections from other neurons may range from a few hundreds to 10^4.

The cell body of a neuron sums the incoming signals from dendrites as well as the signals from numerous synapses on its surface. A particular neuron will send an impulse to its axon if sufficient input signals are received to stimulate the neuron to its threshold level. However, if the inputs do not reach the required threshold, the input will quickly decay and will not generate any action. The biological neuron model is the foundation of an artificial neuron as will be described in detail in the next section.

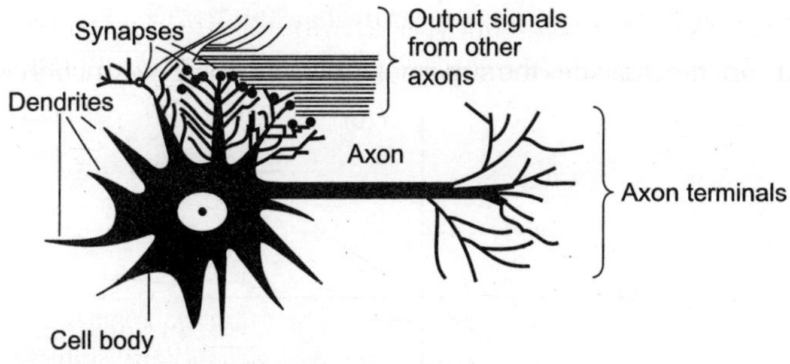

Fig. 11.20 *A biological neuron.*

11.9.2.2 Elements of Neural Networks

An artificial neuron as shown in Fig. 11.21, is the basic element of a neural network. It consists of three basic components that include weights, thresholds, and a single activation function.

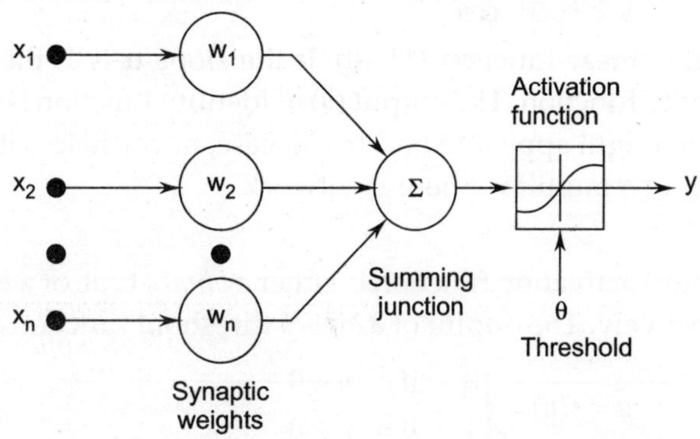

Fig. 11.21 *Basic elements of an artificial neuron.*

Weighting Factors

The values W_1, W_2, W_3, ..., W_n are weight factors associated with each node to determine the strength of input row vector $X = [x_1\, x_2\, x_3 \,......, x_n]^T$. Each input is multiplied by the associated weight of the neuron connection X^TW. Depending upon the activation function, if the weight is positive, X^TW commonly excites the node output ; whereas, for negative weights, X^TW tends to inhibit the node output.

Threshold

The node's internal threshold θ is the magnitude offset that affects the activation of the node output y as follows :

$$y = \sum_{i=1}^{n} (X_i\, W_i) - \theta_k \qquad ...(11.9)$$

Activation Function

In this subsection, five of the most common activation functions are presented. An activation function performs a mathematical operation on the signal output. More sophisticated activation functions can also be utilized depending upon the type of problem to be solved by the network.

1. Linear Function

As is known, a linear function satisfies the superposition concept. The function is shown in Fig. 11.22.

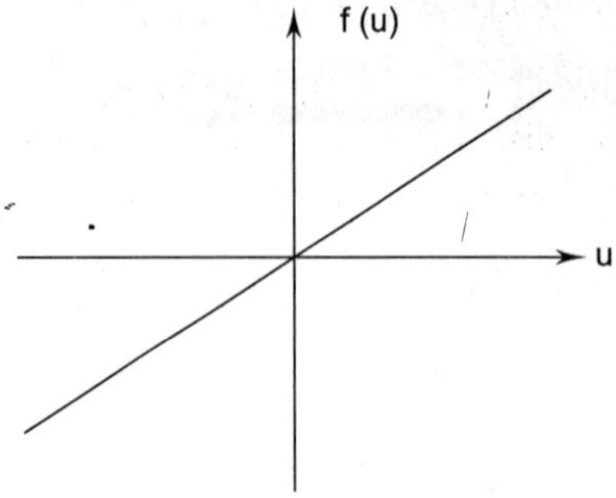

Fig. 11.22 *Linear activation function.*

The mathematical equation for the above linear function can be written as

$$y = f(u) = \alpha.u \qquad \text{... (11.10)}$$

where α is the slope of the linear function (11.10). If the slope α is 1, then the linear activation function is called the identity function. The output (y) of identity function is equal to input function (u). Although this function might appear to be a trivial case, nevertheless it is very useful in some cases such as the last stage of a multilayer neural network.

2. Threshold Function

A threshold (hard-limiter) activation function is either a *binary* type or a *bipolar* type as shown in Fig. 11.23 and 11.24 respectively. The ouptut of a *binary* threshold function can be written as :

$$y = f(u) = \begin{cases} 0 & \text{if} \quad u < 0 \\ 1 & \text{if} \quad u \geq 0 \end{cases} \qquad \text{... (11.11)}$$

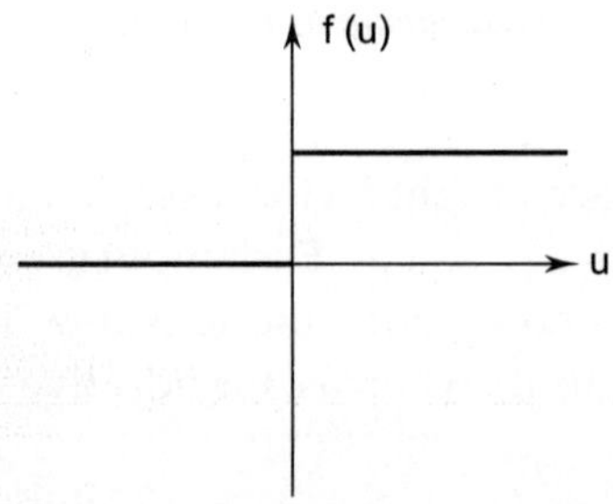

Fig. 11.23 *Binary threshold activation function.*

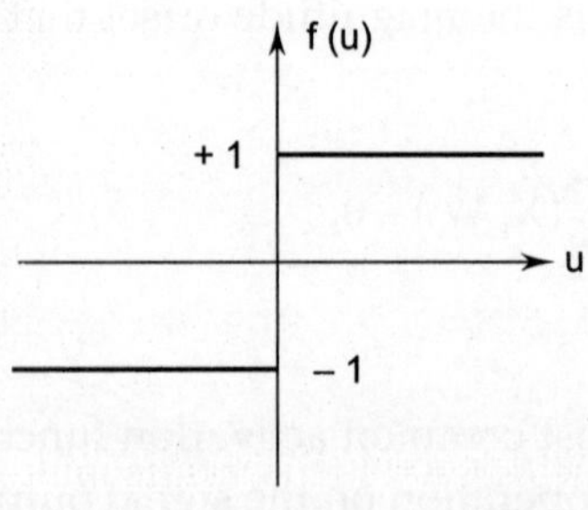

Fig. 11.24 *Bipolar threshold activation function.*

The neuron with the hard limiter activation function is referred to as the McCulloch-Pitts model.

3. Piecewise Linear Function

This type of activation function is also referred to as saturating linear function and can have either a binary or bipolar range for the saturation limits of the output. The mathematical model for a symmetric saturation function (Fig. 11.25) is described as follows :

$$y = f(u) = \begin{cases} -1 & \text{if} \quad u < -1 \\ u & \text{if} \quad -1 \geq u \geq 1 \\ 1 & \text{if} \quad u \geq 1 \end{cases} \qquad \text{... (11.12)}$$

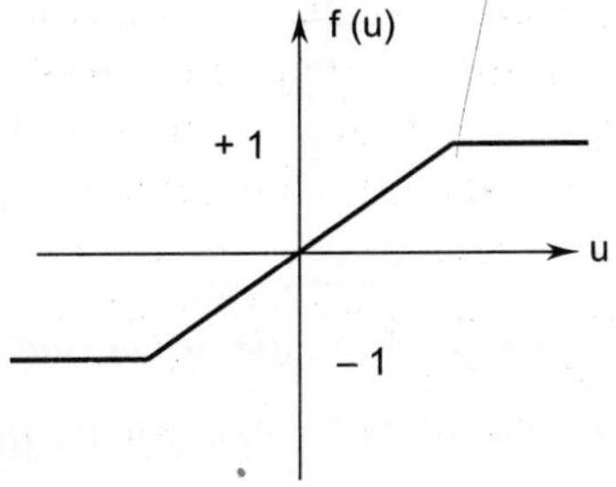

Fig. 11.25 *Piecewise linear activation function.*

4. Sigmoidal (S shaped) Function

This nonlinear function is the most common type of the activation used to construct the neural networks. It is mathematically well behaved, differentiable and strictly increasing function. A sigmoidal transfer function can be written in the following form :

$$f(x) = \frac{1}{1+e^{-\alpha x}}, 0 \leq f(x) \leq 1 \qquad \text{... (11.13)}$$

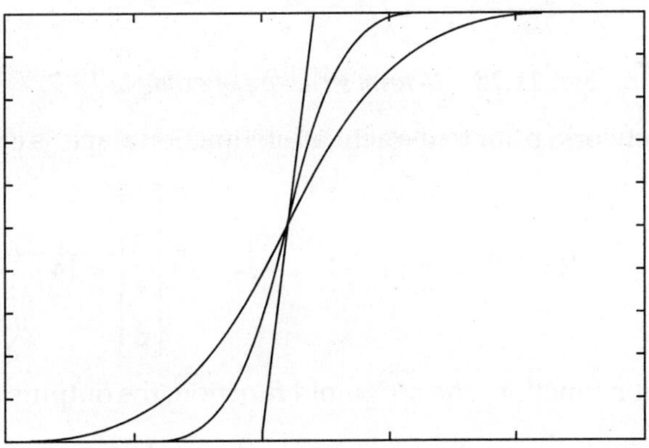

Fig. 11.26 *A sigmoid activation function.*

where α is the shape parameter of the sigmoid function. By varying this parameter, different shapes of the function can be obtained as illustrated in Fig. 11.26. This function is continuous and differentiable.

5. Tangent Hyperbolic Function

This transfer function is described by the following mathematical form :

$$f(x) = \frac{e^{\alpha x} - e^{-\alpha x}}{e^{\alpha x} + e^{-\alpha x}} \; -1 \leq f(x) \leq 1 \qquad \text{... (11.14)}$$

It is interesting to note that the derivatives of Equations (11.13) and (11.14) can be expressed in terms of the individual function itself.

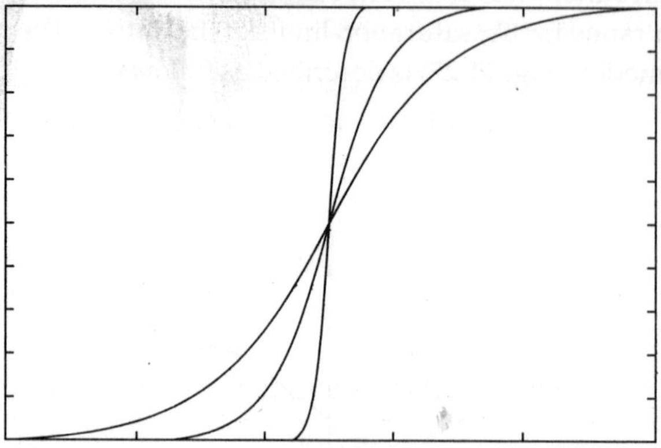

Fig. 11.27 *A tangent hyperbolic activation function.*

Example 11.7. *Consider the following network consists of four inputs with the weights as shown*

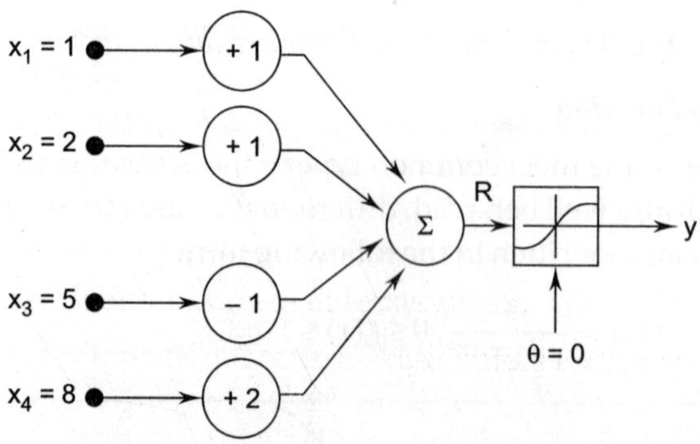

Fig. 11.28 *Neuron structure of example 11.7.*

The output R of the network, prior to the activation function stage, is calculated as follows :

$$R = W^T . X = \begin{bmatrix} 1 & 1 & -1 & 2 \end{bmatrix} . \begin{bmatrix} 1 \\ 2 \\ 5 \\ 8 \end{bmatrix} = 14 \qquad \text{... (11.15)}$$

With a binary activation function, and a sigmoid function, the outputs of the neuron are respectively as follow :

y (Threshold) = 1 ;

y (Sigmoid) = $1.5 * 2^{-8}$

11.9.3 Adaline

An ADAptive LINear Element (ADALINE) consists of a single neuron of the MuCulloch-Pitts type, where its weights are determined by the normalized least mean square (LMS) training law. The LMS learning algorithm was originally proposed by Widrow and Hoff. This learning rule is also referred to as delta rule. It is a well-established supervised training method that has been used over a wide range of diverse applications. Curve fitting approximations can also be used for training a neural network. The learning objective of curve fitting is to find a surface that best fits to the training data. In the next heading the implementation of LMS algorithms for backpropagation, and curve fitting algorithms for radial basis function network, will be described in detail.

The architecture of a simple ADALINE is shown in Fig. 11.29. It is observed that the basic structure of an ADALINE is similar to a linear neuron (Fig. 11.22) with the activation function $f(.)$ to be a linear one with an extra feedback loop. Since ADALINE is a linear device, any combination of these units can be accomplished with the use of a single unit.

During the training phase of ADALINE, the input vector $X \in R^1 : X = [x_1 \quad x_2 \quad x_3 \quad \ldots \quad x_n]^T$ as well as desired output are presented to the network. The weights are adaptively adjusted based on delta rule. After the ADALINE is trained, an input vector presented to the network with fixed weights will result in a scalar output. Therefore, the network performs a mapping of an n dimensional mapping to a scalar value. The activation function is not used during the training phase. Once the weights are properly adjusted, the response of the trained unit can be tested by applying various inputs, which are not in the training set. If the network produces consistent responses to a high degree with the test inputs, it said that the network could *generalize.* Therefore, the process of training and generalization are two important attributes of the network.

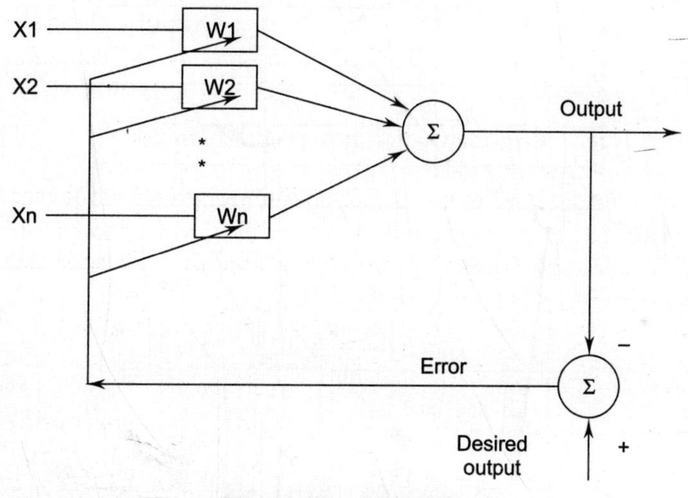

Fig. 11.29 *ADALINE.*

In practice, an ADALINE is usually used to make binary decisions. Therefore, the output is sent through a binary threshold as shown in Fig. 11.29. Realizations of several logic gates such as AND, NOT and OR are common applications of ADALINE. Only those logic functions that are linearly separable can be realized by the ADALINE, as is explained in the next section.

11.9.4 Linear Separable Patterns

For a single ADALINE to function properly as a classifier, the input pattern must be linearly separable. This implies that the patterns to be classified must be sufficiently apart from each other to ensure the decision surface consists of a single hyperplane such as a single straight line in two-dimensional space. This concept is illustrated in Fig. 11.30 for a two-dimensional pattern.

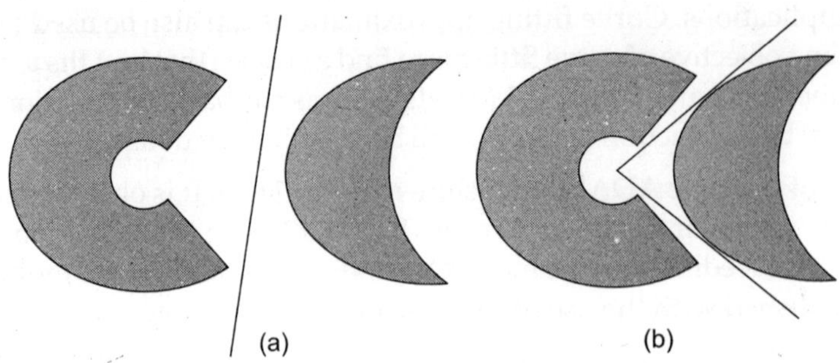

Fig. 11.30 *A pair of linearly separable (a), and non-linearly separable patterns (b).*

A classic example of a mapping that is not separable is XOR (the exclusive or) gate function. Table 11.1 shows the input-output pattern of this problem. Fig. 11.31 shows the locations of the symbolic outputs of XOR function corresponding to four input patterns in X_1-X_2 plane. There is no way to draw a single straight line so that the circles are on one side of the line and the triangular sign on the other side. Therefore, an ADALINE cannot realize this function.

Table 11.1 ***Inputs/Outputs Relationship for XOR.***

X1	X2	Output
0	0	0
0	1	1
1	0	1
1	1	0

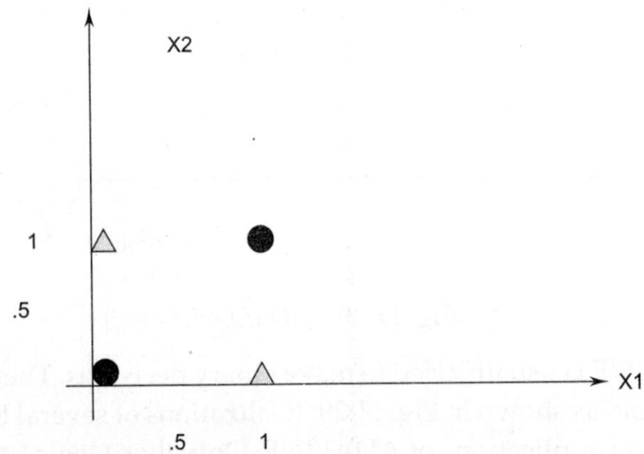

Fig. 11.31 *The output of XOR in X_1-X_2 plane.*

One approach to solve this nonlinear separation problem is to use MADALINE (Multiple ADALINE) networks. The basic structure of a MADALINE network consists of combining several ADALINE with their correspondence activation functions into a single forward structure. When suitable weights are chosen, the network is capable of implementing complicated and nonlinear separable mapping such as XOR gate problems.

11.9.5 Single Layer Perceptron

11.9.5.1 General Architecture

The original idea of the perceptron was developed by Rosenblatt in the late 1950s along with a convergence procedure to adjust the weights. In Rosenblatt's perceptron, the inputs were binary and no bias was included. It was based on the McCulloch-Pitts model of the neuron with the hard limitation activation function. The single layer perceptron as shown in Fig. 11.32 is very similar to ADALINE except for the addition of an activation function.

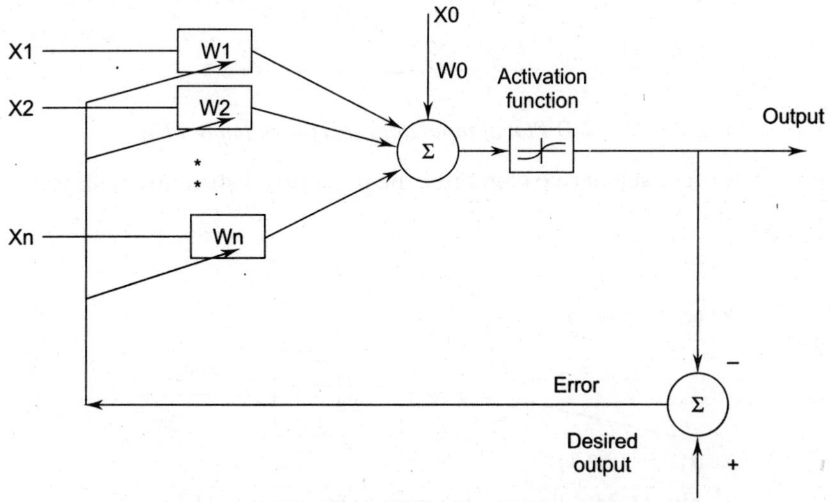

Fig. 11.32 *A perceptron with a sigmoid activation function.*

Connection weights and threshold in a perceptron can be fixed or adapted using a number of different algorithms. Here the original perceptron convergence procedure as developed by Minsky and Papert is described. First, connection weights $W_1, W_2, \ldots\ldots, W_n$ and the threshold value W_0 are initialized to small non-zero values. Then, a new input set with N values received through sensory units (measurement devices) and the input is computed. Connection weights are only adapted when an error occurs. This procedure is repeated until the classification of all inputs is completed.

11.9.5.2 Linear Classification

For classification of the above concept, consider two input patterns classes C_1 and C_2. The weight adaptation at the *k*th training phase can be formulated as follow :

1. If *k* member of the training vector $x(k)$ is correctly classified, no correction action is needed for the weight vector. Since the activation function is selected as a hard limiter, the following conditions will be valid :

   $$W(k+1) = W(k) \text{ if output} > 0 \text{ and } x(k) \in C_1, \text{ and}$$
   $$W(k+1) = W(k) \text{ if output} < 0 \text{ and } x(k) \in C_2.$$

2. Otherwise, the weight should be updated in accordance with the following rule :

   $$W(k+1) = W(k) + \eta\, x(k) \text{ if output} \geq 0 \text{ and } x(k)\, \varepsilon\, C_1$$
   $$W(k+1) = W(k) - \eta\, x(k) \text{ if output} \leq 0 \text{ and } x(k)\, \varepsilon\, C_2$$

Where η is the learning rate parameter, which should be selected between 0 and 1.

Example 11.8. Let us consider pattern classes C1 and C2, where C1 : {(0, 2), (0, 1)} and C2 : {(1, 0), (1, 1)}. The objective is to obtain a decision surface based on perceptron learning. The 2-D graph for the above data is shown in Fig. 11.33.

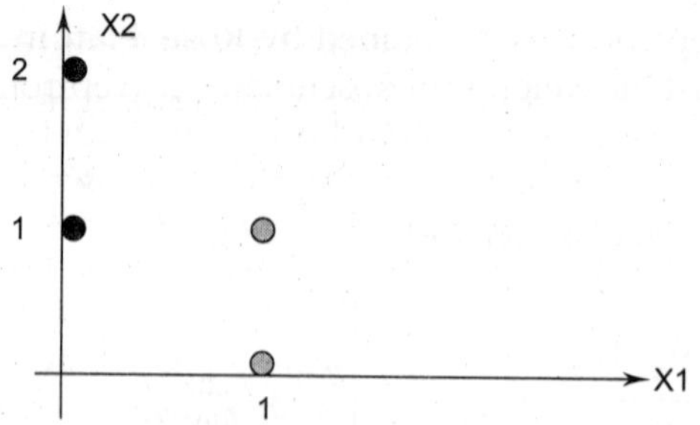

Fig. 11.33 *2-D Plot of input data sets for example 11.8.*

Since, the input vectors consist of two elements, the perceptron structure is simply as follows :

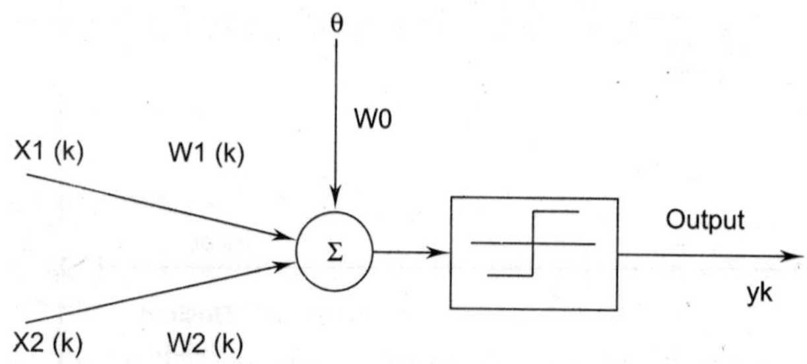

Fig. 11.34 *Perceptron structure for example 11.8.*

For simplicity, let us assume $\eta = 1$ and initial weight vector W (1) = [0 0]. The iteration weights are as follow :

Iteration 1 : $W^T(1)\,x(1) = \begin{bmatrix}0 & 0\end{bmatrix}\begin{bmatrix}0\\2\end{bmatrix} = 0$

Weight Update : $W(2) = W(1) + x(1) = \begin{bmatrix}0\\0\end{bmatrix} + \begin{bmatrix}0\\2\end{bmatrix} = \begin{bmatrix}0\\2\end{bmatrix}$

Iteration 2 : $W^T(2)\,.\,x(2) = \begin{bmatrix}0 & 2\end{bmatrix}\begin{bmatrix}0\\1\end{bmatrix} = 2 > 0$

Weight Update : $W(3) = W(2)$

Iteration 3 : $W^T(3).x(3) = \begin{bmatrix}0 & 2\end{bmatrix}\begin{bmatrix}1\\0\end{bmatrix} = 0$

Weight Update : $W(4) = W(3) - x(3) = \begin{bmatrix}0\\2\end{bmatrix} - \begin{bmatrix}1\\0\end{bmatrix} = \begin{bmatrix}-1\\2\end{bmatrix}$

Iteration 4 : $W^T(4)\,.\,x(4) = \begin{bmatrix}-1 & 2\end{bmatrix}\begin{bmatrix}1\\1\end{bmatrix} = 1$

Weight Update : $W(5) = W(4) - x(4) = \begin{bmatrix}-1\\2\end{bmatrix} - \begin{bmatrix}1\\1\end{bmatrix} = \begin{bmatrix}-2\\1\end{bmatrix}$

Now if we continue the procedure, the perceptron classifies the two classes correctly at each instance. For example for the fifth and sixth iterations :

Iteration 5: $W^T(5) \cdot x(5) = [-2 \quad 1]\begin{bmatrix}0\\2\end{bmatrix} = 2 > 0$ Correct Classification

Iteration 6: $W^T(6) \cdot x(6) = [-2 \quad 1]\begin{bmatrix}0\\1\end{bmatrix} = 1 > 0$ Correct Classification

In a similar fashion for the seventh and eighth iterations, the classification results are indeed correct.

Iteration 7: $W^T(7) \cdot x(7) = [-2 \quad 1]\begin{bmatrix}1\\0\end{bmatrix} = -2 < 0$: Correct Classification

Iteration 8: $W^T(8) \cdot x(8) = [-2 \quad 1]\begin{bmatrix}1\\1\end{bmatrix} = -1 < 0$: Correct Classification

Therefore, the algorithm converges and the decision surface for the above perceptron is as follows:

$$d(x) = -2X_1 + X_2 = 0 \qquad \text{... (11.16)}$$

Now, let us consider the input data {1, 2}, which is not in the training set. If we calculate the output:

$$Y = W^T \cdot X = [-2 \quad 1]\begin{bmatrix}2\\1\end{bmatrix} = -3 < 0 \qquad \text{... (11.17)}$$

The output Y belongs to the class C2 as is expected.

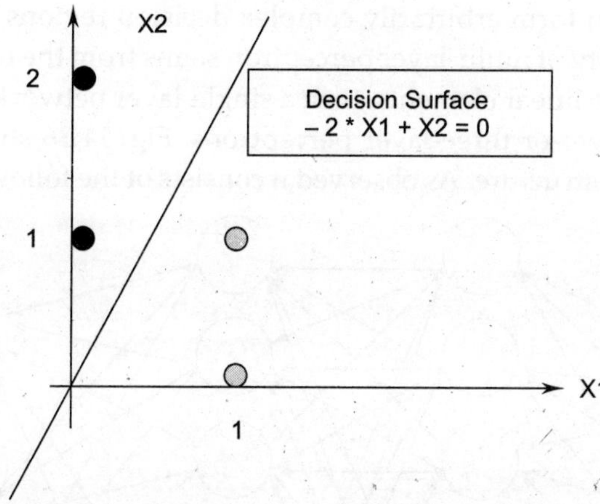

Fig. 11.35 *Decision surface for example 11.8.*

11.9.5.3 Perceptron Algorithm

The perceptron learning algorithm (Delta rule) can be summarized as follows :

Step 1 : Initialize the weights $W_1, W_2, \ldots\ldots, W_n$ and threshold θ to small random values.

Step 2 : Present new input $X1, X2, \ldots\ldots, Xn$ and desired output d_k.

Step 3 : Calculate the actual output based on the following formula :

$$y_k = f_h\left(\sum_{i=1}^{n}(X_i W_i) - \theta_k\right) \qquad \text{... (11.18)}$$

Step 4 : Adapt the weights according to the following equation :

$$W_i(\text{new}) = W_i(\text{old}) + \eta\,(d_k - y_k)\,x_i,\ 0 \le i \le N \qquad \text{... (11.19)}$$

Where η is a positive gain fraction less than 1 and d_k is the desired output. Note that the weights remain the same if the network makes the correct decision.

Step 5 : Repeat the procedures in steps 2–4 until the classification task is completed.

Similar to ADALINE, if the presented inputs pattern is linearly separable, then the above perceptron algorithm converges and positions the decision hyperplane between two separate classes. On the other hand, if the inputs are not separable and their distribution overlaps, then the decision boundary may oscillate continuously. A modification to the perceptron convergence procedure is the utilization of Least Mean Square (LMS) in this case. The algorithm that forms the LMS solution is also called the Widrow-Hoff. The LMS algorithm is similar to the procedure above except a threshold logic nonlinearity, replaces the hard limited non-linearity. Weights are thus corrected on every trail by an amount that depends on the difference between the desired and actual values. Unlike the learning in the ADALINE, the perceptron learning rule has been shown to be capable of separating any linear separable set of the training patterns.

11.9.6 Multi-Layer Perceptron

11.9.6.1 General Architecture

Multi-layer perceptrons represent a generalization of the single-layer perceptron as described in the previous section. A single layer perceptron forms a half-plane decision region. On the other hand multi-layer perceptrons can form arbitrarily complex decision regions and can separate various input patterns. The capability of multi-layer perceptron stems from the non-linearities used within the nodes. If the nodes were linear elements, then a single-layer network with appropriate weight could be used instead of two-or three-layer perceptrons. Fig. 11.36 shows a typical multi-layer perceptron neural network structure. As observed it consists of the following layers :

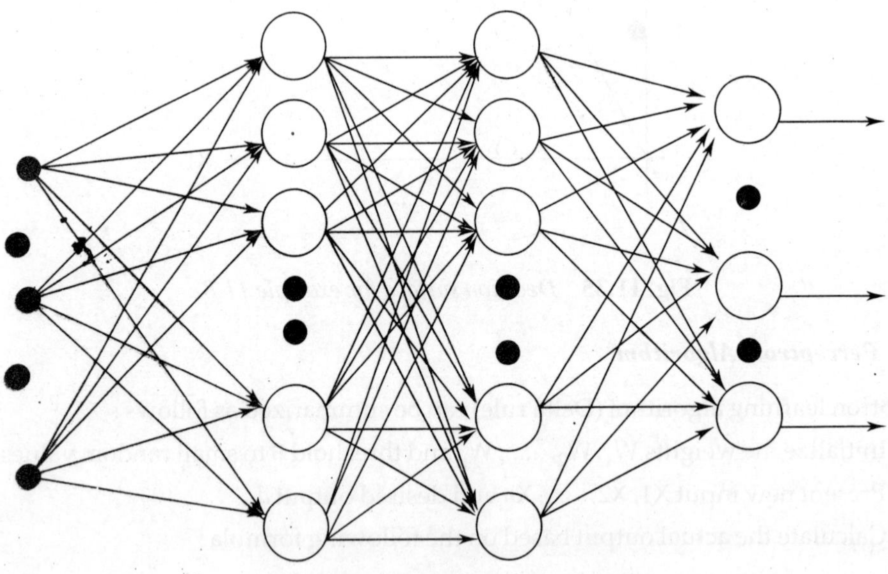

Fig. 11.36 *Multi-layer perceptron.*

Input Layer : A layer of neurons that receives information from external sources, and passes this information to the network for processing. These may be either sensory inputs or signals from other systems outside the one being modeled.

Hidden Layer : A layer of neurons that receives information from the input layer and processes them in a hidden way. It has no direct connections to the outside world (inputs or outputs). All connections from the hidden layer are to other layers within the system.

Output Layer : A layer of neurons that receives processed information and sends output signals out of the system.

Bias : Acts on a neuron like an offset. The function of the bias is to provide a threshold for the activation of neurons. The bias input is connected to each of the hidden and output neurons in a network.

11.9.6.2 Input-Output Mapping

The input/output mapping of a network is established according to the weights and the activation functions of their neurons in input, hidden and output layers. The number of input neurons corresponds to the number of input variables in the neural network, and the number of output neurons is the same as the number of desired output variables. The number of neurons in the hidden layer(s) depends upon the particular NN application. For example, consider the following two-layer feed-forward network with three neurons in the hidden layer and two neurons in the second layer.

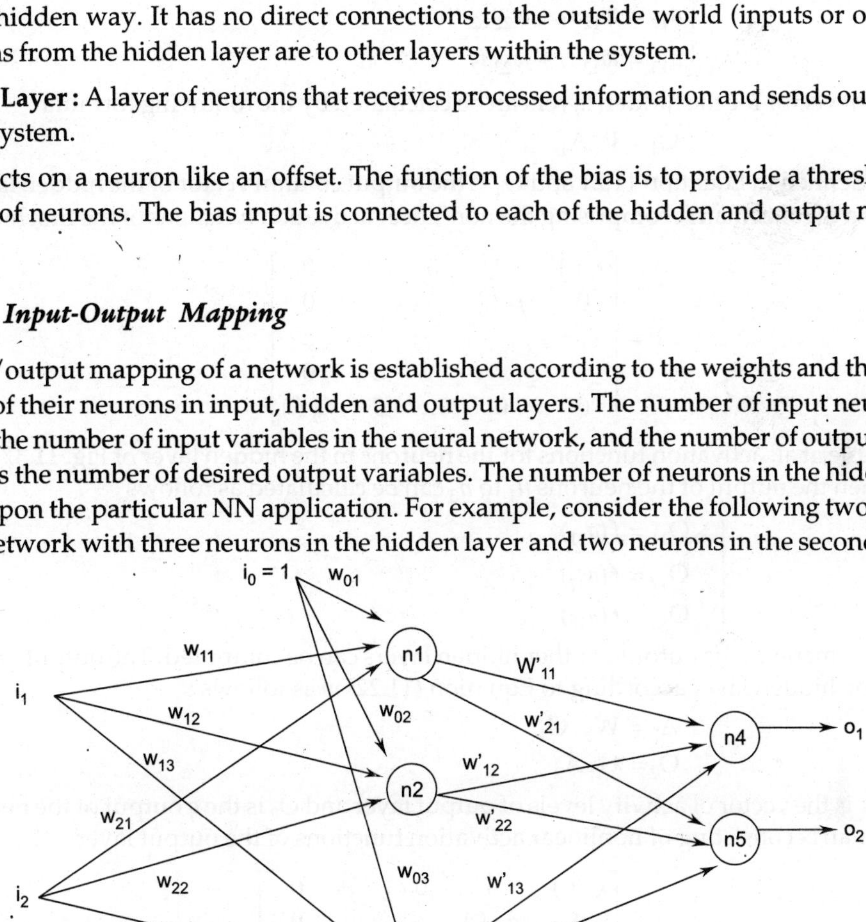

Fig. 11.37 *An example of multi-layer perceptron.*

As is shown, the inputs are connected to each neuron in hidden layer via their corresponding weights. A zero weight indicates no connection. For example, if $W_{23} = 0$, it is implied that no connection exists between the second input (i_2) and the third neuron (n_3). Outputs of the last layer are considered as the outputs of the network.

The structure of each neuron within a layer is similar to the architecture as described in section 11.9.5. Although the activation function for one neuron could be different from other neurons within a layer, for structural simplicity, similar neurons are commonly chosen within a layer. The input data sets (or sensory information) are presented to the input layer. This layer is connected to the first hidden layer. If there is more than one hidden layer, the last hidden layer should be connected to the output layer of the network. At the first phase, we will have the following linear relationship for each layer :

$$A_1 = W_1 X \quad \text{... (11.20)}$$

where A_1 is a column vector consisting of m elements, W_1 is an $m \times n$ weight matrix and X is a column input vector of dimension n. For the above example, the linear activity level of the hidden layer (neurons n_1 to n_3) can be calculated as follows :

$$\begin{cases} a_{11} = w_{11}\, i_1 + w_{21}\, i_2 \\ a_{12} = w_{12}\, i_1 + w_{22}\, i_2 \\ a_{13} = w_{13}\, i_1 + w_{23}\, i_2 \end{cases} \quad \text{... (11.21)}$$

The output vector for the hidden layer can be calculated by the following formula :

$$O_1 = F \cdot A_1 \quad \text{... (11.22)}$$

where A_1 is defined in Equation 11.21 and O_1 is the output column vector of the hidden layer with m element. F is a digonal matrix comprising the non-linear activation functions of the first hidden layer:

$$F = \begin{bmatrix} f_1(.) & 0 & 0 & \dots & 0 \\ 0 & f_2(.) & & & 0 \\ . & & .. & & .. \\ . & & & .. & 0 \\ 0 & 0 & \dots & 0 & f_m(.) \end{bmatrix} \quad \text{... (11.23)}$$

For example, if all activation functions for the neurons in the hidden layer of Fig. 11.37 are chosen similarly, then the output of the neurons n_1 to n_3 can be calculated as follows :

$$\begin{cases} O_{11} = f(a_{11}) \\ O_{12} = f(a_{12}) \\ O_{13} = f(a_{13}) \end{cases} \quad \text{... (11.24)}$$

In a similar manner, the output of other hidden layers can be computed. The output of a network with only one hidden layer according to Equation (11.22) is as follows :

$$A_2 = W_2 \cdot O_1 \quad \text{... (11.25)}$$

$$O_2 = G \cdot A_2 \quad \text{... (11.26)}$$

Where A_2 is the vector of activity levels of output layer and O_2 is the q output of the network. G is a diagonal matrix consisting of nonlinear activation functions of the output layer:

$$G = \begin{bmatrix} g_1(.) & 0 & 0 & \dots & 0 \\ 0 & g_2(.) & & & 0 \\ . & & .. & & .. \\ . & & & .. & 0 \\ 0 & 0 & \dots & 0 & g_q(.) \end{bmatrix} \quad \text{... (11.27)}$$

For Fig. 11.37, the activity level of output neurons n_4 and n_5 can be calculated as follows :

$$\begin{cases} a_{21} = W'_{11}\, O_{11} + W'_{12}\, O_{21} + W'_{13}\, O_{31} \\ a_{22} = W'_{21}\, O_{11} + W'_{22}\, O_{21} + W'_{23}\, O_{31} \end{cases} \quad \text{... (11.28)}$$

The two outputs of the network with the similar activation functions can be calculated as follows:

$$\begin{cases} O_1 = g\,(a_{21}) \\ O_2 = g\,(a_{22}) \end{cases} \quad \text{... (11.29)}$$

Therefore, the input-output mapping of a multi-layer perceptron is established according to relationships (11.20 - 11.29). In sequel, the output of the network can be calculated using such nonlinear mapping and the input data sets.

11.9.6.3 XOR Realization

As it was shown in section 11.9.4, a single-layer perceptron cannot classify the input patterns that are not linearly separable such as an Exclusive OR (XOR) gate. This problem may be considered as a special case of a more general non-linear mapping problem. In the XOR problem, we need to consider the four corners of the unit square that correspond to the input pattern. We may solve the problem with a multi-layer perceptron with one hidden layer as shown in Figure 11.38.

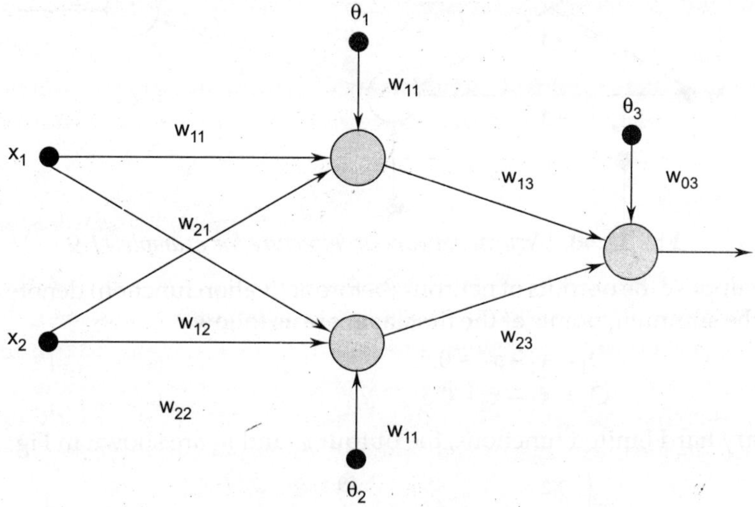

Fig. 11.38 *Neural network architecture to solve XOR problem.*

In the above configuration, a McCulloh-Pitts model represents each neuron, which uses a hard limit activation function. By appropriate selections of the network weights, the XOR could be implemented using decision surfaces as shown in Fig. 11.39.

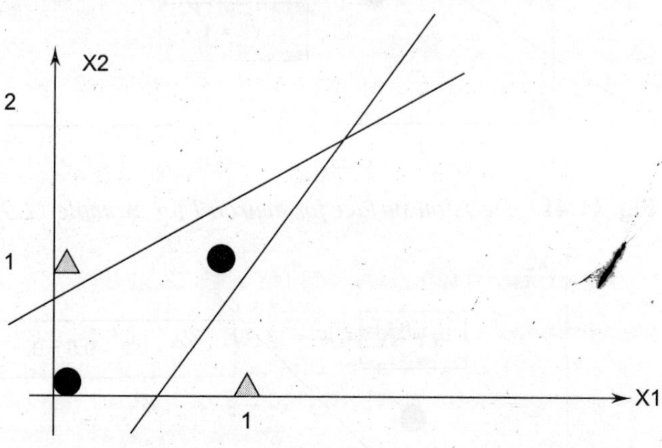

Fig. 11.39 *Decision surfaces to solve XOR problem.*

Example 11.9. Suppose weights and biases are selected as shown in Fig. 11.40. The McCulloh-Pitts model represents each neuron (binary hard limit activation function). Show that the network solves XOR problem. In addition, draw the decision boundaries constructed by the network.

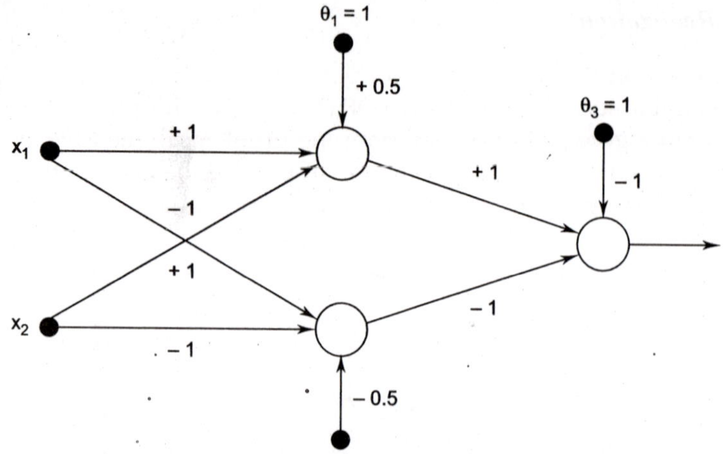

Fig. 11.40 *Neural network architecture for example 11.9.*

In Fig. 11.40, suppose the outputs of neurons (before activation function) denote as O_1, O_2, and O_3. The outputs of the summing points at the first layer are as follow :

$$O_1 = x_1 - x_2 + 0.5 \quad \text{... (11.30)}$$

$$O_2 = x_1 - x_2 - 0.5 \quad \text{... (11.31)}$$

With the binary hard limited functions, the output y_1 and y_2 are shown in Fig. 11.41 and 11.42.

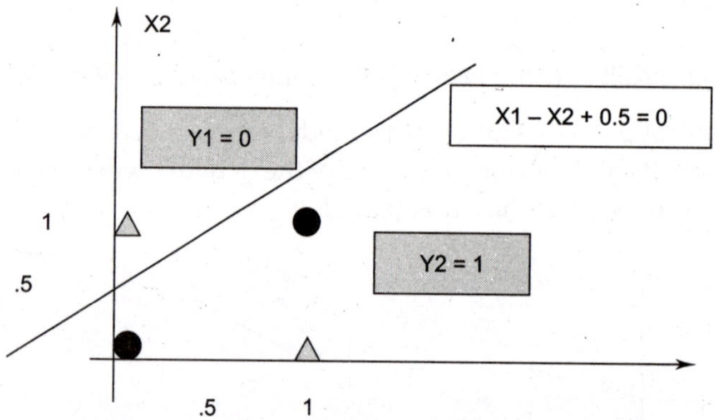

Fig. 11.41 *Decision surface for neuron 1 for example 11.9.*

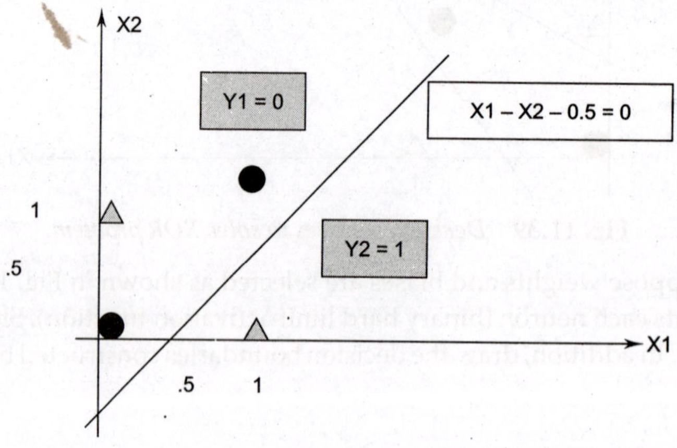

Fig. 11.42 *Decision surface for neuron 2 of example 11.9.*

The outputs of the summing points at the second layer are :

$$O_3 = y_1 - y_2 - 1 \qquad \text{... (11.32)}$$

The decision boundaries of the network are shown in Fig. 11.43. Therefore, XOR realization can be accomplished by selection of appropriate weights using Fig. 11.40.

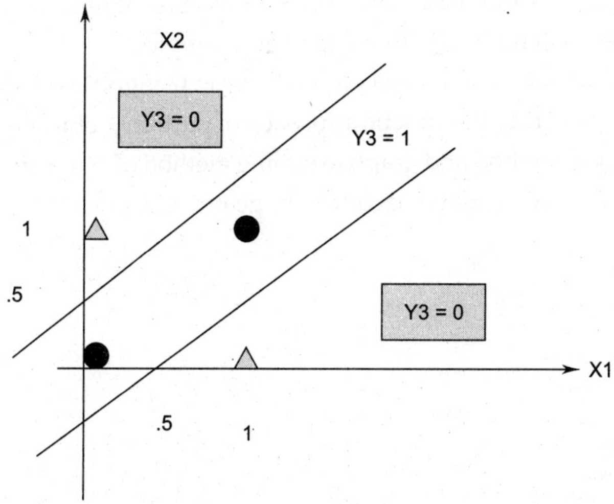

Fig. 11.43 *Decision surfaces for example 11.9.*

11.10 CONCLUSION

In this chapter, the fundamentals of neural networks were introduced. The perceptron is the simplest form of neural network used for the classification of linearly separable patterns. Multi-layer perceptron overcome many limitations of single-layer perceptron. They can form arbitrarily complex decision regions in order to separate various nonlinear patterns.

Summary

1. The basic purpose of object recognition is to classify data based on either a prior knowledge 'or' on statistical information extracted from pattern/object.
2. General approaches for object/pattern recognition are—Template matching, statistical classification, structural (syntactic) matching and neural network.
3. In template matching, every pattern in image is matched to a prototype pattern and according to matching ; objects are classified.
4. In statistical approach; the pattern is represented by a d-feature space and then we decide the boundaries between features of object based on similarities.
5. In syntactic / structural approach ; a complex pattern is divided in relatively small and easy primitive. Then to represent / describe the whole pattern, we find some rules according to those rules, we describe the whole image by primitives.
6. By neural network ; we can recognize more complex pattern. In neural network, before applying neural network for pattern recognition, we have to trained them.

Review Questions

1. What do you understand by object/pattern ? What is the need of object/pattern recognition ?
2. What are the different approaches for pattern / object recognition ? Compare them.
3. Describe template matching with the help of an example.
4. Draw the system model for statistical pattern/object recognition. Explain them.
5. What do you understand by syntactic approach of pattern / object recognition.
6. Explain grammatical method and graph matching method of syntactic approach of recognition.
7. How may the neural network be used for image recognition ? What is multi-layered neural network ?

INDEX

EXERCISE 17.11

Indicate if the following reactions (Scheme 17.59a) are allowed or forbidden.

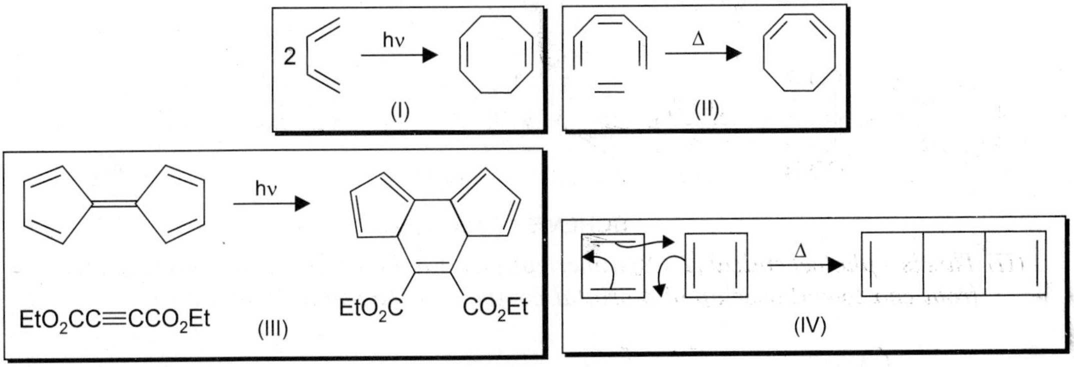

SCHEME 17.59a

> **Hint.** *If in a reactant more π electrons are involved in the cyclization, the nonparticipating π electrons are not counted for the classification (see Table 17.3). A reaction involving odd number of electron pairs requires heat while a reaction involving even number of electron pairs requires light.*

ANSWER. *(I) A[4 + 4] cycloaddition, involves 4 electron pairs is photochemically allowed (see Table 17.3).*

(II) A[6 + 2] cycloaddition, involves 4 electron pairs is photochemically allowed and thermally forbidden.

(III) Since it is a [10 + 2] cycloaddition and involves 6 electron pairs, is photochemically allowed.

(IV) It is the allowed thermal dimerization [4 + 2].

EXERCISE 17.12

One of the reactions (Scheme 17.59b) requires heat and the other light. Which is which ? Explain.

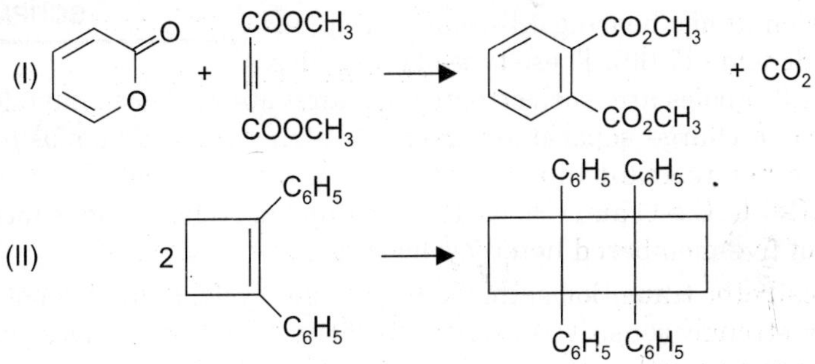

SCHEME 17.59b

ANSWER. *(I) This reaction is thermally allowed ; it being a [4 + 2] cycloaddition. The initially formed intermediate then undergoes a thermally allowed reverse Diels Alder reaction (Scheme 17.59c).*

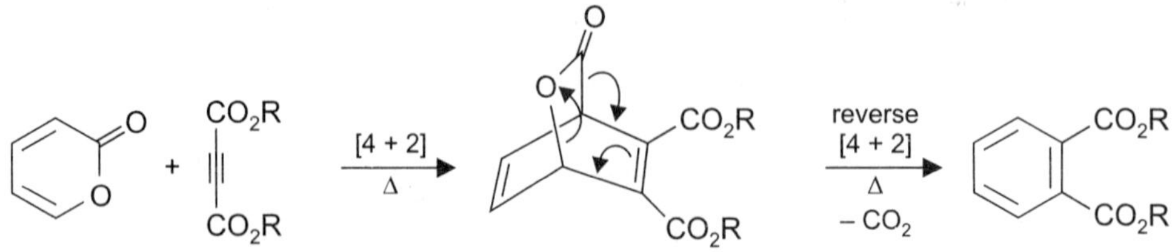

SCHEME 17.59c

(II) This is a photochemical [2 + 2] dimerization with the stereochemistry as dictated from end-to-end overlap of p-orbital components (Scheme 17.59d).

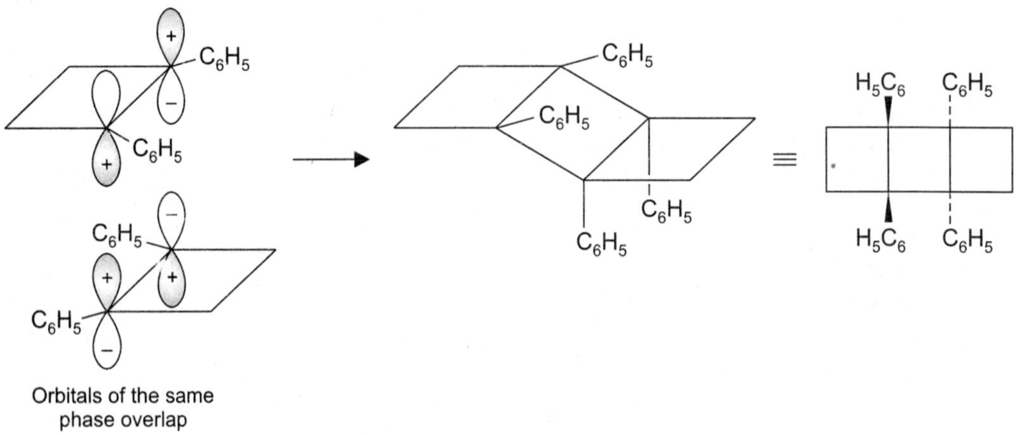

SCHEME 17.59d

17.5 1, 3-DIPOLAR CYCLOADDITIONS

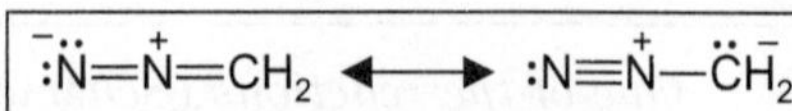

'1,3-dipolar' compound diazomethane

SCHEME 17.60

These cycloadditions are analogous to the Diels-Alder reaction in that they are concerted [$\pi^{4s} + \pi^{2s}$] reactions. The 1,3-dipolar components are compounds whose representation requires ionic structures which include ones with charges on atoms bearing 1,3-relationship, as in diazomethane (Scheme 17.60). These type of molecules which are called, 1,3-dipoles are isoelectronic with allyl anion. These have four π electron and each has at least one charge separated resonance structure with opposite charges in a 1,3 relationship. The other reactant (dipolarophile) in a dipolar cycloaddition has unsaturated bonds like, C=C, C≡C, C=O and C≡N. The 1,3-dipolar cycloadditions form useful reactions for the synthesis of five membered heterocyclic rings.

Mechanistically the transition state for 1, 3-dipolar cycloaddition is not very polar and the reaction rate is not strongly sensitive to solvent polarity. The loss of charge separation which is implied, is more apparent rather than real, since most 1, 3-dipolar compounds are not highly polar. The polarity associated with a single structure is balanced by other contributing structures.

A 1, 3-dipole represents a structural variant of the diene component in the Diels-Alder reaction; in the dipolar compound, four π-electrons are distributed over three atoms instead of the four in a diene. Moreover, the HOMO and LUMO of a 1, 3-dipole are similar in symmetry to that in a diene with respect to the two-fold axis and to the mirror plane which bisects the molecule (Scheme 17.61), a concerted cycloaddition *e.g.*, to an alkene is a symmetry allowed process. The reaction of an alkene with diazomethane to give a pyrazoline (Scheme 17.62 pyrazole derivative) belongs to this class.

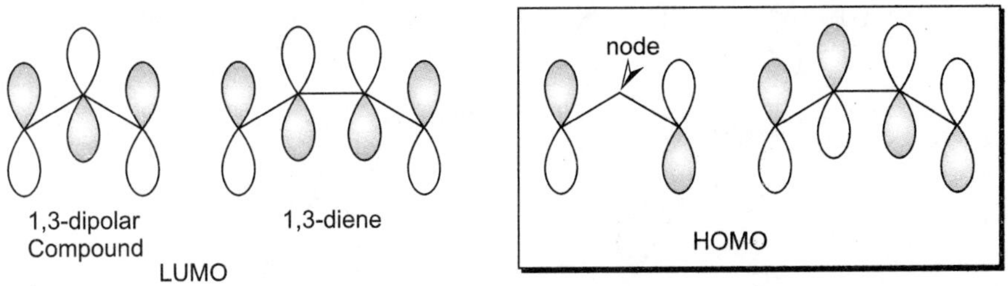

SCHEME 17.61

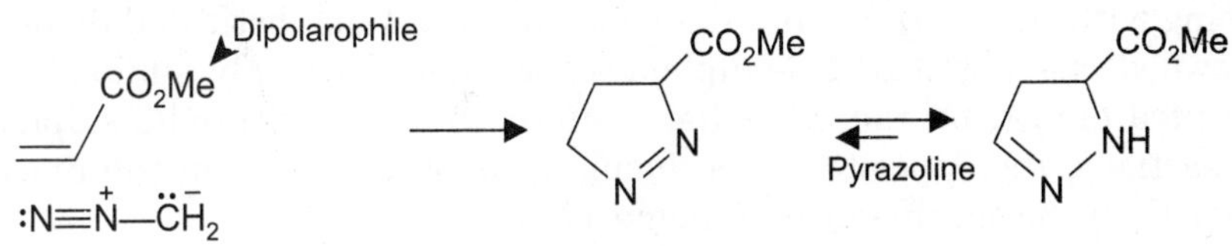

SCHEME 17.62

17.6 CHELETROPIC REACTIONS

In a cheletropic reaction two σ bonds that terminate at a single atom are made or broken during a concerted reaction (Scheme 17.63). In the case of molecules, sulphur dioxide or carbon monoxide the HOMO is that which has a lone pair of electrons in the plane having the atoms, while the LUMO represents the *p* orbital perpendicular to this plane (Scheme 17.64).

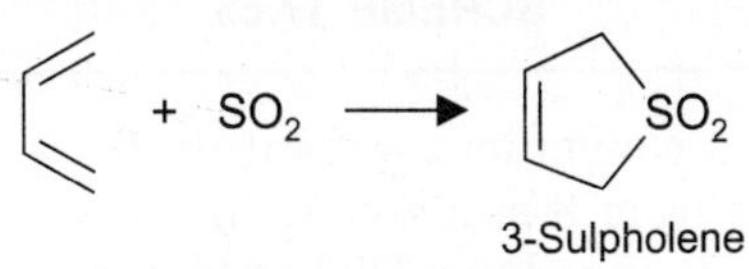

(a cheletropic reaction)

SCHEME 17.63

For a symmetry allowed cycloaddition of *e.g.*, SO_2 to a diene, the molecule of SO_2 must lie in a plane which bisects the *s-cis* conformation of the diene (Scheme 17.64). The interaction is suprafacial for diene and SO_2. In the transition state, the terminal carbon atoms of the diene must move in the disrotatory manner in order that the HOMO of SO_2 can interact with the LUMO of the diene, or the LUMO of SO_2 with the HOMO of the diene.

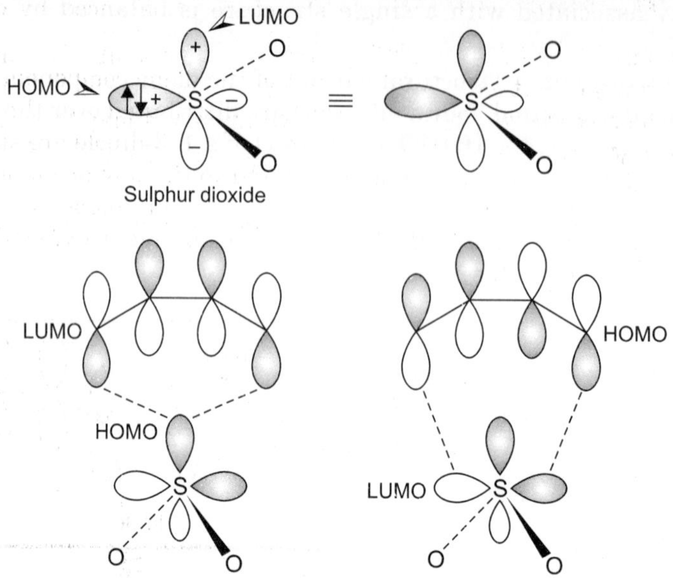

SCHEME 17.64

In keeping with these arguments the *trans, trans*-1,4-disubstituted dienes give specifically more crowded *cis*-substituted 3-sulphones (Scheme 17.65). By similar arguments *cis, trans*-disubstituted dienes, on the other hand afford *trans*-substituted-3-sulphones. As with electrocyclic reactions, the opposite stereochemistry is observed when the reaction is photochemical rather than thermochemical (Scheme 17.65).

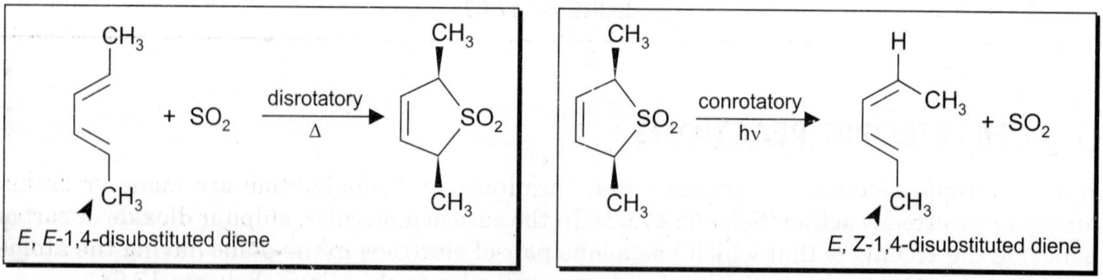

SCHEME 17.65

3-Sulpholene, a solid, is a convenient substitute for geseous butadiene. Butadiene is generated at high temperatures from 3-sulpholene in a reverse reaction (Scheme 17.66) and when a dienophile is present it is trapped in a Diels-Alder reaction. The Diels-Alder reaction in itself is usually reversible and has been used to protect double bonds (see Exercise 17.11).

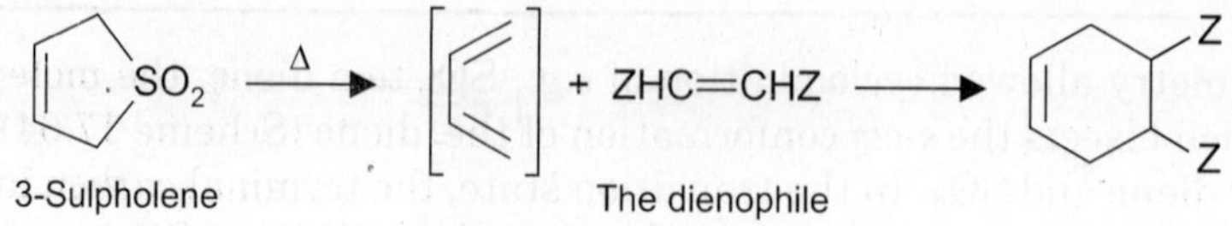

SCHEME 17.66

17.7 SIGMATROPIC REARRANGEMENTS

A sigmatropic rearrangement is a concerted intramolecular shift of an atom or a group of atoms. During this arrangement a σ bond is broken in the reactant and a new σ bond is formed in the product and the π bonds rearrange. The following points may be noted:

- The number of π bonds does not change, both the reactant and the product contain the same number of π bonds.
- The σ bond that cleaves can be in the middle of the π system or at end of the π system (Scheme 17.67).

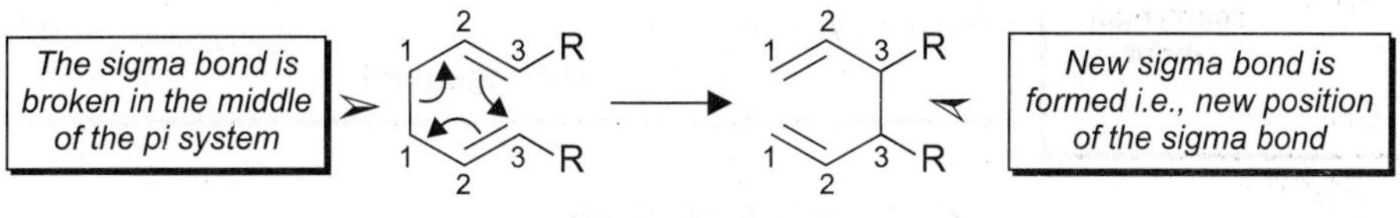

a [3,3] sigmatropic rearrangement

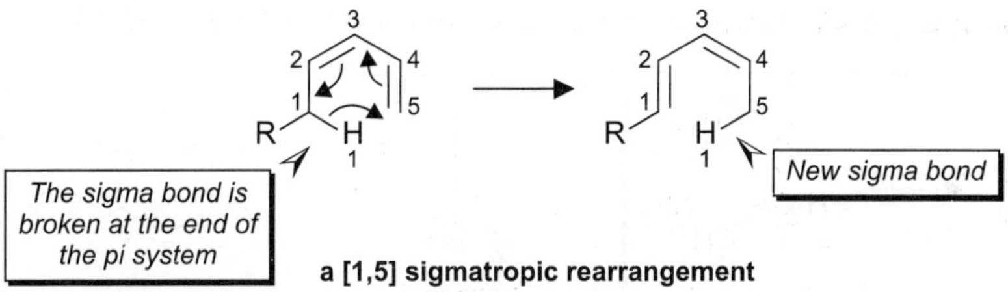

a [1,5] sigmatropic rearrangement

SCHEME 17.67

- The σ bond that breaks is bonded to an allylic carbon.
- To identify the order of a sigmatropic shift [*i*, *j*] first identify the σ bond which is broken in the reaction. Then assign number 1 to both the atoms involved in this bond, then the atoms in each direction from the bond being cleaved, upto and including the atoms which form the new σ bond in the product are numbered as atoms 2,3 and so on. The numbers assigned to the atoms that form the new bond, separated by commas are put within the brackets to show the reaction order (Scheme 17.67). Similarly the migration of hydrogen (Scheme 17.68) is another example of [1,5] sigmatropic shift. The order [1,5] is not due to the fact that hydrogen migrates from C1 to C5 but since the hydrogen (one of the two atoms given the number 1) forms part of the new σ bond and had also formed part of the old σ bond. Only all the atoms taking part in the reaction have to be counted. Thus the rearrangement of cyclohexadiene (Scheme 17.68) cannot be labelled as [1,3] shift since the methylene group linking 1 and 5 is not involved in the reaction.

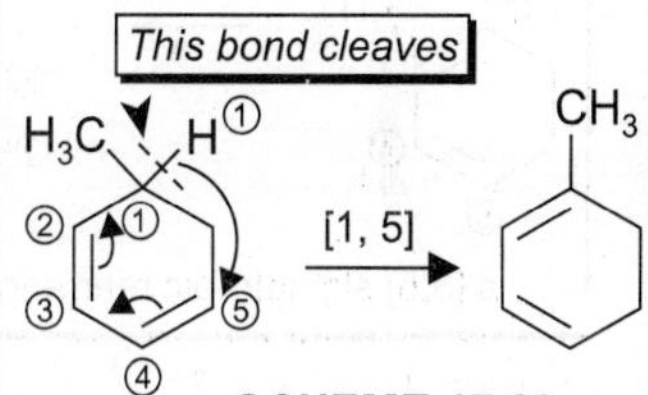

SCHEME 17.68

- Since in these reactions a change in the position of one σ bond takes place, Woodward and Hofmann coined the term "sigmatropic shifts".
- A [3,3] sigmatropic rearrangement of a 1,5-diene (when the six atoms involved are all carbons) is known as the Cope rearrangement (I, Scheme 17.69).

- The oxygen analog of the Cope rearrangement is called the Claisen rearrangement. Often one of the π bonds is part of an aromatic ring (II, Scheme 17.69). Allyl vinyl ethers also undergo Claisen rearrangement.

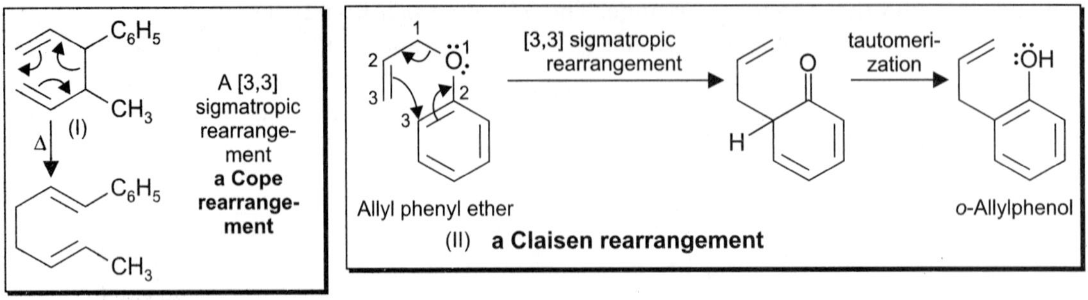

SCHEME 17.69

- More examples of sigmatropic rearrangements are in (Scheme 17.69*a*).

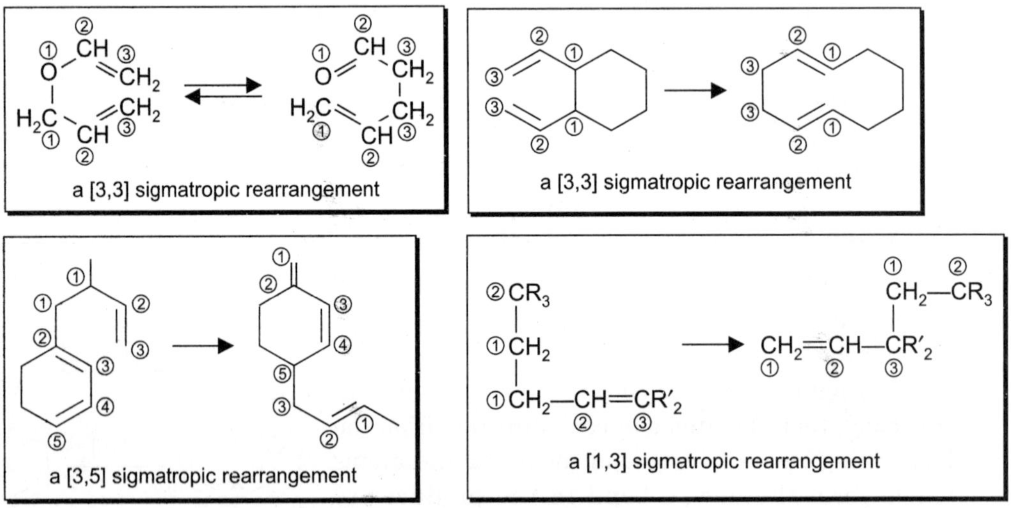

SCHEME 17.69a

A. Sigmatropic Migration of Hydrogen

(i) Introduction.

A hydrogen atom is reported to migrate from one end of a system of π bonds to the other, under thermal or photochemical rearrangements. In the transition state the hydrogen must be in contact with both ends of the chain at the same time. There are two distinct processes by which a sigmatropic migration can occur. If the hydrogen moves along the top or bottom face of the π-system *i.e.,* migrating group remains associated with same face of the conjugated system throughout the process, the migration is termed *suprafacial.* When the hydrogen moves across the π system either from top to bottom or vice versa *i.e.,* the migrating group moves to the opposite face of the π-system during the course of migration then it is called *antarafacial.*

In a given sigmatropic rearrangement, the migrating group is bonded to both the migration source and the migration termini in the transition state. It is imagined that the migrating H atom breaks away from the rest of the system which is treated as a free radical. Thus in a simplest case involving a [1,3] shift of hydrogen (Scheme 17.70), the frontier orbital analysis treats this system as a hydrogen atom interacting with an allyl radical. The electron of the hydrogen atom is in a 1*s* orbital which has only one lobe. The HOMO of an allylic free radical depends on the number of carbons in the π-framework (Scheme 17.71).

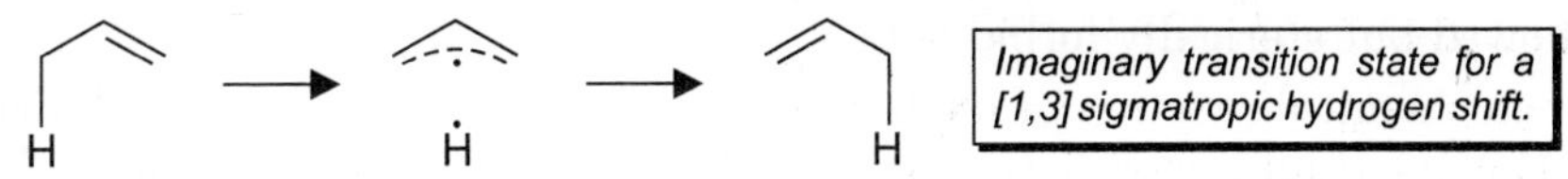

SCHEME 17.70

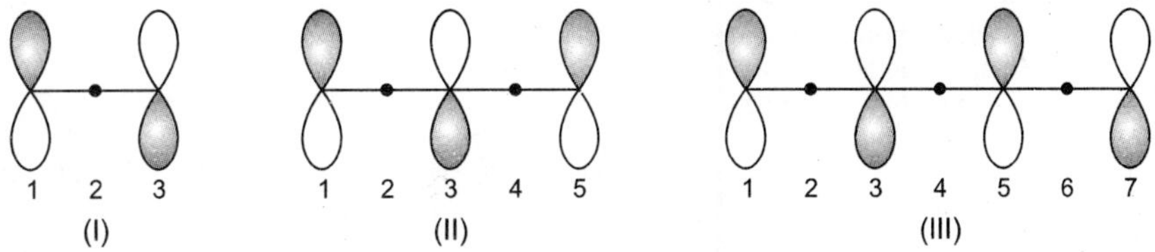

The HOMO of the *allylic* radicals

SCHEME 17.71

(ii) [1,3] Sigmatropic Rearrangement (Hydrogen Shift).

In the migration of hydrogen the H must move from a plus to plus or from minus to a minus lobe of the HOMO, it cannot move to a lobe of opposite sign.

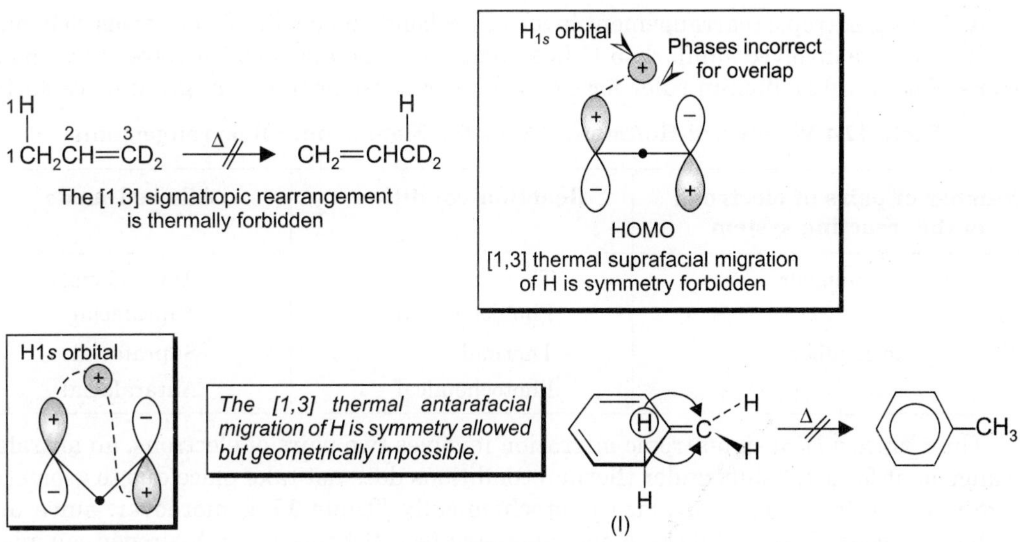

SCHEME 17.72

During a thermal [1,3] sigmatropic migration of a hydrogen, the overlap of the hydrogen 1*s* orbital with the HOMO of the allyl radical (I, Scheme 17.71, asymmetric) is bonding at one end and antibonding at the other end for the suprafacial migration (Scheme 17.72). Thus [1,3] sigmatropic suprafacial migration of hydrogen (under thermal conditions) is symmetry-forbidden (Scheme 17.72). However, in the antarafacial process (Scheme 17.72) the hydrogen atom shall have to cross over the *pi* system to the other face to form a four membered ring transition state, a geometrically very difficult situation. Thus over all thermal [1,3] sigmatropic rearrangements are rare. The stability of the triene (I, Scheme 17.72) which is not thermally isomerized to toluene, which is thermodynamically more stable is due to a symmetry-forbidden process (suprafacial H migration is symmetry forbidden, antarafacial H migration though symmetry allowed but sterically forbidden).

In a photochemical reaction promotion of an electron means that now (I, Scheme 17.73) becomes the HOMO. Suprafacial pathway for [1,3] shift now becomes an allowed process and antarafacial pathway forbidden. Thus, the compound (II, Scheme 17.73) displays a [1,3] hydrogen shift under photochemical conditions.

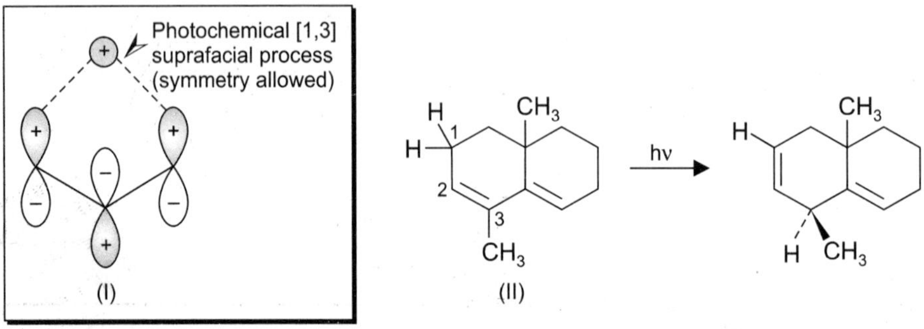

The [1,3] sigmatropic rearrangement is photochemically allowed

SCHEME 17.73

A [1,3] sigmatropic rearrangement involves a π bond and a pair of σ electrons so in all two pairs electrons are involved similarly a [1,5] sigmatropic rearrangement involves three pairs of electrons. Woodward Hoffmann rules for sigmatropic rearrangements are given in Table 17.4.

Table 17.4 Woodward-Hoffmann Rules for Sigmatropic Rearrangements

Number of pairs of electrons in the reacting system	Reaction condition	Allowed mode
Even number	Thermal	Antarafacial
	Photochemical	Suprafacial
Odd number	Thermal	Suprafacial
	Photochemical	Antarafacial

Thus, since a [1,3] sigmatropic migration involves two pairs of electrons, an antrafacial rearrangement for a 1,3-shift under thermal conditions does not take place due to geometrical constraints. 1,3-Shifts do take place photochemically [Table 17.4, moreover, since under photochemical conditions HOMO becomes symmetric (see, Scheme 17.73) hydrogen can migrate by suprafacial pathway].

(iii) [1,5] Sigmatropic Hydrogen Shift.

The [1,5] sigmatropic shift of hydrogen or deuterium atoms is well known. These involve three pairs of electrons, thus these occurs via a suprafacial pathway under thermal conditions (see Table 17.4). These shifts can be analyzed by examining a hydrogen atom and a pentadienyl radical whose HOMO (see III, Scheme 17.71) is bonding at both the migration origin and the migration terminus. Thus the migration maintains orbital symmetry when the migrating group remains on the same side of the conjugated system (suprafacial process, Scheme 17.74).

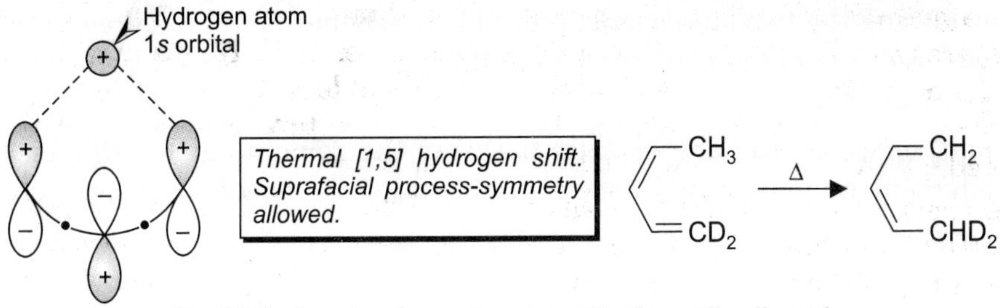

The [1,5] sigmatropic rearrangement is thermally allowed

SCHEME 17.74

Another remarkable example of suprafacial [1,5] hydrogen shift thermally, is in the 1,3-diene (I, Scheme 17.75) of known stereochemistry both at the double bond and at the stereocenter. This 1,3-diene gave a two component mixture compatible with only suprafacial migration. These results are explained as under:

- One has to consider two rotational isomers (I and I*a*, Scheme 17.75) for the reaction.
- Recall, a compound can have an infinite number of conformations but only one configuration.
- In (I) the methyl group is directed toward C4-C5 double bond while in (I*a*) it is now ethyl group that is directed toward C4-C5 bond.

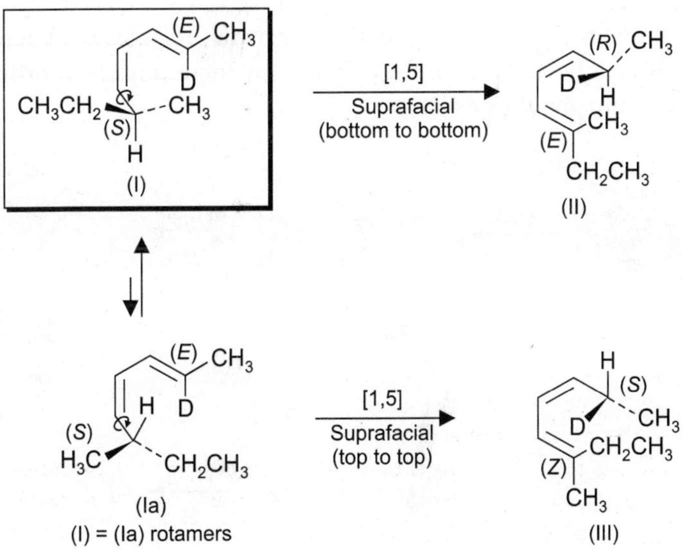

SCHEME 17.75

- There are two suprafacial [1,5] pathways for the hydrogen in these two conformations (I and I*a* Scheme 17.75) "top to top" as in (I) or "bottom to bottom" as in (Ia).
- Each of these suprafacial pathways gives a product with specific stereochemistry and both are formed.

- Considering the two stereogenic units in (I, Scheme 17.75) 4 stereoisomers could be considered. Two (II and III) are formed during suprafacial migration by the symmetry allowed pathway.
- If one considers, the antarafacial pathway the remaining two stereoisomers (as a diastereomeric pair) would have been formed (Scheme 17.76) which however, is not the case.

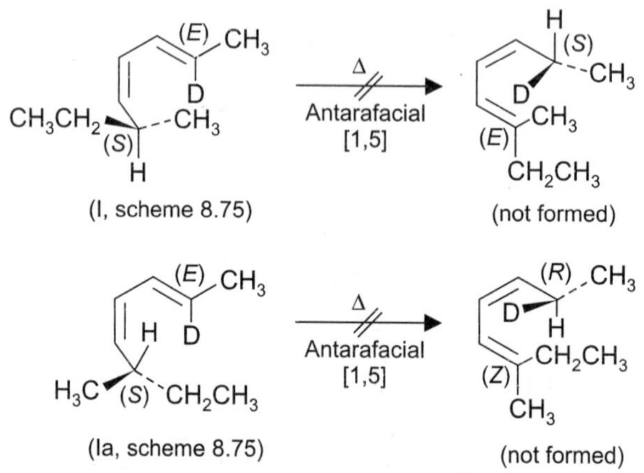

SCHEME 17.76

Heating of indene (Scheme 17.77) causes the scrambling of the label to all the three non-aromatic positions. It is only via [1,5] shift of H or D (by including the *p*-orbitals of the benzene ring) that one can account for the results.

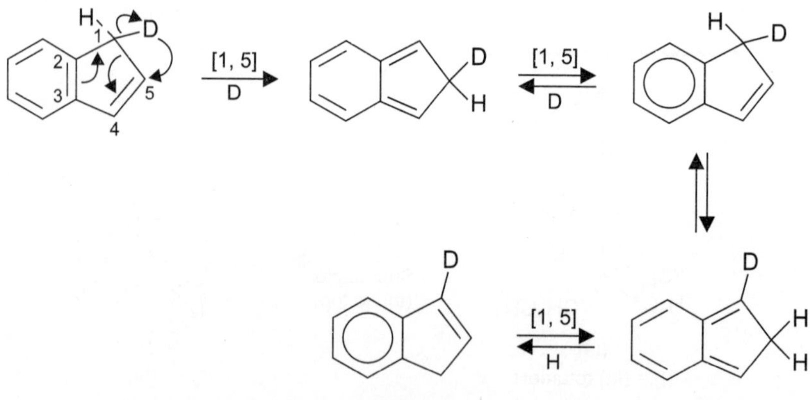

SCHEME 17.77

(iv) [1,7] Sigmatropic Hydrogen Shift

In the case of [1,7] hydrogen shifts, in a triene, the orbital symmetry rules (see III, Scheme 17.71) predict that the transfer of hydrogen must be antarafacial compared to [1,3] shift, the transition state is not much strained and the shift is sterically feasible. This is seen in the thermal interconversion of vitamin D series (Scheme 17.78).

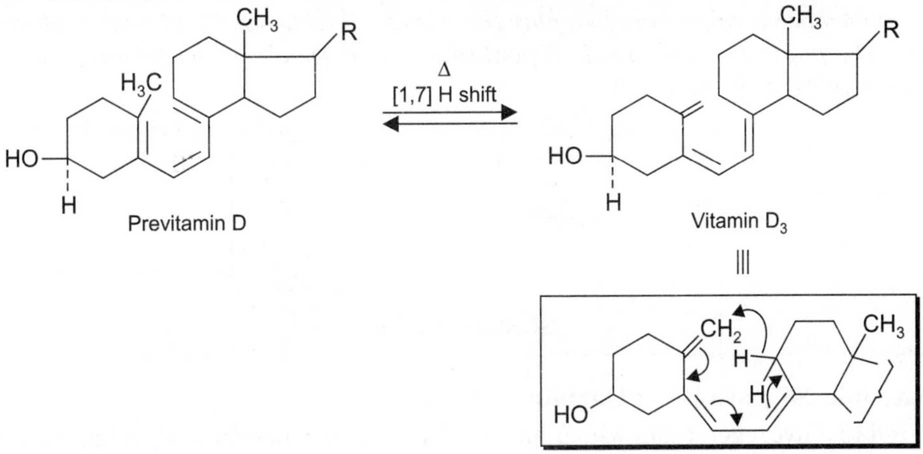

SCHEME 17.78

More on sigmatropic rearrangements (Degenerate rearrangements)

1, 3–Pentadiene on heating regenerates itself via a [1, 5] shift of hydrogen, this kind of process in which a reactant rearranges to itself is termed degenerate rearrangement (Scheme 17.78a). Significantly as expected the [1, 3] shift is symmetry forbidden.

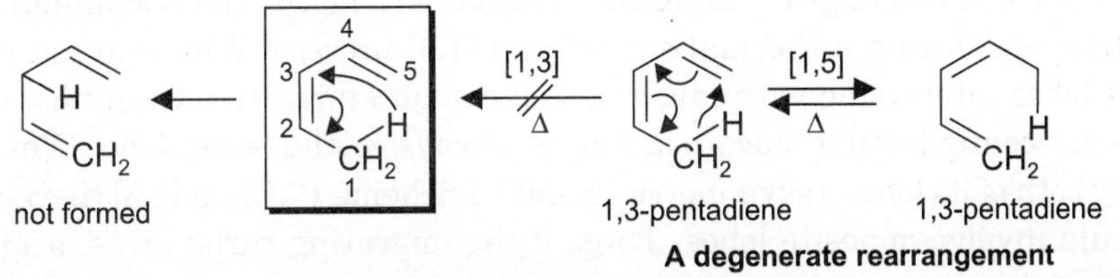

SCHEME 17.78a

The degenerate rearrangement can be established either by isotopically labeled molecules or suitably substituted molecules (Scheme 17.78b).

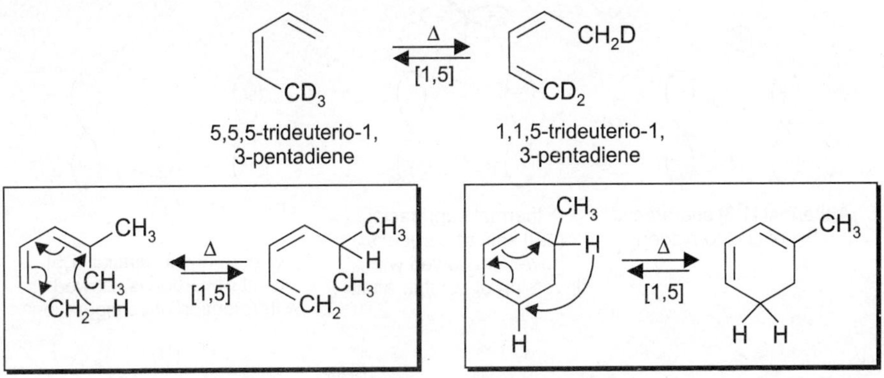

SCHEME 17.78b

Three membered rings can often play the role of a double bond and a [1, 5] H shift can take place just like in 1, 3-pentadiene and involves the opening of the cyclopropane (Scheme 17.78c).

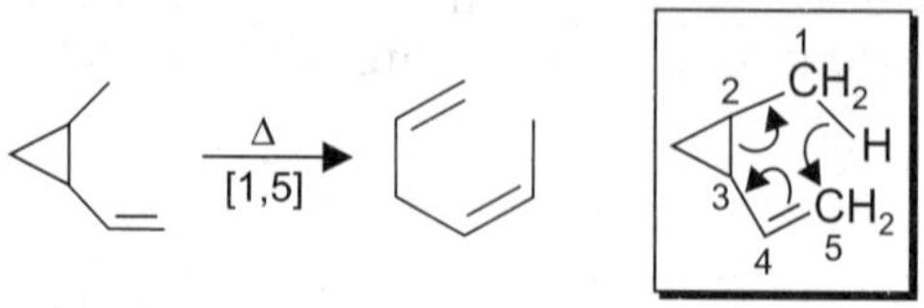

SCHEME 17.78c

B. Sigmatropic Migrations of Carbon

As compared to a hydrogen atom which has its electrons in a 1*s* orbital that has only one lobe, a carbon free radical (free imaginary transition state) has its odd electron in a *p* orbital which has two lobes of opposite sign. Recall that a [1,3] sigmatropic suprafacial migration of hydrogen (thermally) is symmetry forbidden while an antarafacial reaction though allowed is geometrically improbable (see Schemes 17.72–17.74). Interestingly an additional possibility would exist if an alkyl group (carbon) rather than a hydrogen was potential migrator. A [1,3] shift can now be suprafacial migration (I, Scheme 17.79) if the migrating group does so antarafacially *i.e.*, it would result in inversion of configuration of the migrating group. Thus carbon can simultaneously interact with the migration source and the migration terminus using either one of its lobes or both of its lobes (Scheme 17.79). Considering suprafacial rearrangement, carbon will migrate using one of its lobes if the HOMO is symmetric (II, Scheme 17.79). This happens during a thermal suprafacial [1,5] process. When carbon migrates with only one of its lobes interacting with migration source and migration terminus, the migrating group retains its configuration since bonding is always to the same lobe. When the carbon migrates using both of its lobes. (asymmetric HOMO, I Scheme 17.79), a [1,3] thermal suprafacial migration would involve opposite lobes. Thus, if the migrating carbon was originally bonded *via* its positive lobe, it must now use its negative lobe to form the new C—C bond. The stereochemical outcome of such a process is the inversion of configuration in the migrating group.

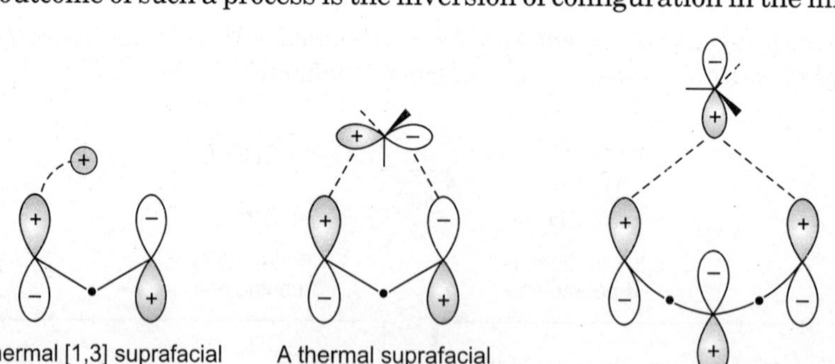

A thermal [1,3] suprafacial shift of H is forbidden

A thermal suprafacial [1,3] shift of carbon is however allowed with inversion of configuration

(I)

A thermal suprafacial [1,5] shift of carbon is allowed with retention of configuration

(II)

SCHEME 17.79

In summary, a suprafacial [1,5] thermal rearrangement proceeds with retention of configuration at the migrating carbon, while the related [1,3] suprafacial process proceeds with inversion. In the thermal conversion of (I, Scheme 17.80) to (II) a carbon atom migrates across an allyl system to leave C-1 and ending up at C-3 via a [1,3] shift. The inversion of configuration is observed using suitable substrates (Scheme 17.81). The [1,3] shifts of carbon

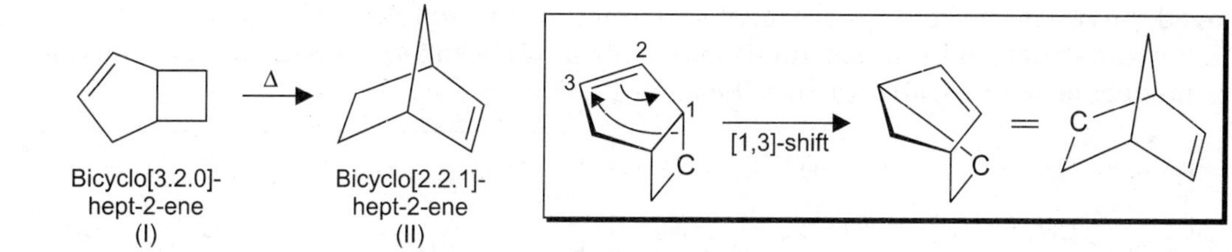

SCHEME 17.80

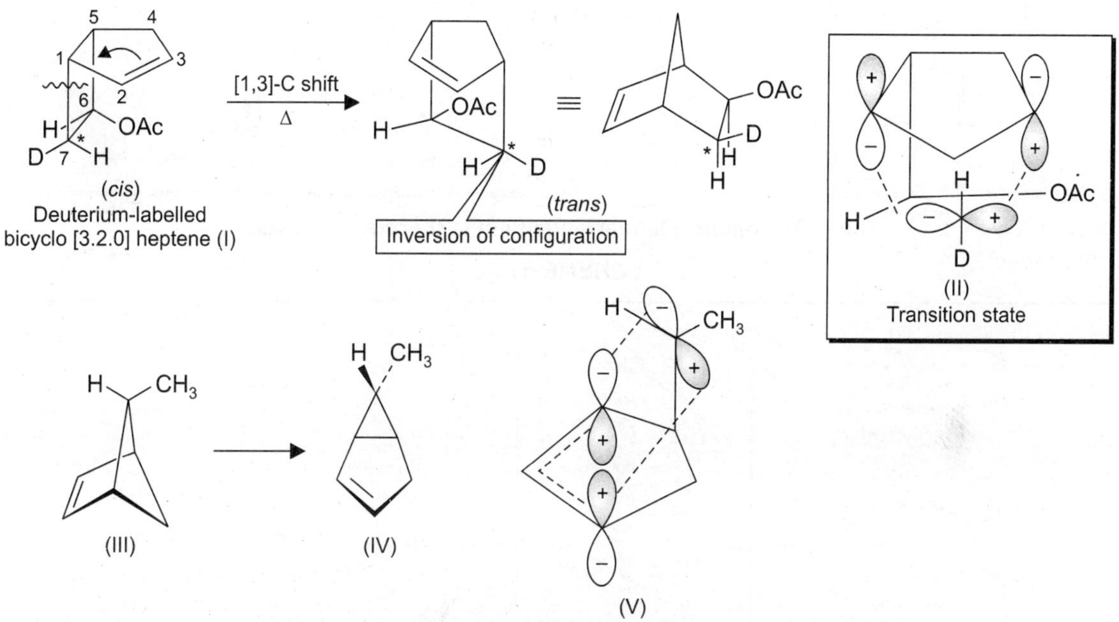

SCHEME 17.81

(*i.e.*, alkyl groups) in such reactions involve expansions of strained three-or four-membered rings. As predicted by orbital symmetry conservation rules these reactions proceed almost entirely with inversion of configurations in the migrating group as in (I, Scheme 17.81). In this case, a label deuterium was placed at C7 which was *trans* to the acetoxy group. After the reaction, it was found to be exclusively *cis* due to inversion of configuration at C7. The transition state (II, Scheme 17.81) shows that it is a [1,3] sigmatropic shift of carbon. Similarly (III, Scheme 17.81) gives (IV) via the transition state (V) by a suprafacial [1,3] shift with inversion at the migrating carbon under thermal conditions.

C. The Cope Rearrangement

A 1,5-diene on heating is rearranged to another 1,5-diene by concerted formation of a 1, 6-bond, breaking of the 3,4-bond and migration of both double bonds in a [3,3] sigmatropic rearrangement known as Cope rearrangement (see, Scheme 17.69). The compound rearranges by a [3,3] sigmatropic pathway and is also hypothetically pictured as split into two allyl radicals (Scheme 17.82). Interaction of the HOMO's of these allyl radicals is bonding at both ends, so the reaction is thermally allowed. The stereochemical outcome of this rearrangement is in keeping with their occurrence generally through the chair-shaped transition states (Scheme 17.83). *Meso* 3,4-dimethyl-1, 5-hexadiene gives *cis*, *trans*-2, 6-octadiene (in the starting compound the two methyl groups are having *cis*-relationship, in the chair form of a cyclohexane only 1, 2-axial, equatorial relationship is *cis*) while a boat shaped transition state would give *cis*, *cis*-product or *trans*, trans-product (Scheme 17.84).

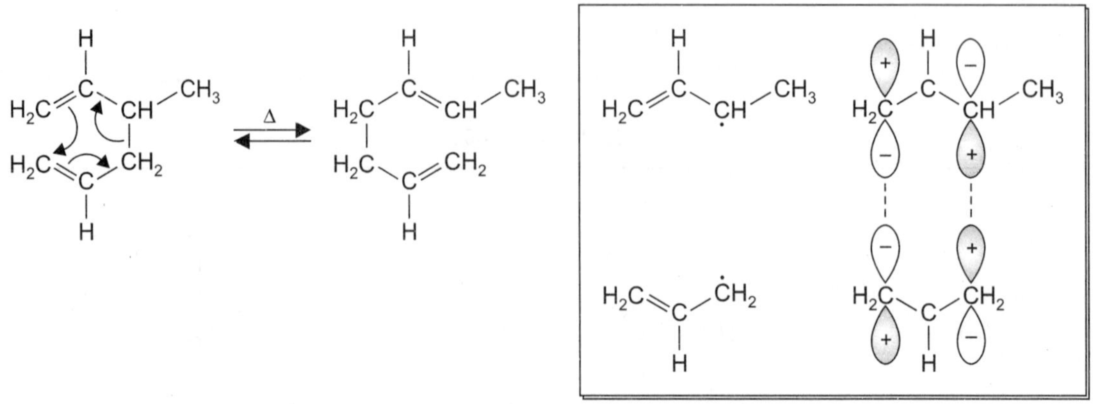

The [3,3] sigmatropic rearrangement is thermally allowed

SCHEME 17.82

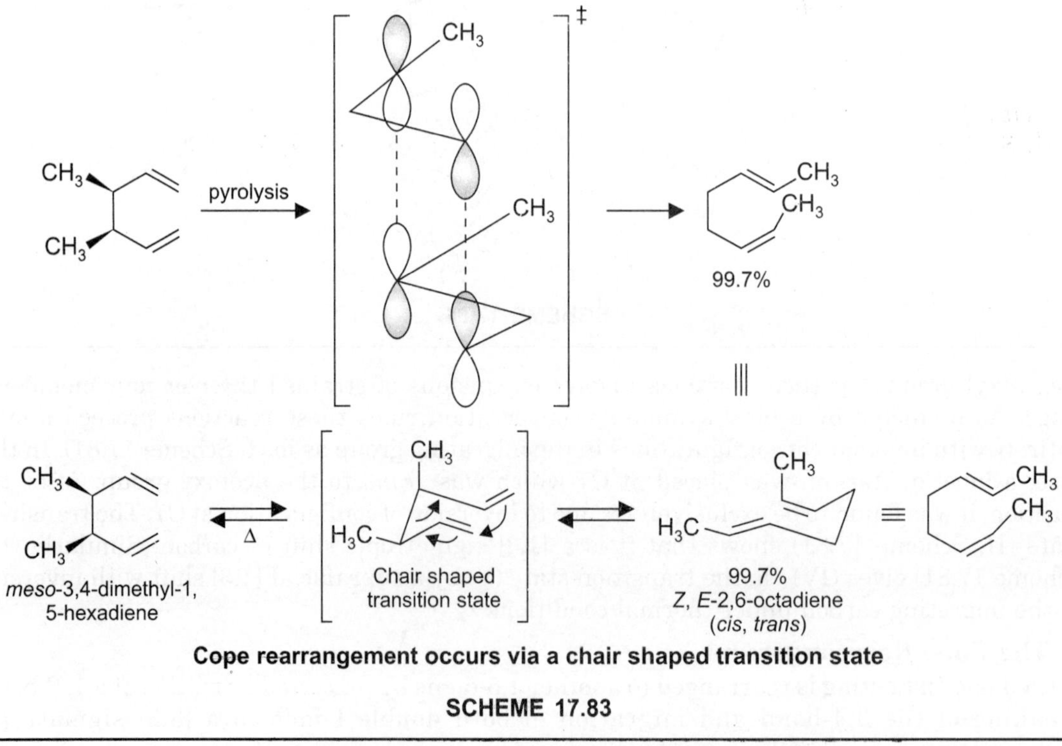

Cope rearrangement occurs via a chair shaped transition state

SCHEME 17.83

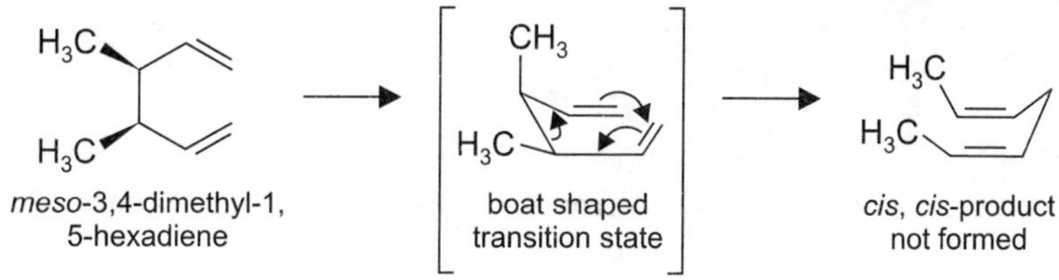

SCHEME 17.84

EXERCISE 17.13

Which diene you expect on pyrolysis of trans-3, 4-dimethylcyclohexadiene ?

ANSWER. *A Cope rearrangement occurs through a chair shaped transition state and the diene expected is E, E isomer of 2, 6-octadiene (Scheme 17.85).*

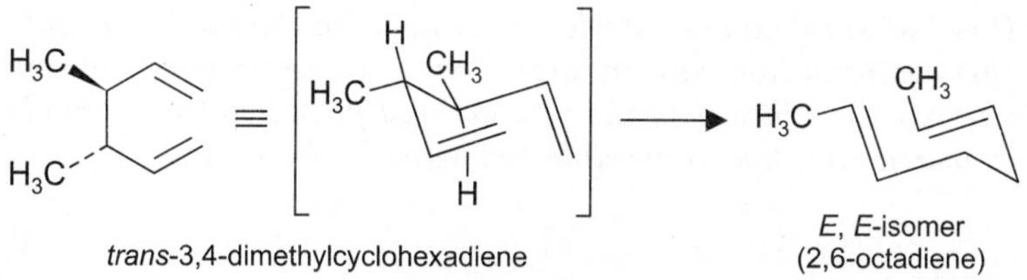

SCHEME 17.85

EXERCISE 17.14

Why Z, Z-2, 6-octadiene is not the product of pyrolysis of trans-3,4-dimethylcyclohexadiene ?

ANSWER. *The transition state (I, Scheme 17.86) with two pseudoequatorial groups is far more stable than (II) with two pseudoaxial groups. The Z, Z-isomer would arise from the less stable chair shaped transition state (II, Scheme 17.86).*

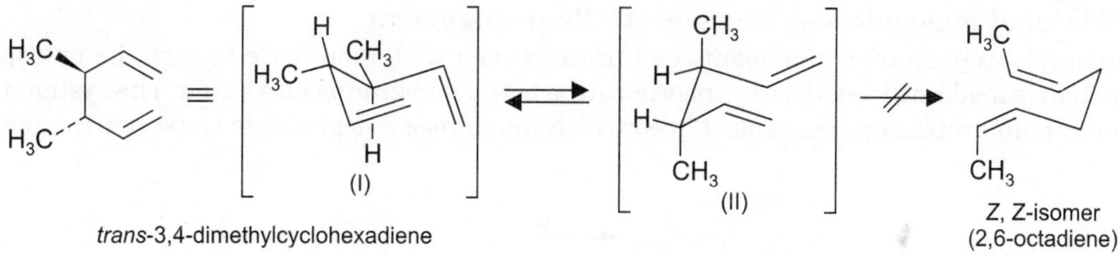

SCHEME 17.86

On introducing strain into the reactant, rate accelerations are observed and *cis*-divinylcyclopropane rapidly undergoes Cope rearrangement (Scheme 17.87). Similar reaction is however, not observed with *trans*-isomer where the reacting ends of the double bonds are too far apart. Thus the Cope rearrangement occurs at low temperatures in *cis*-1, 2-divinyl cyclopropane compared to Cope rearrangement of 1, 5-hexadiene itself which requires temperatures in the range of 200–300°C.

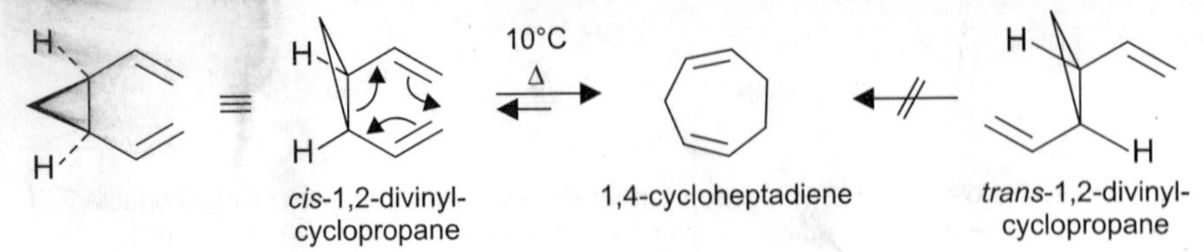

SCHEME 17.87

EXERCISE 17.15

Which two conformations of cis-1, 2-divinylcyclopropane can be considered for a possible Cope rearrangement ?

Which of these conformations is capable of undergoing this rearrangement ?

ANSWER. *See Scheme 17.87a. Two conformations can be adopted (I and II, Scheme 17.87a), (I) is less stable due to steric strain between double bond and a H atom and only this conformation can undergo Cope rearrangement. The conformation (II) will be unreactive since then the product will have two trans double bonds in a seven membered ring (an impossible geometrical situation).*

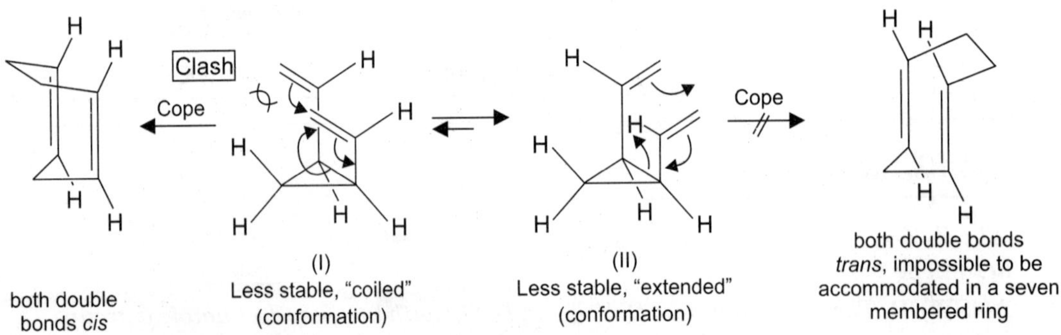

SCHEME 17.87a

D. Fluxional Molecules—A Degenerate Rearrangement

Divinylcyclopropane rearrangements can proceed even with more ease in case the entropy of activation is made still negative by incorporating both vinyl groups into a ring. The system then becomes homotropilidene (Scheme 17.88) which undergoes a degenerate Cope rearrangement

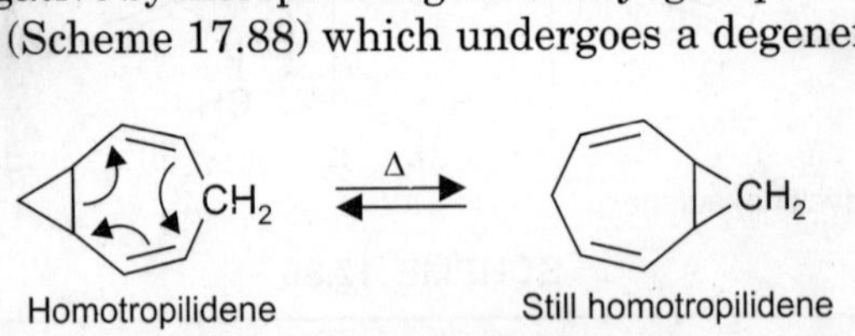

The *degenerate* Cope rearrangement of homotropilidene

SCHEME 17.88

A degenerate rearrangement leads to a product which is indistinguishable from the reactant. By bridging the two methylene groups in homotropilidene one gets a molecule of bullvalene (Scheme 17.89). This is converted into itself at 25°C. At 100°C the ^{1}HNMR spectrum of bullvalene